Crisis Ministries

THOMAS C. ODEN

Classical Pastoral Care

VOLUME FOUR
CRISIS MINISTRIES

Baker Books

A Division of Baker Book House Co
Grand Rapids, Michigan 49516

In memory of Will Herberg—
incomparable mentor
whose friendship transcends death and time

© 1994 by Thomas C. Oden
Originally published 1987 by The Crossroad Publishing Company

Published by Baker Books
a division of Baker Book House Company
P.O. Box 6287, Grand Rapids, MI 49516-6287

Printed in the United States of America

ISBN 0-8010-6766-9

Library of Congress Cataloging-in-Publication data on file in Washington, D.C.

Contents

Preface to the Baker Edition   vii

Introduction   1

1   Special Situations of Crisis Counseling   3

2   Pastoral Visitation and Care of the Sick   26

3   The Enigma of Suffering   57

4   Marriage and Family Counseling   96

5   Care of the Poor   144

6   Care of the Dying   164

Conclusion   186

Abbreviations   187

Appendix: The Pastoral Writers

   Biographical-Bibliographical Summaries   193

Acknowledgments   246

Index   247

Contents

Preface to the Baker Edition

EVANGELICALS STAND POISED to rediscover the classical pastoral tradition. This series seeks the revitalization of a discipline once familiar to evangelical Protestant scholarship, but now regrettably crippled and enervated.

It has been commonly observed that there is a deep hunger and profound readiness among evangelicals for neglected classical Christian roots as a resource for counsel, teaching, exegesis, and the work of ministry (see the writings of Robert Webber, Mark Noll, Ward Gasque, Donald Bloesch, James I. Packer, Michael Horton, Clark Pinnock, and Os Guinness).

It is well known that classic Protestant and evangelical teachers made frequent and informed references to the ancient Christian pastoral writers. Calvin was exceptionally well grounded in Augustine, but was also thoroughly familiar with the texts of Cyprian, Tertullian, John Chrysostom, Ambrose, Jerome, Leo, and Gregory the Great, and ecumenical council definitions such as those of Nicea, Constantinople I, and Chalcedon. Philipp Melancthon and Martin Chemnitz were especially gifted scholars of classical pastoral care. This tradition was carried forth and deepened by Reformed pastoral theologians (Gerhard, Quenstedt, Bucanus, Ursinus, Wollebius, and Cocceius), and survived healthily well into the eighteenth-century evangelical revival among leading teachers like J.A. Bengel, Philip Doddridge, Jonathan Edwards, John Wesley, and Johann Neander, all of whom read classic Christian writers handily in their original languages. Not until the late nineteenth century did the study of the ancient pastoral writers atrophy among Protestant pastors.

What is notably missing in today's picture is the classic pastoral texts themselves in accessible form, and a vital community of pastors and care-givers in living dialogue with these foundational prototypes.

A major long-range objective of this edition is the mentoring of young evangelical pastors and counselors toward greater competence in the classical pastoral tradition. Deliberately included in this collection are the voices of women from the classic Eastern and Western traditions of spiritual formation, exegesis, martyrology, catechesis, and piety. While the documentation of their poignant utterances is regrettably infrequent, they still are exceedingly powerful commentators on care-giving—I am thinking of such voices as Amma Theodora, Julian of Norwich, Hildegaard of Bingen, and Teresa of Avila.

Will benefits accrue to persons in teaching and helping professions who have no evangelical commitments or interests? The study of classical pastoral care is fitting not only for pastors and professionals, but for lay readers interested in their own inward spiritual formation. The arguments contained in this series tend to elicit ripple effects on diverse readers in such widely varied fields as psychology, Western cultural history, liturgies, homiletics, and education. Classical pastoral care is long overdue in contributing something distinctive of its own to the larger dialogue on care-giving, empathy, behavioral change, and therapeutic effectiveness.

By the early eighties it began to be evident that someone needed to pull together a substantial collection of essential sources of classic Christian writers on major themes of pastoral care. The series was first published by Crossroad/Continuum Publishing Company, a general academic publisher of religious books with strong ties to the erudite Herder tradition of Catholic scholarship. In the intervening years, no serious rival or alternative to this collection has appeared. There exists no other anthology of texts of classical pastoral care that presents the variety of textual material offered in this series. I am now deeply pleased to see it come out in an edition more accessible to Protestants. This is the first time the series has been made available in paperback.

The four books can be read either as a single, unified sequence or separately as stand-alone volumes. To this day some readers know of only one or two volumes, but are not aware that each volume is part of a cohesive series. Baker has made this unity clearer by offering the four volumes as a series.

I am deeply grateful for the interest that many working pastors, counselors, and lay persons have shown in this Classical Pastoral Care series. Even though these volumes were chosen as a Religious Book Club selection over several years, the circulation has been disseminated largely through academic audiences. I am pleased that it is now being offered by Baker for the first time to evangelical pastors and evangelically oriented pastoral and lay counselors and lay readers.

These texts are sometimes hard to locate if one is approaching them topically in crumbling, antiquated editions with poor indexes. This edition provides for the first time a well-devised index for the whole series that makes the anthology much more accessible to readers who wish to dip into it thematically.

These four volumes are designed to display the broad range of classical Christian reflections on all major questions of pastoral care. Many practical subjects are included, such as care of the dying, care of the poor, marriage and family counseling, pastoral visitation and care of the sick, counsel on addictive behaviors, vocational counsel, the timing of good counsel, the necessary and sufficient conditions of a helping relationship, body language in pastoral counsel, pastoral care through preaching, pastoral care through prayer, the pastor as educator of the soul, preparing for the Lord's table, clergy homosexuality and sexual ethics, equality of souls beyond sexual difference, the path to ordination, charismatic, healing ministries, and preparation for the care of souls.

The four volumes are:

I. *On Becoming a Minister* (first published 1987)
II. *Ministry Through Word and Sacrament* (1989)
III. *Pastoral Counsel* (1989)
IV. *Crisis Ministries* (1986)

This edition for the first time identifies the order of volumes more clearly. Since in the first edition the fourth volume (*Crisis Ministries*, with its bio-bibliographical addendum) appeared first, the sequential order of the series has been confusing to some readers. Many have never seen the four volumes in a collection together, and do not yet realize that the whole sequence is constructed in a well-designed order to cover all major topics of pastoral theology.

There is reason to believe that this series is already being regarded as a standard necessary accession of theological seminary libraries, as well as of the libraries of most colleges and universities in which religious studies are taught, and in many general public libraries.

Meanwhile, out of rootless hunger the prefix "pastoral" has come to mean almost anything. There is no constraint on ascribing any subject matter to the category of pastoral care. In this game pastoral can mean my ultimate concern, transcendental meditation, or worse, my immediate feeling process or group hugging or my racial identity or crystal-gazing—you name it, anything. Then what is called pastoral is no longer related to the work of Christian ministry at all.

The preaching and counseling pastor needs to know that current pastoral care stands in a tradition of two millennia of reflection on the tasks of soul care. If deprived of these sources, the practice of pastoral care may become artificially constricted to modern psychotherapeutic procedures or pragmatic agendas. During the sixties and seventies, these reductionistic models prevailed among many old-line Protestant pastors, and to some degree as the eighties proceeded they also took root among evangelicals. This anthology shows the classic historic roots of contemporary approaches to psychological change, and provides to some degree a critique of those contemporary models.

Pastors today are rediscovering the distinctiveness of pastoral method as distinguished from other methods of inquiry (historical, philosophical, literary, psychological, etc.). Pastoral care is a unique enterprise that has its own distinctive subject-matter (care of souls); its own methodological premise (revelation); its own way of inquiring into its subject-matter (attentiveness to the revealed Word through Scripture and its consensual tradition of exegesis); its own criteria of scholarly authenticity (accountability to canonical text and tradition); its own way of knowing (listening to sacred Scripture with the historic church); its own mode of cultural analysis (with worldly powers bracketed and divine providence appreciated); and its own logic (internal consistency premised upon revealed truth).

The richness of the classic Christian pastoral tradition remains pertinent to ministry today. The laity have a right to competent, historically grounded pastoral care. The pastor has a right to the texts that teach how pastors have understood their work over the centuries. Modern chauvinism has falsely taught us a theory of moral inferiority: that new ideas are intrinsically superior, and old patterns inferior. This attitude has robbed the laity of the pastoral care they deserve, and the ministry of the texts that can best inform the recovery of pastoral identity.

Thomas C. Oden
June, 1994

Introduction

THE PASTOR STRUGGLES for the health of the person and the life of the soul through major life crises. Six principal arenas of crisis ministries are discussed in this volume. Our purpose is to show that soul care occurs not merely in theory but in the life and death situations in which the soul's growth and happiness are risked; not merely in words but in faith that becomes active in love; not merely in the church but where life is being lived out physically, sexually, habitually, interpersonally, vocationally, economically, and relationally; and finally where life is relinquished in death.

The six *key questions* of this volume are:

- How shall the pastor best function in interpersonal conflict mediation, and in such critical moments as *vocation* decision, *addictive and compulsive behaviors,* and thoughts of *suicide?*
- How shall the pastor most effectively visit and care for the *physically ill?*
- If God is proclaimed as unsurpassably powerful and good, how shall the pastor deal with the *suffering* of parishioners, and what sort of care and reasoning shall be provided for inquiries concerning the justice of God amid suffering, temptation, and inequality?
- How shall the pastor minister to crises in *marriage and family* living: premarital counsel, marital counsel, divorce counsel, celibacy counsel, parental counsel, youth counsel, abortion counsel, and adultery counsel?

1

- How shall the pastor effectively care for the *poor* and needy, the stranger, those deprived of familial and economic resources, orphans, widows, the destitute, the imprisoned, and the enslaved?
- Finally, how shall the pastor care for souls amid the crisis of terminal illness, *death,* and burial, and the grieving process?

1 Special Situations of Crisis Counseling

A CRISIS CONTAINS both hazard and opportunity. This assumption is central to classical pastoral wisdom, whether the crisis referred to is economic, emotive, interpersonal, or spiritual; whether chronic or acute; whether mild, desperate or suicidal.

Crisis derives from the Greek *krinein*, to decide. In medicine it is that point in the progress of a disease when a change takes place which decisively points toward recovery or death. Generally a crisis is a turning point or crossroad in the development of something, a crucial time, a decisive point. The pastor deals frequently with such decisive moments in the lives of persons. Much daily energy of the pastor is devoted to helping persons deal with personal crises.

I ❧ THE PASTOR'S PRESENCE AMID CRISIS

A major premise of pastoral care amid crisis is *presence*. Care of souls first requires simply being there. Simple, empathic, listening presence is a primary pastoral act, the presupposition of all other pastoral acts.

It is hoped that the pastor will be immediately responsive to the onset of a crisis, rather than wait to be signaled, or specifically invited. While the pastor cannot be ubiquitously present at all times throughout the parish, there is no part of the parish which cannot be lifted up in prayer. Thus we find in the earliest liturgies of the Christian tradition (as in the following one dating to second or third century traditions) a wide-ranging spiritual concern for those critical moments. They are lifted up before God in prayer:

> Remember, O Lord, Christians sailing, travelling, sojourning in strange lands; our fathers and mothers, brothers and sisters, who are in bonds, prison, captivity, or exile; who are in mines, or under torture, or in bitter slavery.
>
> Remember, O Lord, the sick and afflicted, and those troubled by twisted imaginings. Enable their speedy healing, O God, and their salvation.
>
> Remember, O Lord, every Christian soul in affliction and distress, needing Thy mercy and comfort, O God; and enable the return of all of those who have erred. (*Early Liturgies,* III.xxxiv, ANF VII, p. 545)*

3

The task of the soul guide is not to circumvent or avoid the crisis, but to face it, to listen for the divine claim speaking through it, and to learn from it constructively. Strength of soul is only known through passing through, not evading, these experiences, according to Minucius Felix (third century):

That we feel and suffer the human mischiefs of the body is not punishment—it is warfare. For fortitude is strengthened by infirmities, and calamity is very often the discipline of virtue. In addition, strength both of mind and body grows torpid without the exercise of labour. . . . In adversity God looks into and searches out each one, weighing the disposition of every individual amid dangers. . . . Therefore, as gold is tried by the fires, so are we declared by our critical moments. (Minucius Felix, *The Octavius,* Ch. XXXVI, ANF IV, pp. 195-196)*

We do not adequately know ourselves until we pass through these moments of challenge and testing. Then we have an opportunity to test our strengths and limitations in the crucible of crisis.

Crisis can come suddenly upon those who appear in every other way healthy. The pastor must be ready to attend persons in his charge who face crisis unexpectedly. The astonishing metaphor of epilepsy was used by Origen (early third century) to reveal the sudden and radical nature of crisis, made more dramatic by the fact that the individual prior to the crisis looked fine, functioned well, and appeared in superb health:

Now this malaise attacks sufferers at distant intervals. During the intervening time, one who suffers from it seems in no way to differ from one in good health, at the season when the epilepsy is not working on him. Similar disorders you may find in certain souls, which are often supposed to be healthy in point of temperance and the other virtues; then, sometimes, as if they were seized with a kind of epilepsy arising from their passions, they fall down from the position in which they seemed to stand. (Origen, *Commentary on Matthew,* Bk. XIII, sec. 4, ANF X, p. 477)*

The epilepsy analogy suggests that even those who seem to live a tranquil life can suddenly be stricken with crisis. No one is immune. Hugh of St. Victor (early twelfth century) viewed crisis under the metaphor of the "sea (of passions) within us," later to be further explored by Carl Jung (CW, 11, pp. 444ff.). Hugh played humorously with the analogy of the emotive flood and Noah's ark in relation to types of persons facing crises:

Here we may well consider three kinds of people, those who have a flood within them, but no ark; those who have both a flood and an ark, but are not in the ark; and those who in the flood have an ark and stay in it. . . . This is what the Psalm says, "Here is the great immeasurable

sea, in which move creatures beyond number. Here ships sail to and
fro" (Ps. 104:25,26). For the "sea" in us is the concupiscence of this
world. . . . Let a man return to his own heart, and he will find there
a stormy ocean lashed by the fierce billows of overwhelming passions
and desires, which swamp the soul as often as by consent they bring it
into subjection. For there is this flood in every man, as long as he lives
in this corruptible life, where the flesh lusts against the spirit. Or rather,
every man is in this flood, but the good are in it as those borne in ships
upon the sea, whereas the bad are in it as shipwrecked persons at the
mercy of the waves. (Hugh of St. Victor, *SSW,* pp. 141-143, NEB)*

The assumption is that within each one of us is a potentially turbulent sea
of passionate, libidinal energy, which is subject on occasion to storm. The
seaworthy believers are those who have learned to chart, navigate and survive
the storms of passion that are endemic to human experience, as a well-made
ship survives the tempest.

George Herbert, the poet and Anglican country parson, thought that the
better pastor was one who had learned to distinguish those parishioners engaged in mortal spiritual combat under conditions of affliction from those
relatively at peace. Pastoral care for each is different:

The Country Parson knows that there is a double state of a Christian
even in this life; the one military, the other peaceable. The military is,
when we are assaulted with temptations, either from within or from
without. . . . Now the parson must exercise good spiritual discernment,
according to whether he discovers one of his flock to be in one and the
other state. Only then can he apply himself to them fittingly. . . .
Particularly, he counsels [the tranquil] to . . . make sure that their
seeming tranquillity does not betray them. . . . and secondly, not to
take the full compass and liberty of their peace. . . . Those the parson
finds in the military state, he fortifies and strengthens with his utmost
skill. . . . If he sees them nearer desperation than atheism, not so much
doubting a God as that he is theirs, then he dives into the boundless
ocean of God's love, and the unspeakable riches of his loving kindness.
(Geo. Herbert, *CP,* Ch. XXXIV, CWS, pp. 105-106, 108)*

It is best not to seek to change one's life abruptly or radically during periods
of intense depression, according to Ignatius Loyola. Listening carefully to
oneself during times of peak experiencing is more reliable than making critical
decisions during times of bleakness:

In time of desolation one should never make a change, but stand firm
and constant in the resolutions and decision which guided him the day
before the desolation, or to the decision which he observed in the

preceding consolation. For just as the good spirit guides and consoles us in consolation, so in desolation the evil spirit guides and counsels. Following the counsels of this latter spirit, one can never find the correct way to a right decision. (Ignatius Loyola, *Spiritual Exercises,* p. 130)

With these few selections, we enter the stormy arena of crisis counsel. They already make clear that the better pastor is one who has learned to become vulnerably and accessibly present amid crisis, to pray for those in his charge confronting crisis, to face and learn from the particular crisis, to navigate the seas of passion, to help persons follow more their intuitive experiences of consolation than desolation, and recognize which ones are desperately embattled, and not treat them on the pretense that their lives are tranquil. Now we turn to another metaphor that pervades this literature: *pilgrimage.*

II ❧ THE JOURNEY OF THE PILGRIM

Since each soul is like a pilgrim, the care-giver is called to offer good counsel on the road, to reduce hazards, maintain the right direction, and provide helping encouragement. Support and guidance may be needed at any point along the way.

This complex metaphor of pilgrimage which occurs so frequently among the pastoral writers, views critical human decision-making under a collage of motifs: The way of the pilgrim is something like leaving of one's former place (correlated with repentance), turning in a new direction (often calling for a change of heart or conversion), setting out on a partially unknown journey to a promised habitation (requiring trust or faith), facing the hazards of the road (temptation), caring for others along the way (love), and living in expectation of the journey's ultimate fulfillment (hope). Crises may occur at any point along the way. The soul friend may be called upon at any time to offer aid and direction.

Is it not in the midst of the pilgrimage that its meaning is finally grasped and fully understood, however, but only at its conclusion. Therefore, there is a strong element of risk, expectation, and promise in the metaphor that cannot be prematurely or theoretically resolved. The daily walk of the pilgrim is made understandable only in relation to its expected destination, its hope, its end vision (eschatological expectation), which becomes its central motive.

"My soul has long been on pilgrimage" (Ps. 119:54). Understand, then, if you can, what the pilgrimages of the soul are, especially when it laments with groaning and grief that it has been on pilgrimage so long. We understand these pilgrimages only dully and darkly so long as the pilgrimage still lasts. But when the soul has returned to its rest, that is, to the homeland of paradise, it will be taught more truly and will understand more truly what the meaning of its pilgrimage was. (Origen, Homily XXVII On Numbers, sec. 4, CWS, p. 250)*

Encouragement is often needed to continue the journey to avert the syndrome of despairing over the fantasy of return. The biblical prototype of not looking back is Lot:

When Lot went to the mountains, he left behind the sins of Sodom, but the woman who looked back could not reach the higher ground. Your feet should not turn back, neither should your actions turn back. Your hands should not hang idle, nor should the knees of your devotion and faith become weak. Let no weakness cause your will to backslide, nor evil deeds recur. You have made your beginning, now stay with it. (Ambrose, *Letters,* 79, To Irenaeus, FC 26, p. 446)*

Those who have been long embattled and wearied by the journey may despair of ever reaching the hoped for destination. Gregory the Great employed two ironic metaphors, that of a physician giving up on a terminal patient, and of a parent purposefully withholding money from a beloved child:

When a physician gives up hope for a patient, he allows him to have whatever he fancies; but a person whose cure he deems possible, is forbidden much that he desires. We take money away from our children, yet at the same time reserve for them, as our heirs, the whole patrimony. Therefore, let those who are humbled by temporal adversity, take joy from the expectation of an eternal inheritance. (Gregory the Great, *Pastoral Care,* Part III, Ch. 26, ACW 11, p. 185)

The pilgrim lives in hope of meanings not yet revealed. Nonetheless, this hope makes the present struggle meaningful. The temptation to abandon the journey is a meaningful test of faith, hope and love. At times these enticements may seem overwhelming. There are two views of the role of pleasure, one for immediate enjoyment, the other for the sublimation of immediate enjoyment looking toward a higher joy through righteousness and behavioral excellence:

It is disgraceful to the wise and good if they themselves become slaves to their appetites, if they walk along smeared with unguents and crowned with flowers. Those who do these things are plainly foolish and senseless. Their actions are fruitless, and they have not even reached the barest notion of moral excellence. Perhaps someone will say, Why, then, have these things been made, except that we may enjoy them? However, it has often been said that there would have been no virtue unless it had become a virtue by overpowering some challenge. Therefore God made all things to supply a contest between two things. Those enticements of pleasures, then, are the instruments of that Deceiver whose only business it is to subdue virtue and bar many from righteousness, who with these soothing influences and enjoyments captivates their souls, who very well knows that pleasure dies. For as God calls us to life only through virtue and effort, so the other calls us to death by delights and pleasures. As humanity arrives at real good only through deceitful evils, so they arrive at real evil through deceitful goods. (Lactantius, *The Divine Institutes,* Bk. VI, Ch. XXII, ANF VII, pp. 188-189)*

No pilgrim can fully explain the soul's pilgrimage through various stages while the story itself is yet incomplete. This is why pilgrims live in hope. Origen emphasized the complexity and uniqueness of each individual journey, under the prototype of the journey of Israel in the wilderness. He appealed to a partially unknowable but utterly kind providence in attempting to describe varied stages:

When the soul sets out from the Egypt of this life to go to the promised land, it necessarily goes by certain roads and, as we have said, observes certain stages. . . . The stages are those by which the soul journeys from earth to heaven. Who will be found worthy and so understanding of the divine mysteries that he can describe the stages of that journey and ascent of the soul and explain either the toils or the rest of each different place? For how will he explain that after the first and second stages Pharaoh is still in pursuit; the Egyptians are in pursuit? And while they do not catch them, they keep on pursuing; while they have been drowned, they still pursue. How will he interpret the fact that the people of God who had been saved only after a few stages first sang the song, saying, "Let us sing to the Lord, for He has triumphed gloriously. The horse and his rider has He thrown into the sea" (Ex. 15:1)? But, as I have said, I do not know who would dare to explain the stages one by one, and also to guess at the special properties of the stages by contemplating their names. I am uncertain whether the understanding of the preacher would be sufficient for such weighty mysteries or the hearing of the listeners capable of understanding. How will he explain the wars encountered with the Amalekites or the different temptations? How will he explain those whose limbs fell in the wilderness (cf. Heb. 3:17; 1 Cor. 10:5) and that it was not at all the children of Israel but the children's children of Israel that were able to enter the holy land? (Origen, Homily XXVII On Numbers, sec. 4, CWS, pp. 250-251)

The history of the soul is like a journey that has a promised, but as yet not experienced, conclusion. While in the midst of the journey we may not yet see how the road could possibly wind toward a fitting conclusion, so evidently does it seem to be going contrary ways. The function of the soul guide is to help interpret, insofar as possible, the whole journey. This interpretation is better made by observing carefully the path already taken, both by humanity and the individual, by accurately reading the present situation, and by providing hope and encouragement that the final destination will provide a full understanding of the prevailing absurdities of the present and past.

III ❦ INTERPERSONAL CRISIS COUNSELING AND CONFLICT MANAGEMENT

Many pastoral conversations hinge primarily on interpersonal crises. They arise out of the challenge and potential conflict of persons meeting persons. What happens there affects their capacity to trust, their happiness, self-esteem, and fulfillment. For this reason, interpersonal conflict resolution is a crucial occupation of soul care. The wise pastor does not make the assumption that the smarter people are, the more effectively will they live in concord interpersonally.

When superior knowledge exalts certain people, it separates them from the society of others, and the greater the knowledge, the less wise they are in the virtue of concord. (Gregory the Great, *Pastoral Care,* Part III, Ch. 22, ACW 11, pp. 162-163)

John Chrysostom argued that friends need each other if they are to increase the justice of their interpersonal relationships. They must not withhold corrective love. Candor is required for moral improvement. Frank disclosures may temporarily elicit conflict, but in time they will be healing and constructive if grounded in love:

To invite someone to our table, to treat him with civil speeches, with routine greetings and with entertainments—these are no signal proofs of friendship. . . . You must not hide your talent for friendship from each other. It is for this that you have been given speech. It is for this you have a mouth and a tongue, that you may correct your neighbor. It is dumb and reasonless creatures only that have no care for their neighbor, and take no account of others. But while you are calling God your Father and the neighbor your brother, when you see him entangling himself in numerous misdeeds, do you prefer his outward affirmation to his genuine welfare? Please do not do this. There is no evidence that friendship is true when it closes its eyes to the deficiencies of the companions' behavior. Do you see them fighting? Reconcile them. Do you see them coveting what each other possesses? Then stand against that tendency. Do you see them wronged? Stand up in their defense. In doing so, you are conferring the chief benefit not on them but on yourself. It is for this we are friends, that we may be of real use one to another. One will listen in a different spirit to a friend. . . . So do not hold back your corrective judgment from a friend, and do not show displeasure when your friend does you the favor of correcting you. For as long indeed as anything is carried on in the dark, it seems carried on with greater security; but when it has many to witness what is done, it is brought to light. (Chrysostom, *Homilies on Ephesians,* Hom. XVIII, NPNF 1, XIII, p. 136)*

Coercive acts and threatening gestures are potentially very damaging to the quality of friendships, as Luther noted:

It is a very foolish saying: I have a right to it, therefore I will take it by storm and keep it, although all sorts of misfortune may come to others thereby. So we read of the Emperor Octavianus, that he did not wish to make war, however just his cause might be, unless there were sure indications of greater benefit than harm, or at least that the harm would not be intolerable, and said: "War is like fishing with a golden net; the loss risked is always greater than the catch can be." (Luther, *Treatise on Good Works,* WML I, p. 265)

The enjoyment of friendship in the community of faith was a characteristic theme expressed in the writings of Cyprian, who lived during the period of death-dealing persecution which tested the strength of many friendships:

I greet you, dearly beloved Brethren, hoping also myself to enjoy your society if circumstances permit me to come to you. For what more agreeable or more joyful thing could happen to me than now to be close to you that you might embrace me with those hands which, pure and innocent and keeping faith in the Lord, have scorned sacrilegious worship? What would be more delightful and sublime than now to kiss your lips, which have confessed the Lord with a glorious voice, than to be seen present by your eyes which, having despised the world, have appeared worthy in the sight of God? (Cyprian, *Letters,* 6, sec. 1, FC 51, p. 16)

Since the soul grows only in community, the care of souls is attentive to the quality of interpersonal relations. Soul care that focusses only upon private, individual, inward existence is distorted. The early pastoral writers were deeply invested in studying and counseling human relationships. Commenting upon the Parable of the Prodigal Son, Origen employed the metaphor of a symphony of intricately coordinated music in order to express the complex nature of interpersonal relationships formerly broken and now harmonized:

The word symphony is strictly applied to the harmonies of sounds in music. There are indeed among musical sounds some that are in accord, and other that are in discord. But the gospel writings are familiar with the term symphony as applied in the passage, "He heard a symphony [*symphonia*] and dancing" (Luke 15,25). For it was fitting that when the son who had been lost and found came by penitence into concord with his father, a symphony should be heard on the occasion of the joyous mirth of the house. But the wicked Laban was not acquainted with the word symphony in his saying to Jacob, "And if thou hadst told me I would have sent thee away with mirth and with music and with drums and a harp" (Gen. 31:27). But akin to the symphony of this nature is that which is written in the second Book of Kings when "the brethren of Aminadab went before the ark, and David and his son played before the Lord on instruments artistically fitted with might and with songs" (2 Sam. 6:4-5). . . . But perhaps also not even few but only two or three can make a symphony as Peter and James and John, to whom as making a symphony the Word of God showed His own glory. But only two, Paul and Sosthenes, made a symphony when writing the first Epistle to the Corinthians; and after this Paul and Timothy when sending the second Epistle to the same. And only three made a symphony when Paul and Silvanus and Timothy gave instruction by letter to the Thessalonians. . . . But if you wish still further to see those who are making symphony on earth look to those who heard the exhortation, "that ye may be perfected together in the same mind and in the same judgment" (1 Cor. 1:10), and who strove after the goal, "the soul and the heart of all the believers were one" (Acts 4:32) who have become such, if it be possible for such a condition to be found in more than two or three, that there is no discord between them, just as there is no discord between the strings of the ten-stringed psaltery with each other. . . . If we are the body of Christ and God has set each member in the body so that the members may have the same care one for another, and may agree with one another, and when one member suffers, all the members suffer with it, we ought to practise the symphony which springs from the divine music, that when we are gathered together in the name of Christ, He is in the midst of us. (Origen, *Commentary on Matthew,* Bk. XIV, sec. 1, ANF X, pp. 494-495)*

Among the very earliest letters of the pastoral tradition are those of Ignatius of Antioch, who appealed to Christians (c. 105 A.D.) to view their lives as fundamentally bonded and covenanted together:

Labor together with one another, strive together, run together, suffer together, rest together, rise up together—as God's stewards and assistants and servants. . . . Be patient with one another in gentleness, as God is with you. (Ignatius of Antioch, *Letter to Polycarp,* sec. 6, AF, p. 118)

The way the pastor deals with his own conflicted relationships is an important signal to others as to whether he may or may not be a trustworthy guide through their interpersonal conflicts. The avid conflict-avoider is not likely to be entrusted with the guidance of others' conflicts.

Pastoral writers have long understood the importance of the pastoral role as mediator of differences between persons, as a sign of God's reconciliation of human enmities in Christ. An early form of the pastoral mandate to personal peacemaking is found in the Apostolic Constitutions:

> Thou shalt make peace between those that are at variance, as Moses did when he persuaded them to be friends (Ex. 2:13). (*Constitutions of the Holy Apostles,* Bk. VII, Sec. I, ch. x, ANF VII, p. 467)

The Apostolic Constitutions set forth a preferred procedure for counseling and dealing with perennially quarrelsome persons—analyze causes accurately, seek dialogue, don't escalate:

> When you know such persons to be foolish, quarrelsome, passionate, and such as delight in mischief, observe carefully their behavior. . . . Consider diligently the accuser, wisely observing his mode of life, his activities, what sort of life he leads. If you find him to be one who tells the truth, then proceed according to the teaching of our Lord to go to the offending party and give pertinent admonitions hoping for a quiet repentance. But if he is not persuaded, take with you one or two more, and so show him his fault, and admonish him with mildness and instruction. "The wicked is overthrown through his evil-doing, but the righteous finds refuge through his integrity" (Prov. 14:32). (*Constitutions of the Holy Apostles,* Bk. II, Sec. V, ch. xxxvii, ANF VII, p. 414, RSV)*

Classical pastoral writers urged the faithful not to prompt situations that could lead to unnecessary conflict, especially during periods of persecution. The pastoral writers of the early third century, who faced bitter persecutions, learned the value of withdrawal. Origen, who himself had faced exile and imprisonment, commented on this passage from Matthew:

> "Then John's disciples came and took away the body, and buried it; and they went and told Jesus. When he heard what had happened Jesus withdrew privately by boat to a lonely place" (Matt. 14:12,13). . . . The scripture teaches us to withdraw as far as it is in our power from those who would persecute us, and from anticipated conspiracies through words. For this would be to act according to prudence. When you are able to keep outside of critical positions, to rush to meet them is rash and headstrong. If anyone still has doubts about avoiding such fruitless situations, then read again about Jesus who not only went into retreat when John was beheaded, but also taught his disciples: "When you are persecuted in one town, take refuge in another" (Matt. 10:23). When a trial comes which is not in our power to avoid, we must endure it with

exceeding nobility and courage. But when it is in our power to avoid it, not to do so is rash. (Origen, *Commentary on Matthew,* Bk. X, sec. 23, ANF X, p. 429, NEB)*

Origen's counsel: unavoidable conflicts must be courageously met; unnecessary conflicts must be avoided. Interpersonal conflicts may begin small, only to end with a flood of needless recriminations. One remedy is a moritorium period to regain composure. Gregory the Great, who mediated many conflicts—both interpersonal and international, thought that acrimony tends to move through several distinguishable stages:

At first we are satisfied to talk about the affairs of others, then the tongue gnaws with detraction the lives of those of whom we speak, and finally we break out into open slanders. Hence provocations are sown, quarrels arise, the torches of hatred are lit, peace of heart is extinguished. Therefore it is well said by Solomon: "The beginning of strife is like letting out water; so quit before the quarrel breaks out" (Prov. 17:14). . . . Solomon says again: "When words are many, transgression is not lacking" (Prov. 10:19). For this reason Isaiah said: "The effect of righteousness will be peace, and the result of righteousness, quietness" (Isa. 32:17), that is, he indicates that the righteousness of the mind is lacking where there is no restraint on immoderate speaking. Hence James says: "If any one thinks he is religious, and does not bridle his tongue but deceives his heart, this man's religion is vain" (James 1:26). James also wrote: "Let every man be quick to hear, slow to speak, slow to anger" (James 1:19) and again, describing the power of the tongue, he notes that animals can be tamed, "but no human being can tame the tongue—a restless evil, full of deadly poison" (James 3:8). (Gregory the Great, *Pastoral Care,* Part III, Ch. 14, ACW 11, pp. 132-133; cf. BPR, p. 38, RSV)*

St. Thomas thought the major types of discord could be sorted out into intentional (conscious) versus accidental (with unconscious motivation), and collusive quarrels (where both initiate the quarrel) versus unilateral quarrels (where one initiates the quarrel).

Concord is destroyed by discord in two ways: first, directly; secondly, accidentally. Now, human acts and movements are said to be direct when they are according to one's intention. . . . The accidental in human acts is that which occurs beside the intention. . . . Discord is sometimes the sin of one party only, for instance, when one wills a good which the other knowingly resists; while sometimes it implies sin in both parties, as when each dissents from the other's good, and loves his own. . . . Just as discord denotes contrariety of wills, so contention signifies contrariety of speech. Thomas Aquinas, *Summa Theologica*, Part II-II, Q. 37, Art. 1, Vol. II, pp. 1352-1354)

The appeal to scripture in settling controversies and questions of conscience has very ancient precedent, as this pre-Nicene tradition indicates:

We shall, as is needful, collect into one mass whatever passages of the Holy Scriptures are pertinent to this subject. And we shall manifestly harmonize, as far as possible, those which seem to be differing or of various meaning. And we shall to the extent of our poor ability examine both the usefulness and advantage of each viewpoint, that we may recommend to all communicants that the most wholesome form and peaceful custom be adopted in the Church. (Anonymous, *A Treatise on Re-baptism*, sec. 1, ANF V, p. 668)*

Wherever the pastor can become an interpersonal peacemaker with hope of reconciliation, it is a pastoral duty to do so in a world torn by enmities. Jesus pronounced the peacemaker blessed. Menno viewed interpersonal peacemaking on a cosmic-eschatological scale:

The Scriptures teach that there are two opposing princes and two opposing kingdoms: the one is the Prince of peace; the other the prince of strife. Each of these princes has his particular kingdom and as the prince is so is also the kingdom. The Prince of peace is Christ Jesus; His kingdom is the kingdom of peace, which is His church; His messengers are the messengers of peace; His Word is the word of peace; His body is the body of peace; His children are the seed of peace; and His inheritance and reward are the inheritance and reward of peace. In short, with this King, and in His kingdom and reign, it is nothing but peace. Everything that is seen, heard, and done is peace. (Menno Simons, Reply to False Accusations, *CWMS*, p. 554)

St. Francis de Sales' Treatise on Antipathies argued that aggressiveness ("repugnance" is his term) is to some degree an instinctive human response. It should be realistically recognized as such. He offered a proof of this hypothesis, the so-called "tennis court proof," which he thought any one could test out for himself. He discussed the dynamics of "first impressions" leading to repugnance, why conflicts grow, and how they may be mitigated:

What is antipathy? Antipathies are certain inclinations which are sometimes natural, and which excite in us a certain repugnance towards those for whom we entertain these feelings; a repugnance which prevents us from liking their conversation, or at least from taking that pleasure in it which we feel with regard to others, for whom we have a certain attraction, because there is between their mind and ours a reciprocity and union of tastes and feelings, which makes us feel for them a natural affection.

Here is a proof that it is perfectly natural that we should love some people and not others by a kind of instinct. Is it not often the case (so say the philosophers who advance this proposition) that two men enter a tennis-court where two others are playing tennis, and at once make up their minds which of the two players they wish should win? They have never seen either of them before, they have never heard them spoken of, and not knowing which is the superior in skill, they have no reason to like one better than the other. . . . Now, we must not dwell too much upon these instinctive antipathies or attractions, provided all are kept in reasonable subjection. If I feel a repugnance to conversing with a person whom yet I know to be most excellent, and from whom I might learn much that would do me good, I must not give way to the antipathy which prompts me to avoid his society. On the contrary, I must force myself to listen to the voice of reason telling me rather to seek his company, or at least, if I am already in it, to remain there with a quiet, peaceful mind. (Francis de Sales, Conference XVI, *SC*, pp. 298-300)

Here Francis offered a specific strategy for reaching out to others toward whom one has already developed a preliminary antipathy: Actively seek out the company of one who is felt to be repugnant, somewhat like the implosive strategy of behavior therapists who urge an immersion in the dreaded behavior in order to more quickly dissipate and overcome it.

It is not always the case, however, that peacemaking is preferable to bringing persons together. John Climacus (seventh century) must have been amused as he reported a provident case of creating an antipathy:

Blessed are the peacemakers. No one will deny this. But I have also seen enemy-makers who are blessed. A certain two developed impure affection for one another. But one of the discerning fathers, a most experienced man, was the means whereby they came to hate each other, by setting one against the other, telling each that he was being slandered by the other. And this wise man, by human roguery, succeeded in parrying the devil's malice and in producing hatred by which the impure affection was dissolved. (Climacus, *The Ladder of Divine Ascent*, Step 26, sec. 149, p. 185)

Normally hatred, stealth, slander, roguery and intentionally fostered conflict would be viewed as regrettable by the pastoral writers. But when one pays careful attention to context, all these tricks at times may be used to "parry the devil's malice," in this case to divert a relationship of "impure affection" that would have harmed both participants more than it did them good.

IV ✿ COUNSEL ON ALCOHOLISM AND ADDICTIVE BEHAVIORS

Pastoral wisdom has long had to struggle with persons caught in the crisis of alcoholism and addictive behaviors. Traditionally pastors have provided moral guidance concerning the use and abuse of alcohol and drugs. Alcohol and drug abuse has power to affect many lives beyond that of the user (wives of alcoholic husbands, children of the alcoholic, the pregnant alcoholic mother's child, friends, business relationships, etc.). Persons affected rank high among the crises that most pastors are called upon to deal with in some way. In this respect, modernity is not different from previous periods where people have struggled with debilitating addictive and compulsive behaviors, even though the chemical agents may have changed.

The pastoral writers have sought first to sort out the question of whether deeds done while intoxicated are to be considered voluntary deeds, and therefore deeds for which one is responsible. The ensuing reasoning is clear and penetrating:

> For example, a man does some ill deed when drunk, or in a rage. In the one case, drunkenness, and in the other anger, is responsible for what he did, and yet did voluntarily. For it lay in his power not to get drunk. So he was his own reason for not knowing what he did. Things of that sort are said to be done not in ignorance but in blindness; and those are not termed involuntary, but voluntary. For this reason, those who do such things are censured by good men. For if such a one had not got drunk, he would not have done what he did. Getting drunk was voluntary on his part, and so, clearly, those things that he did when drunk were voluntary. (Nemesius, *Of the Nature of Man,* Ch. XXXI.47, LCC IV, p. 387)

Addictive alcoholism may elicit a long chain of secondary complications, as indicated by Clement of Alexandria:

> Those pitiable people who exile temperance from their gatherings deem life the happiest when it turns into a wild drinking bout. Their life is nothing but carousing, drunken headaches, baths, undiluted wine, chamber-pots, idleness, and drinking. You can see some of them, in- deed, halfdrunk, stumbling over themselves, with wreathes around their necks as though they were bottles, spitting wine on one another in the name of good-fellowship; and others, too, suffering from the after- effects, unwashed, pallid, with flushed faces, yet, despite yesterday's spree, still gulping down one drink after the other. It is worth while, my friends, worth while indeed, to study this ridiculous yet pitiful picture, but at as great a distance as we can manage, and mend ourselves for the better, lest we ourselves some time may make a similar spectacle of

ourselves, as ridiculous as they. It has been well said: "As the kiln trieth the hard iron dipped in it, wine makes the heart arrogant" (in drunkenness) [Cf. Eccl. 31:31; but in the Septuagint, from which this text is taken, 34:26].

The excessive use of undiluted wine is intemperance; the disorderliness resulting from it is drunkenness; and the discomfort and indisposition felt after indulgence is called the after-effect. The Greek name for this is a word that etymologically means "to lose control of the head." This sort of life—if it can be called living—is sluggish, intent only on enjoying pleasure, yet feverish in its passion for wine. . . . Christ turned water into wine at the mariage feast, but He did not encourage them to become drunk. (Clement of Alexandria, *Christ the Educator,* Bk. II, Ch. 2.25-29, FC 23, pp. 116-118)

Clement commended the temperate use of wine, but was keenly aware of its potential for abuse. He proposed these guidelines for the use of wine:

Those who have already passed the prime of life may be permitted more readily to enjoy their cup. . . . They can even indulge in the merriment of feasts with composure. But, even for them, there is a limit: the point where they can still keep their minds clear, their memories active, and their bodies steady and under control, despite the wine. Those who know about these things call this the last drop before too much. It is well to stop short before this point, for fear of disaster.

A certain Artorius, I recall, in a book on longevity, is of the opinion that we should drink only so much as is needed to moisten our food, if we would live a long life. It is certainly a good idea to use wine, as some do, only for the sake of health, as a tonic, or for relaxation and enjoyment, as others do. Wine makes the man who drinks more mellow toward himself, better disposed toward his servants, and more genial with his friends. But, when he is overcome by wine, then he returns every offense of a drunken neighbor.

Wine is warm and gives out a sweet smell; therefore, in the proper mixture it thaws out the constipation of the intestines and with its sweetness dilutes every pungent or offensive odor. A quotation from Scripture will express it aptly: "Wine drunken with moderation was created from the beginning as the joy of the soul and of the heart" (Eccl. 31:36). (Clement of Alexandria, *Christ the Educator,* Bk. II, Ch. 2.22-23, FC 23, pp. 113-114)

Clement urged local wines to be used for medicinal purposes, and warned against the fostering of luxurious tastes for imported wines:

It is in conformity with right reason that those who are very susceptible to cold use wine during the winter to keep from shivering and at other seasons of the year to take proper care of their stomach. Just as food is permitted to relieve hunger, so drink is to ease thirst, provided the greatest caution is taken against any abuse. . . . There should never be any wild search for Chian wine when it is not available, nor for Ariousian when that fails. Thirst is simply the awareness of a need and requires only a relief corresponding to the need, one that will satisfy it, not deluge the mind. Importing wines from across the seas indicates cupidity grown soft from self-indulgence and a soul deranged by passion before it took to drink. There is the Thasian wine, which is sweet-smelling; Lesbian wine, which is fragrant; the Crean sweet wine; Syracusan pleasant-tasting wine; Mendesian wine from Egypt; insular Nazian wine; and Italian wine that is redolent of flowers. There exist all these various brands of wine, but for the temperate drinker it is only wine cultivated by the one only God. Why in the world is native wine insufficient to satisfy the taste? (Clement of Alexandria, *Christ the Educator,* Bk. II, Ch. 2.29-30, FC 23, pp. 119-120)

There are proper uses of wine, but none without potential abuse:

"Use a little wine," the Apostle cautions the waterdrinking Timothy, "use a little wine for thy stomach's sake" (1 Tim. 5:23). Shrewdly, he recommends a stimulating remedy for a body become ill-disposed and requiring medical attention, but he adds "a little," lest the remedy, taken too freely, itself come to need a cure. . . . But toward evening, near the time for supper, we may use wine, since we are no longer engaged in the public lectures which demand the absence of wine. At that time of day, the temperature has turned cooler than it was at midday, so that we need to stimulate the failing natural heat of the body with a little artificial warmth. (Clement of Alexandria, *Christ the Educator,* Bk. II, Chs. 19, 22, FC 23, pp. 110, 113)

Especially young people had best not be too early introduced to strong drink, according to Clement:

It is conceded that boys and girls should, as a general rule, be kept from this sort of drink. It is not well for flaming youth to be filled with the most inflammable of all liquids, wine, for that would be like pouring fire upon fire. When they are under its influence, wild impulses, festering lusts, and hot-bloodedness are aroused. (Clement of Alexandria, *Christ the Educator,* Bk. II, Ch. 2.20, FC 23, p. 112)

Can addictive behaviors undermine other efforts toward improving one's behavior patterns? Valerian showed how the vices of gluttony, drunkenness and covetousness may mutually affect and support each other:

We have often stated, dearly beloved, that drunkenness and covetousness are sources of vices. From them rushing torrents of sins well forth, and drag along to the depths a great part of the human race. Drunkenness stirs the whirlpool of gluttony, and covetousness enkindles a frenzy for odious thefts. . . . After the manner of some depraved business agreement, covetousness suggests a reward for furtive love, and drunkenness provides the occasion. . . . Clearly, therefore, drunkenness and covetousness ought to be attacked before all the other vices; for these two claim a primacy among the rest. Thus, those which trail these two will be in danger of losing their function. (Valerian, *Homilies,* Hom. 6, secs. 1-2, FC 17, pp. 336-337)

Luther conceded that mere exhortation or hortatory preaching would not stop alcoholic abuse, which he thought had reached an unconscionable point in his own time:

Next comes the abuse of eating and drinking which gives us Germans a bad reputation in foreign lands, as though it were our special vice. Preaching cannot stop it; it has become too common, and has got too firmly the upper hand. The waste of money which it causes would be a small thing, were it not followed by other sins,—murder, adultery, stealing, irreverence and all the vices. The temporal sword can do something to prevent it; or else it will be as Christ says: "The last day shall come like a secret snare, when they shall be eating and drinking, marrying and wooing, building and planting, buying and selling" (Luke 21:34,35). It is so much like that now that I verily believe the judgment day is at the door, though men are thinking least of all about it. (Luther, *An Open Letter to the Christian Nobility,* WML II, p. 161)

V ❧ VOCATIONAL COUNSEL

Pastors are called upon to advise persons making life-forming decisions. One of the most far-reaching decisions persons make is that of how and where they will work. Questions of vocational counseling have long occupied the pastoral writers.

As early as the fourth century tradition, pastors were making clear to their parishioners the value of work, the scriptural basis of its importance, and the consequences of disvaluing it.

Mind your business with all becoming seriousness, that so you may always have sufficient to support yourselves and those that are needy, and not burden the Church of God. For we ourselves, besides our attention to the word of the Gospel, do not neglect our temporal employments. For some of us are fishermen, some tentmakers, some gardeners, that so we may never be idle. So says Solomon somewhere: "Go to the ant, thou sluggard; consider her ways diligently, and become wiser than she. . . . How long wilt thou lie on thy bed, O sluggard? . . . Then poverty comes on thee like an evil traveller, and want as a swift racer" (Prov. 6:6ff.). . . . And again: "He that manages his own land shall be filled with bread" (Prov. 12:11). . . . But "if any one does not work, let not such a one eat" (2 Thess 3:10) among you. For the Lord our God detests sloth. Not one of those who are dedicated to God ought to be idle. (*Constitutions of the Holy Apostles,* Bk. II, Sec. VIII, ch. lxiii, ANF VII, p. 424-425)*

Although much traditional Christian vocational counseling has argued that persons should stay in their appointed place, and bloom where they are planted, some persons may be planted in the wrong spot, and should not fear transplant:

Look closely whether there is in your field a tree that "cumbereth the ground," (Cf. Luke 8:7) which, perhaps, might bear fruit elsewhere. In such a case, let us not hesitate to transplant it, lovingly uprooting it by our counsel. (Climacus, *To the Shepherd,* sec. 86, p. 243)

Not only helping persons decide where to work, but advising them on how to carry out their duties, is a part of pastoral counsel on vocation. Here is an example from a very early period of the pastoral tradition, from Theonas of Alexandria (writing about 300 A.D.). He is, as bishop, advising a friend, Lucianus, on how he is to assume and understand his extraordinary new responsibilities as chief chamberlain of the Emperor.

Bishop Theonas to Lucianus, The Chief Chamberlain of Our Most Invincible Emperor.

I give thanks to Almighty God and our Lord Jesus Christ, who has not neglected to manifest His faith throughout the whole world. In order to make clear our salvation, God has extended his revelation even through the course of the persecutions of despots. Yea, like gold reduced in the furnace, it has only been made to shine the more under the storms of persecution. . . . Wherefore, my Lucianus, I neither suppose nor desire that you should make it a matter of boasting, that by your means many persons belonging to the palace of the emperor have been brought to the knowledge of the truth. Rather it is more fitting that we give thanks to our God who has made you a good instrument for a good work, and has raised you to great honour with the emperor, that you might diffuse the sweet savour of the Christian name to His own glory and to the salvation of many. . . .

Therefore you ought to strive to the utmost of your power not to fall into a base or dishonourable, not to say an absolutely villainous way of thinking, lest the name of Christ be thus blasphemed even by you. Be it far from you that you should sell the privilege of access to the emperor to any one for money, or that you should by any means place a dishonest account of any affair before your prince. . . . Let all things be done with modesty, courteousness, affability, and uprightness, so that the name of our God and Lord Jesus Christ may be glorified in all.

Discharge the official duties to which you are severally appointed with the utmost fear of God and affection to your prince, and complete confidence. Regard every command of the emperor which does not offend God as if it were proceeding from God Himself. Execute it in love as well as in fear and with all cheerfulness. (Theonas of Alexandria, *Epistle to Lucianus*, secs. 1-2, ANF VI, pp. 158-159)*

Bishop Theonas further encouraged this vocational counselee to develop qualities of patience and courtesy in fulfilling fiduciary duties to an employer:

For there is nothing which so well refreshes a man who is wearied out with weighty cares as the seasonable cheerfulness and benign patience of an intimate servant; nor, again, on the other hand, does anything so much annoy and vex him as the moroseness and impatience and grumbling of his servant. . . . Be clothed with patience and courtesy. (Theonas of Alexandria, *Epistle to Lucianus*, sec. 2, ANF VI, pp. 158-159).

VI ❧ SUICIDE COUNSEL

While there may be many persons in a given parish who are in varying degrees depressed or severely depressed or potentially suicidal, there may be rare occasions, but very important ones, in which the pastor will be present amid the crisis of an immediate attempted suicide or near-suicide, or contemplation of suicide. Whatever the degree of immediacy, the pastor will be called upon to deal with persons who despair deeply over their lives, and at times wish to end their lives. This crisis calls for the best resources of empathy, firmness, wit, and care grounded in God's own caring. In this section we will bring together several passages from the struggle of classical pastoral writers to deal with the challenge of potential and actual suicide, and with the grief accompanying it.

Luther urged not judging too harshly those who take their own life in order to avoid a perceived greater evil:

Mention was made of a young girl who, to avoid violence offered her by a nobleman, threw herself from the window, and was killed. It was asked, was she responsible for her death? Doctor Luther said: No: she felt that this step formed her only chance of safety, it being not her life she sought to save, but her chastity. (Luther, *Table-talk,* WLS 1, p. 303)

Much classic pastoral reasoning about suicide has focused, not upon the immediate resolution of an imminent crisis, but rather upon teaching and understanding the value of life so as to avert such a crisis. One question faced by the suicidal is that of courage, whether there be courage to continue living, or whether there may be another kind of inverted courage to take one's life which amounts to an absence of the courage to live. Thomas Aquinas thought carefully about the relation of courage and suicide. He specifically reflected upon whether suicide could be considered an act of courage:

What courage entails is being ready to suffer death at another's hands for the sake of realizing virtue and avoiding sin. But inflicting death on oneself in order to avoid the evil of punishment is indeed a sort of courage, and this is why some people, including Razis, have killed themselves thinking that they are acting courageously. This is, however, not true courage, but, on the contrary, softness of spirit, i.e., the inability to bear penal afflictions, as both Aristotle and Augustine make clear. (Thomas Aquinas, *Summa Theologica,* Part II-II, Q. 64, Art. 5, Vol. II, p. 1469)

Others who struggle over whether their lives are worth living may be passing through stages of inordinate idealism. They may be more inclined to a different sort of rationalization with which the pastor must deal: that it might represent a higher ideal or a great-hearted act if one took one's own life. Augustine carefully considered whether suicide could ever be prompted by magnanimity, or viewed justly as a magnanimous (*magnus + animus* = great-souled) act:

Some who have laid violent hands on themselves may be admired by others to some degree because of their power of self-determination, even when they cannot be affirmed for the soundness of their judgment. However, if you look at the matter more closely, you will scarcely call it greatness of soul or freedom which prompts one to kill oneself rather than bear up against some hardships of fortune, or sins for which one is not responsible. Is it not rather an indication of a weakened soul to be unable to bear either the pains of bodily servitude or the foolish opinion of the vulgar? And is not that to be pronounced the greater soul which rather faces than flees the ills of life? Doesn't the greater soul evaluate itself by the light and purity of conscience, and not merely in terms of the esteem of men, and specially of popular opinion which is so frequently involved in a cloud of error? And, therefore, if suicide is to be esteemed an act of a great soul, a magnanimous act, none can take higher rank for magnanimity than that Cleombrotus, who (as the story

goes), when he had read Plato's book in which he treats of the immortality of the soul, threw himself from a wall, and so passed from this life
to that which he believed to be better. He was not being hard pressed
by calamities, nor by any accusation, false or true, which he could not
very well have lived down. There was, in short, no motive but only a
skewed sense of idealism urging him to seek death, and break away from
the sweet detention of this life. And yet Plato himself could have commented on whether this was a magnanimous or justifiable action. Plato,
whom he had read, would have told him, for he would certainly have
been forward to commit, or at least to recommend, suicide. For the
same bright intellect which saw that soul was immortal, discerned also
that to seek immortality by suicide was to be prohibited rather than
encouraged. (Augustine, *The City of God,* Bk. I.22, NPNF 1, II, p. 15)*

The poignant story of Cleombrotus' suicide after reading Plato's *Phaedo* re-
minds us today of high suicide rates among youth, who though favored by
prosperous circumstances may take their own lives out of either a temporarily
heightened despair or a distorted idealism.

To some it may seem that classical pastoral reason on suicide is too abstractly
reasoned to be practically helpful. And yet the pastoral writers have insisted
that unless one has learned to reason properly about life and its value, one cannot serve pastorally another who is considering denying life and its value.
Thomas Aquinas set forth in their most concise form the principal classical
Christian arguments from reason, Scripture and Christian antiquity against
the moral legitimacy of taking one's own life. Thomas raises the question
"whether it is lawful to kill oneself?" and begins with five paragraphs showing
the arguments that have been used for suicide, and then answers them:

It would seem to be legitimate for somebody to kill himself. Because
homicide is a sin in so far as it is opposed to justice. But nobody can
commit an injustice against himself, as Aristotle showed in his *Ethics*
[V.11]. Therefore, nobody can sin by killing himself.

He who holds public authority may legitimately kill malefactors. But
sometimes he who holds such authority is himself a malefactor. Such a
person may, therefore, legitimately kill himself.

A person may legitimately expose himself to a lesser danger in order
to avoid a greater, just as it is legitimate to cut off one limb in order to
save a body as a whole. But it sometimes happens that by committing
suicide a person avoids a greater evil, whether this be a wretched life
or the shame of some sin. A person may, therefore, legitimately kill
himself.

Judges records how Samson killed himself, and yet he is numbered
among the saints, as Hebrews makes clear.

The second book of Maccabees (14:42) relates that Razis fell upon his own sword preferring to die nobly rather than to fall into the hands of sinners and suffer outrages unworthy of his noble birth. But no noble and courageous act is illicit. Therefore suicide is not illicit. . . .

On the other hand, Augustine states, "It remains that the precept, Thou shalt not kill, refers to man. And this means both other men and oneself. For nobody but a man is killed when a person commits suicide" (*City of God,* I.20).

Reply: Suicide is completely wrong for three reasons. First, everything naturally loves itself, and it is for this reason that everything naturally seeks to keep itself in being and to resist hostile forces. So suicide runs counter to one's natural inclination, and also to that charity by which one ought to cherish oneself. Suicide is, therefore, always a mortal sin in so far as it stultifies the law of nature and charity. Second, every part belongs to the whole in virtue of what it is. But every man is part of the commmunity, so that he belongs to the community in virtue of what he is. Suicide therefore involves damaging the community, as Aristotle makes clear. Third, life is a gift made to man by God, and it is subject to him who is master of death and life. Therefore a person who takes his own life sins against God, just as he who kills another's slave injures the slave's master, or just as he who usurps judgement in a matter outside his authority also commits a sin. And God alone has authority to decide about life and death, as he declares in Deuteronomy, "I kill and I make alive." (Thomas Aquinas, *Summa Theologiae,* Part II-II, Q. 64, Art. 5, Vol. 38; cf. ST, Dominican Fathers ed., Vol. II, pp. 1468f.)

Others with whom the pastor speaks may feel that the depths of their suffering justifies taking their own life. Again the arguments of the pastoral writers may recede far to the background in actually dealing with such pastoral conversations, and we refer the reader to subsequent sections on suffering, but the heart of their reasoning may come to impinge profoundly on such a context. For to take one's own life, even amid great suffering, is to choose a greater evil in order to avoid a lesser, as Thomas Aquinas concisely stated:

Therefore to bring death upon oneself in order to escape the other afflictions of this life, is to adopt a greater evil in order to avoid a lesser. (Thomas Aquinas, *Summa Theologica,* Part II-II, Q. 64, Art. 5, Vol. II, p. 1469)

A helpful approach, first proposed by Augustine, centers on the assumption that everyone, even the suicidal individual, wants happiness. Part of the pastoral task amid thoughts of suicide is a teaching task at a highly personalized level, helping the individual see how much he wants happiness, and how that desire is built into his very being, and how that desire requires life in order to be fulfilled. This is a tightly constructed argument, and may require several readings, but the heart of it is this: that all persons wish to be happy, even if they do not at the moment perceive that wish accurately, and to be happy requires being. Thus no one who wishes to be happy can at the same time reasonably will to end the condition of his happiness—life:

As there is no one who does not wish to be happy, so there is no one who does not wish to be. For how can he be happy, if he is nothing?

As a rule, the very fact of existing is by some natural spell so pleasant, that even those most unhappy are, for no other reason, unwilling to die. Even when they feel that they are hopelessly unhappy, they still do not wish that they themselves be annihilated, but only that their misery be so. Consider even those who both in their own judgment and in point of fact, are utterly wretched, and who are viewed as such not only by caring individuals who may know something of their misdeeds, but also by those who misunderstand them superficially by thinking that they are unhappy only because their outward circumstances are poor and destitute, etc. Let us suppose that these wretched ones should be given an option in which their misery should continue on endlessly. Suppose they were offered this alternative: if they shrank from existing eternally in the same misery, then they would be completely annihilated, and exist nowhere at all, nor in any condition whatever. The evidence is abundant that they would instantly, even joyfully, nay exultantly, make election to exist always, even in such a condition, rather than not exist at all. There is plenty of evidence about us that witnesses to this inveterate human tendency. For when we see that persons fear to die, and will rather live in such misfortune than end it by death, is it not obvious enough how nature shrinks from annihilation? (Augustine, *The City of God,* Bk. XI.26-27, NPNF 1, II, p. 220)*

Although these few selections cannot do justice to a question so difficult, a pastoral task so demanding, and a pastoral tradition that has searched so long for answers, they at least provide the central direction of suicide counsel by pastors. It centers on the recognition of the value of life, the delay of any action that would foreclose the further disclosure of life values as yet unrecognized, and deep, empathic caring for those who suffer despair.

※

In this Part we have seen how ministry is present amid human crises to empathize, understand, console, challenge, warn, and guide. The overarching metaphor is that of the pilgrim travelling along a road that contains many hazards. The pastor is out there on that road offering help, direction, encouragement, and admonition. The crises thus far addressed are those of interpersonal conflict management, alcoholism and addictive behaviors, vocational struggles, and depressive and suicidal crises. Next we turn to the crisis of physical illness.

2 Pastoral Visitation and Care of the Sick

UNDER THE ANALOGY of shepherd and flock, the care-giver is particularly concerned with those in the flock who are ailing and vulnerable. The pastor does not passively wait for the sick to come to the pastoral office or residence for pastoral advice. Rather like the shepherd, the pastor goes out to look and care for them.

Physical illness is one of the most frequent crisis situations with which the pastor must deal. A significant portion of the pastor's time will be given to caring for the sick. In reaching out for the physically ill, the pastor shares directly in Jesus' own ministry. According to the parable of the Last Judgment (Matt. 25), Christ is present incognito in the sick. In caring for the sick one in effect cares for Christ's living body.

Care of the sick must first be placed in the context of the general need for the minister to visit parishioners, to walk among the people, to "perambulate" in the parish. For how are crises to be recognized if the pastor is not attentively there to see them arise.

I ❧ PASTORAL VISITATION

In the second century, the *Didache* assumed a pattern of regular conversation with the faithful. It spoke of peacemaking, dispensing equitable justice, and corrective love, as crucial to ministry.

Wherever the Lord's attributes are the subject of discourse, there the Lord is present. Frequent the company of the saints daily, so as to be edified by their conversation. Never encourage dissensions, but try to make peace between those who are at variance. Judge with justice, reprove without fear or favour, and never be in two minds about your decisions. Do not be like those who reach out to take, but draw back when the time comes for giving. (*Didache*, sec. 4, ECW, p. 29)

Few today would make a connection between pastoral visitation and care of the poor, yet these two tasks were thought to be inseparable, according to Anglican Bishop Burnet (1692). For how can one know the poor unless one visits them?

As the foundation upon which all the other parts of the pastoral care may be well managed, he ought frequently to visit his whole parish from house to house, that he may know them, and be known of them. This I know will seem a vast labour, especially in towns where parishes are large; but that is no excuse for those in the country, where they are generally small. If parishes are larger, the process of going on this round will take a little longer. Nonetheless, about an hour a day, two or three times a week, is no hard duty. This in the compass of a year will go a long way, even in a large parish. In these visits, one need not spend much time in a given place. A short word for stirring them up to mind their souls, to attune their conscience to their ways, and to pray earnestly to God, may begin it, and almost end it. After one has asked in what union and peace the neighbourhood lives, the pastor will inquire into their physical necessities. If they seem very poor, those to whom that care belongs should be put in mind to see how they may be relieved. (Gilbert Burnet, *Of the Pastoral Care,* Ch. VIII, p. 173)*

Burnet made the surprising assumption that pastoral visits to the poor and needy are the foundation upon which all other parts of pastoral care depend. Through such visits one engages in dialogue and gains understanding. The pastor learns about the people, and the people learn about the pastor. According to the analogy of the injured sheep, the more troubled persons require more time than others. Among the canons of the *Apostolic Constitutions* (compiled 350-400 A.D.) is the following pastoral instruction:

Like a compassionate shepherd, be a diligent feeder of the flock. Search out, and keep an account of the flock. Seek out the one that has need, just as the Lord God our gracious Father has sent His own Son, the good Shepherd and Saviour, to seek us. Our Master Jesus said: "If one of you has a hundred sheep and loses one of them, does he not leave the ninety-nine in the open pasture and go after the missing one until he has found it? How delighted he is then! He lifts it on to his shoulders, and home he goes to call his friends and neighbours together, and says, 'I have found my lost sheep'" (Luke 15:4-6). (*Constitutions of the Holy Apostles,* Bk. II, Sec. III, ch. xx, ANF VII, p. 405, NEB)*

There are strong mandates in scripture and tradition to go out and visit in some regularized, intentional manner, those committed to one's care. *How* this is done is less important than *that* it be done in a disciplined, consistent, and deliberate way. Pastoral visitation has often been resisted, either by the pastor or the people. Burnet urged that pastors confront these resistances both within themselves and others, in order that they might better clarify the reasons for visitation. He proposed that deliberate preaching on the biblical grounding and practical rationale for pastoral visitation would undercut much of its opposition:

I know this way of parochial visitation is so worn out that, perhaps, neither priest nor people will be very desirous to see it taken up. It will put the one to labour and trouble, and bring the other under a closer inspection, which bad men will no way desire, nor perhaps endure. But if this were put on the clergy by their bishops, and if they explained in a sermon before they began it the reasons and ends of doing it, that would remove the prejudices which might arise against it. (Gilbert Burnet, *Of the Pastoral Care,* Ch. VIII, p. 174)

Hence, by the end of the seventeenth century (1692) the practice of regular pastoral visitation of the parish in order to be attentive to human crises had fallen into relative confusion and disuse, and deliberate attempts were being made to revive it. One such suggestion was that the pastor visit around the parish particularly on Rogation Days (the early summer days of prayer for the harvest). Archbishop Laud urged that this telling question be asked annually of every congregation by its bishop:

Does your minister in the Rogation Days go in perambulation of the circuit of the parish, saying and using the prayers, suffrages, and thanksgiving to God, appointed by law, according to his duty, thanking God for His blessings, if there be plenty on the earth; or otherwise, to pray for His grace and favour, if there be a fear of scarcity? (William Laud, Visitation Articles, 1635, *Angl.,* p. 706)*

Richard Baxter found that personal interactions were more significant than all his preaching. He suggested a deliberate method for deepening the personal quality of a visit. This passage is among the earliest to suggest a systemic approach to family counseling:

We spend Monday and Tuesday from morning almost to night in the work, taking about fifteen or sixteen families in a week, that we may go through the parish, in which there are upwards of eight hundred families, in a year. I cannot say yet that one family has refused to come to me. Few persons excused themselves, and shifted it off. And I find more outward signs of success with most that do come, than from all my public preaching to them. . . . When the catechisms are ready to deliver, I make a list of all the persons of understanding in the parish. The clerk goes a week before to every family to tell them what day to come, and at what hour (one family at eight o'clock, the next at nine, and the next at ten, etc.). And I am forced by the number to deal with a whole family at once. Ordinarily I do not admit any of another family to be present.

Fellow clergy, would I invite you to this work without the authority of God, without the consent of all antiquity, without the consent of the Reformed Divines, or without the conviction of your own consciences? Note what the Westminster Assembly spoke occasionally in the Directory about the visitation of the sick: "It is the duty of the minister not only to teach the people committed to his charge in public, but privately, and particularly to admonish, exhort, reprove, and comfort them upon all seasonable occasions, so far as his time, strength, and personal safety will permit. He is to admonish them in time of health to prepare for death. And for that purpose, they are often to confer with their minister about the estate of their souls." (Baxter, *RP,* pp. 43-44)*

George Herbert described the unpretentious way in which personal visits might best proceed:

The Country Parson, upon the afternoons in the weekdays, takes occasion sometimes to visit in person, now one quarter of his parish, now another. For there he shall find his flock most naturally as they are, wallowing in the midst of their affairs. . . . When he comes to any house, first he blesses it; and then, as he finds the persons of the house employed, so he forms his discourse. . . . He holds the rule that nothing is little in God's service; if it once have the honor of that name, it grows great instantly. Therefore, neither does he disdain to enter into the poorest cottage, though he even creep into it, and though it smell ever so loathsomely. For both God is there, and also those for whom God died. (Geo. Herbert, *CP,* Ch. XIV, CWS, pp. 75-77)*

These passages show that sick visitation has been classically understood as existing within the context of an already personalized and regular mode of pastoral visitation that meets people where they are. That pastor is best readied to hear of crises and to deal with them who has already reached out, seen, met, and dialogued with the family or person in their own setting.

II ✠ Visitation of the Sick

While all parishioners should at times be visited by an attentive pastor, those in crisis or difficulty should be more immediately and intentionally visited. Illness may constitute a crisis not only for the body, but for self-esteem, hope, understanding, and faith. From its earliest decades, the pastoral tradition has viewed illness, mild or serious, as a special calling and opportunity for spiritual enlargement. The pastoral visit is not perfunctory, but appropriately deep-going where feasible. Here is a general direction for pastoral visitation of the sick, stressing promptness and attentive personal listening:

He is to go as soon as he hears that any of his flock are ill. He is not to satisfy himself with going over the office, or giving them the sacrament when desired. He ought to inform himself of their course of life, and of the temper of their mind, that so he may apply himself to them accordingly. (Gilbert Burnet, *Of the Pastoral Care,* Ch. VIII, p. 175; in *CS,* p. 93)

The visitation of the sick is viewed by pastoral writers as a context in which the teaching office of ministry becomes especially important. For something is to be learned from the limitations of illness. Yet health and knowledge are not the same. For suffering may conflict with learning:

Health and knowledge are not the same; one is a result of study, the other of healing. In fact, if a person is sick, he cannot master any of the things taught him until he is first completely cured. We give instructions to someone who is sick for an entirely different reason than we do to someone who is learning; the latter, we instruct that he may acquire knowledge, the first, that he may regain health. Just as our body needs a physician when it is sick, so, too, when we are weak, our soul needs the Educator to cure its ills. Only then does it need the Teacher to guide it and develop its capacity to know, once it is made pure and capable of retaining the revelation of the Word. (Clement of Alexandria, *Christ the Educator,* Bk. I, Ch. 1.3, FC 23, p. 5)

The Educator to whom Clement referred is Christ, God's own Word addressed to the sufferer, made more plausible and meaningful by God's own participation in human suffering. The purpose of this education is to regain and sustain inward health of soul as one mends bodily. It is not merely to pass along objective data or information.

Long centuries of pastoral experience of visitation of the sick have shown that there are better and worse ways of visiting the sick. The best prayer for the sick will be brief, sincere, and responsive to personal need:

It is fitting and useful that one should "visit orphans and widows," (James 1:27), and especially those poor who have many children. These duties are, by consensus, required of ministers of God, and appropriate and suitable for them. It is also suitable and right and comely for those who are brethren in Christ to visit those who are harassed by evil spirits, and pray and pronounce earnest petitions over them, intelligently offering such prayer as is acceptable before God, yet not with a multitude of fine words, well prepared and arranged, so that one may project the appearance to hearers of having eloquence and a terrific memory. Such persons are "like a sounding pipe, or a tinkling cymbal" (1 Cor. 13:1). They bring no help to those over whom they make their supplications. . . .

In this way let us approach a brother or a sister who is sick, and visit them in a way that is fitting, without guile, and without covetousness, and without noise, and without talkativeness, and without such behaviour as is alien to reverence for God, and without haughtiness, but with the meek and lowly spirit of Christ. Let visitors of the sick, therefore, with fasting and with prayer, make their petitions, not with the elegant and well-arranged and fitly ordered words of learning, but as those who have received the gift of healing from God, confidently, to the glory of God. . . . For the Apostle has said: "Who is sick, and I am not sick? who is offended, and I am not offended?" (2 Cor. 11:29). (Clementina, *Two Epistles Concerning Virginity,* I, Ch. XII, ANF VIII, pp. 59-60)*

Candor, self-constraint, caring attentiveness, and deeply felt empathy with another's suffering: these qualities make up the heart of sick-bed visitation. The following instructions to pastors on how to visit the sick, offered by Philip Doddridge, remain remarkably pertinent today:

First, I shall give you some hints relating to precautions to be taken in order to understand the case of the sick. . . . Inquire of others concerning their character, especially from those who are best acquainted with them, and above all from religious persons; a pious parent, for instance, concerning a child; a master, concerning a servant, etc. Seek to obtain accurate information from them . . . on which you may ground a plain and awakened address.

Send their relations, if you can conveniently, out of the room. Then ask the person seriously whether he has any thing particular to say to you with regard to the state of his soul. Enquire what his hopes are, and especially on what foundation they are built. When you have asked him a few questions on these themes leave him room to talk. Perhaps he may freely and fully tell you his condition.

If he does not, ask him such questions as these: . . . Have you felt the power of scripture upon your heart? Have you been concerned to give your thoughts and affections to God, as well as your external actions? Have you felt a struggle with the temptations of Satan, and the corruptions of your own heart? Have you inquired after the remedies of the particular distempers of your own mind? And so far as you have understood them have you endeavoured to use them? (Doddridge, *Lectures on Preaching,* "On Visiting the Sick," Lect. XXII.7-10, pp. 108-109)*

Doddridge placed high priority upon listening, yet with questions that could open up the patient for a preliminary or deeper spiritual self-examination appropriate to the limitations of the particular ailment.

Pastoral writers have also noted ways *not* to visit the sick. Ambrose pointed to the prototype of Job's so-called "comforters", who completely misunderstood

Job and applied supposed remedies that might be applicable to others, but not to him. Job helped his visitors more than they helped him:

They [the "comforters"] did not know, therefore, what was appropriate to each person. But the holy man Job made distinction in spirit as to how he should speak to each one; therefore he was stronger than those who appeared healthy and sound. . . . For Job was stronger when sick than he had been when healthy, according to that which is written, that "power comes to its full strength in weakness." (2 Cor. 12:9) And so, when Job was suffering weakness, then he had the greater strength. Indeed, he was not sick in spirit, even though he was suffering bodily pain, because his soul was not in bondage to the flesh, nor did it cleave to the passions of the flesh; rather, it was spirit and had covered itself with the strength of the spirit. (Ambrose, *Exegetical Works,* The Prayer of Job and David, Ch. 2, sec. 3, FC 65, p. 354)*

The very language of ministry is intrinsically linked with the act of serving. For there is no ministry without the dimension of *diakonia.* As the offices of ministry became more sharply distinguished, the task of caring for the sick fell to deacons. Here is Calvin's reflection on two kinds of deacons, which he thought distinguishable in scripture:

There were always two kinds in the ancient Church, the one deputed to receive, dispense and hold goods for the poor, not only daily alms, but also possessions, rents and pensions; the other to tend and care for the sick and administer allowances to the poor. This custom we follow again now for we have procurators and hospitallers. . . . The election of both procurators and hospitallers is to take place like that of the elders; and in electing them the rule proposed by Paul for deacons is to be followed.

With regard to the office of procurator, we think the rules which have already been imposed on them by us are good, by means of which, in urgent affairs, and where there is danger in deferment, and chiefly when there is no grave difficulty or question of great expense, they are not obliged always to be meeting, but one or two can do what is reasonable in the absence of the others.

It will be their duty to watch diligently that the public hospital is well maintained, and that this be so both for the sick and the old people unable to work, widowed women, orphaned children and other poor creatures. The sick are always to be lodged in a set of rooms separate from the other people who are unable to work, old men, widowed women, orphaned children and the other poor. (Calvin, *Draft Ecclesiastical Ordinances,* 1541, LCC XX, pp. 64-65)

Accordingly, some deacons focus upon poor relief, while others focus on sick relief. One seeks to sustain persons temporally during economic crisis, while the other seeks to bring the body back to health during the crisis of physical illness. Both are crisis ministries. Both seek to increase spiritual insight while attending to the care of the body amid its personal and/or social situation.

III ✖ The Timing of Sick Visitation

The ethics governing pastoral initiative-taking in sick visitation reflect the fundamental pastoral metaphor of the serving shepherd. If one of the flock falls ill, the pastor does not wait for an invitation or request for help, as the physician's ethics would require. For the pastoral relationship is entirely different from an exchange relationship based upon fees for service. Rather, ministry seeks to manifest the overflowing character of the love of God by responding immediately to need. This passage by Jeremy Taylor expresses the essence of this recurrent theme:

A minister must not stay till he be sent for; but, of his own accord and care, go to them, to examine them, to exhort them to perfect their repentance, to strengthen their faith, to encourage their patience, to persuade them to resignation, to the renewing of their holy vows, to the love of God, to be reconciled to their neighbours, to make restitution and amends. (Jeremy Taylor, *RAC,* sec. 72, p. 77; in *CS,* p. 23)

Once in the presence of the stricken neighbor, the pastor is called to act, not woodenly by a pre-set formula, but responsively to the situation at hand. The situation might variously require encouragement, admonition, behavioral redirection, acts of reparation, or simply letting-be.

Poverty may combine with sickness to intensify the crisis. In this case, early canon law called the minister to seek remedies for both limitations of the body and for its temporal-economic sustenance, as a requisite and implication of soul care:

No priest shall neglect the sick which are in the streets without making enquiry after them. And if the sick man be poor, let him give him what he needs. (*Athanasian Canons,* sec. 47, p. 35)*

It sometimes occurs that the family waits too long, until a patient is extremely ill, before calling the pastor. Calvin considered this problem to be so serious that he proposed the following rule to the diaconate of Geneva:

There are many people negligent in comforting themselves in God by his Word when they are afflicted with sickness, and so many die without the admonition or teaching which is more salutary for a man then than at any other time. It will be good therefore that their Lordships ordain and make public that no one is to be totally confined to bed for three

days without informing the minister, and that each be advised to call
the ministers when they desire it in good time in order that they be not
diverted from the office which they publicly discharge in the Church.
Above all it is to be commanded that parents, friends and attendants do
not wait until the patient is about to die, for in this extremity consolation
is in most cases hardly useful. (Calvin, *Draft Ecclesiastical Ordinances,*
1541, "Of the Visitation of the Sick," *SW,* p. 239)

Although seldom has the pastoral tradition been so specific as this Calvinist
rule of informing the minister within three days of serious illness, at least this
document is a case in point showing the importance of working out some
reasonable system by which the pastor is well-informed about the physical well-
being of his curacy. Luther made this pungent remark in 1527 during the time
of a deadly plague, concerning those who wait too long for pastoral care and
then expect the pastor to do the impossible:

If, after all, a chaplain or pastor is desired, he should be called or the
need of the sick person should be reported betimes and at the beginning
before the disease gets the upper hand and while the patient still has his
mind and reason. I say this because some are so negligent that they do
not call a spiritual counselor or report the sickness until the soul sits on
the tongue of the patient and he can no longer talk and little reason is
left. Then they beg: Tell him what is best. But before this, when the
sickness begins, they do not want us to come. (Luther, WA, 23, p. 372;
in WLS 3, p. 1286)

IV ❧ THE SINGULAR, UNREPEATABLE OPPORTUNITY

In centuries past the onset of illness more often meant the possibility of facing
death more immediately than it does today. This in part explains why sick
visitation has been considered so urgent and imperative by pastoral writers.
For any sickness might bring one starkly into the awareness of the fragility of
all bodily life. Sickness is an unwelcome, yet potentially growth-laden opportunity for decisive spiritual formation. Whether it asks us absolutely about our
death or relatively about the numerous limitations in terms of which we constantly live our lives, any illness may become a spiritual test. Sick visitation
may be the only service the pastor is permitted to render to some.

You will remember that this part of a minister's work is very important. With regard to some it is the only kind office you will ever be able
to perform for them. Perhaps if you neglect it, they may go into the
presence of God with a testimony against you. Sometimes you will have
to visit persons who have been entirely thoughtless of religion, to whom
you may prove of singular advantage. At other times good persons may
end life in a manner more tranquil and more honourable to religion on

account of sickness. Or if they live, they may make a better improvement of their future moments. The conversations you have had with them in health, which were at the time reviving cordials to their drooping spirits, will not be entirely without a relish on their sick-beds. But do not let this relax your purpose of visiting them. At these times, more than when they were healthy, you ought to attend to them, remembering that when sorrow makes the heart droop, then a good word makes it glad. (Doddridge, *Lectures on Preaching,* "On Visiting the Sick," Lect. XXII.1, pp. 106-107)*

The extent to which physical affliction may come to have spiritual meaning has been debated throughout the tradition. The building-construction metaphor (especially the hammering of stone materials before fitting) helped Gregory the Great to clarify this connection. It emerged textually out of the New Testament image of the church as a building in which every part is intricately fitted together by divine forethought, but which must be carefully hewn before fitting (1 Kings 6:7; Eph. 2:20-22):

The stones for building the Temple of God were hammered outside, that they might be set in the building without the sound of hammer. Similarly we are now smitten with scourges outside, that afterwards we may be set into the Temple of God without the stroke of discipline, and that the strokes may now cut away whatever is inordinate in us, and that then only the concord of charity may bind us together in the building. . . . The sick are to be admonished to consider what great health of the heart is bestowed by bodily affliction, for it recalls the mind to a knowledge of itself and renews the memory of our infirmity, which health commonly disregards. . . . To preserve the virtue of patience, the sick are to be admonished ever to bear in mind how great were the evils endured constantly by our Redeemer at the hands of those whom He had created, how many horrible insults and reproaches He endured, how many blows in the face He received at the hands of scoffers. (Gregory the Great, *Pastoral Care,* Part III, Ch. 12, ACW 11, pp. 123-125)*

The hammering in the analogy is like the poundings of suffering that fit one for the praise of God. The healthy easily lose sight of their own mortality. Sickness has the power to challenge and remind them of their actual situation of vulnerability, transcience and physical limitation. In doing so it may render a potentially valuable service, a situation-specific learning that otherwise might never be grasped. The vulnerability of the body may ironically bring a singular opportunity for the cleansing and renewal of spirit. Misunderstood, this point may risk masochistic distortion. Rightly understood, it points to a potentially great gift:

Affliction can in the penitent cleanse sins done and restrain those that might have been done, as well as encourage those troubled in mind to move from outward pain to inward penitence. Thus it is written that "Blows and wounds cleanse away evil, and beatings purge the inmost being" (Prov. 20:30). . . . When we are smitten outwardly, we may be silently and painfully recalled to the memory of our sins and bring back before our eyes all our past misdeeds, so that through what we suffer outwardly we grieve inwardly the more for what we have done. (Gregory the Great, *BPR,* Part III, Ch. XII, NPNF 2, XII, p. 35, NIV)*

Sickness tests strength of soul. Excellent habitual behaviors may be either made stronger or weakened by disease:

When pain is present, the soul appears to diminish in its presence, and view release from present pain as an unparalleled value. At that moment the soul slackens from studies, as supporting virtues are neglected. Yet it does not occur to us to say that it is virtue itself that suffers. For strictly speaking, virtue is not being attacked by disease. Rather it is that one who is partaker of both (virtue and disease) finds that virtue is affected by the stress of the disease. And at that point the person will be distraught who has not attained the habit of self-control, if he does not have exceptional natural vitality. (Clement of Alexandria, *The Stromata, or Miscellanies,* Bk. IV, Ch. V, ANF II, pp. 412-413)*

Sickness may bring a temptation to lose ground that one had gained. Clement's distinction is surgically precise: it is, strictly speaking, not the virtue or behavioral excellence that is directly diminished by disease, but rather the self-determining person who feels the stress put by illness upon the nurturing of virtue. Anyone who is not already under effective spiritual discipline will therefore find disease more difficult and more profoundly tempting.

V ❧ STRENGTH FOUND AMID WEAKNESS

Insofar as pastoral writers view illness as both spiritual opportunity and challenge, much of their energies focus upon helping persons to respond to both the positive and negative challenge of illness. They sought to help people see the ways in which the compassionate God is addressing, assisting, strengthening, comforting, correcting and befriending persons amid illness. Numerous counsels and prayers reflect this kind of reasoning. Ambrose wrote to a friend, Bellicius, who had promised to make important behavioral changes, yet delayed them inordinately, and then had fallen seriously ill:

You tell me that while you lay very ill you believed in the Lord Jesus and soon began to grow better. This sickness was intended for your health . . . . Although, perhaps, you did not hear Him, He as God spoke imperceptibly, and if you did not see Him, there is no possible doubt that He visited you though without a body. You saw Him, for you believed in Him; you saw Him, for you received Him into the dwelling of your mind; you saw Him in spirit; you saw with inner eyes. Hold fast your new Guest, long awaited but lately received, in whom "we live and have our being and move" (Acts 17:28). You have tasted the first fruits of faith; let not the word be hidden in your heart. (Ambrose, *Letters,* 66, To Bellicius, FC 26, p. 401)

This does not imply, however, that sick patients should avoid treatment or do nothing for themselves under the pretense of trusting in God. Against this excess Luther warned:

You should not say: No matter what I do, I cannot hinder the will of God so that because of my conduct less happens than God has determined. For this is the language of the devil, and it is forever damned. Rather you should go on in simple faith, and when you are in danger and trouble, you should use whatever means you can, lest you tempt God. (Luther, "Lectures on Genesis, Chapters 38 to 44, 1535," WA 44, pp. 527f.; in WLS 3, p. 1287; cf. LW 7, p. 308)

Doing nothing amid illness, while piously expecting God to do everything, puts God on trial, and is strongly admonished. Temptations to believe the worst about God may be increased during illness. While some patients may think of sickness as an unambiguous, ominous indication of the anger of God, Luther wanted to make a finer distinction:

Although He *appears* to be angry, it is nonetheless not true that He *is* angry. . . . When God sends us tribulation, Satan suggests: See there, God flings you into prison, endangers your life. Surely, He hates you. He is angry with you; for if He did not hate you, He would not allow this thing to happen. In this way Satan turns the rod of a Father into the rope of a hangman and the most salutary remedy into the deadliest poison. (Luther, WA 25, pp. 178-179; in WLS 1, pp. 29-30)

In this way illness may lead to self-deception. Pastors, like everyone else, must from time to time face physical illness. The following letter was written by Calvin during an extended illness which involved not only hallucinations, pain, exhaustion, indigestion, and fevers, but in addition the dubious treatments of physicians (quarantine, laxatives, bed rest, bodily manipulation, medications, etc.). In such circumstances it may happen that the pastor's own struggle with illness becomes a context of intensive spiritual ferment and self-examination:

Nearly six weeks have now elapsed since I became acquainted with the nature of my complaint, during which I have been in the hands of the doctors, who keep me shut up in my bed-room and pretty generally confine me to bed in which I am protected by a double coverlet, while every now and then they keep dinning in my ears the verse of Sophocles, "the belly has become so hard bound that it will not relax unless aided by a clyster," which is a state very alien to my usual habits. They prescribe to me all the best and most digestible kinds of food, none of which flatter my taste, so that my strength gets gradually more and more feeble. I struggle against my illness, nevertheless, and recruit my exhausted stomach with the most insipid of food, nor do I either allow my loathing to get the better of me, nor like most people, do I coax myself into an appetite by employing stimulants that are pernicious to my complaint. Nay, in everything I take care not to deviate one hair-breadth from the doctor's prescription, except that in my burning thirst I allow myself to drink a little more copiously. And even this excess I impute to their fault, for they most pointedly exact of me to drink Burgundy wine, which I am not allowed to temper with water or any more common beverage. Nay, unless I had obstinately protested, they wanted to kill me outright with the heating fumes of Malmsey and Muscat wine. But as I know that they are men of no common skill in their profession, persons of sound good sense moreover, and experienced from a long practice of their art, I not only from motives of polite-ness pay implicit attention to their orders, but even willingly permit myself to be guided by such masters. They mix my wine with spleen-wort or wormwood. They fortify my stomach by fomenting it with syrups of hyssop, or elecampane, or citron bark, at the same time applying to it a certain pressure, that the novelty of the sensation may give greater energy to the remedy and cause it to act more speedily. They only once attempted to expel the bilious humours from my spleen. But though I seem now to be abusing your leisure moments with too much indifference, and in dictating these details during the heat of the fever, I was not very judiciously consulting my own health; yet, as the issue of my complaint is still doubtful, I wished to assure you that I am now making it the principal subject of my meditation, how at a moment's warning I may be prepared to meet any lot which God intends for me. (Calvin, To Melanchthon, *SW,* pp. 69-71)

Here Calvin pictures himself as the ambivalent patient, needing yet resisting physicians' ploys, miserable with his sickness and even a little more miserable with the proposed cures.

The excessively scrupulous conscience has often presented a difficult pastoral challenge, especially during illness. When guilt is ever poised for intensifica-tion, it may be helpful to point out to those with inordinate scruples that misdeeds and infirmities tend to be virtually universally endemic to the human situation, so that the believer does not inordinately focus upon a direct cause-effect speculation concerning a particular sin and a particular ailment. Here is such a letter of pastoral counsel to a sick woman from Menno Simons, the founder of the Mennonites:

I understand that your conscience is troubled because you have not and do not now walk in such perfection as the Scriptures hold before us. I write the following to my faithful sister as a brotherly consolation from the true Word and eternal truth of the Lord. The Scripture, says Paul, has concluded all under sin. There is no man on earth, says Solomon, who does righteously and sins not. At another place: A just man falls seven times and rises up again. Moses says: The Lord, the merciful God, merciful and gracious, longsuffering and abundant in goodness and truth, keeping mercy for thousands, forgiving iniquity and transgression and sin, before whom there is none without sin. O dear sister, notice, he says, none are without sin before God. And David says: Lord, enter not into judgment with thy servant; for in thy sight shall no man living be justified. And we read, If they sin against thee (for there is no one that does not sin). We are all as an unclean thing, and all our righteousness is as filthy rags. Christ also said, There is none good but one, that is God. The evil which I would not, that I do. In many things we all offend. If we say that we have no sin, we deceive ourselves, and the truth is not in us.

Since it is plain from all these Scriptures that we must all confess ourselves to be sinners, as we are in fact; and since no one under heaven has perfectly fulfilled the righteousness required of God but Christ Jesus alone; therefore none can approach God, obtain grace, and be saved, except by the perfect righteousness, atonement, and intercession of Jesus Christ, however godly, righteous, holy, and unblamable he may be. We must all acknowledge, whoever we are, that we are sinners in thought, word, and deed. Yes, if we did not have before us the righteous Christ Jesus, no prophet nor apostle could be saved. Therefore be of good cheer and comforted in the Lord. (Menno Simons, Letter of Consolation to a Sick Saint, *CWMS,* pp. 1052-1053)

Menno's counsel focusses upon the joyful reality of divine forgiveness, instead of a wretched, continual awareness of sin.

Far from limiting prayer, illness may elicit and illumine prayer. John Donne, with remarkable powers of metaphorical imagination, spoke of being knocked off his feet by illness, only to discover "the knees of the heart":

O Most mighty and merciful God, who, though thou hast taken me off of my feet, hast not taken me off of my foundation, which is Thyself. Though thou hast removed me from that upright form in which I could stand and see thy throne, the heavens, yet thou hast not removed from me that light by which I can lie and see Thyself. Though thou hast so weakened my bodily knees that they cannot bow to thee, yet thou hast left me the knees of my heart; . . . I come to thee, by embracing thy coming to me. (John Donne, *Devotions,* p. 21)*

The fantasia of visions presented to the mind during sickness may frighten. Assuming that the human person is a microcosm of the cosmos, Donne drew a brilliant analogy between natural processes of destruction and the destructive power of physical illness.

As the other world produces serpents and vipers, malignant and venomous creatures, and worms and caterpillars, that endeavour to devour that world which produces them, and monsters compiled and complicated of divers parents and kinds; so this world, ourselves, produces all these in us, in producing diseases, and sicknesses of all those sorts: venomous and infectious diseases, feeding and consuming diseases, and manifold and entangled diseases made up of many several ones. (John Donne, *Devotions,* p. 24)

Nonetheless, God would not have improved creation if He had made sickness absolutely impossible:

It is true that the weakness of the flesh sharpens our mental faculties. When muscular strength is weakened, the strength of the body is transferred into invigoration of the soul. Thus, to me it seems a kind of health that man at times should not be healthy. (Salvian, *Letters,* 5, FC 3, p. 252.)

As a muscle is made stong not by relaxation but by pushing against something, so human health, in the providence of God, is capable of being made stronger by physical infirmity, by the absence of health. Donne described how the loneliness of illness may be softened by God's own companionship:

Thou hast said too, "Two are better than one" (Eccl.4:9); and, "Woe be unto him that is alone when he falls" (v. 10). . . . Thy Son did not refuse, but even chose, many, many times, solitariness, aloneness (Matt. 14:23), but at all times . . . he was far from being alone; for, "I am not alone," says he, "but I, and the Father that sent me" (John 8:16) . . . Have I such a leprosy in my soul that I must die alone; alone without thee? . . . Must not it be concluded that Moses "was commanded to come near the Lord alone" (Exod. 24:2); that solitariness, and dereliction, and abandoning of others, disposes us best for God, who accompanies us most alone? May I not remember, and apply too, that though God came not to Jacob till he found him alone, yet when

he found him alone, he wrestled with him (Gen. 32:24,25). (John
Donne, *Devotions,* pp. 32-34)*

VI ❧ The Healing Professions Holistically Viewed

Physicians are companion professionals to ministry, and have been from
earliest recorded history. The physician has been an identifiable professional
role in most previous centuries of Christian pastoral care. There is a long
history of the interfacing of medicine and ministry. Sometimes one has pre-
dominated over the other, at other times they have stood in paradoxical tension
treating the psychosomatic interconnection as best they could. A sixteenth
century Anglican writer urged a cooperative relationship between physician
and pastor:

There is an excellent Canon to this purpose (in *Decretal,* Book 5, Title
38, chapter 13): "By this present Decree we strictly charge and command all physicians, that when they shall be called to sick persons, they
first of all admonish and persuade them to send for the physicians of
souls, that after provision hath been made for the spiritual health of the
soul, they may the more hopefully proceed to the use of bodily medicine. For when the cause is taken away, the effect may follow." That
which chiefly occasioned the making of this good law was the supine
carelessness of some sick persons, who never used to call for the physician of the soul till the physician of the body had given them over. And
if the physician did, as his duty was, timely admonish them to provide
for their soul's health, they took it for a sentence of death and despaired
of remedy, which hastened their end and hindered both the bodily
physician from working any cure upon their body and the spiritual
physician from applying any effectual means to their soul's health. It is
good counsel that Ecclesiasticus gives (38:9), where we are advised not
first to send for the physician and when we despair of his help and are
breathing our last then to send for the priest, when our weakness has
made him useless; but first to make our peace with God by spiritual
offices of the priest, and then give place to the physician. (Anthony
Sparrow, A Rationale or Practical Exposition of the Book of Common
Prayer, p. 221; in *Angl.,* pp. 521-522)*

At the time of this writing (1657) the problem had developed, as sometimes
occurs today, that the calling of the minister to the bedside was taken to be a
grave sign, causing the patient to despair. The remedy: bring the minister from
the beginning into the healing team so that body and spirit can be treated
together. Despite this call for cooperation, the willingness to cooperate has
sometimes been lacking. Luther, for example, urged parishioners to follow
their physician's advice, but not slavishly or without discernment of their own:

Miserable is the man who is dependent on the help of doctors. I do not deny that medicine is a gift of God and a science, but where are the perfect medics? A good diet is of great value. (Luther, *Table Talk,* WA-T 3, #3733; in WLS 3, p. 1287; cf. LW 54, #3733, p. 266)

In another recollection from *Table Talk,* Luther developed this point further, seeking the proper balance in affirming the medical role without making an idolatry of it:

In sicknesses doctors observe only the natural causes and want to counteract them with their remedies; and they do well. But they do not consider that in sickness Satan provokes the natural causes. . . . There must, then, be a higher remedy, to wit, faith and prayer, just as Ps. 31:15 says: "My times are in Thy hands". I have really learned to understand this passage in my sickness. I commend doctors who are anxious to defend their rules. But they should not blame me either if I do not always obey, for they want to make a fixed star of me when I am a straying planet. The office of doctors is a responsible one. To them is entrusted human life, which has many hidden emotions, internal and invisible members, and is also exposed to various and sudden dangers so that it can be ruined in an hour. Therefore a doctor should be humble, that is, God-fearing. (Luther, *Table Talk,* WA-T 4, #4784; in WLS 3, pp. 1286-1287)

Since Luther viewed illness as a skirmish in a conflict involving super-personal powers on the vast scale of salvation history, he thought physicians were valuable within the sphere of natural remedies, but could do little about the larger combat. The latent potential clash between physicians and pastors has long existed, as evidenced by this second century argument by Tatian, viz., that we are not healed by chemistry alone, but also by that which transcends chemistry:

But medicine and everything included in it is an invention of the same kind. If anyone is healed by matter, through trusting to it, much more will he be healed by having recourse to the power of God. As noxious preparations are material compounds, so are curatives of the same nature. If, however, we reject the baser matter, some persons often endeavour to heal by a union of one of these bad things with some other, and will make use of the bad to attain the good. But, just as he who dines with a robber, though he may not be a robber himself, partakes of the punishment on account of his intimacy with him, so he who is not bad but associates with the bad, having dealings with them for some supposed good, will be punished by God the Judge for partnership in the same object. Why is he who trusts in the system of matter not willing to trust in God? For what reason do you not approach the more powerful Lord, but rather seek to cure yourself, like the dog with grass, or the stag with a viper, or the hog with river-crabs, or the lion with apes? Why do you deify the objects of nature? . . . Even if you be healed by drugs (I grant you that point by courtesy), yet it behoves you to give testimony of the cure of God. (Tatian, *Address to the Greeks,* Chs. XVIII-XX, ANF II, p. 73)

Tatian was not questioning the potential value of drugs to heal, but he was disturbed, as many remain disturbed today, about the tendency to make an idol out of chemical remedies, to assume that they can do anything for us, even cure the soul's malaise. This, says Tatian, is to worship matter, to make a god of the physical manipulations of chemistry.

Amid his own serious illness, John Donne became acutely aware of his own powerlessness in the hands of the physician. Pensively, he compared humans and animals on this point: Animals take care of themselves, but humans must resort to being taken care of.

O miserable abundance, O beggarly riches! How much do we lack of having remedies for every disease, when as yet we have not names for them? But we have a Hercules against these giants, these monsters. We have the physician. He musters up all the forces of the other world to cure disease, and all nature to relieve man. We have the physician. But we are not the physician. Here we shrink in our proportion, sink in our dignity, in relation to seemingly lowly creatures, who are physicians to themselves. The deer that is pursued and wounded, they say, knows an herb, which being eaten throws off the arrow: a strange kind of vomit. The dog that pursues it, though he be subject to sickness, even proverbially, knows his grass that recovers him. . . . The apothecary is not so near to the patient, nor the physician so near him, as medication and medicine are to other creatures. Man does not have that innate instinct to apply those natural medicines to his present danger, as those inferior creatures have. Man is not his own apothecary, his own physician, as they are. . . . His diseases are his own, but the physician is not. He has them at home, but he must send for the physician. (John Donne, *Devotions,* pp. 24-25)*

The physician may become a curse rather than a blessing if spiritual remedies are neglected. It is better if the two physicians, of body and soul, can learn to work together:

Thou, who sendest us for a blessing to the physician, did not intend that it should be a curse to us to go when thou sendest us. The curse rather lies in this: The only one for whom the trip to the physician becomes a curse is, rather, the one who falls into the hands of the physician, casts himself wholly, entirely upon the physician, confides in him, relies upon him, attends to everything from him, yet neglects that spiritual medicine that thou hast instituted in the church . . . I know that even my weakness is a reason, a motive, to induce thy mercy, and my sickness an occasion of thy sending health. . . . "Give place to the physician, for the Lord hath created him; let him not go from thee, for thou hast need of him" (Ecclus. 38:12). I send for the physician, but I will hear him enter with those words of Peter, "Jesus Christ maketh thee whole" (Acts 9:34). (John Donne, *Devotions,* pp. 26-27)*

Donne gave us a vivid description of how the patient watches the face of the physician for clues. He shrewdly and dialectically analyzed, in a humorous way that anticipated Kierkegaard, the dynamics of accelerating anxiety amid illness and its cure:

I observe the physician with the same diligence as he the disease. I see he fears, and I fear with him; I overtake him, I overrun him, in his fear, and I go the faster, because he makes his pace slow; I fear more, because he disguises his fear, and I see it with the more sharpness, because he would not have me see it. He knows that his fear shall not disorder the practice and exercise of his art, but he knows that my fear may disorder the effect and working of his practice. As the ill affections of the spleen complicate and mingle themselves with every infirmity of the body, so does fear insinuate itself in every action or passion of the mind; and as wind in the body will counterfeit any disease, and seem the stone, and seem the gout, so fear will counterfeit any disease of the mind. It shall seem love, a love of having; and it is but a fear, a jealous and suspicious fear of losing. It shall seem valour in despising and undervaluing danger; and it is but fear in an overvaluing of opinion and estimation, and a fear of losing that. A man that is not afraid of a lion is afraid of a cat; not afraid of starving, and yet is afraid of some joint of meat at the table presented to feed him; . . . I know not what fear is, nor I know not what it is that I fear now; I fear not the hastening of my death, and yet I do fear the increase of the disease. I should belie nature if I should deny that I feared this; . . . It is a fearful thing to fall into thy hands. This fear preserves me from all inordinate fear, arising out of the infirmity of nature, because thy hand being upon me, thou wilt never let me fall out of thy hand. . . . So give me, O Lord, a fear, of which I may not be afraid. . . . Let me not therefore, O my God, be ashamed of these fears, but let me feel them to determine where his fear did, in a present submitting of all to thy will. (John Donne, *Devotions,* pp. 35-42)*

Here many elements of contemporary psychotherapeutic practice are anticipated: the dynamics of intensifying anxiety, the syndrome of disproportionality in symbolizing what one fears, the intricacy of the psycho-somatic interface, the ways disease is affected by anxiety, the capacity of anxiety to mimic symptoms, the need to face fear and analyze its roots, and above all the relativization of objects of human fear in relation to God.

VII ✻ The Management of Pain

Despite all efforts of medicine and ministry there are times when we must bear pain of both body and spirit. The pastoral writers have dealt with this harsh reality frequently and profoundly. Here, for example, is St. Anthony's counsel to those who are suffering (as reported by Athanasius):

"Pray continually; avoid vainglory; sing psalms before sleep and on awaking; hold in your heart the commandments of Scripture; be mindful of the works of the saints that your soul's being put in remembrance of the commandments may be brought into harmony with the zeal of the saints." And especially he counselled them to meditate continually on the apostle's word, "If you are angry, do not let anger lead you to sin; do not let sunset find you still nursing it" (Eph. 4:26). (Athanasius, *Life of Anthony*, sec. 54, NPNF 2, IV, pp. 210-211, NEB)*

The human self is stretched out between heaven and earth as if it were a microcosm of all things. This vast range of the body/soul struggle appears even more clearly during illness:

Earth is the centre of my body, heaven is the centre of my soul; these two are the natural places of these two; but those go not to these two in an equal pace: my body falls down without pushing; my soul does not go up without pulling; ascension is my soul's pace and measure, but precipitation my body's. . . . It was part of Adam's punishment, "in the sweat of thy brows thou shalt eat thy bread" (Gen. 3:19). It is multiplied to me, I have earned bread in the sweat of my brows, in the labour of my calling, and I have it; and I sweat again and again, from the brow to the sole of the foot, but I eat no bread, I taste no sustenance: miserable distribution of mankind, where one half lacks meat, and the other stomach! (John Donne, *Devotions*, pp. 12-13)

Does the willed response of the patient to some extent influence the experience of pain? St. Catherine of Siena used the literary device of speaking in the voice of Christ as she argued that freedom transcends pain:

No one born passes this life without pain, bodily or mental. Bodily pain My servants bear, but their minds are free, that is, they do not feel the weariness of the pain; for their will is accorded with Mine, and it is the will that gives trouble to man. (Catherine of Siena, *A Treatise of Discretion,* p. 125)

Although some modern readers may find St. Catherine's language implausible, there is a growing body of evidence that spiritual adepts both in eastern and western ascetic traditions have learned to activate natural bodily censures of pain by means of focussed meditation and the disciplining of the will. Modernity has much more to learn about pain. Much has been many times discovered and forgotten in pre-modern periods. Acupuncture, placebo healing, varied pain thresholds, and spontaneous remission are among phenomena awaiting further modern research. Luther argued that the faithful perceive suffering differently by focussing consciousness upon hope:

In our suffering we should so act that we give our greatest attention to the promise, in order that our cross and affliction may be turned to good, to something which we could never have asked or thought. And this is precisely the thing which makes a difference between the Christian's suffering and afflictions and those of all other men. For other people also have their afflictions, cross, and misfortune, just as they also have their times when they can sit in the rose garden and employ their good fortune and their goods as they please. But when they run into affliction and suffering, they have nothing to comfort them, for they do not have the mighty promises and the confidence in God which Christians have. Therefore they cannot comfort themselves with the assurance that God will help them to bear the afflictions; much less can they count on it that he will turn their affliction and suffering to good.

So it is, as we see, that they cannot endure even the small afflictions. But when the big, strong afflictions occur, they despair altogether, destroy themselves, or they want to jump out of their skin because the whole world has become too cramped for them. Likewise they cannot observe moderation either in fortune or misfortune. When things go well, they are the most wanton, defiant, and arrogant people you can find. When things go wrong, they are utterly shattered and despondent. (Luther, "Sermon at Coburg on Cross and Suffering, 1530," LW 51, p. 201)

VIII ❧ COMMUNION FOR THE SICK

If Christ himself is truly present in the Eucharist, it has been thought unseemly to carry around these mysteries from place to place. However, an exception has been made in the case of the seriously ill:

No priest shall carry forth the mysteries and go with them about the streets, except for a sick man, when the end and death's hour of need draw nigh. (*Athanasian Canons,* sec. 36, p. 32)

It was out of this need that the practice of a reserved communion developed:

But for the Sick, it was always sent them at home, though the distance be ever so great. And against the time of extremity it was thought not amiss to have kept it in reserve, so that, if the priest should not then be in state to go to the sick party, and there to consecrate it for him, yet at least it might be sent him, as in the case of Serapion. For it is sure they made far greater account of the receiving it as their *viaticum* than some do now. (William Forbes, *Considerationes Modestae,* 1658; in *Angl.,* p. 502)*

This Anglican writer was appealing to St. Serapion, bishop of Thumis (d. after 369), who in his *euchologian,* or *Sacramentary,* compiled ancient prayers and rites. These included the embryonic ideas of reserved communion and *viaticum* (journey beyond) for the dying communicant. Another Anglican pastoral writer, Anthony Sparrow, commented on the rubrics for communion of the sick:

The Rubric at the Communion of the Sick directs the Priest to deliver the Communion to the sick, but does not there (i.e. in the pre-1662 Book of Common Prayer) set down how much of the Communion Service shall be used at the delivering of the Communion to the sick; and therefore seems to me to refer us to former directions in times past. Now the direction formerly was this:—

"If the same day (that the sick is to receive the Communion) there be a Celebration of the Holy Communion in the Church, then shall the Priest reserve, at the open Communion, so much of the Sacrament of the Body and Blood, as shall serve the sick person and so many as shall communicate with him. And as soon as he may conveniently, after the open Communion ended in the Church, shall go and minister the same, first to them that are appointed to communicate with the sick, if there be any; and last of all to the sick" (King Edward VI's First Liturgy). (Anthony Sparrow, A Rationale or Practical Exposition of the Book of Common Prayer, pp. 223f.; in *Angl.,* pp. 502f.)

If a person is sick, especially gravely ill, it is thought to be the reponsibility of the pastor to make communion available to him or her, yet to do so under conditions which conserve the essential mystery of the holy communion.

The sick may feel drastically cut off from community, as poignantly expressed by John Donne. The analogy is powerful: the bed is a grave; illness like death; bedside comforters like graveside visitors; speaking to others like trying to reach out from a grave:

A sick bed is a grave, and all that the patient says there is but a varying of his own epitaph. . . . In the grave I may speak through the stones, in the voices of my friends, and in the accents of those words which their love may afford my memory. Here I am mine own ghost, and rather affright my beholders than instruct them . . . . Miserable, and (though common to all) inhuman posture, where I must practise my lying in the grave by lying still, and not practise my resurrection by rising any more. . . . How shall they come to thee whom thou hast nailed to their bed? Thou art in the congregation, and I in solitude: when the centurion's servant lay sick at home, his master was pleased to come to Christ; the sick man could not (Matt. 8:6). . . . I lie here and say, "Blessed are they that dwell in thy house" (Ps. 84:4); but I cannot say, "I will come into thy house." . . . There is another station (indeed they are less stations than prostrations) lower than this bed: To-morrow I may be laid one story lower, upon the floor, the face of the earth; and next day another story, in the grave, the womb of the earth. As yet, God suspends me between heaven and earth, as a meteor; and I am not in heaven because an earthly body clogs me, and I am not in the earth because a heavenly soul sustains me. (John Donne, *Devotions,* pp. 17-21)*

Few pastoral writers have described with more depth and pathos the way in which loneliness may compound with the misery of sickness than John Donne:

As sickness is the greatest misery, so the greatest misery of sickness is solitude; . . . When I am dead, and my body might infect, they have a remedy, they may bury me; but when I am but sick, and might infect, they have no remedy but their absence, and my solitude. . . . It is an outlawry, an excommunication upon the patient, and separates him from all offices, not only of civility but of working charity . . . to be left alone . . . this makes an infectious bed equal, nay, worse than a grave, that though in both I be equally alone, in my bed I know it, and feel it, and shall not in my grave. (John Donne, *Devotions,* pp. 30-32)

IX ❦ CARE OF THE GRAVELY ILL

The pastor who neglects parishioners faced with serious or life-threatening illness is fleeing from a primary responsibility. The opportunity for pastoral service may be exhausted or diminished if the pastor is not promptly responsive. Not only readiness, but quality of relationship is crucial to this ministry. When bishops made annual visitations to parishes, they did well to ask parishioners concerning pastors, according to Archbishop William Laud:

When any person has been dangerously sick in your parish, has the pastor neglected to visit him, and when any have been parting out of this life, has he omitted to do his last duty in their behalf? (William Laud, Visitation Articles, 1635; in *Angl.,* p. 708)*

Philip Doddridge thought it appropriate that the pastor should speak carefully with gravely ill patients about the desirability of defining wishes about their temporal affairs. But this should be done proportionally to the physical strength of the patient, and with spiritual ends in view. Doddridge was keenly aware of the egocentric distortions that could enter into pastoral counsel on temporal affairs:

If their sickness be threatening, some advice as to their temporal affairs may be needful; but your main business relates to their spiritual concerns. As to temporal affairs, advise them as briefly as possible to make a disposition of them by will. Sometimes this is of great importance; at others, however, it is not. If there be any suspicion of ill-gotten wealth or property, urge them to an immediate restitution, as absolutely necessary; and should they refuse, warn them of their danger and pray for them; but in other respects show them but little attention. Be very cautious that you do not give the smallest intimation that you wish to turn the will into such a channel as may be most for your own interest. When you know that legacies have already been designed, have as little as possible to do with the will. As to spiritual concerns, your advice must be regulated by the state and character of each individual. (Doddridge, *Lectures on Preaching,* "On Visiting the Sick," Lect. XXII.12-13, p. 109)*

Many near-death experiences are reported in the pastoral tradition, some with remarkable effect upon the patient and others. This account by Dame Julian of Norwich is a case in point:

And when I was thirty and one-half years old, God sent me a bodily sickness, in which I lay three days and three nights. On the fourth night I received all the rites of holy Church, and I believed I would not live until morning.

After that I lay sick two more days and nights. On the third night, I thought many times that I would die, and so did those who were with me. Since I was still young, I thought it a great hardship to die, but not because there was anything on earth I wanted to live for, nor because I feared the pain, for I trusted in God's mercy. I would have preferred to live so that I could have loved God better, for a longer time, and thus, by the grace of God, have been able to know and love him better in the bliss of heaven. . . .

Thus I endured until daylight, and by then my body, from the middle downward, was dead, having no feeling at all. Then I was moved to ask to be set upright, and, with help, propped up, so that I could have more freedom of heart to be at God's disposal, and to think about him while my life should last.

My curate had been sent for to be at my deathbed, but by the time he came my eyes had become fixed and I could not speak. He set the cross before my face and said, "I have brought you the image of your Maker and Savior. Look on it, and be comforted by it." . . . After this, the other part of my body began to die, to the point where I had scarcely any feeling, and my greatest pain was shortness of breath. At that point, I was sure I was going to die.

And then, suddenly, all my pain was taken from me, and I was as whole and healthy in every part of my body as I had ever been before. I marveled at this sudden change, for it seemed to me that this was a secret working of God, and not the work of nature. (Juliana of Norwich, *Revelations of Divine Love,* Ch. 3, pp. 84-86)

John Donne provided this model of petitionary prayer during severe illness:

O most gracious God, . . . by dulling my bodily senses to the meats and eases of this world, thou hast whet and sharpened my spiritual senses to the apprehension of thee; by whatever steps and degrees it shall please thee to go, in the dissolution of this body, hasten, O Lord, that pace, and multiply, O my God, those degrees, in the exaltation of my soul toward thee now, and to thee then . . . . O my God, who madest thyself a light in a bush, in the midst of these brambles and thorns of a sharp sickness, appear unto me so that I may see thee, and know thee to be my God, applying thyself to me, even in these sharp and thorny passages. (John Donne, *Devotions,* pp. 15-16)*

There are times when life hangs in the balance, when one can only pray:

Whether it be thy will to continue me long thus, or to dismiss me by death, be pleased to afford me the helps fit for both conditions, either for my weak stay here, or my final transmigration from hence. (John Donne, *Devotions,* p. 34)

X ❧ Health of Soul

Modern psychologists and psychotherapists have found it easier to provide an analysis of emotive sickness than of health. The early pastoral writers, too, debated the perplexity of the definition of health, particularly as it relates to a society that itself may have become sick. Abba Anthony thought that good health may look like madness to those who are mad:

Abba Anthony said, "A time is coming when men will go mad, and when they see someone who is not mad, they will attack him saying, 'You are mad, you are not like us.'" (Anthony the Great, in *Sayings of the Desert Fathers,* p. 5)

John Chrysostom also remarked that a healthy person in a sick society may be completely misunderstood:

Among many healthy persons, a healthy man will not be noticed. But when there is one healthy man among many who are sick, the report will quickly spread and reach the king's ears. (Chrysostom, *Homilies on Ephesians,* Hom. XX, NPNF 1, XIII, p. 155)*

This raises the perplexity as to how likely it is that those who are sick will rightly recognize and understand their sickness. Those who are trapped by their own unexamined passions and emotions are not in the best position to understand their emotions. The metaphor Climacus applied is slavery:

We are like bought slaves under contract to unholy passions; we, therefore, know to some extent the whims, ways, will and wiles of the spirits that rule over our poor souls. But there are others who through the operation of the Holy Spirit, and by reason of their liberation from those spirits, are enlightened as to their tricks. The former, being in a painful state of sickness, can only guess about the relief which would come with good health; while the latter, being in a healthy condition are able to recognize and draw conclusions about the miseries attendant on sickness. That is why we, who are weak and infirm, hesitate to philoso-phize in our discourse about the haven of stillness. (Climacus, *The Ladder of Divine Ascent,* Step 27, sec. 1, p. 197)

The healthy are harder to counsel than the sick, in Gregory's view:

The hale are to be admonished in one way, the sick in another. The hale are to be admonished to employ bodily health in behalf of mental health. Otherwise, if they divert the favour granted them of their good condition to the doing of evil and thus become the worse for the gift, they will merit punishment, which will be the graver in proportion as they do not shrink from putting to an evil use the bountiful gifts of God.

The hale are to be admonished not to set aside the opportunity of win-ning eternal salvation, for it is written: Behold, now is the acceptable time, behold, now is the day of salvation (2 Cor. 6:2). They are to be admonished that if they are unwilling to please God when they can, they may not be able to please Him when, too late, they decide to do so. This is why it is said that Wisdom afterwards deserts those who disregard her call too long, for she says: "I called and you refused, I stretched out my hand and there was none that regarded. You have despised all my

counsel and have neglected my reprehensions" (Prov. 1:24,25). . . .
Commonly the gift of health is spent by vices; and when it is suddenly
withdrawn, when the flesh is worn out with afflictions, when the soul is
on the point of being forced to go forth from the body, then the health,
enjoyed for long in evil, is sought once more on the plea of living a good
life. Men then moan for having refused to serve God, when it is utterly
impossible for them to serve Him and thus repair the losses due to their
neglect. (Gregory the Great, *Pastoral Care,* Part III, Ch. 12, ACW 11,
pp. 120-122)*

Health was regarded as a perishable gift to be used responsibly while it is
given, and not wasted away in the neglect of rarely given opportunities.

What is health? It is from Isaac Barrow, the seventeenth century Anglican,
that we find one of the most moving and richly hewn statements of personal
and social health. The question he addressed was: What most engenders interpersonal health, and what most powerfully counteracts interpersonal and
social sickness?

To be just and faithful in our dealings, to be sober and modest in our
minds, to be meek and gentle in our demeanours, to be staunch and
temperate in our enjoyments, and the like principal rules of duty, are
such that the common reason of man and continual experience do
approve them as hugely conducible to the public good of men and to
each person's private welfare. So notoriously beneficial they appear,
that for the justification of them we might appeal even to the judgement
and conscience of those persons who are most concerned to derogate
from them. . . . The understanding of men can hardly be so corrupted
that piety, charity, justice, temperance, meekness, can in good earnest
considerately by any man be disallowed, or that persons apparently
practising them can be despised; but rather, in spite of all contrary prej-
udice and disaffections, such things and such persons cannot but in
judgement and heart be esteemed by all. . . . If we look on a person
sticking to those rules, we shall perceive him to have a cheerful mind
and composed passions, to be at peace within and satisfied with himself,
to live in comely order, in good repute, in fair correspondence, and firm
concord with his neighbours. If we mark what preserves the body sound
and lusty, what keeps the mind vigorous and brisk, what saves and
improves the estate, what upholds the good name, what guards and
graces one's whole life, it is nothing else but proceeding in our demean-
our and dealings according to the honest and wise rules of piety. If we
view a place where these commonly in good measure are observed, we
shall discern that peace and prosperity do flourish there; that all things
proceed on sweetly and fairly; that men generally thrive on conversation

and commerce together contentedly, delightfully, advantageously, yielding friendly advice and aid mutually, striving to render one another happy; that few clamours or complaints are heard there, few contentions or stirs do appear, few disasters or tragedies do occur; that such a place has indeed much of the face, much of the substance of Paradise.

But if you take note of those who neglect them, you will find their minds galled with sore remorse, racked with anxious fears and doubts, agitated with storms of passion and lust, living in disorder and disgrace, jarring with others, and no less dissatisfied with themselves. If you observe what impairs the health, weakens and frets the mind, wastes the estate, blemishes the reputation, and exposes the whole life to danger and trouble, what is it but thwarting these good rules? If you consider a place where these are much neglected, it will appear like a wilderness of savage beasts, or a sty of foul swine, or a hell of cursed fiends, full of roaring and tearing, of factions and feuds, of distractions and confusions, of pitiful objects, of doleful moans, of tragic events. Human beings are there wallowing in filth, wildly revelling, bickering and squabbling, defaming, circumventing, disturbing and vexing one another; as if they affected nothing more than to render one another as miserable as they can. It is from lust and luxury, from ambition and avarice, from envy and spite, and similar dispositions, which religion chiefly interdicts, that all such horrid mischiefs do spring.

In fine, the precepts of religion are no other than such as physicians would prescribe for the health of our bodies, as politicians would avow needful for the peace of the state, as Epicurean philosophers do recommend for the tranquility of our mind and pleasure of our lives; such as common reason dictates and daily trial shows conducible to our welfare in all respects: which consequently, were there no law exacting them of us, we should in wisdom choose to observe, and voluntarily impose on ourselves, confessing them to be fit matters of law, as most advantageous and requisite of the good (general and particular) of mankind. (Isaac Barrow, *Works,* Vol. 1, pp. 21-22; in *Angl.,* pp. 746-748)*

It is a repeated theme of pastoral writers that interpersonal justice is the soundest basis of interpersonal health. The rules of justice are best undergirded by religion, without which their depth is not reached.

XI ✸ THE GIFT OF HEALING

Christ's own ministry and the apostolic ministry were accompanied by remarkable events of healing of both body and spirit. This has given rise to a continuing examination of the proper grounding and understanding of alleged occurrences of healing in the Christian community. For without doubt the temptations to fraud and abuse are great. When healings have occurred, the question has been raised: Who heals in Christian healing? Is it the human agent or Christ's living presence?

Antony, at any rate, healed not by commanding, but by prayer and speaking the name of Christ. So that it was clear to all that it was not he himself who worked, but the Lord who showed mercy by his means and healed the sufferers. But Antony's part was only prayer and discipline, for the sake of which he stayed in the mountain, rejoicing in the contemplation of divine things, but grieving when troubled by much people, and dragged to the outer mountain. (Athanasius, *Life of Antony*, sec. 84, NPNF 2, IV, p. 218)

It is not uncommon in early accounts of healing that healing occurs non-verbally, and without preparation, but with a vital awareness of the presence of Christ. Here is a fourth century rendering of an oral tradition of an alleged recollection by Clement of Peter's healing ministry:

When Peter had said this, the crowds dispersed; and when we also were intending to go to our lodging, the master of the house said to us: "It is demeaning and wrong that such great men should stay in a hostelry when I have almost my whole house empty, many beds spread, and all necessary things provided." But when Peter refused, the wife of the householder prostrated herself before him with her children, and pleaded with him, saying, "I beg of you, stay with us." But even then Peter did not consent, until he met the daughter of these people who begged him to stay. She had been for a long time troubled by a corrupting spirit, had been left bound with chains, shut up in a closet. When Peter came near, the evil spirit was instantly torn away from her, the door of the closet opened, and she came with her chains and fell down at Peter's feet, saying: "It is right, my lord, that you keep my deliverance-feast here to-day, and not sadden me or my parents." But when Peter asked what was the meaning of her chains and of her words, her parents, gladdened beyond hope by the recovery of their daughter, were, as it were, thunderstruck with astonishment, and could not speak. The servants who were in attendance said: "This girl has been troubled by an evil spirit since her seventh year. She used to cut, bite, and even tear into anyone who might even attempt to approach her, and this she has never ceased to do for twenty years until the present time. Nor could anyone cure her, or even approach her, for she rendered many helpless, and even destroyed some; for she was stronger than any man, being doubtless strengthened by the power of the demonic. But now, as you see, the evil spirit has fled from your presence, and the doors which were shut with the greatest strength have been opened, and she herself stands before you with sound mind, asking of you to make the day of her recovery gladsome both to herself and her parents, and to remain with them." When one of the servants had made this statement, and the chains of their own accord were loosened from her hands and feet, Peter, being aware that it was due to his presence that soundness had been restored to the girl, consented to remain with them. (Clementina, *Recognitions of Clement,* Bk. X, ch. xxxviii, ANF VIII, p. 192)*

The Clementina is best read as a novel. It is a part of a vast literature in early Christianity reporting remarkable healings. This one is included here because of its exceptionally dramatic reversal, and because of the surprisingly passive role of Peter, who did not even want to go to the house in the first place. No special words were spoken or rite observed or action taken. Only the presence of the apostle, attesting the presence of the living Christ, according to this account, called forth health and renewal of spirit, unbinding the demonic powers.

Julian of Norwich prayed that sickness might become a means to increased health. She described this account of a near-death experience, out of which came her remarkable visions and a ministry of healing:

These revelations were showed to a simple, uneducated creature living in mortal flesh in the year of our Lord 1373, on the eighth day of May. . . . I desired a vision in which I might have more knowledge of the bodily pains of our savior, and of the compassion of our Lady and of all his true lovers who were living at that time and saw his pains, for I wanted to be one of them and suffer with him. I never desired any other vision or showing from God until my soul should be parted from my body, for I believed I would be saved by the mercy of God.

I made this first petition so that after the showing I might have a truer understanding of the passion of Christ.

As for the second petition, it came to my mind with contrition, freely, without my seeking it in any way. It was a fully willed desire to have as God's gift a bodily sickness so severe it would bring me to the point of death. I asked that in that sickness I might receive all the rites of holy Church, and that I, and everyone else who saw me, should really believe I was dying. I asked this because I wanted absolutely no human or earthly comfort in this sickness. I desired to have all the kinds of bodily and spiritual pain I would have had if I had actually been dying. I wanted all the terrors, the temptations of devils, and every kind of pain except the actual departure of the soul. I asked all this so that by it I might be purged, by God's mercy, and afterward live more for the glory of God, because of that sickness. I also hoped it would assist me in my death, for I desired to be soon with my God and maker. (Juliana of Norwich, *Revelations of Divine Love,* Ch. 2, pp. 83-84)

Dame Julian is not speaking of a morbid death wish, but of an experience of the soul's illumination that Julian thought could have occurred only through a concrete meeting with death. It may seem masochistic to the modern view to wish to suffer as Christ suffered in order more vitally to witness to his resurrected life through and beyond human life. But to Julian it was the central premise of her receptivity to the divine self-disclosure.

The pastoral tradition stores a vast historical and practical wisdom on the care of the sick. For nineteen centuries it has recurrently dealt with the challenge of sickness and the nurture of health. This has occurred through regular visiting of the sick, through seeking a clearer perception of the divine purpose amid illness, through cooperation with physicians in the conjoint psychosomatic healing of both body and soul, through the ministry of the sacrament amid illness—especially grave illness, and through participating in the larger healing activity of God in Jesus Christ.

3 The Enigma of Suffering

PASTORAL WORK DRAWS CLOSE to human suffering. The pastoral tradition has repeatedly faced the most harsh and undeniable realities of suffering, and has been required to respond to them in deed and word.

The technical name for the reasoning of the pastoral tradition on suffering is theodicy. Theodicy seeks to vindicate the justice and goodness of God in the face of the disturbing facts of evil and suffering. Pastoral theodicy seeks to answer the recurrent, sometimes urgent, existential question: If God is so good and powerful, why is so much evil and suffering permitted?

No working pastor can avoid this question for long. Nor could the classical pastoral writers. What follows is a brief selection of texts that indicate the main lines of reflection and response by the pastoral tradition to this most demanding theological issue of pastoral care. It is fitting first to make clear how limited rational argument is in the face of suffering.

I ❧ ACKNOWLEDGING THE LIMITS OF RATIONAL ARGUMENT AMID SUFFERING

The season of the reasonable argument is not in the midst of acute suffering, but rather in due preparation for it. Pastoral consolations cannot substitute for concrete acts of caring service to sufferers. The time to reflect deeply upon the theological arguments concerning God's justice amid suffering is not after, but before illness has overtaken one. Reasonable arguments should not be assumed to have undue efficacy in the midst of actual suffering:

All things have their proper season. So it is proper to ply men with words which strengthen the soul prior to evil events, so that if at any time evil comes upon them, the mind, being forearmed with the right argument, may be able to bear up under that which happens to it. For at that point the mind still is capable of having recourse to the One who sustains it by good counsel, prior to the crisis of struggle with evil. (Clementina, *Homilies,* Hom. II, Ch. III, ANF VIII, p. 229)*

The person who is well-grounded in reflection about the providence and goodness of God is more likely to be able to bear whatever comes. The pastoral writers did not conform to the stereotype of a pastor who goes into a sickroom

57

with a neatly devised but personally insensitive argument for the justice of God. The sickroom may be too late. Luther downplayed the competence of reason in helping persons to face actual suffering. Something more than natural reason is needed:

Reason holds that if God had a watchful eye on us and loved us, He would prevent all evil and let us suffer nothing. But now, since all sorts of calamities come to us, it concludes: Either God has forgotten me, or God is hostile to me and does not want me; otherwise He would help me and would not permit me to lie here and struggle in such misery. Against such thoughts, which we harbor by nature, we must arm ourselves with God's Word; and we must not judge according to our opinion but according to the saying of the Word. For if we judge without the Word, our judgment is wrong and misleads us.

What, then, does the Word say? First, that not a hair can fall from our head unless it is the will of God (Matt. 10:30). . . . But then another thought arises, one still more dangerous. For if I hold that God has laid upon me the trouble I am suffering, reason goes on to conclude: God cannot wish me well; otherwise He would not let me be plagued in this way; He would relieve me of my suffering and be gracious to me. If conscience then raises its voice, too, and our sins become clear to us, then there is real trouble, so that one despairs of God. . . . We must then again be armed with God's Word and not follow reason and its judgment. For then we would certainly either fall into despair or become hostile to God and ignore Him altogether. Well, what does the Word say about this? Paul says, 1 Cor. 11:31f: "If we examined ourselves, we should not then fall under judgment. When, however, we do fall under the Lord's judgment, he is disciplining us, to save us from being condemned with the rest of the world." This is certainly a clear passage, telling us that God chastises and disciplines those whom He intends to keep and preserve for eternal life, that He cannot be hostile to them, but that they must nonetheless suffer all sorts of trouble, crosses, and temptations. (Luther, WA 52, pp. 284f.; in WLS 1, p. 21, NEB)*

In crisis, the Word of scripture counts more than our inadequate attempts at rational consistency. Luther urged the faithful to rely on the Word when their feeling processes or judgment leads to despair. The manner of framing the question of theodicy may be crucial to a meaningful outcome:

If you truly want to learn then you must first learn this: How unskillfully you have framed your question. For you say, "Since God has created all things, where does evil come from?" But before you asked this, three sorts of questions should already have been previously asked: First, Whether there be evil? Secondly, What evil is? Thirdly, To whom it is, and then whence? . . . Only on this basis can you rightly inquire, Whence comes evil—whether from God, or from nothing? Whether it has always been, or has had its beginning in time? Whether it has purpose or is without purpose? . . . It is God who made the world, not in order that we should inquire into God as if we were capable of knowing everything, but that, being met by God we should ask about his will and righteousness, for it is in our power to search into these things, that searching we may come to find and do what is required of us. Therefore God calls us not to try to fathom where evil comes from, as you asked just now, but rather to seek the righteousness of the good God, and His kingdom; and all these things, he promises, shall be added to you. (Clementina, *Recognitions of Clement*, Bk. III, ch. xvi-xx, ANF VIII, pp. 118-119)*

One cannot meaningfully and rightly inquire of the ground or origin of evil without first probing whether evil may be said to have any being of its own, and to what extent it may be said to be purposeful. The Petrine figure of this oral tradition invites an inquiry into the conditions under which evil comes to confront us, rather than prematurely asking in an oversimplified way: Whence evil? If the question is ill-framed from the beginning, the conclusion is likely to be inadequate.

II ❧ WHY DID GOD PERMIT THE WILL TO FALL?

Despite the previous disclaimer—that argumentation has limited efficacy amid suffering—the questions of sufferers remain too urgent and difficult for the pastor to ignore or dismiss with unreflective appeals to piety. The pastor will often be asked to speak meaningfully to these perplexing issues that trouble parishioners deeply. They deserve thoughtful responses.

If much suffering comes from the distortions of human freedom, it is important to try to understand classical reasoning on why such a vulnerable freedom would have been permitted by God in the first place. Why not a freedom that always chooses the good? Would not there have been less suffering as a consequence? On these answers hinge many implications for intelligent response in pastoral care amid suffering.

Tertullian, in answering why God permitted evil, laid down the intellectual groundwork for a more deliberate pastoral theodicy, hinging primarily on the value of human self-determination. Note how carefully Tertullian takes into account the arguments against his own position:

If God is good, and foreknowing of the future, and powerful enough to avert evil, why did He permit human beings, the very image and likeness of Himself, who by virtue of the gift of their souls share in God's own being, to be deceived by the devil and fall from obedience of the law into death? For if God had been completely good, would he not have been unwilling that such a catastrophe should happen? And if fore-knowing, God would hardly have been ignorant of what was coming to pass. And surely would not God be powerful enough to hinder sin's occurrence, so that the consequence of evil would never have come about? All this seemingly should have been impossible under these three conditions of the divine greatness. From this the contrary proposition might appear to be more certainly true: that God must be deemed either not good or not foreknowing or not powerful. For one could argue that no evil could possibly have come about if God had been that which he is reputed—good, and foreknowing, and mighty. Yet we have on our hands this question of evil, to make us wonder whether God is as reported.

In reply, we must first vindicate those attributes in the Creator which are thereby called into question—namely, God's goodness, foreknowl-edge and power. But I shall not linger long over this point, since Christ's own definition comes to our aid at once: From evidences must proofs be obtained. The Creator's works testify at once to His goodness, since they are good, as we have shown, and to His power, since they are mighty, and spring indeed out of nothing. . . . But what shall I say of God's foreknowing, which has for its witnesses as many prophets as it inspired? After all, what title to prescience do we look for in the Author of the universe, since it was by this very attribute that He foreknew all things when He appointed them their places, and appointed them their places when He foreknew them? . . .

We affirm human beings' self-determining power over their own wills. If so, then what happens to free individuals must be laid to their own charge and not to God's. Some may argue that human beings ought never to have been constituted with will, since their liberty and power of will always had the possibility of turning out to be injurious. I will first of all maintain that human beings were rightly so constituted, in order that I may with the greater confidence commend both the actual human constitution, and the additional fact of its being worthy of the Divine Being.

The cause which led to man's being created with a constitution cap-able of willing is a very great cause indeed. For with this freedom, human life thus constituted still stood under the protection of God's goodness and God's purpose. For in God, goodness and intent always agree. For God does not have any intention except goodness. And God's goodness is never a goodness without a plan (except in the silly case of Marcion's hypothesis of a purposelessly good divine being).

Now if what God intends is good, is it not fitting that God's intention should become known? Wouldn't it also be proper that there should be some being capable of knowing God? If so, what sort of creature could be more fitting for this than one who is capable of imaging or reflecting the goodness of God? If so, it was good and reasonable that God create just such a creature. This is why it was proper that creatures who are formed with a capacity to reflect God's goodness should be formed with a free will and a capacity for self-control. The point is that this very ability—free will and the capacity for self-control—is precisely that which is referred to as humanity made in God's image and likeness. (Tertullian, *Against Marcion*, Bk. II, Chs. V-VI, ANF III, pp. 300-302)*

The heart of Tertullian's argument is that it is fitting that God, being good, foreknowing and almighty, should be known, and freely responded to by his creatures. But who can freely respond unless free? Self-determinating will is that which most clearly shows that humanity is made in God's image, able to reflect God's goodness not by coercion but by free response, without which God's goodness and love could not be properly celebrated. Thus it is better that humanity is constituted free, and therefore fallible, than the alternative which would imply an unresponsiveness unworthy of God.

It is fitting to ask whether there is purpose in temptation and the human potentiality that freedom can be corrupted. The Westminster Confession pointed to three levels of purposefulness in the divine permission to allow the human will to be tempted: a corrective purpose, a humbling purpose, and a reconciling purpose:

The most wise, righteous, and gracious God does oftentimes leave for a season his own children to manifold temptations and the corruption of their own hearts, to chastise them for their former sins, or to help them discover the hidden strength of corruption and deceitfulness of their own hearts, that they may be humbled; and to raise them to a more close and constant dependence for their support upon God himself, and to make them more watchful against all future occasions of sin, and for sundry other just and holy ends. (Westminster Confession, Ch. V, sec. v, *CC*, pp. 200-201)

God did not make a mistake in making humanity free. But what is that agency or efficient cause by which the evil will is caused? Augustine brilliantly argued that there was no *efficient* cause, but only a *deficient* cause of the self-alienating will:

Let no one, therefore, look for an efficient cause of the evil will; for it is not efficient, but deficient, as the will itself is not an effecting of something, but a defect. For defection from that which supremely is, to that which has less of being—this is to begin to have an evil will. . . . For those things which are known not by their actuality, but by their want of it, are known, if our expression may be allowed and understood, by not knowing them, that by knowing them they may be not known. For when the eyesight surveys objects that strike the sense, it nowhere sees darkness but where it begins not to see. And so no other sense but the ear can perceive silence, and yet it is only perceived by not hearing. Thus, too, our mind perceives intelligible forms by understanding them; but when they are deficient, it knows them by not knowing them. (Augustine, *The City of God,* Bk. XII.7, NPNF 1, II, p. 230)

This is a crucial argument that pastors do well to grasp. To say that there is no *efficient* cause of the evil will, but only *deficient* causes, is to say that evil exists only as a diminution of some good upon which it depends, and that evil can therefore be properly viewed only as a defect of good, or a lack of good (*privatio boni*), according to Augustine.

Lactantius, writing earlier, had sought to understand whether any finite good could exist at all without some possibility of its becoming defective or corrupted. In pursuing this thought, Lactantius provided a definitive statement of classical pastoral reasoning about why God permitted evil, in order that good might be better seen through it:

God permitted evil only for this reason: that good might shine forth through and beyond it. For, as I have previously said, Christian teaching understands that the one exists only with the other. Think of it in relation to this analogy: The world is made up of elements that oppose and connect with each other, as fire and water. Light could not be light unless one posits darkness. No high place can exist without positing lower places. No sun could ever rise without setting. There is no warmth without cold, or softness without hardness. (Lactantius, *The Divine Institutes,* Bk. VII, Ch. XV, ANF VII, p. 272)*

This perplexity may emerge in pastoral conversation: Is God's power diminished by even positing the possibility of evil? How can God be all powerful if evil exists or even could exist? Are these assertions suggesting potential limits on the divine omnipotence? Augustine faced this dilemma head-on:

We do not put the life of God or the foreknowledge of God under necessity if we should say that it is necessary that God should live for ever, and foreknow all things. Neither is God's power diminished when we say that God cannot die or fall into error—for this is in such a way impossible to Him, that if it were possible for Him, He would be of less power. But assuredly God is rightly called omnipotent, though He can neither die nor fall into error. For He is called omnipotent on account of His doing what He wills, not on account of His permitting what he does not directly will. For if it should be the case that God could not do what he wills, God would by no means be omnipotent. Therefore God "cannot" do some things precisely because God is omnipotent. (Augustine, *The City of God,* Bk. V.10, NPNF 1, II, p. 92)*

Language becomes strained when we hypothesize something that God "could not do" precisely because God is omnipotent. God does not will to do that which is inconsistent with the divine character. God in a sense "cannot" be unfair or less than good or die or do something inconsistent with himself— all of these are things that exist only in the hypothetical imagination, if it is the case that God is incomparably just, good, and eternally consistent with himself.

The Christian community in Athanasius' time was troubled with the question of whether the soul has the power to create evil heretofore uncreated. It was being asked: When the soul does evil deeds, do they have reality, so as to belong to God's world? Athanasius answered:

> The truth of the Church's theology must be manifest: that evil has not from the beginning been with God or in God, nor has any substantive existence; but that men, in default of the vision of good, began to devise and imagine for themselves what was not, after their own pleasure. For as if a man, when the sun is shining, and the whole earth illumined by his light, were to shut fast his eyes and imagine darkness where no darkness exists, and then walk wandering as if in darkness, often falling and going down steep places, thinking it was dark and not light,—for, imagining that he sees, he does not see at all;—so, too, the soul of man, shutting fast her eyes, by which she is able to see God, has imagined evil for herself, and moving therein, knows not that, thinking she is doing something, she is doing nothing. For she is imagining what is not, nor is she abiding in her original nature; but what she is is evidently the product of her own disorder. For she is made to see God, and to be enlightened by Him; but of her own accord in God's stead she has sought corruptible things and darkness, as the Spirit says somewhere in writing, "God made man upright but they have sought out many inventions" (Eccl. 7:29). (Athanasius, *Against the Heathen,* sec. 7, NPNF 2, IV, p. 7)

III ❧ THE AFFIRMATION OF DIVINE MYSTERY

Amid all these efforts to make reasonable sense out of the power and goodness of God amid evil and suffering, a modest note on human finitude is repeatedly sounded. Those who imagine that they can comprehend the divine mystery have not even begun to apprehend it.

The pastoral writers have celebrated purposefulness amid mystery. This is not merely a desperate act of acquiescence, but more so a heartfelt response to

God's goodness even when that goodness far outdistances narrow, culturally-shaped understandings and misunderstandings of it. This has profound relevance for pastoral care. For every experienced pastor knows those moments of quiet awareness of affirmable mystery.

Dame Julian of Norwich spoke in this way to the question of whether God wills that we with finite minds should learn and know everything about his purpose:

> He gave me understanding of two parts (of truth). . . . In this first part our Lord wills that we be occupied rejoicing in him, for he rejoices in us. The more fully we take from this source with reverence and meekness the more thanks we earn from him and the more success we gain for ourselves. Thus we can say, rejoicing, that our part is our Lord.
>
> The second part of truth is hidden and barred from us—that is to say, everything that is unrelated to our salvation. These are our Lord's secret purposes. It belongs to the royal lordship of God that he have his secret purposes in peace; to his servants belong obedience and reverence, not full knowledge of his purposes.
>
> Our Lord has pity and compassion on us, because there are some of us who so busy ourselves in his secret purposes; I am sure if we knew how very greatly we would please him and ease ourselves by abandoning this curiosity, we would do so. The saints who are in heaven will to know nothing but what our Lord wills to show them. (Juliana of Norwich, *Revelations of Divine Love,* Ch. 30, p. 128)

This is far from an anti-intellectual appeal to simplistic piety without any effort at intelligent reflection. Rather it is an appeal to affirm what lies beyond all our finite capacities for comprehensive reflection, viz., the divine goodness. Does God want us to know everything about his providence, if we were capable of it? Luther answered similarly yet with a different set of metaphors: God is not immobilized until he gets popular consensus on his design for history. What general would succeed if every strategy were published in advance?

> Would you expect a prince to divulge all his plans and decisions to his people and confide all his policies to his subjects? Should a general reveal, make known, and publish his tactics and strategy in an encampment? That would be some army and business! And yet we fools, in the devil's name, will not believe our God unless He has previously initiated us into the why and the wherefore of His doctrines! . . . In the Garden of Eden the devil acted like that when he said to Adam and Eve (Gen. 3:1): "Why did God do this?" (Luther, "Sermon on the Gospel of St. John, Chapter Six," LW 23, p. 81; cf. WA 33, pp. 120ff.)

History would be boring if the direction of every struggle were accurately foreknown to all. Are some things, therefore, deliberately and meaningfully hidden, according to the divine intention? This is a pivotal question for pastoral theodicy, an arena in which many speculative pseudo-answers and theories abound. John Chrysostom wrote:

> Some people, out of restless curiosity, want to elaborate idly and irresponsibly doctrines which are of no benefit to those who understand them, or else are actually incomprehensible. Others call God to account for his judgements and struggle to measure the great deep. For the Psalmist says: "Thy judgements are a great deep" (Ps. 36:6). You will find that few are deeply concerned about faith and conduct, but the majority go in for these elaborate theories and investigate questions to which there is no answer and whose very investigation rouses God's anger. For when we struggle to learn things which God himself did not will us to know, we shall never succeed—how can we, against God's will?—and we shall gain nothing but our own peril from the investigation.

> But, for all that, when anyone uses authority to silence people who pursue these enigmas, he gets a reputation for arrogance and ignorance. So here, too, the president needs great tact to dissuade others from inappropriate speculations and to escape the criticisms I have mentioned. For all these matters no other help has been vouchsafed but that of the word. And if anyone is deprived of this power, the souls of those under him (I mean the weaker and more speculative of them) will be not better off than ships storm-tossed at sea. (Chrysostom, *On the Priesthood*, Ch. IV.4-5, pp. 118-119)*

It was comforting to the pastoral writers that finite intelligence need not know everything about the divine purpose in order to believe in it on the basis of its abundant and adequate disclosures of meaning. It was hardly viewed as a matter for demoralizing frustration to them that they could not answer everything. Rather they rejoiced that God had not disclosed everything about his will for human history, and that human intelligence was relieved of the impossible task of understanding providence exhaustively.

IV ❧ KEY ISSUES OF CLASSIC PASTORAL THEODICY: VINDICATING THE JUSTICE OF GOD AMID PAIN

When pastors hear parishioners blame God for allowing evil, or wonder whether God takes pleasure in human suffering, or despair that God allows innocents to suffer, they may at least be reassured that these complaints are not new. For each of these issues has repeatedly confronted pastors of the Christian tradition. There has been no generation of Christians in which these questions have not been earnestly raised. Eight perennial questions are raised and dealt with in the following texts:

(1) Is God culpable for not making us incapable of evil?

Man has free-will and is mutable. He is mutable because he is a creature. He has free-will because he is endowed with reason. Anyone, therefore, that finds fault with God for not making man incapable of evil, while at the same time being endowed with free-will is, though he may not know it, blaming God for making man rational, and not irrational. It has to be in one way or the other. Either man must be irrational, or, if he is rational, then liable to act now in one way and now in another, and so he must have free-will. (Nemesius, *Of the Nature of Man,* Ch. XLI.58, LCC IV, pp. 418-419)

(2) Is God responsible for human infirmities?

Irrational, therefore, in every respect, are they who await not the time of increase, but ascribe to God the infirmity of their nature. Such persons know neither God nor themselves, being insatiable and ungrateful, unwilling to be at the outset what they have also been created—men subject to passions. (Irenaeus, *Against Heresies,* Bk. IV, Ch. XXXVIII, sec. 4, ANF I, p. 522)

(3) Is God made happy by our suffering?

It is not that God is regaled by our tortures; no, He heals the diseases of our sins by their contrary antidotes, so that we who have departed from Him by the delight of pleasures, may return to Him in tearful grief, and after having fallen by losing ourselves amid sinful things, we may rise up by restraining ourselves even in what is lawful. (Gregory the Great, *Pastoral Care,* Part III, Ch. 30, ACW 11, p. 207)

(4) Did God's holiness become corrupted by coming into contact with human corruption?

For just as the rays of the sun's light undergo no suffering, though they fill all things, and touch dead and unclean bodies, much less could the unembodied Power of God suffer in its essence, or be harmed, or ever become worse than itself, when it touches a body without being really embodied. For what of this? Did He not ever and everywhere reach through the matter of the elements and of bodies themselves, as being the creative Word of God, and imprint the words of His own wisdom upon them, impressing life on the lifeless, form on that which is formless and shapeless by nature, stamping His own beauty and unembodied ideas on the qualities of matter, moving things by their own nature lifeless and immovable, earth, air, fire, in a wise and harmonious motion, ordering all things out of disorder, increasing and perfecting them, pervading all things with the divine power of reason, extending through all places and touching all, but yet receiving hurt from naught, nor defiled in His own nature. (Eusebius, *The Proof of the Gospel,* Bk. IV, Ch. 13, p. 188)

(5) Is God less than just in allowing animals to suffer?

These casuists, who ask questions of that kind not because they want to examine them seriously but because they are loquacious and want to ventilate them, are wont also to trouble the faith of the less learned by pointing to the pains and labours of animals. What evil, they say, have the animals deserved that they suffer such woes, or what good can they hope for in having such troubles imposed on them? They say that or feel like that because they have a perverted sense of values. They are not able to see what the chief good is, and they want to have everything just as they conceive the chief good to be. They can think of no chief good except fine bodies like the celestial bodies which are not subject to corruption. And so without any sense of order they demand that the bodies of animals shall not suffer death or any corruption, as if forsooth they were not mortal, being lowly bodies, or because celestial bodies are better. The pain which the animals suffer commends the vigour of the animal soul as admirable and praiseworthy after its own fashion. By animating and ruling the body of the animal it shows its desire for unity. For what is pain but a certain feeling that cannot bear division and corruption? Hence it is clearer than day that the animal soul is eager for unity in the whole body and is tenacious of unity. Neither gladly nor with indifference, but reluctantly and with obstinate resistance it meets bodily suffering which it is grieved to know destroys the unity and integrity of the body. We should never know what eagerness there is for unity in the inferior animal creation, were it not for the pain suffered by animals. (Augustine, *On Free Will,* Bk. III, ch. xxiii.69, LCC VI, pp. 211-212)

(6) Is God unjust when innocent infants suffer?

A greater complaint, and one with a show of pity about it, is often occasioned by the bodily torments which infants suffer, for by reason of their tender age they have committed no sins, at least if the souls which animate them have had no existence prior to their birth as human beings. People say: What evil have they done that they should suffer such things? As if innocence could have any merit before it has the power to do any hurt. . . . By the torments of their children parents have their hard hearts softened, their faith exercised and their tenderness proved. Who knows what good compensation God has reserved in the secrecy of his judgments for the children themselves who, though they have not had the chance of living righteously, at least have committed no sin and yet have suffered? Not for nothing does the Church commend for honour as martyrs the children who were slain by the orders of Herod when he sought to slay the Lord Jesus Christ. (Augustine, *On Free Will,* Bk. III, ch. xx.68, LCC VI, p. 211)

(7) Is all misery intrinsically unjust?

If you are in your own power either you will not be miserable, or you will be justly miserable because you rule yourself unjustly. If you wish to rule yourself justly and cannot, you will not be in your own power. You will then be in the power of no one or in the power of another. If you are in no one's power you will act willingly or unwillingly. It cannot be unwillingly, unless some superior force overpowers you. But he who is in the power of no one cannot be overpowered by any force; if willingly, you are in no one's power, and you must be in your own power, and either you will be miserable by ruling yourself unjustly, or, seeing you can be what you wish, you have cause to give thanks for the goodness of your Creator. If you are not in your own power, then someone must have you in his power who is either more powerful or less powerful than yourself. If he is less powerful the fault is your own and the misery just. But if someone more powerful than you are holds you in his power, you will not rightly think so rightful an order to be unjust. It is true, therefore, that you will not be miserable if it is unjust, and if it is just, let us praise him whose laws bring it to pass. (Augustine, *On Free Will,* Bk. III, ch. vi.18, LCC VI, p. 182)

(8) Why does God permit human freedom to be tempted?

There are five reasons, they say, why God permits us to be attacked by demonic temptation: (1) that by means of the attacks and counter-attacks we may come to distinguish virtue and vice; (2) that possessing virtue in such combat and struggle, we shall hold it firm and steadfast; (3) that with advance in virtue we do not become high-minded but learn to be humble; (4) that having had some experience of vice, we will detest it with a consummate revulsion; and (5) above all that when we become detached we forget not our own weakness nor the power of Him who has helped us. (Maximus the Confessor, *The Four Centuries of Charity,* Ch. 2, sec. 67, ACW 21, p. 166)*

V ❄ THE PEDAGOGY OF SUFFERING

It is a widely-held view of pastoral writers that the sufferer has something important to learn from his suffering. Although there are different interpretations of what is to be learned, there is greater agreement that suffering is not in itself meaningless, but that it has a pedagogical function.

There is nothing about pain that automatically increases virtue, although pain may become the occasion for excellent behaviors to be challenged and tested:

For the Scriptures state that nothing is good but what is virtuous, and declare that virtue is blessed in every circumstance, and that it is never enhanced by either corporal or other external good fortune, nor is it weakened by adversity. . . . A blessed life can rise up in the midst of pain. This can easily be shown when we read: "How blest are you, when you suffer insults and persecution and every kind of calumny for my sake" (Matt. 5:11). . . . And again: "If anyone wishes to be a follower of mine, he must leave his self behind; he must take up his cross and come with me" (Matt. 16:24). . . . There is, then, a blessedness even in pains and griefs. . . . There is, then, in pain a virtue that can display the sweetness of a good conscience, and therefore it serves as a proof that pain does not lessen the pleasure of virtue. As, then, there is no loss of blessedness to virtue through pain, so also the pleasures of the body and the enjoyment that benefits give add nothing to it. (Ambrose, *Duties of the Clergy,* Bk. II, Chs. III-IV, secs. 8, 9, 10, 12, NPNF 2, X, p. 45, NEB)*

Suffering may continue after learning has effectively occurred. So the pedagogy of suffering does not necessarily mean an abrupt end to suffering. Luther made this clear:

It teaches us, not how to get rid of evil and to enjoy peace but how to live with it and yet conquer it. It teaches us, not how to avert it by our effort and resistance but patiently to endure it till it wearies and exhausts itself upon us, can do no more, and of its own accord ceases and drops from us in impotence, as the ocean waves dash against the shore, turn back and disappear. Not yielding but perseverance counts in this conflict. (Luther, "Exposition on Rom. 12:7-16, Second Sunday After Epiphany," WA 17 II, p. 49; in WLS 1, p. 22)

Since human life is lived out in social interaction, and not in isolation, one person's or society's suffering may become the basis of another's moral education:

The suffering the Sodomites endured was a judgment passed on those who sinned, but for those who hear the story, it is education. (Clement of Alexandria, *Christ the Educator,* Bk. III, Ch. 8.43, FC 23, p. 235)

Thus one must have an intergenerational and historical view of social suffering if one is to see how its teaching function can endure from one generation to another. For we can still learn from the suffering Israel endured in the Babylonian captivity or from the holocaust. Those lessons do not end with the immediate sufferers. Luther was questioned as to whether God's "strange work of affliction" was necessary to his purpose:

Therefore to destroy such works of ours as well as the old Adam in us, God overwhelms us with those things which move us to anger, with many sufferings which rouse us to impatience, and last of all, even with death and the abuse of the world. By means of these he seeks nothing else but to drive out of us anger, impatience, and unrest, and to perfect his own work in us, that is, his peace. Thus Isaiah 28 (:21) says, "He takes upon himself an alien work, that he may do his own proper work." What does this mean? He sends us suffering and unrest to teach us to have patience and peace. He bids us die that he may make us live. (Luther, "Treatise on Good Works, 1520," LW 44, p. 77; cf. WA 6, p. 248)

The assertion that God hardened Pharaoh's heart is made meaningful only by the teaching that followed it:

That he might be able to say what he did when no longer hardened, "The Lord is in the right, and I and my people are in the wrong" (Ex. 9:27). (Origen, *On Prayer,* XXIX.16, CWS, p. 160)

VI ❦ THE MEANING OF SUFFERING

Suffering can be our teacher only because it bears meaning. It is difficult to find any voice in the central pastoral tradition that has suggested that suffering is absurd or meaningless. Yet the range of interpretations of meaning in suffering has been vast. Here are some of the viewpoints expressed. We will begin with three commonplace metaphors. The meaning of suffering is like melting wax, the gardener's pruning sheers, and the parent who does not give up.

A little fire softens a large piece of wax. So, too, a small indignity often softens, sweetens and wipes away suddenly all the fierceness, insensibility and hardness of our heart. (Climacus, *The Ladder of Divine Ascent,* Step 4, sec. 88, p. 44)

From suffering indignities we learn kindness, sensitivity, caring. The point of the metaphor is that even from a little suffering we can learn a lot—a large degree of hardness in the heart can be melted away. The gardening analogy favored by Luther may help us to grasp the meaning of suffering as a divine pruning of human insensitivities:

[It] requires the art of believing and being sure that whatever hurts and distresses us does not happen to hurt or harm us but is for our good and profit. We must compare this to the work of a vinedresser who hoes and cultivates his vine. If the vine were able to be aware of this, could talk, and saw the vinedresser coming along and chopping about its roots with his mattock or his hoe and cutting the wood from its branches with his clipper or his pruning hook, it would be prompted by what it saw and felt to say: "Ah, what are you doing? Now I must wither and decay, for you are removing the soil from my roots and are belaboring my branches with those iron teeth. You are tearing and pinching me everywhere, and I will have to stand in the ground bare and seared. You are treating me more cruelly than one treats any tree or plant." But the vinedresser would reply: "You are a fool and do not understand. For even if I do cut a branch from you, it is a totally useless branch; it takes away your strength and your sap. Then the other branches, which should bear fruit, must suffer." (Luther, "Sermon on the Gospel of St. John, Chapter Fifteen, 1537," LW 24, p. 194; cf. WA 45, p. 635, WLS 1, p. 17)

What looks like harm from the viewpoint of the plant is purposeful and helpful from the viewpoint of the gardener. What looks like absurd suffering from the viewpoint of humanity actually is meaningful and redemptive from the viewpoint of God. Lactantius thought the principal meaning in suffering was that it provided evidence that God's corrective love was still trying to reach us. It is only where sin abounds that God seems to have given up on us. That is when we are no longer within range of hearing of his corrective love:

If anyone shall wish to know more fully why God permits the wicked and the unjust to become powerful, happy, and rich, and, on the other hand, suffers the pious to be humble, wretched, and poor, let him take the book of Seneca which has the title, "Why many evils happen to good men, though there is a providence;" in which book he has said many things, not assuredly with the ignorance of this world, but wisely, and almost with divine inspiration. "God," he says, "regards men as His children, but He permits the corrupt and vicious to live in luxury and delicacy, because He does not think them worthy of His correction. But He often chastises the good whom He loves, and by continual labours exercises them to the practice of virtue: nor does He permit them to be corrupted and depraved by frail and perishable good." From which it ought to appear strange to no one if we are often chastised by God for our faults. Yea, rather, when we are harassed and pressed, then we especially give thanks to our most indulgent Father, because He does not permit our corruption to proceed to greater lengths, but corrects it with stripes and blows. . . . Therefore, lest they should be as much corrupted by ease as their fathers had been by indulgence, it was His will that they should be oppressed by those in whose power He placed them, that He may both confirm them when wavering, and renew them to fortitude when corrupted, and try and prove them when faithful. (Lactantius, *The Divine Institutes,* Bk. V, Ch. XXIII, ANF VII, p. 160)

This is a hard argument for moderns to grasp. It appears masochistic. Yet its deeper strain is based upon another analogy: the corrective love of the parent who does not give up on the child prematurely. Thus the best evidence of meaning in suffering is that it shows the continuing effort of the divine caring Parent to re-direct our self-assertive, fallen will, and through humility to bring us back into a deeper reconciliation. There is at least one meaningful act that can be done amid any situation of affliction, in Luther's view: praise God.

This is truly the noblest directive of all in times of tribulation, a teaching of pure gold and the best of advice, which can rescue us from every evil, when in tribulation we can say that God is in the right and can bless and praise Him, as the example of the three men in the fiery furnace shows (Daniel 3). "O Lord, righteousness belongeth unto Thee, but unto us confusion of faces, as at this day" (Dan. 9:7). It is incredible how efficacious a remedy this praise of God is in times of danger; for as soon as you begin to praise God, the evil lessens, confidence grows, and calling upon God in faith follows. (Luther, WA 5, p. 494; in WLS 3, p. 1380)

Luther was not merely beginning from the subjective, human side of the divine-human relationship and courageously projecting praise upon an un-praiseworthy situation out of personal courage. Rather he was affirming the essential praiseworthiness of the situation, due to God's trustworthy (but at times hidden) purpose. Faith is precisely that response which affirms that purpose, despite temporary prevailing evidence to the contrary. So what faith can always meaningfully do is praise. But when sufferings become great and terrible, doesn't this approach finally have to be abandoned?

Therefore the fiercer our sufferings are, the greater and more wonderful are the things that are worked in the saints. It is a proof of grace and God's goodwill when they are disciplined by the cross and afflictions. For when they persevere by faith in the promise and endure, great and incredible blessings follow. (Luther, "Lectures on Genesis, Chapters 31 to 37, 1544," LW 6, p. 355; cf. WA 44, p. 265)

In the best of the pastoral tradition there is no pretending that pain is avoidable or unreal, nor that all bodily life is miserable, nor that any suffering is beyond God's power to transform into some good. Ambrose held all these points in careful tension in his *Duties of the Clergy:*

Some, however, are who think a blessed life is impossible in this body, weak and fragile as it is. . . . Suppose that things come which are accounted terrible as regards the grief they cause, such as blindness, exile, hunger, violation of a daughter, loss of children. Who will deny that Isaac was blessed, who did not see in his old age, and yet gave blessings with his benediction? (Gen. 27:28). . . . A wretched thing is slavery, but Joseph was not wretched; nay clearly he was blessed. . . . All these felt their own weakness, but they bravely prevailed over it. . . . True it is that in these sufferings there is something bitter, and that strength of mind cannot hide this pain. I should not deny that the sea is deep because in shore it is shallow, nor that the sky is clear because sometimes it is covered with clouds, nor that the earth is fruitful because in some places there is but barren ground, nor that the crops are rich and full because they sometimes have wild oats mingled with them. So, too, count it as true that the harvest of a happy conscience may be mingled with some bitter feelings of grief. (Ambrose, *Duties of the Clergy*, Bk. II, Ch. V, secs. 19-21, NPNF 2, X, pp. 46-47)

The soul, in being subject to desolation due to its very contingencies, dependencies, and finitude, may also be consoled amid temporal losses by awareness of divine care. Ignatius Loyola distinguished consolation from desolation in this way:

I call it consolation when the soul is aroused by an interior movement which causes it to be inflamed with love of its Creator and Lord, and consequently can love no created thing on the face of the earth for its own sake, but only in the creator of all things. . . . I call consolation any increase of faith, hope, and charity and any interior joy that calls and attracts to heavenly things, and to the salvation of one's soul, inspiring it with peace and quiet in Christ our Lord.

I call desolation all that is contrary to the third rule, as darkness of the soul, turmoil of the mind, inclination to low and earthly things, restlessness resulting from many disturbances and temptations which lead to loss of faith, loss of hope, and loss of love. It is also desolation when a soul finds itself completely apathetic, tepid, sad, and separated, as it were, from its Creator and Lord. For just as consolation is contrary to desolation, so the thoughts that spring from consolation are the opposite of those that spring from desolation. (Ignatius of Loyola, *Spiritual Exercises*, pp. 129-130)

VII ❧ Avoiding the Trap of Masochism

Whenever the pastoral tradition has spoken about the meaning of suffering, the question has arisen as to whether there might be a regrettable masochistic ring in the entire apology. Is there some hidden desire in Christianity to suffer not less but more? Because God suffered for humanity, does that make true believers want to suffer? If so, is not the whole problem of a Christian pastoral theodicy subject to a major psychological distortion, a tendency to desire sickness, to be fascinated with death-wish and self-pity? The traditions following Nietzsche and Freud have seen little deeper in Christian theodicies than these themes.

The pastoral writers have recognized these potential misunderstandings, and have tried sharply to counter them. Whatever Luther may have said above about the meaning of suffering, he did not think that suffering could be conceived as inevitably productive or growth-eliciting. Some are made distinctly worse by suffering.

For the elect all things work together for good (Rom. 8:28), even the rod and the cross. The flesh is mortified, faith is strengthened, and the gift of the Holy Spirit is increased. On the other hand, when the ungodly are burdened with a cross, they become worse; for the German proverb holds good, that after a sickness people rarely become better. (Luther, "Lectures on Genesis, Chapters Six to Fourteen, 1536," LW 2, pp. 378-79; cf. WA 42, p. 533)

Some theodicies get caught in the syndrome of implying that "if affliction strengthens, then why should not suffering be sought?" This misconception was countered by Luther:

The Donatists, about whom Augustine writes, turned to verses that speak of suffering and killed themselves. They hurled themselves into the sea. God does not want us to search for misfortune and to choose it ourselves. Walk in faith and love. If the cross comes, accept it. If it does not come, do not search for it. (Luther, "Sermons on the First Epistle of St. Peter, 1522," LW 30, pp. 109-110; cf.WA 12, pp. 364f.)

That suffering bears a teaching function does not imply that it should be sought. For there is enough suffering already under the conditions of finitude to teach us all we need to know, without suggesting *reductio ad absurdum* that one must create more to learn more.

Gregory was pastorally concerned about those persons who, having endured much affliction, still have not learned anything from it. He thought that the furnace of affliction tended to elicit different responses from different temperaments, just as the metal-worker's furnace has different effects on different types of metals. Some persons are more like brass, others like tin, lead or iron, whom God wishes to make silver or gold:

Hence the Lord reproaches the people of Israel, captive yet not converted from their iniquity, saying: "The house of Israel is become dross to me; all these are brass, and tin and iron, and lead, in the midst of the furnace" (Ezek. 22:18). This is as though he said unmistakably: "I wished to purify them in the fire of tribulation, and I wanted them to become silver or gold. But they have turned from me in the furnace into brass, and tin, and iron, and lead, because even in tribulation they have rushed forward not to virtue but to vices." When brass is struck, it gives off a greater sound than do other metals. A man, therefore, who when chastised breaks forth into sounds of murmuring, has turned to brass in the midst of the furnace. Tin, however, when skilfully treated, presents the deceptive appearance of silver. He, therefore, who is not free from the vice of pretence in the midst of tribulation, has become tin in the furnace. But a man uses iron who plots against the life of the neighbour, and he is iron in the furnace when he does not put away in his tribulations the wickedness of doing harm to neighbours. Lead, again, is heavier than the other metals. He, then, is found to be lead in the furnace who is so weighed down by the burden of his sin, that even in tribulation he is not raised above earthly desires. Therefore, it is again written: "Great pains have been taken, and the great rust thereof has not gone out, not even by fire" (Ezek. 24:12). God brings on us the fire of tribulation that He may purge out from us the rust of vices; but not even by fire do we lose the rust, when even amid scourges we are not without vices. Hence the Prophet says again: "The founder hath melted in vain, for their wicked deeds are not consumed" (Jer. 6:29).

We must realise, however, that sometimes when such men remain uncorrected amidst severe scourgings, they are to be soothed by loving admonition. For those whom torments do not correct, are sometimes restrained from evil-doing by gentle blandishments. As is known, frequently sick people who cannot be cured by a strong potion of drugs, have been restored to their former state of health by tepid water; and some wounds that cannot be cured by incisions, are healed by fomentations with oil. (Gregory the Great, *Pastoral Care,* Part III, Ch. 13, ACW 11, pp. 128-129)

Gregory urged gentle pastoral care for those who, having been afflicted, have not positively learned from it. They may need placebos (tepid water) or a warm bath with soothing oils more than anything else.

Origen was worried that some well-intended attempted theodicies run the risk of making evil look good:

Celsus has made a statement regarding evils of the following nature, viz., that "although a thing may seem to you to be evil, it is by no means certain that it is so; for you do not know what is of advantage to yourself, or to another, or to the whole world." Now this assertion is made with a certain degree of caution; and it hints that the nature of evil is not wholly wicked, because that which may be considered so in individual cases, may contain something which is of advantage to the whole community. However, lest anyone should mistake my words, and find a pretence of wrongdoing, as if his wickedness were profitable to the world, or at least might be so, we have to say, that although God, who preserves the free-will of each individual, may make use of the evil of the wicked for the administration of the world, so disposing them as to conduce to the benefit of the whole; yet, notwithstanding, such an individual is deserving of censure, and as such has been appointed for a use, which is subject of loathing to each separate individual, although of advantage to the whole community. It is as if one were to say that in the case of a city, a man who had committed certain crimes, and on account of these had been condemned to serve in public works that were useful to the community, did something that was of advantage to the entire city, while he himself was engaged in an abominable task, in which no one possessed of moderate understanding would wish to be engaged. Paul also, the apostle of Jesus, teaches us that even the very wicked will contribute to the good of the whole, while in themselves they will be amongst the vile. (Origen, *Against Celsus,* Bk. IV, Ch. LXX, ANF IV, p. 528)

If evil and suffering may be turned secondarily to good use, there is a temptation to some apologists to therefore make evil and suffering appear in some inverted sense to be primarily good in themselves. This Origen refuted by arguing that evil itself is not made good, simply because it can be a component out of which a new configuration of good emerges. God is determined to preserve free will, even though the will is always liable to fall. When it does fall, God still uses its fallenness redemptively within the larger ordering of providence, so that even evil eventually serves the larger good. But this can be no excuse to affirm evil as directly good, or the one who does evil as inculpable.

VIII ❧ On Inequalities in Created Beings

Extreme forms of equalitarianism have always been offended at the idea that the creator does not treat all of creation exactly alike. There have been numerous attempts in the pastoral tradition to account meaningfully for the obvious fact that all beings are not the same, that variety in the universe is the intentional purpose of God, that different strata of beings have different challenges, capacities, limitations and sufferings, and that the dissimilarity of beings is not inconsistent with the justice and goodness of God.

Origen was among the first to probe the question of whether all rational creatures are created equal. Does diversity in the world result from freedom, he asked, without which there would be no diversity?

God in the beginning created those beings which He desired to create, i.e., rational natures. He had no other reason for creating them than on account of Himself, i.e., His own goodness. He Himself, then, was the cause of the existence of those things which were to be created—He in whom there was neither any variation nor change, nor lack of power—He created all whom He made equal and alike, because there was in Himself no reason for producing variety and diversity.

But since those rational creatures themselves, as we have frequently shown, and will yet show in the proper place, were endowed with the power of free-will, this freedom of will incited each one either to progress by imitation of God, or through negligence fell below their higher capacities. And this, as we have already stated, is the cause of the diversity among rational creatures, deriving its origin not from the will or judgment of the Creator, but from the freedom of the individual will. . . . And these are the causes, in my opinion, why that world presents the aspect of diversity, while Divine Providence continues to regulate each individual according to the variety of his movements, or of his feelings and purpose. This is why the Creator will neither appear to be unjust in distributing (for the causes already mentioned) to all according to their merits; nor will the happiness or unhappiness of each one's birth, or whatever be the condition that falls to his lot, be deemed accidental. (Origen, *De Principiis,* Bk. II, Ch. IX, sec. 6, ANF IV, p. 292)*

Indeed all human beings are equal in dignity, but due to freedom of the will there are great varieties of responses, competencies, and abilities. No two seem to be in fact equal in knowing or doing well. Should every one of these inequalities be the grounds for despair? Is it fair that some should have more power or security than others? One of Clement of Rome's reasons for appealing to the rich to care for the poor was precisely the *de facto* diversity of creation. He held an organic view of community that strongly affirmed the value of each person within a whole that necessarily must remain diverse:

The great cannot exist without the small, nor the small without the great. Every organism is composed of various different elements; and this ensures its own good. Take the body as an instance; the head is nothing without the feet, nor are the feet anything without the head. Even the smallest of our physical members are necessary and valuable to the whole body; yet all of them work together and observe a common subordination, so that the body itself is maintained intact.

In Christ Jesus, then, let this corporate body of ours be likewise maintained intact with each of us giving way to his neighbor in proportion to our spiritual gifts. The strong are not to ignore the weak, and the weak are to respect the strong. Rich men should provide for the poor and the poor should thank God for giving them somebody to supply their wants. (Clement of Rome, *To the Corinthians,* secs. 37-38, ECW, pp. 42-43)

Christianity has been criticized from the beginning on the grounds that it justified injustice on the basis of providence. This critique is not just a modern invention of Marx, but a complaint as old as the second century, as we see in Origen:

They object to us, with regard to terrestrial beings, that a happier lot by birth is the case with some rather than with others . . . . That one man is born among the Hebrews, with whom he finds instruction in the divine law; another among the Greeks, themselves also wise, and men of no small learning; and then another amongst the Ethiopians, who are accustomed to feed on human flesh; or amongst the Scythians, with whom parricide is an act sanctioned by law; or amongst the people of Taurus, where strangers are offered in sacrifice,—is a ground of strong objection. Their argument accordingly is this: If there be this great diversity of circumstances, and this diverse and varying condition by birth, in which the faculty of free-will has no scope (for no one chooses for himself either where, or with whom, or in what condition he is born); if, then, this is not caused by the difference in the nature of souls, i.e., that a soul of an evil nature is destined for a wicked nation, and a good soul for a righteous nation, what other conclusion remains than that these things must be supposed to be regulated by accident and chance? And if that be admitted, then it will be no longer believed that the world was made by God, or administered by His providence. (Origen, *De Principiis,* Bk. II, Ch. IX, sec. 5, ANF IV, p. 291)

Thus the moral dilemmas of social and cultural determinism, and the "scandal of particularity," were stated at a very early stage of Christian pastoral care: If we do not choose where we are born, if birth determines whether we are barbaric or civilized, cannabalistic or rational, and if birth makes the soul evil or good, then how could a good God devise such an evil plan? How does Origen answer this? Is it a fundamental challenge to the justice of God that inequalities exist in God's world?

Now, when we say that this world was established in the variety in which we have above explained that it was created by God, and when we say that this God is good, and righteous, and most just, there are numerous individuals, especially those who, coming from the school of Marcion, and Valentinus, and Basilides, have heard that there are souls of different natures, who object to us, that it cannot consist with the justice of God in creating the world to assign to some of His creatures an abode in the heavens, and not only to give such a better habitation, but also to grant them a higher and more honourable position; to favour others with the grant of principalities; to bestow powers upon some, dominions on others; to confer upon some the most honourable seats in the celestial tribunals; to enable some to shine with more resplendent glory, and to glitter with a starry splendour; to give to some the glory of the sun, to others the glory of the moon, to others the glory of the stars; to cause one star to differ from another star in glory. And, to speak once for all, and briefly, if the Creator God wants neither the will to undertake nor the power to complete a good and perfect work, what reason can there be that, in the creation of rational natures, i.e., of beings of whose existence He Himself is the cause, He should make some of higher rank, and others of second, or third, or of many lower and inferior degrees? (Origen, *De Principiis,* Bk. II, Ch. IX, sec. 5, ANF IV, pp. 290-291)

Origen argued that variety in creation is part of God's design. To seek absolute equality invariably sustained among all creatures would be to deny to human freedom the power to assert itself individually, and to divine providence the joy of seeing all varied creatures working as a whole. If God desires many strata of rational creatures, some finite and some angelic, some having more and some less power, then is this rich variety of rational beings a diminution of the justice of God? No, because the freedom of rational creatures is a greater value than a rigidly bound order of absolute equality.

Variety is the hallmark of the divine gardener. According to Prosper of Aquitaine, the husbandry of God requires not uniformity of response but variety and a grasp of the beauty, usefulness and purpose of the variegated whole:

Even in our own day when streams of ineffable gifts flood the whole world, grace is not bestowed on all in the same measure and intensity. Though the ministers of the word and of God's grace preach the same truth to all and address to all the same exhortations, yet this is *God's husbandry* and *God's building,* and it is He whose power invisibly acts and gives growth to what they build or cultivate. . . . The Author of all growth raises them; for in the Lord's field the plants are not all uniformly developed nor is there one kind of plant only. Again, although the structure of the whole temple makes for all the beauty that it has, yet the places and functions of the stones that go into it, are not the same for all. (Prosper of Aquitaine, *The Call of All Nations,* Bk. II, Ch. 6, ACW 14, pp. 98-99)*

Do these differences in power or status among creatures make talk of God's justice scandalous? Are sand crabs treated less justly than hawks? Was Esau treated less fairly than Jacob? Origen wrote:

> The Apostle Paul, in discussing the case of Jacob and Esau, says: . . . "'The elder shall be servant to the younger,' and that accords with the text of Scripture, 'Jacob I loved and Esau I hated'" (Rom. 9:11,12). And after that, he answers himself, and says, "What shall we say then? Is there unrighteousness with God?" And in order that he might furnish us with an opportunity of inquiring into these matters, and of ascertaining how these things do not happen without a reason, he answers himself, and says, "God forbid!" For the same question, it seems to me, which is raised concerning Jacob and Esau, may be raised regarding all celestial and terrestrial creatures. . . . Diversity was not the original condition of the creature, but that, owing to causes that have previously existed, a different office is prepared by the Creator for each one. . . . Nevertheless, some of those who are possessed of greater merit are ordained to suffer with others for the adorning of the state of the world, and for the discharge of duty to creatures of a lower grade, in order that by this means they themselves may be participators in the endurance of the Creator, according to the words of the apostle: "For the created universe waits with eager expectation for God's sons to be revealed. It was made the victim of frustration, not by its own choice, but because of him who made it so" (Rom. 8:20,21). (Origen, *De Principiis,* Bk. II, Ch. IX, sec. 7, ANF IV, p. 292, NEB)*

Origen was viewing the diversity of creation, as Paul, within the larger framework of salvation history, which includes the tragic alienation of the will, not only in the case of Esau, but of Adam, of all humanity and finally of all creation. The premise of Origen's argument must be understood in order to grasp its scope: What God wisely and rightly creates, though subject to fallenness, is not viewed by us in the same way that it is viewed by God. God's equities transcend our inequities. Only in the mode of prayer, finally, may one rightly seek an explanation:

> Now we term world everything which is above the heavens, or in the heavens, or upon the earth, or in those places which are called the lower regions, or all places whatever that anywhere exist, together with their inhabitants. This whole, then, is called world. In this world certain beings are said to be super-celestial. . . . Certain beings are called earthly, and among them, for example, among human beings, there are no small differences. For some are Barbarians, others Greeks; and of the Barbarians some are savage and fierce, and others of a milder disposition. Certain of them live under laws that have been widely affirmed. Others, again, live under laws of a more common or severe kind; while

some, again, possess customs of an inhuman and savage character, rather than fair laws. And certain of them, from the hour of their birth, are reduced to humiliation and subjection, and brought up as slaves, being placed under the dominion either of masters, or princes, or tyrants. Others, again, are brought up in a manner more consonant with freedom and reason: some with sound bodies, some with bodies diseased from their early years; some defective in vision, others in hearing and speech; some born in that condition, others deprived of the use of their senses immediately after birth, or at least undergoing such misfortune on reaching manhood. And why should I repeat and enumerate all the horrors of human misery, from which some have been free, and in which others have been involved, when each one can weigh and consider them for himself. . . . In the Psalm also it is written, "In wisdom hast Thou made them all" (Ps. 104:24); —seeing then that Christ is the Word and Wisdom, and so also the Righteousness of God, it will undoubtedly follow that those things that were created in the Word and Wisdom are said to be created also in that righteousness which is Christ; that in created things there may appear to be nothing unrighteous or accidental, but that all things may be shown to be in conformity with the law of equity and righteousness. How, then, so great a variety of things, and so great a diversity, can be understood to be altogether just and righteous, I am sure no human power or language can explain, unless as prostrate suppliants we pray to the Word, and Wisdom, and Righteousness Himself. (Origen, *De Principiis,* Bk. II, Ch. IX, sec. 3, ANF IV, pp. 290-291)*

There is no rational answer that finite minds can readily grasp and state in a few words. Yet it remains clear that the only alternative to such variety in the world would have been the elimination of human freedom, which elicits these varieties, which, although sometimes horrifying, are nonetheless all embraceable within the providence of God. This is not an apology for the abuses of freedom, such as slavery and murder, but rather an appeal to the goodness of God in granting freedom which is able to stand, but liable to fall.

Could other worlds have existed that are precisely the same as or radically different from ours? Was this cosmic order preceded by any others, and may there be ages left to come? Origen found it entirely unconvincing that (a) a subsequent world would be precisely like this one, and (b) that such worlds must be ruled out altogether:

And now I do not understand by what proofs they can maintain their position, who assert that worlds sometimes come into existence which are not dissimilar to each other, but in all respects equal. For if there is said to be a world similar in all respects to the present, then it will come to pass that Adam and Eve will do the same things which they did before: there will be a second time the same deluge, and the same Moses will again lead a nation numbering nearly six hundred thousand out of Egypt; Judas will also a second time betray the Lord; Paul will a second time keep the garments of those who stoned Stephen; and everything which has been done in this life will be said to be repeated,—a state of things which I think cannot be established by any reasoning, if souls are actuated by freedom of will, and maintain either their advance or retrogression according to the power of their will. For souls are not driven on in a cycle which returns after many ages to the same round, so as either to do or desire this or that, but at whatever point the freedom of their own will aims, there they direct the course of their actions. For what these persons say is much the same as if one were to assert that if a tiny bit of grain were to be poured out on the ground, the fall of the grain would be on the second occasion identically the same as on the first, so that every individual grain would lie for the second time close beside that grain where it had been thrown before, and so the exact bits of grain would be scattered in the same order, and with the same results as formerly. . . . It seems to me impossible for a world to be restored for the second time, with the same order and with the same amount of births, and deaths, and actions; but that a diversity of worlds may exist with changes of no unimportant kind, so that the state of another world may be for some unmistakeable reasons better (than this), and for others worse, and for others again intermediate. But what may be the number or measure of this I confess myself ignorant, although, if any one can tell it, I would gladly learn.

But this world, which is itself called an age, is said to be the conclusion of many ages. Now, the holy apostle teaches that in that age which preceded this, Christ did not suffer, nor even in the age which preceded that again; and I know not that I am able to enumerate the number of anterior ages in which He did not suffer. . . . We have clearly learned from Paul himself that after this age, which is said to be formed for the consummation of other ages, there will be other ages again to follow, "So that he might display in the ages to come how immense are the resources of his grace, and how great his kindness to us in Christ Jesus" (Eph. 2:7). He has not said, "in the age to come," nor "in the two ages to come," from which I infer that by his language many ages are indicated. (Origen, *De Principiis,* Bk. II, Ch. III, sec. 5, ANF IV, pp. 272-273, NEB)*

In Origen's view there may be many worlds, and judging by the varieties in this world, we should not expect other worlds to be exactly like ours. Again, this is a testimony to the goodness of God in the creation of variety and the permission of freedom to emerge within that variety.

What is the pastoral relevance of these arguments? It is particularly acute in our modern culture that tends to be obsessed with simple equalitarianism, that all judgments about the justice of God fall under the spell of equality as a simple, absolute norm, so as to imply that if God does not create everything equal, and thereby do away with variety, God could not be good or just. Although the pastor may have to listen carefully to spot this prevailing assumption, it will often be plaintively voiced in serious discussions with parishioners about suffering. This is particularly to be expected of well-educated parishioners who have been strongly impacted by sociological and psychological studies of social and cultural determinants of human behavior, and by simplistic equalitarian idealism. That many fit into this category makes the seventeen hundred year old arguments of Origen all the more pertinent to ponder.

IX ✹ TEMPTATION AND RESPONSIBLE FREEDOM

We have seen a consistently strong emphasis in pastoral writings upon freedom. Since behavioral excellences can only emerge out of freedom, moral accountability is absurd without the premise of freedom, and arguments about the justice of God amid historical evils hinge on the gift of freedom.

But freedom is prone to more complications than its more generalized theories imply. For freedom faces temptation, according to the virtually unanimous opinion of the pastoral writers. This means that in order to become more assuredly free, freedom must be tested in order to strengthen its growth toward goodness and its rootage in divine grace. At this point the story of freedom becomes layered with complexity and irony. The only freedom we human beings have is a freedom that from time to time is sorely and vulnerably *tempted.*

Perfectionistic equalitarianism returns once more to ask whether all persons are tempted equally:

Nor is there here any room for the excuse that some have lighter, others heavier, evils to bear. For to everyone is given his temptation according to measure, and never beyond his strength. As it is written in Psalm 80:5: "Thou shalt feed us with the bread of tears, and give us for our drink tears in measure," and as Paul says, "God is faithful, who will not suffer you to be tempted above that ye are able; but will with the temptation also make a way to escape, that ye may be able to bear it" (I Cor. 10:13). Where there is, therefore, a greater evil, there is also more of divine help, and an easier way to escape; so that the unequal distribution of sufferings appears to be greater than it actually is. (Luther, *The Fourteen of Consolation,* WML I, p. 134)

There is no guaranteed equality of temptation, but there is faith's confidence that God will not allow more than we can bear, according to scripture's promise. In Luther's view, there is a proportionality at work in temptation: the greater evil, the greater the divine help. There is no guarantee, given the variable conditions of human freedom in developing history, that one will face less temptation than Job or more than St. Anthony. But is it probable that one who has had fifty years to exercise freedom and risk its potential abuse is more likely to have been tempted more often than the infant who is only six months old? Doubtless there is a correlation between the length of time freedom has to operate, and the probability it will face serious temptation to lose its bearings and fall into corruption and despair. Yet temptation, fallenness and despair also apply proportionally in some primitive sense to the newborn. Is temptation, therefore, endemic to human freedom?

"And lead us not into temptation, but deliver us from the Evil One" (Matt. 6:13). The petition "but deliver us from the Evil One" is omitted by Luke. If the Savior orders us to pray for things that are not impossible, it seems to me worth asking how we are commanded to pray not to enter into temptation, when the whole of men's life on earth is temptation. We are in temptation by the very fact that we are on earth. . . . We learn from Job that the whole of human life on earth is temptation. He says, "Is not the life of men on earth a temptation?" (Job 7:1 LXX). . . . Moreover, Paul wrote to the Corinthians not that they would not be tempted, but that God would favor them with not being tempted beyond their power. . . . And David shows in a general way what happens to all righteous when he says, "Many are the afflictions of the righteous" (Ps. 34:19). And the Apostle in Acts says, "Through many tribulations we must enter the kingdom of God" (Acts 14:22). . . . In Psalm 26 it says, "Prove me, O Lord, and tempt me, try with fire my reins and my heart" (Ps. 26:2). . . . Whoever supposed that he was beyond human temptations by having fulfilled the tally of those he knew? And what time is there when he can presume he does not have to struggle to keep from sinning? . . . Therefore, in the times of relief between temptations let us stand firm for their onset, and let us be prepared for everything that can happen, so that whatever comes to pass, we may not be tested as though unready, but may be revealed as those who have disciplined themselves with extreme care. For when we have accomplished all we can by ourselves, God will fulfill what is lacking because of human weakness. (Origen, *On Prayer,* XXIX.1-5, 19, CWS, pp. 152-153, 161)

Human life brings with it temptation as a perennial concomitant of freedom, accompanying freedom intermittantly from beginning to end, although at times it may recede or remit temporarily. Why temptation?

It is sometimes good for the servants of God to be tempted, so that the very temptations may practise them and make them more wary; for struggles with the vices are exercises in the virtues. And just as a man learns by falling often how to tread firmly and walk warily, or as the man who has often been wounded in battle is on the look-out for the coming blow, so he who has been frequently deluded by the devil presently perceives his wiles more readily. (Hugh of St. Victor, *SSW*, p. 113)

The early pastoral tradition reflected deeply on the promise of scripture that we will not be tempted beyond our strength. The metaphor of fairness in setting the rules of athletic competition was employed to interpret this promise:

"You may fall. So far you have faced no trial beyond what man can bear. God keeps faith, and he will not allow you to be tested above your powers, but when the test comes he will at the same time provide a way out, by enabling you to sustain it" (1 Cor. 10:13). For as the officials of public games do not allow the competitors to enter the lists indiscriminately or fortuitously, but after a careful examination, pairing in a most impartial consideration either of size or age, this individual with that— boys, e.g., with boys, men with men, who are nearly related to each other either in age or strength; so also must we understand the procedure of divine providence, which arranges on the most impartial principles all who come to engage in the struggles of this human life, according to the nature of each individual's power, which is known only to Him who alone beholds the hearts of men: so that one individual fights against one temptation of the flesh, another against a second; one is exposed to its influence for so long a period of time, another only for so long; one is tempted by the flesh to this or that indulgence, another to one of a different kind; one has to resist this or that hostile power, another has to combat two or three at the same time. . . .

He who contends in the lists of competitors, although paired with his adversary on a just principle of arrangement, will nevertheless not necessarily prove conqueror. But unless the powers of the combatants are generally on the same level, the prize of the victor will not be justly won; nor would any reproach be justly attached to the vanquished. On the basis of this analogy, God allows us indeed to be tempted, but not "beyond what man can bear" (1 Cor. 10:13). Rather it is in proportion to our strength that we are tempted. Paul does not here write that in temptation God will make also a way of escape so that we could circumvent temptation, but a way of escape so as that we might be enabled to bear temptation. . . . For there is no doubt that under every temptation we gain a power of endurance, if we employ properly the strength that is granted us. . . . If such a power were absolutely given us in such a way that we would in every case prove victorious, and never be challenged, what further reason for a struggle could remain to one who could not therefore be overcome? Or what merit would there be in a victory where the power of successful resistance is taken away? (Origen, *De Principiis,* Bk. III, Ch. II, sec. 3, ANF IV, pp. 330-331)*

This is an argument based on God's justice: God, being just, would not design an unfair competition in which small children must run against experienced adults. Since God is just, you can count on it that you will not be placed in a contest that is completely beyond your competence, even though it may require you to make a great effort.

Let us take the opposite hypothesis. Suppose that no temptation were allowed to exist, no rational creatures (human or angelic) would be allowed to fall, and no challenge would be allowed to human freedom. Would that improve the human condition?

Let us consider . . . whether if there were no devil, it were possible for human experience to exhibit such restraint in partaking of food as never to exceed the proper limits; i.e., that no one would either take otherwise than the case required, or more than reason would allow; and so it would result that men, observing due measure and moderation in the matter of eating, would never go wrong. I do not think, indeed, that so great moderation could be observed by men (even if there were no instigation by the devil inciting thereto), as that no individual, in partaking of food, would go beyond due limits and restraint until he had learned to do so from long usage and experience. (Origen, *De Principiis,* Bk. III, Ch. II, sec. 2, ANF IV, p. 330)

The question of whether temptations come from our own constitution or from demonic powers is not an easy one to sort out:

Stupendous, truly stupendous and incomprehensible is the wickedness of the evil spirits. It is not seen by many, and I think that even those few who see it see it only in part. Thus, how is it that, while living in luxury and plenty, we keep vigil and do not sleep? . . . When we are hungry, why are we tempted by dreams? Yet when sated, we do not experience these temptations. In poverty, we become dark and incapable of compunction; but if we drink wine, we are happy and easily come to compunction. He who can do so in the Lord, let him bring light to the unenlightened in this matter. For we are not enlightened about this. At least, we can say that such a change does not always come from the demons. And this sometimes happens to me, I know not how, by reason of the constitution I have been given and the sordid and greedy corpulence with which I am girt about.

With regard to the changes enumerated above, which are so hard to interpret, let us sincerely and humbly pray to the Lord. And if, after prayer and the time which it took, we still feel the same thing at work in us, then let us conclude that this is caused not by demons but by nature. (Climacus, *The Ladder of Divine Ascent,* Step 26, secs. 128-129, p. 181)

John Climacus was keenly aware of the power of the demonic, which he thought was doubtless far deeper than conscious awareness, but he did not want thereby to make of temptation something completely external to human freedom. Although he asks for further enlightenment on this perplexity, he at least attributed some significant level of temptation to his own constitution, his nature as a dynamic body/soul relationship.

St. Catherine thought that the essence of demonic temptation was that a lesser good appears to be better:

The soul, from her nature, always relishes good, though it is true that the soul, blinded by self-love, does not know and discern what is true good, and of profit to the soul and to the body. And, therefore, the Devil, seeing them blinded by self-love, iniquitously places before them diverse and various delights, coloured so as to have the appearance of some benefit or good. (Catherine of Siena, *A Treatise of Discretion,* p. 122)

Penitence seeks to restore the equilibrium that temptation has taken away:

Practically every sin is committed for pleasure; it is taken away by the suffering of hardships and grief, whether this be voluntary or involuntary, through penitence, or some trial disposed by Providence. . . . When a temptation comes upon you unexpectedly, do not accuse him through whom it came; but seek the why of it and you will find correction. . . . Some temptations bring men pleasure, some grief, some bodily pain. The physician of souls by means of His judgments applies the remedy to each soul according to the cause of its passions. (Maximus the Confessor, *The Four Centuries of Charity,* Ch. 2, secs. 41-44, ACW 21, pp. 161-162)

X ❧ THE POTENTIALLY CONSTRUCTIVE USES OF TEMPTATION

The pastoral writers viewed temptation as permitted by Almighty God and within the larger framework of God's providential purposes, however dimly perceived. This is why they sought so diligently to grasp the positive uses and effects of temptation. Origen speculated that demonic resistance to the will actually had the paradoxical effect of strengthening it:

Now the use of temptation is something like this. What our soul has received escapes everyone's knowledge but God's—even our own. But it becomes evident through temptations, so that we no longer escape the knowledge of what we are like. And in knowing ourselves we are also conscious, if we are willing, of our own evils; and we give thanks for the good things that have been made evident to us through temptation. (Origen, *On Prayer,* XXIX.17, CWS, pp. 160-161)

Origen's speculation on the fundamental purpose of temptation is far-reaching: It is to increase self-knowledge, to bring the soul to an awareness of itself that had previously been hidden, or one might say, similarly to Freud, to make the unconscious conscious, to behold our erotic energies clearly. This cannot occur without the testing of freedom, which is what temptation is. For this reason, according to Anglican martyr Hugh Latimer, we do better not always to hope for simplistic tranquility and absence of temptation:

David said, "Examine me, O God, and know my thoughts; test me, and understand my misgivings" (Ps. 139:23). He knew that to be tempted (or tested) of God is a good thing, since temptations perform the ministry of providing the occasion to run to God and ask divine help. Therefore David desired to have an occasion whereby he might exercise his faith. For there is nothing so dangerous in the world as to be without trouble, without trial. And notice: It is when we are most at ease, when all things go with us according to our will and pleasure, then we are commonly furthest off from God. For our nature is so feeble that we cannot bear tranquility. We soon forget God. Therefore we should say, "Lord examine me" and "test me" (Ps. 139:23). (Hugh Latimer, OCC 1, p. 53)

One particular generation may be tried in a quite different way than another generation. St. Anthony viewed his own generation with irony. He thought that it was too weak to bear much temptation, and for that reason had been spared it in a severe form:

Abba Anthony said, "God does not allow the same warfare and temptations to this generation as he did formerly, for men are weaker now and cannot bear so much." (Anthony the Great, in *Sayings of the Desert Fathers,* p. 5)

In a similar vein, Luther observed that those who have been sorely tried may become like jewels of historical experience:

One Christian who has been tried does more good than a hundred who have not been tried. For in trials the blessing grows, so that with its counsels it can teach, comfort, and help many in physical and spiritual matters. (Luther, "Lectures on Genesis, Chapters 26 to 30, 1542ff.," LW 5, p. 146)

So the pastor need not be defensive, cynical or intimidated by profound trials of the spirit, either in himself or others. They are potential sources of great derivative value. One of the Desert Mothers, Amma Theodora, used this powerful metaphor:

Amma Theodora said, "Let us strive to enter by the narrow gate. Just as the trees, if they have not stood before the winter's storms cannot bear fruit, so it is with us; this present age is a storm and it is only through many trials and temptations that we can obtain an inheritance in the kingdom of heaven." (Amma Theodora, in *Sayings of the Desert Fathers*, p. 71)

Anthony expected no end to temptation, so long as freedom lives:

Abba Anthony said to Abba Poemen, "This is the great work of a man: always to take the blame for his own sins before God and to expect temptation to his last breath."

He also said, "Whoever has not experienced temptation cannot enter into the Kingdom of Heaven." He even added, "Without temptations no one can be saved." (Anthony the Great, in *Sayings of the Desert Fathers*, p. 2)

Ignatius Loyola, himself a former soldier, used a metaphor of military strategy in discussing the way temptation hits one's point of greatest weakness and vulnerability:

The enemy's behavior is also like that of a military leader who wishes to conquer and plunder the object of his desires. Just as the commander of an army pitches his camp, studies the strength and defenses of a fortress, and then attacks it on its weakest side, in like manner, the enemy of our human nature studies from all sides our theological, cardinal, and moral virtues. Wherever he finds us weakest and most in need regarding our eternal salvation, he attacks and tries to take us by storm. (Ignatius of Loyola, *Spiritual Exercises*, p. 132)

XI ❧ THE CARE OF SOULS FACING TEMPTATION

We have laid the groundwork for the pastoral care of those facing trials of spirit by discussing freedom, theodicy, temptation and its potential uses and abuses. Now we ask what practical wisdom or specific directives the pastoral tradition has developed to help the pastor care for persons facing difficult spiritual trials.

The theme of making temptation profitable to the spirit is frequently found in the soul care literature, as in this recollection of Amma Theodora:

Amma Theodora asked Archbishop Theophilus about some words of

the apostle saying, "What does this mean, 'Knowing how to profit by circumstances'?" (Col. 4:5). He said to her, "This saying shews us how to
profit at all times. For example: is it a time of excess for you? By humility and patience buy up the time of excess, and draw profit from it. Is
it the time of shame? Buy it up by means of resignation and win it. So
everything that goes against us can, if we wish, become profitable to us."
(Amma Theodora, in *Sayings of the Desert Fathers,* p. 71).

A healthy life of prayer is the first line of defense against temptation. Yet we
tempt God if we ask the impossible:

Seeking for what is beyond us may have perilous results. The Lord's
judgment about us is unfathomable. By His special providence, He
often chooses to hide His will from us, knowing that, even if we were
to learn it, we should disobey it, and should thereby receive greater
punishment. . . . There are courageous souls who, with love and
humility of heart, throw themselves into tasks that are beyond them;
and there are proud hearts who do the same. For our foes often intentionally suggest to us things beyond our powers, so that these should
cause us to lose heart and leave even what is within our power, and
make ourselves a great laughing-stock to our enemies. (Climacus, *The
Ladder of Divine Ascent,* Step 26, secs. 120, 122, p. 180)

According to John Climacus, the devil has an avid interest in leading human
beings to try to do the impossible. Those most sorely tempted may be helped
by a soul guide who can show them how to grow through and make good use
of such trials.

The limit of demonic power in temptation is another prevalent theme. St.
Catherine of Siena spoke of her divine revelation as if in the voice of Christ:

"The Devil, dearest daughter, is the instrument of My Justice. . . .
I have set him in this life to tempt and molest My creatures, not for My
creatures to be conquered, but that they may conquer, proving their
virtue, and receive from Me the glory of victory. And no one should fear
any battle or temptation of the Devil that may come to him, because I
have made My creatures strong, and have given them strength of
will. . . . You therefore, with free arbitration, can hold it or leave it,
according as you please. It is an arm, which, if you place it in the hands
of the Devil, straightway becomes a knife, with which he strikes you and
slays you. But if one does not give this knife of his will into the hands
of the Devil, that is, if he does not consent to his temptations and
molestations, he will never be injured by the guilt of sin in any temptation, but will even be fortified by it, when the eye of his intellect is

opened to see My love which allowed him to be tempted, so as to arrive at virtue, by being proved. For one does not arrive at virtue except through knowledge of self, and knowledge of Me, which knowledge is more perfectly acquired in the time of temptation, because then one knows oneself to be nothing, being unable to lift off oneself the pains and vexations which one would flee. . . . My love permits these temptations, for the devil is weak, and by himself can do nothing, unless I allow him. And I let him tempt, through love, and not through hatred, that you may conquer, and not that you may be conquered, and that you may come to a perfect knowledge of yourself, and of Me, and that virtue may be proved, for it is not proved except by its contrary." (Catherine of Siena, *A Treatise of Discretion,* pp. 118-119)*

Although modern psychology may consider St. Catherine's revelations as hallucinations and her talk of the demonic as pathological, modern pastors may view this language within its historical context as a powerful affirmation of human freedom from demonic determination, and a plausible clarification to the faithful of the purposefulness and meaning of temptation.

John Cassian passed along to others this cure for despair that moves through and beyond temptation:

The formula was given us by a few of the oldest fathers who remained. They did not communicate it except to a very few who were athirst for the true way. To maintain an unceasing recollection of God it is to be ever set before you. The formula is: "Show me favour, O God, and save me; hasten to help me, O Lord" (Ps. 70:1).

This verse has rightly been selected from the whole Bible for this purpose. It fits every mood and temper of human nature, every temptation, every circumstance. It contains an invocation of God, a humble confession of faith, a reverent watchfulness, a meditation upon our frailty, a confidence in God's answer, an assurance of his ever-present support. The man who continually invokes God as his guardian, is aware that he is always at hand. . . . Souls sunk in accidie or worry or melancholy thoughts of any kind find the cure of despair in this verse, which shows them God's watch over their struggles and their prayers. (Cassian, *Conferences,* Conference 10, sec. 10, LCC XII, pp. 239-240)

John Climacus also left this intriguing aphorism:

Just as thieves will not attack a place where they see royal weapons stacked, so he who has united his heart to prayer will not lightly be raided by spiritual thieves. (Climacus, *The Ladder of Divine Ascent,* Step 26, sec. 33, p. 194)

XII ❦ Angelic and Demonic Influences: Superpersonal Energies in the Struggle of the Soul

It is evident by now that virtually all pre-modern pastoral writers viewed the struggle of the soul as involving demonic temptation. The internal battle was thus intrinsically connected with a greater primordial, trans-historical combat among angelic powers fallen and unfallen. These powers were assumed to influence, but not unilaterally determine human choice.

Although this premise is difficult for many modern persons to take seriously as a plausible view of human decision-making, we cannot now change the texts or alter the assumptions of the early pastoral writers. Whether we find it plausible or not, they firmly believed that this overarching supra-historical battle was more fundamental than their own subjective minor skirmishes that echo it. If we wish to enter into dialogue with them, we are compelled to do so first by entering empathically into their sphere of reference, in order to understand what they were thinking, and only on that basis can we meaningfully assess what they were saying. The demonic-angelic combat can be existentially interpreted, whatever one might think about its objective plausibility. Furthermore, our modern empirical analyses are never exhaustive. Parapsychological studies have given us reason to doubt that naturalistic reductionism has fully accounted for all psychological, physical and sociological determinants.

The pastor will serve persons who take the premise of superpersonal influence with deadly seriousness, and others who will regard it as wholly outmoded and implausible. The pastor will not be able to choose either one group or the other exclusively, but is likely to have to deal with both, and not infrequently to confront both mixed together. The pastor has an important teaching function toward both groups: To the modernists he may need to show that an existential interpretation of superpersonal powers is possible; to the others he may need to show that something more subtle than the bare objective reality of these forces may be intended.

In any case the classic pastoral tradition has expressed strong opinions about how these superpersonal forces may affect the soul, its education and development. Luther, for example, assumed with extraordinarily dramatic realism that the devil exists, has power, and never stops harassing the believer:

> The devil takes no holiday; he never rests. If beaten, he rises again. If he cannot enter in front, he steals in at the rear. If he cannot enter in the rear, he breaks through the roof or enters by tunneling under the threshold. He labours until he is in. He uses great cunning and many a plan. When one miscarries, he has another at hand and continues his attempts until he wins. (Luther, WA 17 I, pp. 449f.; in WLS 1, p. 395)

This is one of hundreds of references by Luther to the formidable power of the demonic. Yet in asserting this awesome power, many pastoral writers were already quite aware that talk of the demonic could easily become distorted, and the devil's power could be exaggerated. That point is reached, in the view of

Athanasius, when we assume that evil has a reality independent from God:

Now certain of the Greeks, having erred from the right way, and not having known Christ, have ascribed to evil a substantive and independent existence. In this they make a double mistake: either in denying the Creator to be maker of all things, [as] if evil had an independent subsistence and being of its own; or again, if they mean that He is maker of all things, they will of necessity admit Him to be maker of evil also. (Athanasius, *Against the Heathen,* sec. 6, NPNF 2, IV, p. 6)

Athanasius further probed the question of whether God or the devil elicited or produced evil:

They arbitrarily imagine another god besides the true One, the Father of our Lord Jesus Christ, and that he is the unmade producer of evil and the head of wickedness, who is also artificer of Creation. But these men one can easily refute, not only from the divine Scriptures, but also from the human understanding itself, the very source of these, their insane imaginations. To begin with, our Lord and Saviour Jesus Christ says in His own gospels confirming the words of Moses: "The Lord God is one" (Mark 12:29), and "I thank thee, Father, Lord of heaven and earth" (Matt. 11:25). But if God is one, and at the same time Lord of heaven and earth, how could there be another God beside Him? Or what room will there be for the God whom they suppose, if the one true God fills all things in the compass of heaven and earth? (Athanasius, *Against the Heathen,* sec. 6, NPNF 2, IV, p. 7)

Clement rejected the notion that the devil is able to coerce freedom unilaterally into doing wrong:

Let them not then say, that he who does wrong and sins transgresses through the agency of demons; for then he would be guiltless. But by choosing the same things as demons, by sinning, being unstable, and light, and fickle in his desires, like a demon, he becomes a demoniacal man. Now he who is bad, having become, through evil, sinful by nature, becomes depraved, having what he has chosen. (Clement of Alexandria, *The Stromata, or Miscellanies,* Bk. VI, Ch. XII, ANF II, p. 502)

Clement here made clear his subsequently influential view that the demonic in reality is interlaced with and dependent upon human freedom, so that humanity cannot blame its ills on a power external to freedom. We cannot say: "The Devil made me do it!" We choose our misdeeds. St. Catherine of Siena spoke pointedly:

When the time of discretion is come, the soul can, by her free will, make choice either of good or evil, according as it pleases her will; and so great is this liberty that one has, and so strong has this ability been made by virtue of this glorious inheritance, that no demon or creature can constrain one to the smallest fault without one's own free consent. (Catherine of Siena, *A Treatise of Discretion,* pp. 69-70)*

For if the will is completely impotent in the presence of the demonic, according to Catherine, how could the soul be held responsible? Tertullian strongly affirmed the premise of free will, but argued that it had become fundamentally damaged by corruptions freely chosen in response to demonic temptation:

All the endowments which the soul received at birth are obscured and corrupted by the Devil, who from the very beginning cast an envious eye on them, so that they are not properly cared for nor perform their functions as they ought. For, the Devil lies in wait to trap every human soul from the moment of its birth. (Tertullian, *On the Soul,* Ch. 39, sec. 1, FC 10, p. 270)

Due to the subtlety of superhuman intelligences, it has been thought to be difficult for human intelligence to recognize the differences between angelic and demonic forces. The Shepherd of Hermas argued that it was by visible fruits, overt evidences, and observable activities that one can discern this difference. The pathway of each is strewn with different results:

"The angel of righteousness is gentle and modest, meek and peaceful. When, therefore, he ascends into your heart, forthwith he talks to you of righteousness, purity, chastity, contentment, and of every righteous deed and glorious virtue. When all these ascend into your heart, know that the angel of righteousness is with you. These are the deeds of the angel of righteousness. Trust him, then, and his works. Look now at the works of the angel of iniquity. First, he is wrathful, and bitter, and foolish, and his works are evil, and ruin the servants of God. When, then, he ascends into your heart, know him by his works." And I said to him, "How, sir, I shall perceive him, I do not know." "Hear and understand," said he. "When anger comes upon you, or harshness, know that he is in you; and you will know this to be the case also, when you are attacked by a longing after many transactions, and the richest delicacies, and drunken revels, and divers luxuries, and things improper, and by a hankering after women, and by overreaching, and pride, and blustering, and by whatever is like to these. When these ascend into your heart, know that the angel of iniquity is in you." (*The Pastor of Hermas,* Bk. II, Commandment VI, ANF II, p. 24)

In Part Three we have shown that ministry to persons in crisis requires a rigorous theological reflection upon the meaning of suffering. The pastor must consider carefully how the justice and goodness of God may be declared without neglecting the reality of suffering. This reasoning must occur without falling into a masochistic trap of making evil look good. It must take seriously the inequalities of created beings, the temptations endemic to human freedom, the potential pedagogy of suffering, and the complexity of divine providence.

4 Marriage and Family Counseling

SINCE MARRIAGE IS BLESSED by God and affirmed by the church, and since the family is a crucial arena of spiritual formation, the classical pastoral writers have thought often and written much about marriage and family counseling. This area of pastoral care includes a wide range of reflection upon premarital pastoral counseling, marriage counseling, the single life, parental counseling, youth counseling, and marital crisis counseling (adultery, abortion, divorce, and other topics).

I ❦ PREMARITAL PASTORAL COUNSEL

Pastoral writers have generally assumed that it is exceedingly important for couples considering marriage to understand realistically the nature of monogamous marriage, engagement to marry, the marriage covenant, its meaning, promises, and responsibilities, and its relation to Christian faith and community. These assumptions have for many centuries thrust the pastor in the midst of the arena in which persons are considering Christian marriage. The task is partially one of education, partly counsel, partly friendship and support, and partly one of aiding persons in the making of plans to celebrate the special event of matrimony. The first priority in such a premarital conversation is a clear understanding of the nature of marriage as divinely instituted. One who enters the state of matrimony without due consideration is living hazardously:

> To recognize the estate of marriage is something quite different from merely being married. He who is married but does not recognize the estate of marriage cannot continue in wedlock without bitterness, drudgery, and anguish; he will inevitably complain and blaspheme like the pagans and blind, irrational men. But he who recognizes the estate of marriage will find therein delight, love, and joy without end; as Solomon says, "He who finds a wife finds a good thing," etc. (Prov. 18:22). Now the ones who recognize the estate of marriage are those who firmly believe that God himself instituted it, brought husband and wife together. (Luther, "The Estate of Marriage, 1522," LW 45, p. 38; cf. WA 10 II, p. 297)

John Chrysostom warned against fixing one's attention primarily upon physical attraction in the selection of a spouse:

Seek out soul beauty. Follow the pattern of Christ as Bridegroom of the church. External attractiveness tends toward conceit and license. It hurls people toward jealousy and suspicion. But think about the limits of its pleasure. Do not be surprised if it, considered by itself, lasts one or two months, or perhaps at most a year. What then? This level of admiration fades with familiarity. Meanwhile the problems that arise from deception and false representation still are there: pride, folly, contempt. In one who has soul beauty, the attractiveness does not fade. The love, having been begun on honest grounds, still continues ardent, since its object is beauty of soul, and not of body. . . . Seek in a spouse affection, modesty, gentleness; these are the characteristics of beauty. (Chrysostom, *Homilies on Ephesians,* Hom. XX, NPNF 1, XIII, p. 145; cf. BPEC IV, pp. 303-304)*

Much has been said in Christian ethics about sexual continence before marriage, but often deeper aspects of the question of continence have not been addressed. According to Clement of Alexandria, continence is not focused primarily on sexuality:

One ought to consider continence not merely in relation to one form of it, that is, sexual relations, but in relation to all the other indulgences for which the soul craves when it is ill content with what is necessary and seeks for luxury. It is continence to despise money, softness, property, to hold in small esteem outward appearance, to control one's tongue, to master evil thoughts. (Clement of Alexandria, *On Marriage,* sec. 59, LCC II, p. 67)

The root word, *continentia,* refers to any kind of self-restraint, of which sexual self-restraint is only one kind. But the early pastoral writers indeed speak of sexual self-restraint prior to marriage as an important evidence of the seriousness with which one views the covenant of marriage:

Continence is as worthy of veneration as freedom to marry is worthy of respect, since both are according to the will of the Creator. Continence honors the law of marriage, permission to marry tempers it; the former is perfectly free, the latter is subject to regulation; the former is a matter of free choice, the latter is restricted within certain limitations. (Tertullian, *On Monogamy,* ACW 13, p. 70)

While most pastoral writers assumed that the consummation of sexual intimacy is rightly reserved for the married covenant, some have expressed other views. Luther, for example, took an unusually lenient attitude toward the question of sexual intercourse between those who are firmly committed to marriage:

Secret intercourse of those who are engaged to each other can certainly not be considered fornication; for it takes place in the name and with the intention of marriage, a desire, intention, or name which fornication does not have. (Luther, WA 30 III, pp. 226f.; in WLS 2, p. 896)

The difference between premarital intercourse of the betrothed and the sin of fornication, in Luther's view, is the clear and certain resolve to marry, i.e., the commitment to life-long monogamous fidelity in love.

Bucer employed this analogy in commending premarital pastoral counseling:

. . . [One] acts impiously if he enters the marriage contract, that lasting and highest union of human nature, without the counsel of important and pious men through whom he may be able to know the mind and will of God with more certainty. In less serious matters involving money and other things, the investment of which is often more profitable than the keeping of it, men who do not trust their own judgment use as counselors those whom they judge to have a bit more knowledge than they themselves in such matters. (Bucer, *De Regno Christi,* XVIII, LCC XIX, pp. 321-322)

Prospective marriage partners are well-advised not to fixate inordinately on each others' faults, but to develop early the habit of patiently overlooking each other's minor misdeeds:

It is impossible to keep peace between man and woman in family life if they do not condone and overlook each other's faults but watch everything to the smallest point. For who does not at times offend? Thus many things must be overlooked; very many things must be ignored that a peaceful relation may exist. (Luther, "Exposition on the Ten Commandments, 1516-1517," WA 1, p. 457; in WLS 2, p. 905)

Marriage looks unpleasant to those who reason about it only from a purely egocentric viewpoint, without reference to its fundamental purposes:

Now observe that when that clever harlot, our natural reason (which the pagans followed in trying to be most clever), takes a look at married life, she turns up her nose and says, "Alas, must I rock the baby, wash its diapers, make its bed, smell its stench, stay up nights with it, take care of it when it cries, heal its rashes and sores, and on top of that care for my wife, provide for her, labor at my trade, take care of this and take care of that, do this and do that, endure this and endure that, and whatever else of bitterness and drudgery married life involves? What, should I make a prisoner of myself?" (Luther, "The Estate of Marriage, 1522," LW 45, p. 39; cf. WA 10 II, p. 295)

Viewing marriage in terms of its limitations on personal freedom and its rigorous duties is indeed "reasonable" from an egocentric point of view, but marriage has values that cannot be grasped or understood from this viewpoint. The best premarital counsel will not focus primarily upon merely legalistic rules on how spouses are supposed to act toward each other in detail, but rather upon the relationship and its meaning:

You are her husband to help, support, and protect her, not to harm her. It is impossible to set specific bounds for you. Here you yourself must know how to proceed thoughtfully. (Luther, "Sermon on the First Epistle of St. Peter, 1522," LW 30, p. 92; cf. WA 12, p. 346)

In a moving passage, John Chrysostom commented on the value of clear and open expression of love and fidelity as the relationship emerges and develops:

I am aware that I shall appear perhaps ridiculous to many persons in giving such admonitions. Nevertheless, if you will but listen to me, as time goes on, and the benefit of the practice accrues to you, then you will understand the advantage of it: . . . "I value your affection above all things, and nothing is so bitter or so painful to me as ever to be at variance with you. Even though it should be my lot to lose everything, and become poorer than Irus, and undergo the extremest hazards, and suffer any pain whatever, all will be tolerable and endurable, so long as your feelings are true towards me. And then will my children be most dear to me, while you are affectionately disposed towards me, as long as you feel the same commitment that I do." Then mingle also with your own words the apostle's words, that "this is the way that God would have our affections blend together, as scripture says, 'That is why a man leaves his father and mother, and is united to his wife, and the two become one flesh' (Gen. 2:24). So let us never give each other any pretext for narrowminded jealousy." . . . Show her, also, that you set a high value on her company, that you desire nothing more than to be at home with her, far more than in the market-place. Put her before all your friends. Do not let your love of your children eclipse your love of her, and let these very children be beloved by you for her sake. . . . Pray with her. Go to church with her. And when you return from church ask her about what she thought about it, and be willing to let her call you to accountability for what was said there. (Chrysostom, *Homilies on Ephesians,* Hom. XX, NPNF 1, XIII, pp. 150-151, NEB)*

John Chrysostom thought that if one does well in the choosing of a spouse, one will thereby tend to choose everything else well. His metaphor of the choice of a wife is, surprisingly, not that of choosing a queen, but of choosing a king:

This wife will be a second king in the house, lacking only the diadem; and one who knows how to choose this king will excellently regulate all the rest. (Chrysostom, *Homilies on Ephesians,* Hom. XXII, NPNF 1, XIII, p. 159)

In conjugal love at its best, the whole person is loved, not just some aspect of the person.

But over and above all these is married love, that is, a bride's love, which glows like a fire and desires nothing but the husband. She says, "It is you I want, not what is yours: I want neither your silver nor your gold; I want neither. I want only you. I want you in your entirety, or not at all." All other kinds of love seek something other than the loved one: this kind wants the entire person of the loved one himself. (Luther, "A Sermon on the Estate of Marriage, 1519," LW 44, p. 9; WA 2, p. 167)*

II ❧ THE MEANING OF MARRIAGE

It is intrinsic to the pastor's teaching function to help young persons understand the nature of marriage as viewed by the Christian community. Matrimony is a Christian doctrine. An important part of premarital and marriage counseling by pastors is the clarification of what marriage is, what it promises, and why God blesses it when faithfully pursued.

The minister may be asked about the difference between civil marriage and Christian marriage. The Westminster Confession provided a concise definition of the three-fold purpose of marriage: mutuality in love, propagation, and moral development.

Marriage was ordained for the mutual help of husband and wife; for the increase of mankind with a legitimate issue, and of the church with an holy seed; and for preventing of uncleanness.

It is lawful for all sorts of people to marry who are able with judgment to give their consent. Yet it is the duty of Christians to marry only in the Lord. (Westminister Confession, Ch. XXIV, secs. ii-iii, *CC,* p. 221)

The essence of civil marriage is competent mutual consent, and of Christian marriage is marrying "in the Lord," according to Christ's teaching.

Christian marriage was viewed by Symeon of Thessalonica (d. 1420) as a sign of the joy of divine union received in the Holy Communion. Therefore there is an intrinsic liturgical connection between marriage and Eucharist.

This is why Christian marriage occurs in a church instead of a civil setting. Here is the commentary of Symeon on the liturgy of marriage, describing its spiritual meaning:

And immediately, (the priest) takes the holy chalice with the Presanctified Gifts, and exclaims: "The Presanctified holy Things for the Holy." And all respond: "One is holy, One is Lord," because the Lord alone is the sanctification, the peace and the union of His servants who are being married. The priest then gives Communion to the bridal pair, if they are worthy. Indeed, they must be ready to receive Communion, so that their crowning be a worthy one and their marriage valid. For Holy Communion is the perfection of every sacrament and the seal of every mystery. And the Church is right in preparing the Divine Gifts for the redemption and blessing of the bridal pair; for Christ Himself, who gave us these Gifts and Who is the Gifts, came to the marriage (in Cana of Galilee) to bring to it peaceful union and concord. So that those who get married must be worthy of Holy Communion; they must be united before God in a church, which is the house of God, because they are children of God, in a church where God is sacramentally present in the Gifts, where He is being offered to us and where He is seen in the midst of us. After that the priest also gives them to drink from the common cup; and the hymn "I will receive the cup of salvation," is sung because of the Most Holy Gifts, and as a sign of the joy which comes from divine union, and because the joy of the bridal pair comes from the peace and concord which they have received. (Symeon of Thessalonica, *Against the Heresies and On the Divine Temple,* Ch. 282, MPG clv, cols. 512f.; in J. Meyendorff, *Marriage: An Orthodox Perspective,* pp. 124-125)

Luther emphasized the religiously formative power of the marriage relationship:

The ultimate purpose is to obey God, to find aid and counsel against sin; to call upon God; to seek, love, and educate children for the glory of God; to live with one's wife in the fear of God and to bear the cross; but if there are no children, nevertheless to live with one's wife in contentment. (Luther, "Lectures on Genesis, Chapters 21 to 25," WA 43, p. 310; in WLS 2, p. 884; cf. LW 4, p. 244)

A far different cultural situation prevailed when Clement of Alexandria wrote on the purposes of marriage. For then, marriage was under attack, as some feel it is today. Key thinkers were repudiating marriage because of its numerous petty annoyances. Those who valued their own free time and pleasure were avoiding the trouble marriage brings. Under these circumstances, Clement appealed both to nature and scripture to speak of the purpose of marriage as inclusive of both the species' need for propagation and the natural ordering of sexuality:

> Marriage is the first conjunction of man and woman for the procreation of legitimate children. . . . Of course, not everyone should be married. But there is a time in which marriage is suitable. There are persons for whom marriage is suitable. There is an age up to which it is suitable. . . . Democritus repudiated marriage and the procreation of children on account of the many annoyances arising out of it, and because it caused distractions from things thought to be more important. Epicurus agreed, and most others will agree who imagine their final good to be personal pleasure, and the absence of trouble and pain. According to the opinion of the Stoics, marriage and the rearing of children were a thing indifferent. . . . But they who approve of marriage say, Nature has adapted us for marriage, as is evident from the structure of our bodies, which are male and female. Our bodies constantly proclaim that command: "Increase and replenish" (Gen. 1:28). (Clement of Alexandria, *The Stromata, or Miscellanies,* Bk. II, Ch. XXIII, ANF II, p. 377)*

Later, John Chrysostom set forth the argument that although a woman may seem to be the loser in marriage, due to the unequal position in which childbearing places her, she becomes the beneficiary through receiving the protection of another and being freed to fully give care to another. Chrysostom also in this passage articulated the surprising argument that the child is also "one flesh" with the parents! Thus "one flesh" does not merely refer to sexual union, but also its offspring. Consequently, caring for one's spouse and child is like caring for one's own flesh.

> "Husbands, love your wives, as Christ also loved the church" (Eph. 5:25ff.). . . . If so then take the same provident care for her that Christ takes for the Church. This is so even to the extent that you may need to give your life for her . . . . The partner of one's life, the mother of one's children, the foundation of one's every joy, one ought never to chain down by fear or intimidation. Draw her toward you with love and good temper. For what sort of union is that in which the wife is intimidated by her husband? What sort of pleasure will the husband himself enjoy if he treats his wife as a slave, and not as a free human being? . . . "In the same way men also are bound to love their wives, as they love their own bodies. In loving his wife a man loves himself. For no one ever hated his own body: on the contrary, he provides and cares for it" (Eph. 5:26-29). . . . So a man leaves his parents and his life becomes knit together with his wife. From this they emerge as one flesh: father, mother, and child, from the reality of the two lives commingled. For

indeed by the commingling of their seeds is the child produced, so that
the three are one flesh. . . . Don't you see that the self, viewed individ-
ualistically, has many deficiencies alone? . . . As great love as each
entertains towards oneself, so great would the Apostle have us entertain
towards one's spouse. (Chrysostom, *Homilies on Ephesians,* Hom. XX,
NPNF 1, XIII, pp. 144-146, NEB; cf. BPEC IV, pp. 301-304)*

It was not primarily the rational ideal of rigid equality, but the living
metaphor of an organism of mutually dependent members that shaped Chrysostom's view of the husband-wife relationship:

Where there is equal authority there can never be peace. Neither will
there be peace where a house is a democracy, where everyone presumes
to be the ruler. It is better that guidance be singular than divided. . . .
The wife though seeming to be the loser in that she was charged to obey,
is actually the gainer, because the principal duty, love, is charged upon
the husband. "But what," one may say, "if a wife does not obey?" Never
mind, you are to continue to love, and fulfill your part of the agreement. . . . And even when the wife is not loved, she does well to
continue to respect her husband. And even when the husband is not
respected, he does well to continue to love nevertheless. . . . This then
is marriage when it takes place according to Christ. It is a marriage of
spirit, that elicits birth of spirit. (Chrysostom, *Homilies on Ephesians,*
Hom. XX, NPNF 1, XIII, pp. 146-147; cf. BPEC IV, pp. 308-309)*

While these arguments will hardly satisfy the modern hunger for equality,
the reasoning behind these arguments has often been misunderstood by
modernity. Marriage is a covenant bond that affirms its intention to remain
faithful for life. Although this bond may be broken in divorce, it nonetheless
remains the essence of marital covenant to state its *intent of irrevocability*. This
was clearly set forth in pre-Nicene church canons:

"The Lord was witness to the covenant between you and the wife of
your youth, ... So take heed to yourselves, and let none be faithless
to the wife of his youth. 'For I hate divorce, says the Lord the God of
Israel'" (Mal. 2:14-16). For the Lord says: "What therefore God has
joined together, let no man put asunder." (Matt. 19:6). For the wife is
the partner of life, united by God into one body from two. But one who
divides again into two that which God has made one goes against the
way God has ordered creation, and fights providence. (*Constitutions of the
Holy Apostles,* Bk. VI, Sec. III, ch. xiv, ANF VII, p. 456, RSV)*

Alan of Lille set forth six reasons for the unique dignity of marriage, understood in the broadest possible historical context—salvation history:

How great is the dignity of marriage, which had its beginning in paradise, which takes away the sinfulness from incontinence, which embraces within itself a heavenly sacrament which keeps men faithful to the marriage-bed; which provides between spouses a companionship for life; which redeems the children from the reproach (of illegitimacy); which exculpates carnal intercourse. In this state were the Patriarchs saved, and in this condition were certain of the Apostles chosen. (Alan of Lille, *The Art of Preaching,* ch. xlv, CSS 23, p. 163)

In a cultural context in which marriage itself was under fire by some Christians, Clement of Alexandria argued that the Old and New Testaments do not differ fundamentally in their strong affirmation of the blessing of marriage:

It is not frequent intercourse of the parents which produces birth, but the reception of the seed in the womb. In the workshop of nature the seed is transformed into an embryo. How then can marriage be a state only intended for ancient times and an invention of the law, and marriage on Christian principles of a different nature, if we hold that the Old and the New Testaments proclaim the same God? "For what God has joined together no man may ever put asunder" (Matt. 19:6) for any good reason; if the Father commanded this, so much the more also will the Son keep it. If the author of the law and the gospel is the same, he never contradicts himself. . . . But if marriage according to the law is sin, I do not know how anyone can say he knows God when he asserts that the command of God is sin. If the law is holy, marriage is holy. . . . Thus "the children also are holy," (I Cor. 7:14) they are well-pleasing to God, in that the Lord's words bring the soul as a bride to God. Fornication and marriage are therefore different things, as far apart as God is from the devil. . . . In general all the epistles of the apostle teach self-control and continence and contain numerous instructions about marriage, begetting children, and domestic life. But they nowhere rule out self-controlled marriage. (Clement of Alexandria, *On Marriage,* secs. 83-86, LCC II, pp. 79-81)

Is marriage a permanent and enduring human institution? Could it at some point be phased out by changes in human morality? These questions appear to be modern, but they were also faced by Luther, who argued that the fact that women and men were created so unlike stands as evidence that God has a divine purpose in sexuality that is not likely to be set aside.

[God] wants it honored, maintained, and conducted by us, too, as a divine, blessed estate, because He instituted it first, before all others; and with it in view, He did not create man and woman alike, as is evident, not for lewdness, but that they should live together, be fruitful, beget children, and nourish and rear them to the glory of God. Therefore God has also most richly blessed this estate above all others and, in addition, has made everything in the world serve it and depend on it that this estate might without fail be well and amply provided for. Hence married life is not a jest or an object for inordinate curiosity but a splendid institution and a matter of divine seriousness. (Luther, *Large Catechism,* 1529, Sixth Commandment, WA 30 I, p. 161; in WLS 2, p. 886)

God is serious about marriage, otherwise so much in creation, providence, history and human happiness would not have been made dependent upon it. This is why the pastor as representative of the whole church is called upon to bless marriage, and to pray for grace for married partners:

O Lord God, you have created man and woman, and ordained them for the marriage bond, making them fruitful by your blessing, and have typified therein the sacramental union of Thy dear Son, the Lord Jesus Christ, and the church, His bride: We beseech your infinite goodness and mercy that you will not permit this, your very creation, ordinance, and blessing, to be disturbed or destroyed. Graciously preserve this marriage, we pray, through Jesus Christ, our Lord. Amen (Luther, "The Order of Marriage for Common Pastors, 1529," WA 30 III, p. 80; in WLS 3, p. 1106; cf. LW 53, p. 115)*

III ✠ QUESTIONS CONCERNING MARRIAGE

Good judgment is required of the pastor in offering wise situational counsel on the marriage covenant, its beginning and continuation, its possibilities and limitations, its hopes and realities. It is a pastoral teaching responsibility to instruct parishioners on the Christian doctrine of marriage so as to encourage fidelity in love.

Essential elements of the definition of marriage are consent, public avowal, and consummation. Bonaventure concisely defined its three key elements, its three major benefits, and major impediments to its full functioning:

This union is created through the free consent of each person outwardly expressed in some sensible sign, but it has to be consummated through carnal union. Matrimony is begun by words of promise, ratified by present words, but consummated in carnal union. This sacrament has three benefits, namely, "faith, offspring, and a sacrament," and it has twelve impediments which hamper those uniting and separate those already united as is shown in these verses: Error, disparity in circumstance, vow, blood relationship, crime, disparity in religion, force, orders, existing marital ties, spiritual affinity, if you are affianced, if perchance you shall not be able to be together; these things prevent marriage from being entered into and break up unions already entered into. (Bonaventure, *Breviloquium,* pp. 210-211)

Consent is an element of marriage. Marriage without the untrammeled mutual consent of partners is lacking in one of its essential elements. Parental consent is also ordinarily regarded as highly desirable in marriage. With characteristic vivacity, Luther commented on how he would feel if his own daughter might marry without his consent:

For although a thousand witnesses were present at a secret engagement, entered into without the knowledge and will of the parents, the thousand are to be considered as only one witness, since they have helped to get this matter under way with treachery, under cover, and not out in the open, without consulting the regular and public power of the parents. . . . I have brought up a daughter with great expense and effort, care and peril, diligence and labor, and for many years I have ventured my entire life, my person and possessions, in the undertaking. . . . And now she is not to be better protected for me than my cow, lost in the woods, which any wolf may devour? Who would approve of this? Likewise, is my child to stand there free for all, so that any knave, unknown to me, or perhaps even a former enemy of mine, has the power and the unlimited opportunity secretly to steal her from me and take her away without my knowledge and will? There certainly is no one who would want to let his money and goods stand open to the public in this way, so that they may be taken by the first comer. (Luther, WA 30 III, p. 207; in WLS 2, p. 894)

Are homosexual or bigamist agreements properly to be called marriage?

Marriage is to be between one man and one woman: neither is it lawful for any man to have more than one wife, nor for any woman to have more than one husband at the same time. (Westminister Confession, Ch. XXIV, sec. i, *CC,* p. 221)

John Chrysostom urged special, thoughtful, self-giving efforts to sustain second marriages:

What will be said of those who are knit together in second marriages? I speak not at all in condemnation of them, God forbid; for the Apostle himself permits them, though indeed by way of condescension. Supply her with everything. Do everything and endure difficulties for her sake. (Chrysostom, *Homilies on Ephesians,* Hom. XX, NPNF 1, XIII, p. 148)*

Consanguinity—the degree of closeness of blood relationship—has been an important consideration in canon law concerning the propriety of marriage covenants. Protestant as well as Catholic and Orthodox traditions have sought to define the range of this propriety, as in the following Protestant definition. Luther made it clear, however, that marriage itself was far greater than the laws that seek to guarantee its continuance:

As it is written in Leviticus 18, there are twelve persons a man is prohibited from marrying: his mother, his mother-in-law, his full sister, his half-sister by either parent, his granddaughter, his father's and mother's sister, his daughter-in-law, his brother's wife, his wife's sister, his stepdaughter, and his uncle's wife. Here only the first degree of affinity and the second degree of consanguinity are forbidden; yet not without exception, as will appear on closer examination, for the brother's or sister's daughter, or the niece, is not included in the prohibition, although she is in the second degree. Therefore, if a marriage has been contracted outside of these degrees, it should by no means be annulled on account of the laws of men, since it is nowhere written in the Bible that any other degrees were prohibited by God. Marriage itself, as of divine institution, is incomparably superior to any laws. (Luther, *The Babylonian Captivity*, WML II, pp. 264-265)*

IV ❊ Sex and Marriage

Modern readers may imagine that until recently pastors never dared to provide sex and marriage counseling. Not so. These selections from the earliest period of the Christian pastoral tradition (pre-Nicene, before 325 A.D.), will provide glimpses of the sort of counsel Christian pastors have been giving from the very outset of the tradition. It should be kept in mind that much of the writing of this period was done under hazardous conditions of persecution and social stress, when the Christian community was a tiny minority in a hostile political environment. Our purpose for including these selections is not to imply that a completely adequate view of sexuality was worked out by these earliest pastoral writers, or one that could be adequate for all other historical situations. At least they demonstrate that the need to provide guidance and understanding of sexuality has been perceived from the beginning of Christian pastoral activity.

Clement of Alexandria developed some preliminary theories on the psychology of sexuality. He suggested, for example, that the delay of intercourse tended to make it more desirable:

In the evening, after dinner, it is proper to retire after giving thanks for the good things that have been received. Sometimes, nature denies them the opportunity to accomplish the marriage act so that it may be all the more desirable because it is delayed. (Clement of Alexandria, *Christ the Educator*, Bk. II, Ch. 10.97, FC 23, p. 174)

the intrusion of scholastic ecclesiastical legalism into the privacy of marriage:

Among endless other monstrosities which are supposed to instruct the confessors while they most mischievously confuse them, there are enumerated in this book eighteen hindrances to marriage. If you will examine these with the just and unprejudiced eye of faith, you will see that they belong to those things which the Apostle foretold: "There shall be those that give heed to spirits of devils, speaking lies in hypocrisy, forbidding to marry" (1 Tim. 4:1ff). What is forbidding to marry if it is not this—to invent all those hindrances and set those snares, in order to prevent men from marrying or, if they be married, to annul their marriage? Who gave this power to men? Granted that they were holy men and impelled by godly zeal, why should another's holiness disturb my liberty? Why should another's zeal take me captive? . . .

But what shall I say or do? If I enter into details, the treatise will grow to inordinate length, for everything is in such dire confusion one does not know where to begin, whither to go on, or where to leave off. I know that no state is well governed by means of laws. If the magistrate be wise, he will rule more prosperously by natural bent than by laws. If he be not wise, he will further the evil by means of laws. For he will not know what use to make of the laws nor how to adapt them to the individual case. More stress ought, therefore, to be laid, in civil affairs, on putting good and wise men in office than on making laws; for such men will themselves be the very best laws, and will judge every variety of case with lively justice. And if there be knowledge of the divine law combined with natural wisdom, then written laws will be entirely superfluous and harmful. Above all, love needs no laws whatever. . . . But let them arm themselves with the divine law which says, "What God hath joined together, let no man put asunder" (Matt. 19:6). For the joining together of a man and a woman is of divine law and is binding, however it may conflict with the laws of men; the laws of men must give way before it without hesitation. For if a man leaves father and mother and cleaves to his wife, how much more will he tread underfoot the silly and wicked laws of men, in order to cleave to his wife. (Luther, *The Babylonian Captivity*, WML II, pp. 262-264)

God permits and commends the freedom to marry. This permission stands above any web of legalistic rulings that civil or ecclesiastical judicatories may make to impede the fulfillment of the divine permission.

There is in Tertullian's writings a moving letter to his wife on the beauty of Christian marriage. In it he describes the profound unity of souls that occurs in marriages infused with Christ's spirit. In part, it says:

How beautiful, then, the marriage of two Christians, two who are one in hope, one in desire, one in the way of life they follow, one in the religion they practice. . . . Nothing divides them, either in flesh or in spirit. They are, in very truth, two in one flesh; and where there is but one flesh there is also but one spirit. They pray together, they worship together, they fast together; instructing one another, encouraging one another, strengthening one another. . . . They have no secrets from one another; they never shun each other's company; they never bring sorrow to each other's hearts. (Tertullian, *To His Wife*, ACW 13, p. 35)

Here one gets a rare, personalized glimpse of early Christian marriage: two persons sharing their lives completely, hiding no secrets, providing mutual encouragement, becoming one flesh.

The awareness that women can bring special wisdom to these unions is in part an achievement of developing Christian consciousness. In a male dominated hellenistic cultural environment in which the high virtue of wisdom was often thought to be found only among men, we find Clement of Alexandria surprisingly speaking of the wisdom of women:

The wise woman, then, will first choose to persuade her husband to be her associate in what is conducive to happiness. And should that be found impracticable, let her by herself earnestly aim at virtue. (Clement of Alexandria, *The Stromata, or Miscellanies*, Bk. IV, Ch. XIX, ANF II, p. 432)

To modern ears it may not sound like any wonderful achievement for women to learn to persuade their husbands to be their partners in seeking what is conducive to happiness, but if this passage is assessed only from modern presuppositions, its importance may be missed. For here Clement was arguing in the third century: (1) that women can be wise; (2) that women have the power significantly to influence their spouses and families toward interpersonal associations that elicit excellent behaviors conducive to greater general happiness; and (3) even if the relation with the spouse fails, then women on their own can do the one thing that really matters—aim toward virtue.

The special limitations and disadvantages that may adhere to the married state were not ignored by the pastoral writers. We are familiar with standard modern complaints about the tendency of marriage to miss its goals. These criticisms were realistically anticipated in good humor by Hugh of St. Victor in early twelfth century Paris:

It cannot be denied that marriage has a number of good points in its favour. But, if we are ready to think the matter out, we shall find the number of trials involved to be even greater. For is there anyone who does not know how rare is that harmony of spirit of which you speak?

Nay rather, once the very association that should engender harmony becomes a bore, how quickly does it provide occasions of enmity! And although they disagree with one another, it is not possible for them to part, so that the couple become only the more unhappy in living together. Daily disputes and quarrels consequently become more frequent. Dreadful beatings are the next stage after unkind words. Neither can escape the other; they are obliged to share one home, one table, and one bed, and—what is worse than anything—they have neither a congenial partner nor a separated enemy. For just as to those whose hearts are united in love it does not matter if they be apart in body, so is the physical association a real torment if the couple cannot agree. (Hugh of St. Victor, *SSW,* p. 166)

VI Keeping Faithful Covenant

The pastoral writers had no illusions about the ease of keeping faithful covenants, particularly in the realm of sexuality. The roving eye, the desire for a variety of partners, the dread of boredom, the inconstancy of passion—all of these were taken for granted as recurrent challenges to covenant faithfulness in marriage. There was no easy attempt by pastoral marriage counselors to gloss over these difficulties, or to make these problems sound simple, or to assume they could always be easily managed:

The devil takes no pleasure in harmony among married people, in seeing them live in peace with each other and bring up their children in the fear of God, in decency and honesty. This is one of the reasons why a successful marriage is a rare thing. . . . St. Augustine also speaks of this and says: The great passion of man for woman and, again, of woman for man is exceedingly inconstant. The woman who has been given to me I do not appreciate, my desire does not go out to her; but the woman God has forbidden me is the one I lust for.—An exceedingly strong disobedience, then, inheres in the flesh. This is why it cannot remain constant. The husband soon tires of his wife and thinks: Ah, if you had that one, you would be satisfied. And if he obtained her, his love and lust would again soon be gone and at an end, and he would look around for another. Just so a wife soon tires of the man God has given her and casts her love upon another. But even if she had him, she would not like him for any length of time; for the natural evil and mischief called satiety (that one soon tires of something and is surfeited with it) does not stay away. I have often observed that two people come together in great passion and love and want to devour each other for love. But before a half year had passed, he was an adulterer and she an adulteress. Besides this, I have known people who have become hostile to each other after they had five or six children and were bound to each other not merely by marriage but also by the fruits of their union. Yet they left each other. Nowadays one has more to do with marriage relations than with all other matters. Because of them we can hardly read, preach, or study. (Luther, "Exposition of Matthew 19:10ff., 1537," WA 47, p. 320; in WLS 2, pp. 899-900)

Luther here treated both women and men as equally prone to sexual boredom and the latent desire to look elsewhere for satisfaction. If we today think that sexual experimentation, serial marriages, and inveterate unfaithfulness are unique to modern culture, we do well to listen to Luther, who saw these same patterns in his culture, and recognized them as perennial temptations.

In order to test out the edges of the doctrine of covenant sexual fidelity to the spouse, Luther deliberately explored the borderline question of the sexual responsibility of the husband of an incapacitated wife:

What about a situation where one's wife is an invalid and has therefore become incapable of fulfilling the conjugal duty? May he not take another wife? By no means. Let him serve the Lord in the person of the invalid and await His good pleasure. (Luther, "The Estate of Marriage," LW 45, p. 35)

Dean Colet had pungent words for persons who had freely elected marriage relationships that subsequently turned out to be less than wonderful. If one has a good spouse, it is easier to be grateful, but, he mused, what if the spouse is not so good?

If you are married and have a good wife, thank the Lord therefore, for she is of his sending. If you have an evil wife, take patience, and thank God, for all is for the best, well taken. In that case you are bound to act and pray for her amendment, lest she go to the devil, from whom she came. (John Colet, *Daily Directions,* OCC III, p. 41)

Does the marriage covenant require or imply that a spouse will rigorously keep physical distance from other spouses?

Have you not read, and do you not know, concerning those elders in the days of Susanna, who, because they were constantly with women, and looking upon the beauty which was another's, fell into the depths of wantonness. . . . Should it not therefore cause us to stand in fear and trembling if these elderly individuals, these judges and elders of the people of God, suddenly fell from their dignity because of a woman? They did not keep in mind what Scripture had said: "Do not let your eye linger on a woman's figure or your thoughts dwell on beauty not yours to possess. Many have been seduced by the beauty of a woman, which kindles passion like fire. Never sit at table with another man's wife or join her in a drinking party, for fear of succumbing to her charms and slipping into fatal disasters" (Ecclus. 9:8,9). . . . Elsewhere it asks whether there is anyone who can "kindle fire in his bosom without burning his clothes?" (Prov. 6:27). And, "If a man walks on hot coals, will his feet not be scorched?" (Prov. 6:28). So whoever goes in to another man's wife is not pure from evil. (Clementina, *Two Epistles Concerning Virginity,* II, Ch. XIII, ANF VIII, p. 64, NEB)*

The assumption is that one may collude with another to bring temptation nearer. The pastoral writers knew how prone sexuality is to self-deception. What else could make us think that we can put a lighted match in our coat and not burn our clothes? It is not surprising that prior to the technology of contraception we would have strong injunctions in the pastoral literature against even getting oneself in the position of being tempted by another spouse so as to potentially wreck not one but two marriages. If the injunction seems exaggerated against even looking at the beauty of others who are not one's own life partner, then modern readers do well to remember that these cultures did not have the technological competencies to stop or curb the consequences of sexual experimentation. "The pill" was not yet even a gleam in a medical research assistant's eye.

VII ❧ Breaking Covenant

The major concerns of pastoral marriage counseling today remain much the same as always: encouraging fidelity in sexual covenant while increasing the love and joy of partners and offspring, and averting the potentially devastating consequences of breaking covenant.

There has been from the beginning in Christian views of sex a realism about the tendency of eroticism to wax and wane. Clement speculated that sexual vitality could itself be diminished by breaches of covenant, and love turn to revulsion:

Love, which tends toward sexual relations by its very nature, is in full bloom only for a time, then grows old with the body; but sometimes, if immoral pleasure mars the chastity of the marriage bed, desire becomes insipid and love ages before the body does. The hearts of lovers have wings; affection can be quenched by a change of heart, and love can turn into hate if there creep in too many grounds for loss of respect. (Clement of Alexandria, *Christ the Educator,* Bk. II, Ch. 10.97, FC 23, pp. 174-175)

Love can age prematurely and grow old even in youth. Though love may have wings, its fall may be hard. Clement's observations could serve as lyrics of a plaintive modern love ballad. These hazards caused Luther to be exceptionally cautious about the prospect of "sowing wild oats":

> Many think they can evade marriage by having their fling [*auss bubenn*] for a time, and then becoming righteous. My dear fellow, if one in a thousand succeeds in this, that would be doing very well. He who intends to lead a chaste life had better begin early, and attain it not with but without fornication, either by the grace of God or through marriage. (Luther, "The Estate of Marriage, 1522," LW 45, p. 44)

John Chrysostom urged patience and tolerance in exploring the dynamics of marital jealousy. Should husband and wife be mutually trusting even when there seems to be some evidence of untrustworthiness?

> If someone slanders a husband to his wife, let the wife not be too ready to believe it. Nor let the husband believe anything at random against the wife. Nor should the wife be constantly inquisitive without reason about his goings out and his comings in. No, nor on any account let the husband ever render himself worthy of any suspicion whatever. Tell me, suppose you devote yourself all day to your friends, and then give the evening to your wife, and still you are not able to make her content, and place her out of reach of suspicion? Though your wife complain, do not be annoyed. Remember that it is her love, not her folly, that is at work. For these are the complaints of fervent attachment, burning affection, and anxiety. Yes, she is afraid lest anyone might have stolen her marriage bed, lest anyone have injured her in that which is the summit of her blessings, lest anyone may have taken away from her him upon whom she most depends, lest anyone have broken through her marriage chamber. (Chrysostom, *Homilies on Ephesians,* Hom. XX, NPNF 1, XIII, p. 149)*

Just as it was considered a mark of orthodox teaching that one remain the "husband of one wife," so was it often thought to be a mark of heterodox views not to take sexual covenant seriously. Heretical teachers were frequently faulted for their habit of leaving their wives, and fanatical women spiritualists for leaving their husbands:

> We declare to you, then, that these first [Montanist] prophetesses, as soon as they were filled with the spirit, left their husbands. (Apollonius, *Concerning Montanism,* A Fragment, Remains of the Second and Third Centuries, A.D. 211, Ch. II, ANF VIII, p. 775)

We find this among the complex and delicate cases involving desertion that were examined by the Quinisext Synod (692 A.D.): Suppose a deserted wife marries another man, and her husband returns?

If the wife of a man who has gone away and does not soon reappear, cohabits with another before she is assured of the death of the first, it must be viewed as adultery. The wives of soldiers who have married husbands who simply do not reappear, and yet there is no evidence of death, are in the same situation. So also are those who on account of the wanderings of their husbands do not wait long for their return. But the circumstance changes greatly if the suspicion of the spouse's death becomes very great. For that would allow remarriage.

Suppose a more complex situation: A woman in ignorance has married a man who at the time was deserted by his wife, and then is dismissed because his first wife returns to him. That again must be viewed as fornication, but it has occurred through ignorance. If so, she need not be prevented from marrying, but it is better if she remain as she is. Suppose a soldier returns after a long time and finds that his wife on account of his long absence has been united to another man. If they so desire, they may be remarried, and pardon may be extended in consideration of their ignorance both to her and to the man who took her home in second marriage. (Synod of Quinisext, A.D. 692, Canon XCIII, The Seven Ecumenical Councils, NPNF 2, XIV, p. 404)*

Although cultural values may have shifted and social constraints about sexuality are hardly the same as in the seventh century, nonetheless ethical questions such as these remain debatable among those considering remarriage, who may come for pastoral counsel.

VIII ❧ ADULTERY

Since faithfulness in covenant commitment has been assumed to be central to the Christian teaching of matrimony, the breaking of that faithfulness has been a perennial concern of pastoral care. Adultery (*moicheia*) is sexual intercourse with someone other than one's own spouse, hence outside of the covenant. A clear conception of adultery is only understandable in the light of a clear conception of marriage:

Let us see what marriage is in the eyes of God and we shall then see what adultery is as well. A marriage is this: when God joins two together in one flesh. Or if one finds them already united, a marriage occurs when the union has been blessed and sealed. Adultery is this: when the two having been—in whatever way—disjoined, so that there is commingling with some other—that is to say, alien—flesh, of which it cannot be said; "This is flesh of my flesh and bone of my bone" (Gen. 2:23). (Tertullian, *Monogamy,* sec. 9, ANF IV, p. 66)*

Consequently, adultery has been distinguished from fornication by the fact that only those who are married can commit adultery. The Apostolic Constitutions, having affirmed that married male/female sexuality is part of the intention of the creator and acceptable to the mind of God, then reject homosexuality, adultery and fornication as unacceptable, but distinguish between them:

But we cannot approve as acceptable to the mind of God that sexual activity that is contrary to nature or immoral, since it stands against God's way. Homosexuality is contrary to nature, as is also having sex with animals. Adultery and fornication are immoral, but immoralities of different types, for the one goes against religion and the other goes against justice. . . . For the practisers of fornication attempt to undermine the order of creation, trying to change the natural course of things into that which is unnatural. The adulterers are immoral in a different way, by corrupting others' marriages, and dividing into two what God has made one, rendering the children suspected and exposing the true spouse to the snares of others. And fornication is the destruction of one's own flesh, not being made use of for the procreation of children, but entirely for the sake of pleasure, which is a mark of incontinency, and not a sign of virtue. All these things are forbidden by the laws; for thus say the oracles: "You shall not lie with a man as with a woman" (Lev. 18:22). (*Constitutions of the Holy Apostles,* Bk. VI, Sec. V, ch. xxviii, ANF VII, pp. 462-463, NEB)*

Adultery was thought to have societal effects far beyond those that directly affect the primary persons involved:

Adultery not only destroys the person himself who sins, but those also who share his family and associate with him. It is like the madness of a dog. It has the nature of communicating its own madness. For the sake of chastity, therefore, let not only the elders, but even all, hasten to accomplish marriage. For the sin of him who commits adultery necessarily impinges upon others. (Clementina, *Homilies,* Hom. III, Ch. LXVIII, ANF VIII, p. 250)*

Augustine inquired, in his dialogue with Evodius, into the reasons why adultery is objectionable:

Give this matter your best consideration and tell me the reason why you know that adultery is evil. Ev.—I know it is evil because I should not wish it to be committed with my own wife. Whoever does to another what he would not have done to himself does evil. Aug.—Suppose someone offered his wife to another, being willing that she should be corrupted by him in return for a similar licence allowed him with the other's wife. Would he have done no evil? Ev.—Far from that. He would have done great evil. Aug.—And yet his sin does not come under your general rule, for he does not do what he would not have done to him. You must find another reason to prove that adultery is evil.

Ev.—I think it evil because I have often seen men condemned on this charge. Aug.—But are not men frequently condemned for righteous deeds? Without going to other books, think of scripture history which excels all other books because it has divine authority. If we decide that condemnation is a certain indication of evil-doing, what an evil opinion we must adopt of the apostles and martyrs, for they were all thought worthy of condemnation for their faith. If whatever is condemned is evil, it was evil in those days to believe in Christ and to confess the Christian faith. But if everything is not evil which is condemned you must find another reason for teaching that adultery is evil. Ev.—I have no reply to make.

Aug.—Possibly the evil thing in adultery is lust. So long as you look for the evil in the outward act you discover difficulties. But when you understand that the evil lies in lust it becomes clear that even if a man finds no opportunity to lie with the wife of another but shows that he desires to do so and would do it if he got the chance, he is no less guilty than if he were caught in the act. (Augustine, *On Free Will*, Bk. I, ch. iii.6-8, LCC VI, p. 116)

IX ✠ AFFIRMING THE SINGLE LIFE

There is renewed awareness in our time of the special dignity and value of the single life. That marriage is presumptively normative for human existence, or an absolute precondition of happiness, either for women or men, has been questioned and rejected. These modern views were anticipated by influential voices in the pastoral tradition. For even where marriage was most strongly commended, it was seldom made an absolute domestic value, as if there could be no wisdom or joy without it. This was often joined with a strong affirmation of the single life as an esteemed way of high accountability to God characterized by exceptional joy and freedom.

Tertullian thought it ill-advised to frame human sexual alternatives exclusively as "whether to marry or to burn" with desire:

Scripture says that it is better to marry than to burn (1 Cor. 7:9); but what sort of good, I ask you, can that be which is such only when it is compared to what is bad? Marriage, forsooth, is better because burning is worse! How much better it is neither to marry nor to burn! (Tertullian, *To His Wife*, ACW 13, p. 13)

Singleness is warmly commended, yet without denying the validity of marriage:

"Thus, he who marries his partner does well, and he who does not will do better" (1 Cor. 7:38). Surely Paul's declaration, in which he proposed the special beauty and happiness of celibacy, was not intended to forbid or to take away from marriage. It merely arranges an order, assigning to each condition its peculiar property and advantage. To some the gift has never been given to attain virginity. For others it is God's wish that they no longer preoccupy themselves with the lusts of the flesh, but that henceforth they strive to center their minds upon the spiritual transformation of the body. (Methodius, *The Symposium,* ACW 27, p. 57)*

Methodius, writing at the end of the second century, was one of many during the Diocletian persecution who extolled the excellence of virginity. Tertullian stated dialectically the balance between the competing values of marriage and celibacy in this way:

Are you covenanted with a wife? Do not seek to be free, lest you give adultery an opportunity. Are you freed from marital burdens? Do not seek them, in order that you do not lose the opportunity given by your freedom. (Tertullian, *On Purity,* sec. 16, FC 28, p. 101)*

It should not be assumed that celibacy was valued only by patristic and medieval writers, and not also by Protestants. The value of the single life is clearly affirmed in the moderate Reformed creed, the Second Helvetic Confession of 1566. The Reformers viewed celibacy as a highly valued *charisma* that allows forms of commitment not possible with family responsibilities:

Such as have the gift of chastity given unto them from above, so that they can with the heart or whole mind be pure and continent, and not be grievously burned with lust, let them serve the Lord in that calling, as long as they shall feel themselves endued with that heavenly gift; and let them not lift up themselves above others, but let them serve the Lord daily in simplicity and humility. For such are more apt for attending to heavenly things than they who are distracted with the private affairs of a family. (Second Helvetic Confession, 1566, ch. xxiv, *CC,* p. 188)

X ❧ Pastoral Care of Parents

Pastors historically have been active supporters not only of marital fidelity, but also of parental fidelity to children, of building carefully the fabric of the family, and of providing children with a solid foundation. Pastors are called upon to respond to a wide variety of questions concerning the challenges and tasks of parenting, and the importance of caring well for children.

Ambrose encouraged parents to treat children equally in love, while seeing each one uniquely in relation to his or her own needs. He rejected the concept of a "favorite child." Ambrose did not fail to see realistically that each child is different, and therefore that each child's uniqueness will be loved by the good parent in a different way. But supportive of this affirmation of uniqueness is the moral requirement to be fair, holding each of one's children in equal regard, and to treat all equitably so as not to make one spoiled and the other jealous.

Let children be nurtured with a like measure of devotion. Granted that one's love may fasten more upon some trait in a child who is more agreeable or similar to oneself, the exercise of justice ought to be the same in regard to all. The more that is given to the child that is loved and who seeks his brother's love, the more is taken away from the one who is burdened with jealousy at the unfair preferment. (Ambrose, *Exegetical Works,* Jacob and the Happy Life, Ch. 2, sec. 5, FC 65, p. 149)

To spoil a child is the opposite of loving the child, in Luther's view. Parents can destroy a child's capacity for resilience by spoiling him:

There is another dishonoring of parents, much more dangerous and subtle than this first, which adorns itself and passes for a real honor; that is, when a child has its own way, and the parents through natural love allow it. . . . Thus God's Commandment secretly comes to naught while all seems good, and that is fulfilled which is written in the Prophets Isaiah and Jeremiah, that the children are destroyed by their own parents . . . . O how perilous it is to be a father or a mother! (Luther, *Treatise on Good Works,* WML I, pp. 252-253)

Luther treated this under the rubric of the commandment to honor one's father and mother. There are many ways to dishonor one's parents. In many cases parents collude in the process by which children lose respect and honor for their parents. Giving children what they want is the surest road to the breaking of this commandment, in Luther's view. He argued that parenting is a responsibility of the highest order. For there we meet the needy neighbor and therefore Christ in the most concrete form. This is why the home is so much like the community of faith, in a deep and inconspicuous sense:

Thus it is true, as is often said, that parents, although they had nothing else to do, could be saved by attending well to their own children if they rightly train them to God's service. They will indeed have both hands full of good works to do. For what else are they than the hungry, thirsty, naked, imprisoned, sick, strangers? These are the souls of your own children. With them God makes of your house a hospital, and appoints you as chief nurse, to wait on them, to give them good words and works as meat and drink, that they may learn to trust, believe and have reverence for God. . . . See, what great lessons are these, how many good works you have before you right there in your home, with your child, who needs all these things like a hungry, thirsty, naked, poor, imprisoned, sick soul. That marriage and home are truly blessed where the parents are caring in this way. Truly it would be like a real Church, a chosen cloister, a paradise. (Luther, *Treatise on Good Works*, WML I, p. 255)*

Psychoanalysis seeks to disclose the complex layers of parental influence in neurotic distortions. In the pastoral tradition this sort of analysis was projected upon biblical typologies, as in this case of a pseudonymous pre-Nicene writer who was commenting imaginatively upon the relation of Eve and Cain, in order to show that a parent's egocentricity and possessiveness may increase a child's tendency to deceit and violence:

Note the ambiguous name that Eve gave to her first-born son: Cain, a name that can mean either something possessed or something envied. . . . One might say metaphorically that Eve, being overly possessive toward Cain, brought him certain advantages at first, yet later these led to his becoming a murderer and liar, unwilling to rest at peace with the governance given him by God. As an awesome consequence, those who came after him by his generation also tended to become adulterers . . . and forgers of instruments of war. (Clementina, *Homilies*, Hom. III, Ch. XXV, ANF VIII, p. 243)*

Overly permissive parents are held responsible for their children's misdeeds:

Do not hesitate to counsel those in your charge. Teach them wisdom with toughness. For your corrections will not undermine them, but rather preserve them. As Solomon says somewhere in the book of Wisdom: "Correct your son, and he will be a comfort to you and bring you delights of every kind" (Prov. 29:17). "Chastise your son while there is hope for him" (Prov. 19:18). And again Solomon wrote: "A father who spares the rod hates his son, but one who loves him keeps him in order" (Prov. 13:24). . . . Teach them from their infancy the truth of Christian scriptures which are from God. Deliver to them all the sacred writing. Do not confusingly give them a free reign to question everything arbitrarily out of ignorance. Do not permit them to defy your opinion, or to club together so that they only learn from their peers. If so they will be turned to disorderly courses, and will fall into fornication. If this happens by the carelessness of parents, those that parented them will be responsible for their souls. If the offending children fall into the company of corrupting persons by the negligence of those who parented them, they will not be held reponsible alone. (*Constitutions of the Holy Apostles*, Bk. IV, Sec. II, ch. xi, ANF VII, p. 436, NEB)*

Early Christians were much concerned that their children not be inordinately exposed to bad examples and demoralizing permissiveness:

Childhood is an age of particular vulnerability. To the natural folly of the child is added the bad examples derived from heathen mythology that introduces them to supposed heros, admired by so many, who are slaves to their passions and cowardly in the face of death. Achilles, for example, dies for his concubine, others get drunk, others do worse. Family education should provide some remedy for these distorted values. Isn't it absurd to send young people out into the world of trade and to school and not ever give them a chance to hear of discipline and admonition in the Lord? We ultimately have to reap the harvest of all this neglect, after we have allowed our children to be isolent, profligate, disobedient and vulgar. Don't do this. Listen to the Apostle: "You fathers, again, must not goad your children to resentment, but give them the instruction, and the correction, which belong to a Christian upbringing" (Eph. 6:4). (Chrysostom, *Homilies on Ephesians,* Hom. XXIV, NPNF 1, XIII, p. 154, NEB)*

If children are dependent upon parental wisdom for their guidance, even with respect to their ultimate destiny, then parents cannot justly default on this crucial role:

In fact, all children depend for their birth and during the whole time of their infancy up to the age of reason on the decisions made by others, and the guidance given them must come exclusively from others. Thus it follows that infants share the lot of those persons whose right or wrong dispositions decide their condition. Some of them happen to have the faith through the profession of faith of other people. Others disbelieve through the neglect of others. (Prosper of Aquitaine, *The Call of All Nations,* Bk. II, Ch. 23, ACW 14, p. 131)*

XI ❧ SHEPHERDING OF FAMILIES

Not parents alone, or children alone, but whole families, viewed systemically, are recipients of pastoral care. Richard Baxter outlined an elaborate rationale and practical procedure in terms of which pastors might understand and organize their ministry to families:

We must have a special eye upon families, to see that they are well ordered, and the duties of each relation performed. The life of religion, and the welfare and glory of both the Church and the State, depend much on family government and duty. If we suffer the neglect of this, we shall undo all. . . . I beseech you, therefore, if you desire the reformation and welfare of your people, do all you can to promote family religion. To this end, let me entreat you to attend to the following things: (1) Get information how each family is ordered, that you may know how to proceed in your endeavours for their further good. (2) Go occasionally among them, when they are likely to be most at leisure, and ask the master of the family whether he prays with them, and reads the Scripture, or what he doth? Labour to convince such as neglect this, of their sin; and if you have opportunity, pray with them before you go, and give them an example of what you would have them do. . . . If you find any, through ignorance and want of practice, unable to pray, persuade them to study their own wants, and to get their hearts affected with them, and, in the meanwhile advise them to use a form of prayer, rather than not pray at all. . . . See that in every family there are some useful moving books, besides the Bible. If they have none, persuade them to buy some: if they be not able to buy them, give them some if you can. If you are not able yourself, get some gentlemen, or other rich persons, that are ready to good works, to do it. And engage them to read them at night, when they have leisure, and especially on the Lord's day. . . . Neglect not, I beseech you, this important part of your work. (Baxter, *RP,* pp. 100-102)

Origen, in his debate with Celsus, was quick to point out that children cannot be counseled or treated as if they were already adults. As God has condescended to address humanity in the flesh, so must parents condescend to communicate with children on their own level of understanding:

Celsus, not understanding that the language of Scripture regarding God is adapted to an anthropopathic point of view, ridicules those passages which speak of words of anger addressed to the ungodly, and of threatenings directed against sinners. We have to say that, as we ourselves, when talking with very young children, do not aim at exerting our own power of eloquence, but, adapting ourselves to the weakness of our charge, both say and do those things which may appear to us useful for the correction and improvement of the children as children, so the word of God appears to have dealt with history, making the capacity of the hearers, and the benefit which they were to receive, the standard of the appropriateness of its announcements. (Origen, *Against Celsus,* Bk. IV, Ch. LXXI, ANF IV, p. 529)

Luther placed special importance upon the command to honor parents. Among the commands of the decalogue that teach us "how we are to exercise ourselves in good works toward others," it ranked as the first. It is not unhealthy that children have a certain respect, and honor (*kabed*), even reverence (*yare,* fear), for parents. He explains:

The first work is that we honor our own father and mother. And this honor consists not only in respectful demeanor, but in this: that we obey them, look up to, esteem and heed their words and example, accept what they say, keep silent and endure their treatment of us, so long as it is not contrary to the first three Commandments; in addition, when they need it, that we provide them with food, clothing and shelter. For not for nothing has He said: "Thou shalt honor them"; He does not say: "Thou shalt love them," although this also must be done. But honor is higher than mere love and includes a certain fear, which unites with love, and causes a man to fear offending them more than he fears the punishment. Just as there is fear in the honor we pay a sanctuary, and yet we do not flee from it as from a punishment, but draw near to it all the more. Such a fear mingled with love is the true honor; the other fear without any love is that which we have toward things which we despise or flee from, as we fear the hangman or punishment. There is no honor in that, for it is a fear without all love, nay, fear that has with it hatred and enmity. Of this we have a proverb of St. Jerome: What we fear, that we also hate. With such a fear God does not wish to be feared or honored, nor to have us honor our parents; but with the first, which is mingled with love and confidence. (Luther, *Treatise on Good Works,* WML I, p. 251)

Later Freud would hinge an entire therapeutic procedure upon gaining freedom from this anxiety that one has in the presence of once-powerful parental figures upon whom one's fundamental existence has depended. Yet Luther, more perceptively than Freud, distinguished loveless fear of parents from that appropriate sense of proportional awe mixed with love, which the Bible defines as "honoring thy father and thy mother."

Is it possible that sibling rivalries may, if well-guided, become a means of personal growth and improvement? Ambrose used Jacob and Esau as a biblical type of rivalry that required much parental love and patience:

Hereupon there arose enmity, and Esau threatened that after the death of their father he would kill his brother. But if needs be, let us learn from Rebecca how to make provision that enmity may not provoke wrath and wrath rush headlong into fratricide. Let Rebecca come—that is, let us put on patience, the good guardian of blamelessness—and let her persuade us to give place to the wrath. Let us withdraw somewhat further, until the wrath is softened by time and we are taken by surprise at having forgotten the wrong done us. Therefore patience is not much afraid of exile but readily enters upon it, not so much to avoid the danger to salvation as to escape giving incitement to wrongdoing. The loving mother, too, endures the absence of her dearly beloved son and purposes to give more to the one whom she has harmed, while still consulting the interests of both, to render the one safe against fratricide and the other blameless of crime. (Ambrose, *Exegetical Works,* Jacob and the Happy Life, Ch. 4, sec. 14, FC 65, pp. 154-155)

Luther did not hesitate to poke fun at the excessive religiosity of parents. He was aware that a high intensity in religious commitment could actually harm children. He appealed to parents to put the tasks of child-rearing in their proper proportionality:

Here this husband runs to St. James, that wife vows a pilgrimage to Our Lady; no one vows that he will properly govern and teach himself and his child to the honor of God; he leaves behind those whom God has commanded him to keep in body and soul, and would serve God in some other place, which has not been commanded him. Such perversity no bishop forbids, no preacher corrects; nay, for covetousness' sake they confirm it and daily only invent more pilgrimages, elevations of saints, indulgence-fairs. God have pity on such blindness. . . . Of what help is it, that they kill themselves with fasting, praying, making pilgrimages, and do all manner of good works? God will, after all, not ask them about these things at their death and in the day of judgment, but will require of them the children whom He entrusted to them. This is shown by that word of Christ, Luke 23:28, "Ye daughters of Jerusalem, weep not for me, but for yourselves and for your children." (Luther, *Treatise on Good Works,* WML I, pp. 256-257)

The pastoral care of families in the Protestant tradition owes much to the work of Richard Baxter, who developed a specific practice of conjoint family counsel, accompanied by individual counsel:

When your people come to you, one family or more, begin with a brief preface, to mollify their minds and to take off all offence, unwillingness, or discouragement, and to prepare them for receiving your instructions. . . . The Lord knows how short a time you and I may be together; and therefore it concerns us to do what we can for our own and your salvation before we leave you, or you leave the world. All other business in the world is but as toys and dreams in comparison of this. . . . When you have spoken thus to them all, take them one by one, and deal with them as far as you can in private out of the hearing of the rest; for some cannot speak freely before others. . . . I find by experience, people will better take plain close dealing about their sin, and misery, and duty, when you have them alone, than they will before others; and, if you have not an opportunity to set home the truth, and to deal freely with their consciences, you will frustrate all. If, therefore, you have a convenient place, let the rest stay in one room, while you confer with each person by himself in another room . . . . (Baxter, *RP*, pp. 238-240)

XII ❧ RESPONSIBLE PARENTING

If parenting has this high order of importance, then it is proper for the soul guide to give considerable attention to its specific problems. It was often noted by pastoral writers that parenting and pastoring are similar. Most of the qualities that we have already described as being intrinsic to good counseling or effective therapeutic relationships apply also to the parental nurture of children.

Should one care more for one's own children than other children? Thomas Aquinas thought it right and fitting that parents pay more attention to and love more deeply those with whom they are connected by family and kinship ties. Although this may seem self-evident, it is a question that has emerged frequently in the Christian tradition, which has so emphasized universal love for all humanity. If so, then what reasons may we give for loving our own children more than other children? Here are Thomas' reasons:

We ought out of charity to love those who are more closely united to us more, both because our love for them is more intense, and because there are more reasons for loving them. . . . Friendship among blood relations is based upon their connection by natural origin, the friendship of fellow-citizens on their civic fellowship, and the friendship of those who are fighting side by side on the comradeship of battle. Wherefore in matters pertaining to nature we should love our kindred most, in matters concerning relations between citizens, we should prefer our fellow-citizens, and on the battlefield our fellow-soldiers. . . . If however we compare union with union it is evident that the union arising from natural origin is prior to, and more stable than all others, because it is something affecting the very substance, whereas other unions supervene and may cease altogether. Therefore the friendship of kindred is more stable, while other friendships may be stronger in respect of that which is proper to each of them. (Thomas Aquinas, *Summa Theologica*, Part II-II, Q. 26, Art. 8, Vol. II, pp. 1300-1301)

Although there are many different levels of the intensity of various affections, the intensity of natural love for our own flesh and blood and the permanence of the union between children and parents are key reasons why children are of a different order of loving than friendships, however important friendships may be. For one may change friends, but one cannot biologically negate being a parent to a particular child.

It may surprise modern sensibilities to hear Luther say that not sex but having children really is the most pleasant aspect of marriage:

You will find many to whom a large number of children is unwelcome, as though marriage had been instituted only for bestial pleasures and not also for the very valuable work by which we serve God and men when we train and educate the children whom God had given us. They do not appreciate the most pleasant feature of marriage. For what exceeds the love of children? (Luther, "Lecture on Psalm 128," WA 40 III, p. 297; in WLS 2, p. 906)

It is not unusual to find the pastoral tradition contemplating ecstatically the female body, not out of sexual interests, but because it is so remarkably adapted to parental nurture, far more so than the male, in Luther's view:

To me it is often a source of great pleasure and wonderment to see that the entire female body was created for the purpose of nurturing children. How prettily even little girls carry babies on their bosom! As for the mothers themselves, how deftly they move whenever the whimpering baby either has to be quieted or is to be placed into its cradle! Get a man to do the same things, and you will say that a camel is dancing, so clumsily will he do the simplest tasks around the baby! I say nothing about the other duties which mothers alone can perform. (Luther, "Lectures on Genesis, Chapters 1 to 5, 1535-36," LW 1, p. 202)

Modern individuals may find such sex role stereotyping unfair or offensive, but it is in its cultural context an act of praise of God by a male truly awed by what women could do that men could not. In a similar vein, Luther was quite worried about the trend he saw developing in his time, which saw women tending increasingly to detest child-bearing and child-rearing:

The Jews highly esteemed children. Our women almost detest them. The reason: one does not want the burden of bearing and educating children: women only want leisure. In the comedies we see that the Greeks also loved a progeny. Among the Jews it was a shame not to have children. (Luther, *Table Talk,* WA-T, #5458; in WLS 1, p. 137)

Many pastoral writers have drawn the analogy between the home and the church, and between domestic and ecclesiastical administration. Over a millennium before Luther, John Chrysostom had said:

If we then regulate our own houses, we shall be also fit for the management of the Church. For indeed a house is a little Church. (Chrysostom, *Homilies on Ephesians,* Hom. XX, NPNF 1, XIII, p. 148).

Parents are directly responsible for the spiritual care of their children.

Menno Simons viewed parental counsel as linked closely with pastoral counsel. Most importantly, parental soul care includes corrective love:

All Christian parents should be as sharp, pungent salt, a shining light, and an unblamable, faithful teacher, each in his own home. The high priest Eli was held responsible because he had not reproved his children enough.

If I see my neighbor's ox or ass go astray, I must bring him back to the owner or keep him safe, as Moses teaches. If now it becomes me thus to do with another man's brute beast, how much more should I be concerned for the souls of my children who are so readily misled, and wander so easily from the right way by their willful flesh in which no good dwells. . . . Moses taught Israel saying, "These commandments which I give you this day are to be kept in your heart; you shall repeat them to your sons and speak of them indoors and out of doors, when you lie down and when you rise. Bind them as a sign on the head and wear them as a phylactery on the forehead; write them on the doorposts of your houses and on your gates. The Lord your God will bring you into the land which he so swore to your forefathers Abraham, Isaac, and Jacob that he would give you" (Deut. 6:6ff). . . . Behold, worthy reader, thus the literal Israel was obliged to teach the children from youth and to acquaint them with all the blessings and miracles of the Lord which had happened to them and their fathers, so that they might fear, love, and serve the Lord all their days, and so receive the blessings, and escape the curse, which was contained in the Law.

In like manner we must also do, if we rightly confess Christ, believe His Word, and with our children desire to obtain the worthy and pleasant land. . . . Therefore, all who fear the Lord, love your children with divine love; seek their salvation with all your hearts even as Abraham, Tobit, and the Maccabean mother did. If they transgress, reprove them sharply. If they err, exhort them paternally. If they are childish, bear them patiently. If they are of teachable age, instruct them in a Christian fashion. Dedicate them to the Lord from youth; watch over their souls as long as they are under your care, lest you lose also your own salvation on their account. (Menno Simons, *True Christian Faith, CWMS,* pp. 387-390, NEB)*

In an essay of 1557 on "The Nurture of Children," an early Protestant statement of parental soul care, Menno developed this theme further:

Let us be mindful and solicitous of our own children, and let us display unto them a still greater degree of spiritual love than with others; for they are by nature born of us, of our flesh and blood, and are so solemnly committed to our special care by God. Therefore be sure that you instruct them from their youth in the way of the Lord, that they fear and love God, walk in all decency and discipline, are well-mannered, quiet, obedient to their father and mother, reverent where that is proper, after their speech honest, not loud, not stubborn, nor self-willed: for such is not becoming to children of saints. . . . For if we do not keep a strict watch over our own children, but let them follow their evil and corrupt nature; if we do not correct and chastise them according to the Word of the Lord, then we may verily lay our hands upon our mouths and keep still. For why should we teach those not of our household, seeing we do not take care of our own family in the love and fear of God? Paul says, If any provide not for his own, and specially for those of his own house, he has denied the faith, and is worse than an infidel (1 Tim. 5:8).

Dearly beloved brethren and sisters in Christ Jesus, take heed that you do not spoil your children through natural love, that you do not offend, do not rear them in wickedness, lest in the day of judgment their soul be required at your hands, and it happened unto you, on account of your children, as it did unto Eli, the high priest, who was punished by the hand of the Almighty, on account of his sons. (Menno Simons, The Nurture of Children, c. 1557, *CWMS,* p. 950)

Parents are enjoined to love no creaturely being more than their children. The parent-child relationship is best understood by analogy to the divine-human parental relationship:

Not only do we say that children should be loved, but they should be loved in the first place and above all other things; nothing must be preferred to them in any way except God alone. For this is to love in a special manner, to place Him before our children whom it is not proper to place after them in any way. Why do we say children should be loved and in what manner? In what other manner than that ordained by God Himself? For there is no better love of children than that taught by Him who gave us our children. Neither can offspring be better loved than if they are loved in Him by whom they were given. (Salvian, *The Four Books of Timothy to the Church,* Bk. 1, sec. 4, FC 3, pp. 274-275)

XIII ❧ STRICTNESS AND LENIENCY IN PARENTAL CARE

The pastoral care of families has sought to avoid both legalism and license in guiding children and youth toward responsible actions. Legalism fails by not being flexible enough to respond to the contingencies of living experience.

License fails by not gaining and securing moral strength amid those contingencies. There is a continuing debate in the pastoral tradition as to how parental care can be firm without becoming excessively rigid.

The child that is permissively treated is done great harm, even if one intends to do good:

The first destroyers of their own children are those who neglect them and knowingly permit them to grow up without the training and admonition of the Lord. Even if they do not harm them by a bad example, they still destroy them by yielding to them (*permissione*). They love them too much according to the flesh and pamper them. (Luther, *Sermons on the Ten Commandments*, 1516, WA 1, p. 451; in WLS 1, p. 139)

An over-possessive and controlling parental strictness may backfire and inadvertently elicit rebelliousness and license:

Experience teaches us that youths reared with extreme strictness become much worse when loosed from restraint than those who have not been so strictly reared. So utterly impossible it is to improve human nature with commandments and punishments. More than this is required to do so. (Luther, WA 10 I, p. 451; WLS 3, p. 1563)

If negative reinforcements are to be used, they should be accompanied by positive reinforcements:

One must punish in such a way that the rod is accompanied by the apple. It's a bad thing if children and pupils lose their spirit on account of their parents and teachers. (Luther, *Table Talk*, LW 54, #3566A, p. 235)

Children inordinately indulged by parents are not favored with love. Badly raised children may foreshadow a disastrous result, as suggested by this eerie double entendre on the metaphor of raising:

This is also what the heathen say on the basis of daily experience: "Strict justice is the greatest injustice." The same may also be said of mercy: All mercy is much worse than no mercy at all. A father cannot do a more unfatherly thing for his child than to spare the rod and let the little child have its own way. With such stupid affection he is finally "raising" a son for the executioner, who afterwards will have to "raise" him in another way, namely, with a rope on the gallows. (Luther, "Commentary on Psalm 101, 1535," LW 13, p. 153)

Neither an excess of leniency or rigor is good for children. Menno Simons sought a balance. He was keenly aware of how deeply parents are at times blinded by their natural affections for their children:

Teach and admonish them, I say, in proportion to the extent of their understanding. Constrain and curb them with discretion and moderation, not with anger or bitterness which will make them discouraged. Do not spare the rod if necessity requires. Think on what is written: Parents who love their child may cause him often to feel contraint in order that they may take delight in his life as a result. But those who are too lenient with a child will always take his side, and he will be frightened whenever he hears the slightest cry. A child unrestrained becomes headstrong as an untamed horse. Do not give him free reign during his youth, and do not wink at his follies. Bow down his neck while he is young, in order that he not become stubborn and ungovernable. Correct your children. Keep them from idleness, in order than you not later feel shame from their behavior. . . . Teach them, and instruct them, admonish them, threaten, correct, and discipline them, as circumstances require. Keep them away from good-for-nothing youth, from whom they will hear and learn nothing but lying, cursing, swearing, fighting, and mischief. Guide them toward good reading and writing. Teach them to spin and other handicrafts suitable, useful, and proper to their years and personal development. If you do this, you shall live to see much honor and joy in your children. But if you do not do it, heaviness of heart may finally catch up with you in the end. For a child left to himself, without correction, is not only the shame of his father, but he disgraces his mother also.

This brief little admonition I have written to my beloved, out of hearty love, and that not without reason. For in the course of my ministry, I have unfortunately observed more than enough how disorderly, improperly, and yes even in a barbarian fashion do some parents care for their children. The misguided love of one's own children is so very great with some parents. They are so blinded by the natural affection for their childen that they can neither see nor perceive any evil, error, or defect in them at all, even when they are so frequently full of mischievous tricks and wickedness, disobedient to father and mother, lie right and left, quarrel and fight with other people's children, and mock people as they pass by, crying after them and calling them names. (Menno Simons, The Nurture of Children, c. 1557, *CWMS,* pp. 951-952)*

Faults must be corrected, but constant fault-finding by parents is demoralizing:

Not all trees grow straight, not all waters flow straight; nor is the earth level everywhere. Therefore, the statement is true: *Qui nescit dissimulare, nescit imperare* (He who does not know how to close an eye does not know

how to guide). (Luther, *Table Talk,* WAT-1, #315; WLS 2, p. 907; cf.
LW 54, #315, pp. 43-44)*

Luther was especially concerned to guide parents into an appropriate
balance of strictness and lenience. He remarked with particular poignancy of
the ironic capacity of the children or young people to hurt their parents deeply.
He knew that parents do not have the power absolutely to determine how their
children will develop:

Isaac is a very saintly patriarch, the father of the promise; Rebecca
is a very saintly woman and the mother of the same promise. But Esau
was born from their flesh and blood. He longs for their death, and he
himself plans to bring it about. Of what will we not have to be afraid?
But the grief of parents is far more piercing and far bitterer than that
of children, than that of brothers or relatives. For there are very great
and intense emotions that God has created in the whole nature of things
and has implanted in parents toward their offspring. And if at any time
their hearts are wounded by grief or sorrow on account of a misfortune
suffered by children, this is a very real plague and a poison for their
lives. Therefore parents are easily killed, if not by the sword, then by
sorrow and grief. I myself have seen that many very honorable parents
were slain by godless children because of sadness of heart. Young people
neither consider nor understand this. But children should be taught and
warned, lest they become murderers of mothers and murderers of
fathers. (Luther, "Lectures on Genesis, Chapters 26 to 30, 1542ff.,"
LW 5, pp. 163-164)

XIV ❧ Pastoral Care for Young People

The critical decisions and experiences between adolescence and adulthood hold
many promises and hazards. Good pastors have always been attuned and
attentive to the limits and possibilities of this period of human development.
The first irony, as the classical pastoral literature shows, is how little the complaints of elders toward youth have changed over centuries:

The common complaint now is that youth is ill-bred, wild, and insolent. Children do not want to be subject to parents, pupils to teachers,
servants to masters and mistresses; and obedience and order no longer
exist among the young folk, but only conceit and self-will. Everybody
wants to do whatever he pleases and to be a young lord, free and un-
punished. God will not allow matters to go on like this for any great
length of time. (Luther, "Exposition on 1 Peter 5:4," Erlangen ed., 52,
pp. 193ff.; in WLS 3, p. 1561)

The extent to which young people should be protected and overseen by parents has been variously debated in different periods. One might prematurely imagine that the pastoral writers would typically fall on the side of extreme protectiveness. Take note, however, of this passage from John Chrysostom, which highly values the virtues of independence:

Tell me, which sort of plants are the best? Are they not those that have their strength from themselves and are injured neither by rains, nor by hailstorms, nor by gusts of wind, nor by any other vicissitude of the sort, but stand naked in defiance of them all, and needing neither wall nor fence to protect them? Such is the truly wise person. Such is that wealth of which we spoke. He has nothing, and has all things. He has all things, and has nothing. For a fence is not within, but only without. A wall is not a phenomenon of nature, but only something built around something else from without. And what again, I ask, what sort of body is a strong one? Is it not that which is in good health, and which is therefore not easily overcome by hunger or abundance, by cold or by heat? Or is it that which in view of all these things, stands constantly in need of caterers and weavers, hunters and physicians, to give it health? He is the rich and wise person who can get along fine without any of these secondary supports. It is for this reason that the blessed Apostle said, "Give them the instruction, and the correction, which belong to a Christian upbringing" (Eph. 6:4). Do not surround them with unnecessary outward defenses. For such is wealth, such is glory. For when these fall, and they do fall, the plant stands naked and defenseless, not only having derived no profit from them during the intervening time, but even injury. For those very shelters that prevented its being inured to the attacks of the winds, will now have prepared it for perishing all at once. This is why wealth tends to be injurious, because it renders us undisciplined for the vicissitudes of life. Let us therefore train up our children to be ready and able to bear up against every trial, and not be surprised at what may come upon them. . . . Let us beseech God that He aid us in the work. If God shall see us committed to this work, and eager to learn about it, God will be our helper. But if He shall see us paying no regard to it, He will not give us His hand. . . . For a helper (as the name implies) is not a helper of one that is inactive, but of one who also himself works. (Chrysostom, *Homilies on Ephesians,* Hom. XXI, NPNF 1, XIII, pp. 156-157)*

Each generation calls for new insight and courage from young people, in the view of Clement of Alexandria. He described the Christian community as perpetually and intrinsically young:

The old people were perverse and hard of heart, but we, the new people, the assembly of little ones, are amenable as a child. In the Epistle to the Romans, the Apostle declares that he rejoices in "the minds of innocent people" (Rom. 16:18), but notice that he goes on to set limits, so to speak, to this childlikeness: "Yet I should wish you to be experts in goodness but simpletons in evil" (Rom. 16:19). . . . Little ones are indeed the new spirits, they who have newly become wise despite their former folly. . . . Then the new people, in contrast to the older people, are young, because they have heard the new good things. The fertile time of life is this unaging youth of ours in which we are ever at the prime of intelligence, ever young, ever childlike, ever new. For, those who have partaken of the new Word must themselves be new. But whatever partakes of eternity assumes, by that very fact, the qualities of the incorruptible; therefore, the name "childhood" is for us a life-long spring, because the truth abiding in us is ageless and our being, made to overflow with that truth, is ageless, too. (Clement of Alexandria, *Christ the Educator,* Bk. I, Ch. 5.19-20, FC 23, pp. 20-21)

Youth is indeed a special, joyful period of life, but not one that rightly should be given over to self-indulgence, hedonism, and narcissism, which are prone to elicit sadness of spirit. The right relation of soul and body is the key:

Young people should indeed avoid sadness and solitude. Joy is as necessary to youth as eating and drinking are necessary, for the body is invigorated by a soul that is happy. To be sure, training must be begun, not with the body but with the soul; however, it must proceed in such a way that the body is not neglected. When minds have been correctly instructed, bodies are easily controlled. Therefore we should look with indulgence on the joyousness of youth and its doing everything with a happy heart. Only this must be watched: that they do not become corrupted by the lusts of the flesh. For drinking bouts, drunkenness, and love affairs are not that joyousness of the heart of which Solomon speaks here; rather they make the soul sad. (Luther, "Exposition on Eccl. 11:9, 1526," WA 20, p. 191; in WLS 3, p. 1559)

The analogy between youthfulness and the energetic vitalities of the new birth in Christianity is a familiar theme of scripture and tradition. Clement of Alexandria amassed the biblical imagery reflecting this analogy (chicks, colts, young birds, etc.):

As the hen gathers her chicks under her wings (Luke 13:34). . . . In that sense we are young birds, a name which graphically and mystically describes the simplicity of soul belonging to childhood. At times, He calls us children, at other times, chicks, sometimes, little ones, here and there sons, and very often offspring, a new people, a young people. "A

new name," He says, "will be given My servants" (by new name He
means one that is different, everlasting, pure and simple, suggestive of
childhood and of candor), "which will be blessed upon the earth" (Isa.
65:15,16—Septuagint).

At another time, He speaks of us under the figure of a colt. He means
by that that we are unyoked to evil, unsubdued by wickedness, un-
affected, high-spirited only with Him our Father. We are colts, not
stallions "who whinny lustfully for their neighbor's wife, beasts of
burden unrestrained in their lust" (Cf. Jer. 5.8). Rather, we are free and
newly born, joyous in our faith, holding fast to the course of truth, swift
in seeking salvation, spurning and trampling upon worldliness. "Rejoice
greatly, O daughter of Sion. Shout for joy, O daughter of Jerusalem"
(Zech. 9:9). . . . Such young colts as we little ones are our divine Tamer
trains. . . . Again, it is said: "He tethers his colt to the vine" (Cf. Gen.
49:11). This means He united the simple, new people to the Word,
whom the vine signifies. (Clement of Alexandria, *Christ the Educator*, Bk.
I, Ch. 5.14-15, FC 23, pp. 15-16)

Although the pastoral writers have generally valued highly the potential
contributions of emerging generations of young people, they have also been
aware that immature leadership may impetuously want to change everything
instantly. Luther quipped about the hazards of experimentation among youthful experimenters in various professions:

Hence the German proverbs about the young doctor of medicine who
needs a new cemetery, about the jurist who recently took over a public
office and starts wars all over the place, and about the young theologian
who fills hell with souls. Because these men lack the practical experience
that engenders wisdom, they do everything in accordance with their
own canons and rules. This is why they get into difficulties and make
mistakes to the great detriment of people and affairs. (Luther, "Lectures
on Genesis, Chapters 6 to 14, 1536," LW 2, p. 340)

Many pastoral writers assumed that each developmental period was provi-
dentially designed and destined to have its own special challenges and temptations. Youth, like those in each successive developmental stage, face distinctive
problems that correlate intrinsically with the developmental tasks of their age
group. Ambrose succinctly stated five perennial issues of youth:

Childhood, indeed, possesses innocence; and old age, prudence; and
young manhood, that is so close to youth, a regard for one's good
reputation and a sense of shame at committing sin. But youth alone is
weak in strength, feeble in counsels, ardent in sin, scornful of those who

give counsel, and ready to be seduced by pleasures. (Ambrose, *Exegetical Works,* The Prayer of Job and David, sec. 7.21, FC 65, p. 343)

Despite these difficulties, young souls are especially capable of becoming attracted to the aroma of truth, with greater vitality than their elders. Origen used an erotic image of the hastening of the beloved to meet the lover, allegorically understood as believer and Christ, in order to express the extraordinary intensity of the vitality of young souls:

Now it says that when "Thy name" has been emptied out as ointment, "have they loved Thee," (Song of Songs 1:3), not those little old souls clothed in the old man, nor yet the spotted and wrinkled, but that "the maidens" have done so—that is to say, the young souls growing up in years of beauty, who are always being made new and renewed from day to day, as they put on the new man, who is created according to God.
For the sake of these young souls, therefore, in their growing and abundant life, He who was in the form of God emptied Himself, that His name might be as ointment emptied out. . . . When souls have thus drawn the Word of God to themselves, and have ingrafted Him into their minds and understandings, and have experienced the pleasantness of His sweetness and odour, when they have received the fragrance of His ointments and have grasped at last the reason for His coming, the motives of the Redemption and Passion, and the love whereby He, the Immortal, went even to the death of the cross for the salvation of all men, then these maiden souls, attracted by all this as by the odours of a divine and ineffable perfume and being filled with vigour and complete alacrity, run after Him and hasten to the odour of His sweetness, not at a slow pace, nor with lagging steps, but swiftly and with all the speed they can. (Origen, *The Song of Songs,* Bk. I, ACW 26, pp. 75-76)

Some pastoral writers, among them Luther, have strongly affirmed the legitimate need of young people to have fitting contexts for social interaction, such as dancing, provided the context is not harmful:

Where decency prevails, I let the wedding run its usual and rightful course and dance as much as I please (*tanze immerhin*). If you are decent and moderate in your conduct, you cannot dance or sit away faith and love. Youngsters certainly dance without harm. You may as well do likewise, and become a child; then dancing will not harm you. (Luther, WA 17 II, p. 64; in WLS 3, pp. 1562-1563)*

At times it became a special question of propriety and protocol as to whether the pastor should appear at social occasions such as dances. Luther provided a sample of pastoral reasoning about this:

Dances are arranged and permitted that courtesies in group life may be learned and friendships may be formed among adolescent youths and girls. For in this way moral conduct can be observed, and an opportunity is also given to come together in a decent manner so that in the light of this acquaintance with a girl a young man can thereafter more decently and deliberately court her. . . . But let all be done with modesty. For this reason decent men and matrons should be there to mingle with the dancers that everything may be done more fittingly. At times I myself shall be there so that my presence may keep them from the gyrations of certain dances. (Luther, WA-T 5, #5265; in WLS 3, p. 1563)*

Ambrose was strongly convinced that younger and older generations have important gifts to offer each other:

He who lives in company with wise men is wise himself; but he who clings to the foolish is looked on as a fool too. This friendship with the wise is a great help in teaching us, and also as giving a sure proof of our uprightness. Young men show very soon that they imitate those to whom they attach themselves. . . . Beautiful, therefore, is the union between old and young. The one to give witness, the other to give comfort; the one to give guidance, the other to give pleasure. . . . In the Acts of the Apostles, Barnabas took Mark with him, and Paul took Silas and Timothy and Titus. (Ambrose, *Duties of the Clergy*, Bk. II, Ch. XX, secs. 97, 100, NPNF 2, X, pp. 58-59)

XV ✇ DIVORCE COUNSEL

Since the pastor is a teacher of fidelity in marriage, the pastor also may be consulted when difficulties arise in marriage. There is no absolute injunction against divorce either by Jesus or by the pastoral tradition, but strict constraints have been placed upon the moral legitimacy of divorce. Christian partners whose marriage is in trouble do well to consult at an early stage with the pastor. Joseph Hall set forth a series of priorities in divorce counsel that move from prevention to acceptance:

I should therefore earnestly advise and exhort those whom it may concern, carefully and effectually to apply themselves to the forementioned remedies: reconciliation if it be possible to prevent a divorce; holy endeavours of a continued continence, if it may be obtained, to prevent a second marriage after divorce. But, if these prevail not, I dare not lay a load upon any man's conscience, which God has not burdened. I dare not ensnare those whom God will have free. (Joseph Hall, Cases Matrimonial, Case iii, *Works*, 1837, vol. VII, p. 474; in *Angl.*, p. 666)*

The dissolution of marriage is allowed in the classical Protestant tradition under conditions where adultery, fornication, or willful desertion have irremediably abrogated the covenant, and when all efforts at reconciliation have failed:

Adultery or fornication, committed after a contract, being detected before marriage, gives just occasion to the innocent party to dissolve that contract. In the case of adultery after marriage, it is lawful for the innocent party to sue out a divorce, and after the divorce to marry another, as if the offending party were dead.

Although the corruption of man be such as is apt to study arguments, unduly to put asunder those whom God has joined together in marriage; yet nothing but adultery, or such willful desertion as can no way be remedied by the Church or civil magistrate, is cause sufficient for dissolving the bond of marriage; wherein a public and orderly course of proceeding is to be observed; and the persons concerned in it, not left to their own wills and discretion in their own case. (Westminster Confession, 1646, Ch. XXIV, secs. v-vi, *CC*, p. 221)

The Athanasian canons prevented clergy from assisting persons in ending marriages:

No cleric (*kleros*) shall be go-between (*mesiteuo* or *mesazo*) in any way at all that colludes in dividing marriages. But if one be found to have divided or mediated (*mesiteuo* or *mesazo*) in any matter encouraging divorce (*repoudiou*), he shall be cast forth from the clergy (*kleros*) until that marriage shall be joined together again. (*Athanasian Canons*, sec. 46, p. 120)*

It is assumed that the pastor will make substantial efforts to prevent a divorce. But there may come a time when all efforts fail:

Accordingly, if a spouse has committed adultery and the fact can be publicly proved, I may and dare not keep the other person from being free, from permission to obtain a divorce, and from marrying someone else. But if it can be done, it is very much better to reconcile the two and keep them together. But if the innocent spouse so desires, he or she may in the name of God make use of his or her right and get a divorce. (Luther, WA 30 III, p. 241; in WLS 2, p. 902)

Key biblical mandates on divorce and separation were set forth by Menno Simons in the Wismar Articles of 1554:

If a believer and an unbeliever are in the marriage bond together and the unbeliever commits adultery, then the marriage tie is broken. And if it be one who complains that he has fallen in sin, and desires to mend his ways, then the brethren permit the believing mate to go to the unfaithful one to admonish him, if conscience allows it in view of the state of the affair. But if he be a bold and headstrong adulterer, then the innocent party is free—with the provision, however, that she shall consult with the congregation and remarry according to circumstances and decisions in the matter, be it well understood.

Concerning a believer and a nonbeliever—if the nonbeliever wishes to separate for reasons of the faith, then the believer shall conduct himself honestly without contracting a marriage, for as long a time as the nonbeliever is not remarried. But if the nonbeliever marries or commits adultery, then the believing mate may also marry, subject to the advice of the elders of the congregation. (Menno Simons, The Wismar Articles of 1554, *CWMS,* pp. 1041-1042)

John Chrysostom warned against extending the recognized grounds of divorce inordinately:

Be she drunkard, or railer, or gossip, or evil-eyed, or extravagant, and a squanderer of your substance, you have her for the partner of your life. (Chrysostom, *Homilies on Ephesians,* Hom. XV, NPNF 1, XIII, p. 124)*

Since some biblical patriarchs had many spouses, the question arose as to why this was not permitted in Christian marriage. Tertullian placed this question within the frame of reference of the history of salvation with its two covenants, law and gospel:

Of course, we do not reject the union of man and woman in marriage. It is an institution blessed by God for the reproduction of the human race. It was planned by Him for the purpose of populating the earth and to make provision for the propagation of mankind. Hence, it was permitted; but only once may it be contracted. . . . Now, everybody knows that it was allowed our forefathers, even the Patriarchs themselves, not only to marry but actually to multiply marriages. They even kept concubines. But, although figurative language is used in speaking of both Church and Synagogue, yet we may explain this difficult matter simply by saying that it was necessary in former times that there be practices which afterwards had to be abrogated or modified. For the Law had first to intervene; too, at a later date, the Word of God was to replace the Law and introduce spiritual circumcision. Therefore, the licentiousness and promiscuity of earlier days—and there must needs have been abuses which called for the institution of a law—were responsible for that subsequent corrective legislation by which the Lord through His Gospel, and the Apostle in these latter days did away with excesses or controlled irregularities. . . . We do not read anywhere at all that marriage is forbidden; and this for the obvious reason that marriage is actually a good. (Tertullian, *To His Wife,* secs. 2-3, ACW 13, pp. 11-12)

Tertullian speculated that divorce was unknown in the earliest human history, and only came about in more recent times:

It is adultery, as I have already pointed out, when a man commingles any flesh with his own, outside that first union in which God joined "two in one flesh" (Gen. 2:24) or found them so joined. . . . So true is it that divorce was not from the beginning, that among the Romans it is not until the six hundredth year after the foundation of the city that the first instance of such cruel conduct is recorded. They committed adultery, however, although they did not divorce; we, on the contrary, do not even permit remarriage, though we do allow divorce. (Tertullian, *Monogamy,* ACW 13, p. 90)

By the time of Clement of Alexandria, there was a strong, but not absolute, emphasis on single marriages clearly being taught:

But it is the same man and Lord who makes the old new, by no longer allowing several marriages (for at that time God required it when men had to increase and multiply), and by teaching single marriage for the sake of begetting children and looking after domestic affairs, for which purpose woman was given as a "helpmeet" (Gen. 2:18). And if from sympathy the apostle allows a man a second marriage because he cannot control himself and burns with passion, he also does not commit any sin according to the Old Testament (for it was not forbidden by the Law), but he does not fulfil the heightened perfection of the gospel ethic. But he gains heavenly glory for himself if he remains as he is, and keeps undefiled the marriage yoke broken by death, and willingly accepts God's purpose for him, by which he has become free from distraction for the service of the Lord. (Clement of Alexandria, *On Marriage,* sec. 82, LCC II, pp. 78-79)

Clement stated the prevailing view that grounds for divorce are strictly limited by scripture:

That Scripture counsels marriage and allows no release from the union, is expressly contained in Jesus' teaching: "I tell you, if a man divorces his wife for any cause other than unchastity, and marries another, he commits adultery" (Matt. 19:9). And it regards as unchastity the marriage of those separated while the other is alive. (Clement of Alexandria, *The Stromata, or Miscellanies,* Bk. II, Ch. XXIII, ANF II, p. 379, NEB)*

Luther represented a less prevalent voice in the pastoral tradition when he argued cautiously that divorced persons may be counseled according to scripture, under particular circumstances, to remarry. His argument is complex:

As to divorce, it is still a moot question whether it be allowable. For my part I so greatly detest divorce that I should prefer bigamy to it, but whether it be allowable, I do not venture to decide. Christ Himself, the Chief Pastor, says in Matthew 5:32, "If a man divorces his wife for any cause other than inchastity he involves her in adultery; and anyone who marries a divorced woman commits adultery." Christ, then, permits divorce, but for the cause of fornication only. . . . If Christ permits divorce for the cause of fornication and compels no one to remain unmarried, and if Paul would rather have one marry than burn, then He certainly seems to permit a man to marry another woman in the stead of the one who has been put away. . . . I, indeed, who, alone against all, can decide nothing in this matter, would yet greatly desire at least the passage in 1 Corinthians 7:15 to be applied here—"If on the other hand the heathen party wishes for a separation, let him have it. In such cases the Christian husband or wife is under no compulsion." Here the Apostle gives permission to put away the unbeliever who departs and to set the believing spouse free to marry again. Why should not the same hold true when a believer—that is, a believer in name, but in truth as much an unbeliever as the one Paul speaks of—deserts his wife, especially if he never intends to return? (Luther, *The Babylonian Captivity,* WML II, pp. 271-272)

Similarly wrote Bucer:

They must exercise as vigilant a care as possible in this matter, that marriages be first contracted responsible and in the Lord and then preserved in good faith. When unhappiness demands it, let them be dissolved, but only legitimately, and allow remarriage, as the law of God and of nature as well as the sanctions of pious princes have decreed. (Bucer, *De Regno Christi,* XLVII, LCC XIX, p. 333)

XVI ✤ Abortion Counsel

During some periods of the church's history, abortions were very common. There is a strong tendency in church law to associate abortion with pagan moral barbarity. With almost no exceptions, the pastoral writers regarded abortion as forbidden by the injunction to not kill. Often the early Christian tradition appealed to Jewish precedent in this question:

The first way, therefore, is that of life. . . . "Thou shalt not kill" (Exod. 20:13), that is, you shall not destroy a human being like yourself, for in doing so you destroy what is well made. . . . You shall not slay your child by causing abortion, nor kill that which is alive. For "everything that is shaped, and has received a soul from God, if it be slain, shall be avenged, as being unjustly destroyed" (Exod. 21:23, LXX). (*Constitutions of the Holy Apostles,* Bk. VII, Sec. I, chs. ii-iii, ANF VII, pp. 445-466)*

Is the embryo a human being?

The embryo, therefore, becomes a human being from the moment when its formation is completed. Consequently, Moses imposed punishment in kind for one who was guilty of causing an abortion on the ground that the embryo was a rudimentary "human being," exposed to the chances of life and death. (Tertullian, *On the Soul,* Ch. 37, sec. 2, FC 10, p. 260)*

Since the fetus is regarded as an object of God's care, it cannot be treated as if it were not alive, according to Athenagoras:

Women who induce abortions are murderers, and will have to give account of it to God. For the same person would not regard the fetus in the womb as a living thing and therefore an object of God's care, and at the same time slay it, once it had come to life. (Athenagoras, *A Plea for the Christians,* sec. 35, LCC I, pp. 338-339)

At what point after conception may one be said to have received a soul?

When, therefore, conception follows, that seed is not said to live immediately, because it cannot feel. Soon, however, it has within it that movement, by which it is impelled to take shape and grow. For just as the seed of a tree, planted by nature in the womb of the earth, takes shape by reason of the aforesaid movement and grows and spreads out its branches, so the seed of the beast, infused into the womb of the female, is by the same movement moulded into shape, grows and develops into limbs. Nevertheless, we do not say of it, as we do of trees, that it is alive, because there is another more important life which has to be awaited. But when this life has been added to it, we do not say that there are two lives or two souls in it, but only one possessing a twofold power, one of which lies in the natural movement, by which it becomes a body and lives and grows, and the other of which lies in the spontaneous movement attached to the senses by which it also feels. (Aelred of Rievaulx, *Dialogue on the Soul,* CFS 22, p. 58)

Shall those who abort be readmitted as communicants in the community of faith?

> Concerning women who commit fornication, and destroy that which they have conceived, or who are employed in making drugs for abortion, a former decree excluded them until the hour of death, and to this some have assented. Nevertheless, being desirous to use somewhat greater leniency, we have ordained that they fulfil ten years (of penance), according to the prescribed degrees. . . . Concerning wilful murderers let them remain prostrators; but at the end of life let them be indulged with full communion. (Council of Ancyra, A.D. 314, Canons XXI and XXII, The Seven Ecumenical Councils, NPNF 2, XIV, pp. 73-74)

Minucius Felix (second or third century) contrasted the rigorous early Christian ethic of abortion to pagan abuses:

> There are some women who by drinking medical preparations, extinguish the source of the future human being in their very bodies, and thus commit a parricide before they give birth. These things come directly from the teaching of your pagan gods. . . . To us it is not lawful either to see or to hear of homicide. (Minucius Felix, *The Octavius,* Ch. XXX, ANF IV, p. 192)*

※

In these passages we see the pastor historically as involved in all stages of the life cycle: present at the birth of children, concerned with parental care of souls, helping young people with their life crises, engaged in premarital counseling, teaching the meaning of marriage, nurturing marriages and assisting partners in covenant-keeping, counseling partners concerning the church's teaching on adultery, divorce, and abortion. Now we turn to two final crises of radical loss where pastoral wisdom is needed: poverty and death.

5 Care of the Poor

THE CLASSICAL PASTORAL WRITERS viewed care of the poor as a claim intrinsic to the pastoral office. As God has cared for us in our need, so are we being called to care for others in their needs. Christians are called to love all humanity, yet the poor, hungry and dispossessed constitute a special claim upon faith active in love because they are most urgently and immediately in need.

I ❧ THE SCOPE OF PASTORAL CARE OF THE POOR

In enumerating seven "kinds of almsdeeds," St. Thomas revealed the broad scope of the church's conception of care for the poor. For alms encompass both bodily and spiritual care:

> We reckon seven corporal almsdeeds, namely, to feed the hungry, to give drink to the thirsty, to clothe the naked, to harbor the harborless, to visit the sick, to ransom the captive, to bury the dead; all of which are expressed in the following verse:
> To visit, to quench, to feed, to ransom, clothe, harbor or bury.
> Again we reckon seven spiritual alms, namely, to instruct the ignorant, to counsel the doubtful, to comfort the sorrowful, to reprove the sinner, to forgive injuries, to bear with those who trouble and annoy us, and to pray for all, which are all contained in the following verse:
> To counsel, reprove, console, to pardon, forbear, and to pray.
> . . . The aforesaid distinction of almsdeeds is suitably taken from the various needs of our neighbor: some of which affect the soul, and are relieved by spiritual almsdeeds, while others affect the body, and are relieved by corporal almsdeeds. (Thomas Aquinas, *Summa Theologica*, Part II-II, Q. 32, Art. 2, Vol. II, p. 1324)

In this way a counseling ministry and a ministry to the poor were viewed as integrated, not separable, tasks. Among corporal almsdeeds (acts of mercy toward the bodily needs of others), St. Thomas revealed the extent of accountability. The bodily needs to be responded to are the range of familiar, specific human needs that emerge in risk-laden human existence—needs for food, drink, shelter, clothing, medical care, and lacking all else, burial.

144

The need is either internal or external. Internal need is two-fold: one which is relieved by solid food, viz. hunger, in respect of which we have to feed the hungry; while the other is relieved by liquid food, viz. thirst, and in respect of this we have to give drink to the thirsty. The common need with regard to external help is twofold; one in respect of clothing, and as to this we have to clothe the naked: while the other is in respect of a dwelling place, and as to this we have to harbor the harborless. Again if the need be special, it is either the result of an internal cause, like sickness, and then we have to visit the sick, or it results from an external cause, and then, we have to ransom the captive. After this life we give burial to the dead. (Thomas Aquinas, *Summa Theologica,* Part II-II, Q. 32, Art. 2, Vol. II, p. 1325)

Earlier the Apostolic Constitutions had set forth the wide-ranging vision of the Church's care for the poor:

Be solicitous about their maintenance, being in nothing wanting to them; exhibiting to the orphans the care of parents; to the widows the care of husbands; to those of suitable age, marriage; to the artificer, work; to the unable, commiseration; to the strangers, a house; to the hungry, food; to the thirsty, drink; to the naked, clothing; to the sick, visitation; to the prisoners, assistance; . . . to the maiden, give her in marriage; . . . to the young man, assistance that he may learn a trade and may be maintained by the advantage arising from it. (*Constitutions of the Holy Apostles,* Bk. IV, Sec. I, ch. ii, ANF VII, p. 433)*

In this way, the pastor may become a surrogate family to the oppressed:

Love all your brethren with grave and compassionate eyes, perform-ing to orphans the part of parents, to widows that of husbands, affording them sustenance with all kindliness, arranging marriages for those who are in their prime, and for those who are without a profession, the means of necessary support through employment; giving work to the artificer, and alms to the incapable. (Clementina, *The Epistle of Clement to James,* Ch. VIII, ANF VIII, pp. 219-220)

Ambrose is warmly remembered for having sold sacred vessels to redeem captives from imprisonment. In this autobiographical report, Ambrose stated his view that resources should not be hoarded, but flow through the church to the poor, who are the church's real treasure:

I once brought odium on myself because I broke up the sacred vessels to redeem captives—a fact that could displease the Arians. Not that it displeased them as an act, but as being a thing in which they could take hold of something for which to blame me. Who can be so hard, cruel, iron-hearted, as to be displeased because someone is redeemed from death? . . . He Who sent the apostles without gold also brought together the churches without gold. The Church has gold, not to store up, but to lay out, and to spend on those who need. . . . Is it not much better that the priests should melt it down for the sustenance of the poor, if other supplies fail, than that a sacrilegious enemy should carry it off and defile it? . . . Such gold the holy martyr Lawrence preserved for the Lord. For when the treasures of the Church were demanded from him, he promised that he would show them. On the following day he brought the poor together. When asked where the treasures were which he had promised, he pointed to the poor, saying: "These are the treasures of the Church." (Ambrose, *Duties of the Clergy,* Bk. II, Ch. XXVIII, secs. 136, 137, 140, NPNF 2, X, pp. 64-65)*

II ❧ IMMEDIATE RELIEF FOR THOSE IN IMMEDIATE NEED

The first need of the seriously malnourished is food. Food comes before talk:

If your brother should be weak—I speak of the poor man—do not visit empty-handed such a person as he lies ill. . . . God Himself cries out: Break your bread with the needy. There is no need to visit with words, but with benefits. It is unthinkable that your brother should be sick through lack of food. Do not try to satisfy him with words. He needs food and drink. (Commodianus, *Instructions,* ch. lxxi, ANF IV, p. 217)*

Commodianus in the second century was relying upon a widely available tradition of preaching and care that preceded him. It still remains a key principle of pastoral priorities in care of the poor: bread for the needy must precede talk, and talk cannot be a substitute for bodily sustenance.

Since the poor are God's own concern, they are due a rightful share of the pastor's time and concern:

The poor being God's peculiar care, they ought to have a great share in the concern of his ministers, to relieve, to instruct, and to comfort them. (Thomas Wilson, *Parochialia,* p. 413)

The inner unity underlying mercy, beneficence, liberality, and alms was considered by Jeremy Taylor. He set forth four ways in which the giver may offend against the recipient: by routinization, by hostility, by eliciting guilt, and by demeaning the suffering neighbor:

Love is as communicative as fire, as busy and as active. It has four twin daughters extremely like each other. . . . Their names are Mercy; Beneficence (or Well-doing); Liberality; and Alms. Each has obtained a special privilege to be called after their mother's name: Charity. The first or oldest is seated in the affection; and is that which all the others must attend. For mercy without alms is acceptable when the person is unable to express outwardly what he heartily desires. But alms without mercy are like prayers without devotion, or religion without humility. Beneficence, or well-doing, is a promptness and nobleness of mind, making us to do offices of courtesy and humanity to all sorts of persons in their need, and out of their need. Liberality is a disposition of mind opposite to covetousness, and consists in the contempt and neglect of money upon just occasions, and relates to our friends, kin, associates and others to whom we are related. But alms is a relieving the poor and needy. The first and last only are duties of Christianity. . . .

He that gives alms must do it in mercy; that is, out of a true sense of the calamity of his brother, first feeling it in himself in some proportion, and then endeavoring to ease himself and the other, of their common calamity. Against this rule they offend who give alms out of custom; or to upbraid the poverty of the other; or to make him feel obliged to pay back the money; or with any demeaning circumstance. He that gives alms must do it with a single eye and heart; that is, without designs to get the praise of men. Assuming this is understood, one may give alms either publicly or privately. For Christ's intention was only to resist pride and hypocrisy when he bade alms to be given in secret. For remember that another one of his commands was that "you, like the lamp, must shed light among your fellows, so that, when they see the good you do, they may give praise to your Father in heaven" (Matt. 5:16). To give privately is more excellent; to give publicly is more safe. The one who has done a good turn should so forget it as not to speak of it. The instant one boasts of it, or demeans another through it, it is as if one has done something for oneself, and the charitable act has lost it meaning.

Give alms with a cheerful heart and countenance. "There should be no reluctance, no sense of compulsion; God loves a cheerful giver" (2 Cor. 9:7). Let the gift be given quickly, while the power is in your hand, and the need is being felt by the neighbor, and your neighbor is at your door. One gives twice who relieves speedily. (Jeremy Taylor, *Rule and Exercise of Holy Living,* Ch. 4, sec. 8, PW II, p. 89)*

The pastor is called to be immediately responsive to the concrete situation of need wherever it actually emerges, not where it might fit conceptually into a bureaucratic or rationalistic timetable. George Herbert thought that the pastor had best not too closely interrogate those upon whom hardship has fallen, but rather serve and love that very one "whom God puts in his way."

So doth he also to those at his door; whom God puts in his way, and makes his neighbors. But these he helps not without some testimony, except the evidence of the misery bring testimony with it. For though these testimonies also may be falsified, yet—considering that the law allows these in case they be true, but allows by no means to give without testimony—as he obeys authority in the one, so, that being once satisfied, he allows his charity some blindness in the other; especially since, of the two commands, we are more enjoined to be charitable than wise. But evident miseries have a natural privilege and exemption from all law. (Geo. Herbert, *CP,* Ch. XII, CWS, p. 73)

Since pastors are called to be charitable even when they cannot always be wise, they give "evident miseries" a status of "natural privilege." If food and shelter are given without the compassionate spirit of charity, they are not almgiving in the full and complete sense, according to St. Thomas:

Now the motive for giving alms is to relieve one who is in need. Thus some have defined alms as being *a deed whereby something is given to the needy, out of compassion and for God's sake,* whose motive is therefore mercy . . . . Accordingly almsgiving can be materially without charity, but to give alms formally, i.e. for God's sake, with delight and readiness and completely as one ought, is not possible without charity. (Thomas Aquinas, *Summa Theologica,* Part II-II, Q. 32, Art. 2, Vol. II, p. 1324)*

Richard Baxter pleaded with his fellow pastors to not allow the poor to remain strangers:

Remember, you are obliged to be the servants of all. "Condescend to men of low estate" (Rom. 12:16). Be not strange to the poor of your flock; they are apt to take your strangeness for contempt. . . . Go to the poor, and see what they want, and show your compassion at once to their soul and body. Buy them a catechism, and other small books that are likely to do them good, and make them promise to read them with care and attention. . . . You lose no great advantage for heaven by becoming poor: "In pursuing one's way, the lighter one travels the better." (Baxter, *RP,* pp. 66-67)

Maximus the Confessor thought that in the giving of charity, it is best not to make distinctions between those who seem worthy and those who seem less worthy of care:

He that in imitation of God does almsdeeds knows no difference between evil and good, just and unjust, in regard to the needs of the body, but distributes equally to all according to their need, even though for his good intention he prefers the virtuous to the bad. (Maximus the Confessor, *The Four Centuries of Charity,* Ch. 1, sec. 24, ACW 21, p. 140)

By means of an intensely personal exercise in empathy, Ignatius Loyola set forth a rule for distributing to the poor:

The following rules should be followed in the ministry of distributing alms. . . . The love which moves me and inspires me to give the alms must come from above; that is, from the love of God our Lord. I should feel within myself that the greater or less love that I have for these persons is inspired by God, and that he is clearly the source of the reasons for which I love them more. . . . I will consider that I am at the Day of Judgment and I will reflect on how I should then wish to have fulfilled the duties of my ministry. I will follow now the same rules that I shall then wish to have observed. (Ignatius of Loyola, *Spiritual Exercises*, p. 134)

III ❧ AVERTING THE DEPENDENCY SYNDROME IN CARE OF THE POOR

Temporal assistance and spiritual counsel must be conjoined in care for the poor. To give the poor money but withhold teaching them how to become more self-sufficient—that is to do only half of the task:

There is a twofold liberality: one gives actual assistance, that is, in money. The other is busy in offering active help of a more consequential and ennobling kind. . . . Money is easily spent. Good counsels can never be exhausted. They only grow the stronger by constant use. Money grows less and quickly comes to an end, and has failed even kindness itself; so that the more there are to whom one wants to give, the fewer one can help; and often one has not got what one thinks ought to be given to others. But as regards the offer of good counsel and active help, the more there are to spend it on, the more it returns to its own source. (Ambrose, *Duties of the Clergy*, Bk. II, Ch. XV, secs. 73, 75, NPNF 2, X, pp. 54-55)*

Repeatedly the pastoral writers observed that Christian care of the poor, even with the best motivation, was subject to being distorted and abused by false teachers and "con artists," who would unconscionably take food away from the poor for their own profit. In order to protect the poor, the pastor must be alert to spot those who would exploit poor relief:

It is clear, then, that there ought to be due measure in our liberality, that our gifts may not become useless. Moderation must be observed, especially by priests, for fear that they should give away for the sake of ostentation, and not for justice sake. Never was the greed of beggars greater than it is now. They come in full vigour, they come with no reason but that they are on the tramp. They are willing to empty the purses of the poor—to deprive them of their means of support. Not content with a little, they ask for more. In the clothes that cover them they seek a pretense to make urgent their demands. With lies about their lives they ask for ever greater sums of money. If anyone were to trust their tale too readily, he would quickly drain the fund which is meant to serve for the sustenance of the poor. . . . Many pretend they have debts. Let the truth be looked into. They bemoan the fact that they have been stripped of everything by robbers. Credit such a case only if the misfortune is quite clear and the person is known to you. In that case give help quickly. To those rejected by the church, supplies must be given if they are in need of food. . . . We ought not only to lend our ears to hear the voices of those who plead, but also our eyes to look into their needs. (Ambrose, *Duties of the Clergy,* Bk. II, Ch. XVI, sec. 76, 77, NPNF 2, X, p. 55)*

Ambrose set forth the reasons why charitable acts that engender independence are to be preferred to outright charitable acts that may increase dependency. In doing so Ambrose enunciated a crucial principle of social welfare that has hardly been well-learned in modern society:

The poor to be most sought out are those who are ashamed to be seen. Those in prison must ever be in your thoughts. The cries of those who are ill must reach your ears. . . . Joseph had the power to give away all the wealth of Egypt and spend the royal treasure, but he thought it best not to give wastefully what belonged to another. Rather he preferred to sell the corn than give it away. For if he had given it to a few there would have been none for the most. Thereby the proof of his liberality is seen in the fact that there was enough for all. He opened the storehouses that all might buy their corn supply, lest if they received it for nothing, they should give up cultivating the ground. He who has the use of what is another's often neglects his own. (Ambrose, *Duties of the Clergy,* Bk. II, Ch. XVI, secs. 77, 79, NPNF 2, X, pp. 55-56)*

George Herbert urged that the pastor's care for the poor must seek diligently to avoid creating a syndrome of dependency relationships:

The Country Parson is full of charity; it is his predominant element. For many and wonderful things are spoken to thee, thou great virtue. To charity is given the covering of sins, I Pet. 4:8; and the forgiveness of sins, Matt. 6:14; Luke 7:47; the fulfilling of the law, Rom. 13:10; the life of faith, James 2:26; the blessings of this life, Prov. 22:9; Ps. 41:2; and the reward of the next, Matt. 25:35. In brief, it is the body of religion, John 13:35, and the top of Christian virtues, I Cor. 13. Therefore all of the parson's works relish of charity. When he rises in the morning, he bethinks himself what good deeds he can do that day, and presently does them; counting that day lost, wherein he has not exercised his charity.

He first considers his own parish; and takes care, that there be not a beggar or idle person in his parish, but that all be in a competent way of getting their living. This he effects either by bounty or persuasion or by authority; making use of that excellent statute which binds all parishes to maintain their own. If his parish be rich, he exacts this of them; if poor, and he able, he eases them therein. But he gives no set pension to any; for this in time will lose the name and effect of charity with the poor people, though not with God; for then they will reckon upon it, as on a debt, and if it be taken away, though justly, they will murmur and repine as much, as he that is disseized of his own inheritance. (Geo. Herbert, *CP,* Ch. XII, CWS, pp. 72-73)

The early pastoral writers were not unaware of the systemic syndromes of dependency that cause poverty to be intergenerational:

Therefore, because they are incapable of doing what they really prefer, they do the one thing of which they are capable. They give themselves to the upper classes in return for care and protection. They make themselves the captives of the rich and as it were, pass over into their jurisdiction and dependence.

However, I would not consider this serious or unbecoming, indeed, I would rather thank this public spirit of the powerful to whom the poor entrust themselves, if they did not sell these patrocinia, if, when they say they are defending the poor, they are contributing to humanity and not to greed. It is harsh and severe that the poor seem to be protected by this law in order to despoil them, and they defend the poor by this law in order to make them more wretched by defending them. For, all those who seem to be defended give to their defenders almost all their goods before they are defended; thus, in order that the fathers may have defense, the sons lose their heritage. The safety of the parents is secured by the penury of the offspring. (Salvian, *The Governance of God,* Bk. 5, sec. 8, FC 3, pp. 141-142)

Salvian in the fifth century recognized that an older generation could secure itself at the cost of burdening the ensuing generation, that the law could be used to despoil the poor, that greed could lurk under the disguise of "defending the poor," and that the syndrome of poverty could become intergenerational.

Martin Bucer, chief reformer of Strassbourg, developed an elaborate system for poor relief, without which, he said, "there can be no true communion of the saints." Yet he was aware that the worthiest of the poor were inclined to hide their poverty, and those most prone to deception would be inclined to exaggerate their poverty. Hence, it became necessary for the servants of the poor to make careful inquiry to discern the true condition of recipients:

Each church will have as many of these [deacons to provide for the poor] as is necessary to care for the needy, in proportion to its population and the numbers of the poor.

Their duty and office is contained under these headings: First, they should investigate how many really indigent persons live in each church for whom it is equitable for the church to provide the necessities of life. For the churches of Christ must exclude from their communion those who, when they can sustain themselves by their own power, neglect this and live inordinately, accepting borrowed food (II Thess. 3:6); it certainly is not the duty of the church to foster such people in their godless idleness. Against these, therefore, the saying should prevail: "Whoever does not work, let him not eat" (v. 10). . . . This horrifying pronouncement of the Holy Spirit should resound in the hearts of all: "If anyone does not look after his own, and especially his own household, he has denied the faith and is worse than an infidel" (I Tim. 5:8). For those whom the Lord has given to us in special close relationships fall particularly under the second great commandment, in which the whole law is contained and fulfilled: "Thou shalt love thy neighbor as thyself" (Matt. 22:39). For the Lord gives to each as neighbors in a special sense those whom he associates and unites to him by blood, marriage, domestic service, or other particular custom.

The first requirement of deacons in charge of giving of alms is to inquire as diligently as possible who are really in need and cannot themselves alleviate their own need, and who are the ones who either feign need or invite it by laziness and soft living, and who have or do not have neighbors who can or may undertake their care and provide for them. . . . For just as the wicked are never satisfied, and beggary knows neither moderation nor limit, so also reputable and prudent men dissimulate and conceal their need and judge whatever is provided for them by the churches to be too much. (Bucer, *De Regno Christi,* XIV, LCC XIX, p. 307)

Tax policy may greatly affect the life of the poor, who are often first to be burdened and last to be relieved:

But, surely, those who are wicked in one way are found moderate and just in another, and compensate for their baseness in one thing by goodness in another. For, just as they weigh down the poor with the burden of new tax reliefs; just as the lower classes are oppressed by new taxes, so they are equally relieved by tax mitigations. Indeed, the injustice is equal in taxes and reliefs, for, as the poor are the first to be burdened, so they are the last to be relieved. (Salvian, *The Governance of God*, Bk. 5, sec. 8, FC 3, p. 140)

IV ✹ FAITH AND POSSESSIONS

Spiritual formation may be hindered by wrong use of possessions. The pastor has a teaching role with respect to the use of temporal goods. The health of the soul is in part indicated by how one deals with one's possessions. The pastoral writers have shown a strong interest, on behalf of soul care, in how one understands one's possessions and uses them according to the rule of stewardship. The care of a soul does not take place in a temporal vacuum.

Valerian argued that genuine piety manifests itself in caring for the poor, and in using temporal resources responsibly. The pastor looks for practical ways of applying remedies for social hurts. It is a travesty upon prayer to pray for the poor and do nothing:

What does it profit to bewail another man's shipwreck if you take no care of his body which is suffering from exposure? Or what good does it do to torture your soul with grief over another's wound, if you refuse him a health-giving cup? These flattering remarks do not feed the hungry man; those bootless counsels do not clothe another's nakedness. What good does it do to apply soft poultices to an indigent man, if you will not give a bit of food to one on the point of dying from hunger? What kind of mercy is that, in which you desire the man to live, but are unwilling to save him in his need? Clearly, that piety is a cruel one which knows how to grieve over the wretched, but does not know how to help those about to perish. (Valerian, *Homilies,* Hom. 7, sec. 5, FC 17, p. 349)

In the early church, a lack of caring for the poor showed evidence of distorted, heretical teaching:

Observe well those who hold heterodox views about the grace of Jesus Christ which came to us—how opposite they are to God's purpose. For love they have not regard, none for the widow, none for the orphan, none for the distressed, none for the men imprisoned or released, none for the hungery or thirsty (Ignatius of Antioch, *To the Smyrnaeans,* sec. 6, *AF,* p. 121)

Athanasius described the cruelties to the poor perpetrated by the Arians. Since faith active in love requires care of the poor, Athanasius was convinced that a view so distorted as Arianism could not elicit caring faith. In his view, a broad callousness toward the poor stood as prime evidence that Arian magistrates were heretical, even though they claimed to be Christians, demonstrating that religious zeal could turn to madness:

When the Arians saw that the brethren readily ministered unto them and supported them, they persecuted the widows also, beating them on the feet, and accused those who gave to them before the Duke. This was done by means of a certain soldier named Dynamius. And it was well-pleasing to Sebastian, for there is no mercy in the Manichaeans; nay, it is considered a hateful thing among them to show mercy to a poor man. Here then was a novel subject of complaint; and a new kind of court now first invented by the Arians. Persons were brought to trial for acts of kindness which they had performed, he who showed mercy was accused, and he who had received a benefit was beaten; and they wished rather that a poor man should suffer hunger, than that he who was willing to show mercy should give to him. . . . They thought by treachery and terror to force certain persons into their heresy, so that they might be brought to communicate with them; but the event turned out quite the contrary. The sufferers endured as martyrdom whatever they inflicted upon them, and neither betrayed nor denied the true faith in Christ. . . . Human nature is prone to pity and sympathise with the poor. But these men have lost even the common sentiments of humanity; and that kindness which they would have desired to meet with at the hands of others, had they themselves been sufferers, they would not permit others to receive, but employed against them the severity and authority of the magistrates. . . . These things it is impossible for words to describe, for their cruelty surpasses all the powers of language. What terms could one employ which might seem equal to the subject? What circumstances could one mention first, so that those next recorded would not be found more dreadful, and the next more dreadful still? (Athanasius, *History of the Arians*, Part VII, secs. 61-63, NPNF 2, IV, p. 293)

The pastoral writers had a clear and shrewd grasp of the vulnerability of wealth. For no one, they argued, can possess anything absolutely:

Thus, we receive only the use of those possessions which we hold. We make use of the wealth loaned to us by God. We are, as it were, tenants by precarium. When departing from this world, whether we like it or not, we leave everything behind on earth. Since we are usufructory tenants, why do we attempt to take away and alienate from God's ownership what we cannot take with us? Why do we not use in good faith the little things given us by God? We hold property so long as He has allowed, we hold so long as He has permitted, He who has given us all. (Salvian, *The Four Books of Timothy to the Church,* Bk. 1, sec. 5, FC 3, p. 278)

Modern readers may find it odd that there is a vast literature in the pastoral tradition on the *disadvantages* of wealth. Pastoral writers have pointed to the tendency of possessions to turn into a personal burden of anxiety over having to protect them:

For the more a rich man possesses, the more worry he has. And, above all, because he has to bear the burden of anxiety alone, that which he acquires so eagerly and hoards so carefully is of more benefit to other people than it is to himself. In the fever of his anxiety he tosses unceasingly. He fears the failure of his revenues, for, though his property is great, no less so are the forces at work to dissipate it. He fears the violence of the mighty, doubts the honesty of his own household, lives in perpetual fear of the deceptions of strangers, and, since he knows himself hated by everyone because of his possessions, he tries to avert this by a wretched and unhappy sort of struggle against everyone. And so it comes about that, in cutting himself off from the common fellowship of everyone by this depraved pursuit, he becomes hateful to all men, and a stranger to their love. Moreover, he knows quite well that, if his material prosperity should fail him, he will receive no kindly compassion from anybody else. . . . As long as he keeps it, they speak ill of him; when he gives it away, they mock him with empty adulation, though he is hurt no less by being laughed at than by being cursed. (Hugh of St. Victor, *SSW,* pp. 164-165)

A non-possessive, detached attitude toward worldly goods was encouraged among clergy:

Although the Old Law granted to all copious means of obtaining wealth, nevertheless it bound all Levites and priests to a certain property limit and it did not permit them to possess either corn, or wine, or even any land for tillage.

From this it can be understood whether God wishes His clergy who now live in the Gospel to bequeath wealth, which He was unwilling that those placed in the Law should even possess, to worldly heirs after their own death. Hence, in the Gospel, the Saviour Himself pointed out to the clergy, not a voluntary duty of perfection as to others, but a commanded one. What do we read that He said to the young layman? "If you wish to go the whole way, go, sell your possessions, and give to the poor" (Matt. 19:21). What did He say to His clergy? He says: "Provide no gold, silver, or copper to fill your purse, no pack for the road, no second coat, no shoes, no stick" (Matt. 10:9-10).

See how great is the difference in both these salutary warnings of God. To the layman He says: "If you wish, sell what you possess," but to the cleric: "I do not wish you to possess." (Salvian, *The Four Books of Timothy to the Church,* Bk. 2, sec. 9, FC 3, pp. 306-307, NEB)*

V ❧ CARE OF WIDOWS

From the earliest decades of Christian pastoral care, widows have given much to the Christian community, and have been perceived as a central concern of Christian social service. The directions for care of widows given in 1 Tim. 5:3-16 indicate that widows had a well-defined social role in early Christianity.

It is clear from the pre-Nicene Apostolic Constitutions that widows were thought to share in the church's care of souls, especially by the efficacy of their prayers:

She that will attend to God will sit within, and mind the things of the Lord day and night, offering her sincere petition with a mouth ready to utter the same without ceasing. As therefore Judith, most famous for her wisdom, and of a good report for her modesty "never left the temple, but worshipped day and night, fasting and praying" (Luke 2:37); so also the widow who is like her will offer her intercession without ceasing for the Church to God. And God will hear her, because her mind is fixed on this thing alone, and is not disposed to be either insatiable, or covetous, or wasteful. When her eye is pure, and her hearing clean, and her hands undefiled, and her feet quiet, and her mouth prepared for neither gluttony nor trifling, but speaking the things that are fit, and partaking of only such things as are necessary for her maintenance. So, being serious, and giving no disturbance, she will be pleasing to God; and as soon as she asks anything, the gift will come to her. As Scripture says: "Then, if you call, the Lord will answer; if you cry to him, he will say, 'Here I am'" (Is. 58:9). Let such a one also be free from the love of money, free from arrogance, not given to filthy lucre, not insatiable, not gluttonous, but continent, meek, giving nobody disturbance, pious, modest, sitting at home, singing, and praying, and reading, and watching, and fasting; speaking to God continually in songs and hymns. (*Constitutions of the Holy Apostles,* Bk. III, Sec. I, ch. vii, ANF VII, p. 428, NEB)*

In a "Comforting Letter to a Widow," Menno Simons viewed widowhood as a calling to benefit others through hospitality, holy living, and prayer:

Much grace and peace, and a kind greeting!

Fervently beloved sister in the Lord, whom my soul cherishes and loves! Since the Lord has now called you to widowhood, my fatherly faithful admonition to you is, as my dear children, to walk as becomes holy women, and I hope that you may, even as the pious prophetess Anna, serve the Lord in the holy temple, that is, in His church with a new and upright conscience, with prayer and fasting, night and day serving the needy saints, which the virtuous widow of Sarepta in Sidon did for faithful Elijah in the time of drought and scarcity when she received him in her hospitality and fed him with her tiny bit of meal and oil. So shall the meal of the holy divine Word be not lacking in the vessel of your conscience, and the joyous oil of the Holy Spirit from your soul. (Menno Simons, Comforting Letter to a Widow, c. 1549, *CWMS*, p. 1028)

The vocation of the widow, accordingly, may not fit neatly into modern expectations, but there can be no doubt that in the early church the widow was regarded as having a distinctive, purposeful, significant vocation. Widows are especially called to a ministry of intercession for the whole community. Augustine, in his poignant letter to the widow Proba, sought to understand and describe the special ministry of intercession that may be given to the widow:

Pray in hope, pray in faith, pray in love, pray earnestly and patiently, pray as a widow belonging to Christ. For although prayer is, as He has taught, the duty of all His members, i.e. of all who believe in Him and are united to His body, a more assiduous attention to prayer is found to be specially enjoined in Scripture upon those who are widows. . . . Observe, however, what is written concerning the other Anna, the widow: she "departed not from the temple, but served God with fastings and prayers night and day" (Luke 2:36-37). In like manner, the apostle said in words already quoted, "She that is a widow indeed, and desolate, trusts in God and continues in supplications and prayers night and day" (1 Tim. 5:5). The Lord, when exhorting us to pray always and not to faint, made mention of a widow, who, by persevering importunity, persuaded a judge to attend to her cause. . . . Now what makes this work specially suitable to widows but their bereaved and desolate condition? Whosoever, then, understands that she is in this world bereaved and desolate as long as he is a pilgrim absent from his Lord, is careful to commit her widowhood, so to speak, to her God as her shield in continual and most fervent prayer. Pray, therefore, as a widow of Christ, not yet seeing Him whose help you implore. And though you are very wealthy, pray as a poor person, for you have not yet the true riches of the world to come, in which you have no loss to fear. . . . Regard yourself as desolate, even though all your family are spared to you, and live as you desire. (Augustine, *Letters,* CXXX, To Proba, Ch. XVI, secs. 29-30, NPNF 1, I, pp. 468-469)*

There are spiritual dangers faced by widows that require soul care, according to John Chrysostom. He thought that ministry to widows was shaped by social processes, inclinations and temperaments to some degree particular to widows, whose foibles and vices (here stereotyped) were not to be taken advantage of:

Widows, as a class, owing partly to their poverty, partly to their age, and partly to their sex, use an unbridled freedom of speech—to call it no worse! They scold out of season and find unnecessary fault and lament what they ought to be thankful for and criticize what they ought to welcome. The one in charge of them must bear it all politely and not be provoked by their inopportune fussing or their unreasonable complaints. For persons of this kind deserve to be pitied, not insulted, for their misfortunes. And it would be a mark of utter cruelty to take advantage of their misfortunes and add to the pain of poverty the pain of insult. (Chrysostom, *On the Priesthood,* Ch. III.16, p. 95)*

VI ❧ HOSPITALITY TO STRANGERS

The command to care for strangers is deeply rooted in Hebraic faith, which lived out of an awareness of having been met as strangers by the friendship of God:

Since therefore they were strangers in the land of Egypt, being by birth Hebrews from the land of Chaldaea—for at that time, there being a famine, they were obliged to migrate to Egypt for the sake of buying food there, where also for a time they sojourned; and these things befell them in accordance with a prediction of God—having sojourned, then, in Egypt for 430 years, when Moses was about to lead them out into the desert, God taught them by the law, saying, "You shall not oppress the alien, for you know how it feels to be an alien; you were aliens yourselves in Egypt" (Exod. 23:9). (Theophilus, *To Autolycus,* Bk. III, ch. x, ANF II, p. 114)

Hospitality is a mark of good pastoral care. The constant hospitality of the Anglican divine, Lancelot Andrewes, was described by Henry Isaacson:

From the first time of his preferment to means of any considerable value, even to his dying day, he was ever hospitable, and free in entertainment to all people of quality and worthy of respect, especially to scholars and strangers, his table being ever bountifully and neatly furnished with provisions, and attendants answerable, to whom he committed the care of providing and expending in a plentiful yet orderly way—himself seldom knowing what meat he had, till he came from his study to dinner, at which he would show himself so noble in his entertainment and so gravely facetious, that his guests would often profess they never came to any man's table where they received better satisfaction in all points, and that his Lordship kept Christmas all the year in respect of the plenty they ever found there. (Henry Isaacson, On Andrewes, *Miscellaneous Works,* pp. xxii-xxiv; in *Angl.,* p. 728)

Pastoral hospitality was thought to be as much an inner attitude of openness as an outward act of welcome:

Teach them to welcome strangers willingly rather than to do what they ought merely from necessity. Thus, in offering hospitality they will not reveal an inhospitable state of mind and in the very giving of welcome to a guest spoil their favor by wrong-doing. Rather, let hospitality be fostered by the practice of social duties and by services of kindness. Rich gifts are not asked of you, but a willing performance of duty, full of peace and harmonious agreement. A dinner of herbs is better with friendship and love than a banquet adorned with choice victuals, if sentiments of love are not there. (Ambrose, *Letters,* 35, To Bishop Vigilius, 385 A.D., FC 26, p. 176)

Ambrose thought that hospitality was a distinct gift and virtue of the good pastoral counselor:

Hospitality also serves to recommend many. For it is a kind of open display of kindly feelings, so that the stranger may not lack hospitality, but be courteously received, and that the door may be open to him when he comes. . . . This especially was Abraham's praise, for he watched at the door of his tent, that no stranger by any chance might pass by. He carefuly kept a lookout, so as to meet the stranger, and anticipate him, and ask him not to pass by. . . . Such is the favour in which hospitality stands with God, that not even the cup of cold water shall fail of getting a reward. You know that Abraham, in looking for guests, received God Himself to entertain. Similarly Lot received the angels. And how do you know that when you receive the needy you do not receive Christ? Christ may be in the stranger that comes, for Christ is there in the person of the poor, as He Himself says: "When I was hungry, you gave me food; when thirsty, you gave me drink" (Matt. 25:35); and "when in prison you visited me" (v. 37). (Ambrose, *Duties of the Clergy,* Bk. II, Ch. XXI, secs. 103-107, NPNF 2, X, pp. 59-60, NEB)*

Alan of Lille wrote this instruction to clergy on how to practice hospitality:

Paul says: "Do not neglect to practise hospitality." (Heb. 13:2). Peter, similarly: "Be hospitable to one another without grumbling" (1 Peter 4:9). And Isaiah: "Take wanderers and the needy into your house" (Is. 58:7). Hence Truth says: "I was a sojourner and you took me in" (Mt. 25:35). O man, Christ in his members cries at the gate and asks for hospitality. Take in the pilgrim on earth, that he may receive you rejoicing into the homeland. Abraham deserved to be given his son, because he entertained angels in the guise of sojourners. Lot, because he took in angels as if they were sojourners, deserved to be saved from the destruction of Sodom. The widow who in kindness of hospitality honored Elijah deserved to have her son restored to life. The disciples going to Emmaeus were enlightened through the teaching of Christ, but they deserved to be more fully and more perfectly illuminated by him through the service of hospitality.

O man, if you know yourself to be a stranger and pilgrim in this world, if you recognize your own condition of pilgrimage, do not refuse hospitality to the pilgrim. For, if you shut out the poor man of Christ from under your roof, you shut out Christ himself from the guesthouse of your heart. Hear what he himself says: "What you have done for one of the least of these my brothers, you have done for me" (Mt. 25:40). But hospitality should be joyful, munificent, showing humility, displaying generosity. For a great part of true hospitality is an unruffled countenance. (Alan of Lille, *The Art of Preaching,* ch. xxxvii, CSS 23, pp. 140-141)

The Christian view of hospitality was contrasted by Lactantius to the Stoic view. For hospitality is not to be viewed as a means to gain a return of some kind, but rather a simple means of doing good:

Hospitality is a principal virtue, as the philosophers also used to say. But those who insist upon thinking of it primarily as a source of advantage may miss the insight that hospitality essentially pertains to justice. Cicero says: "Hospitality was rightly praised by Theophrastus. For (as it appears to me) it is highly becoming that the houses of illustrious men should be open to illustrious guests." He has here committed the same error which he later did when he said that we must bestow our bounty on "suitable" persons. For the house of a just and wise man ought not to be open merely to the illustrious, but also to the lowly and abject. For those illustrious and powerful men cannot be in want of anything, since they are sufficiently protected and honoured by their own opulence. But the just person seeks to do nothing than that which is beneficial. Yet if the benefit is returned, it is destroyed and brought to an end; for we cannot possess in its completeness that for which a price has been paid to us. Therefore the principle of justice pertains especially to those benefits which have remained safe and uncorrupted. Benefits to others cannot be better sustained than when they are bestowed upon those who cannot pay one back in return for them. But in receiving illustrious men, Cicero looked to nothing else but usefulness. He pointed openly toward the advantage that he hoped to gain from hospitality. . . . It is not the part of a simple and open man to ingratiate himself in the favour of others, to pretend and allege anything, to appear to be doing one thing when he is doing another, to feign that he is bestowing upon another that which he is bestowing upon himself. (Lactantius, *The Divine Institutes,* Bk. VI, Ch. XII, ANF VII, p. 176)*

Athanasius, who was repeatedly forced to go into hiding to evade tyrants, took note of instances in early Christian antiquity where non-Christians have taken grave risks to protect Christians from persecution:

I have heard from our fathers, and I believe their report to be a faithful one, that long ago, when a persecution arose in the time of Maximian, the grandfather of Constantius, the Gentiles concealed our brethren the Christians, who were sought after, and frequently suffered the loss of their own substance, and had trial of imprisonment, solely that they might not betray the fugitives. They protected those who fled to them for refuge, as they would have done their own persons, and were determined to run all risks on their behalf. (Athanasius, *History of the Arians,* Part VIII, sec. 64, NPNF 2, IV, pp. 293-294)

Bonaventure viewed St. Francis as a consistent model of the radical intent of Christian love to embrace the outsider, and to identify with the alienated:

One day while he was riding on horseback through the plain that lies below the town of Assisi, he came upon a leper. This unforeseen encounter struck him with horror. But he recalled his resolution to be perfect and remembered that he must first conquer himself if he wanted to become a knight of Christ. He slipped off his horse and ran to kiss the man. When the leper put out his hand as if to receive some alms, Francis gave him money and a kiss. Immediately mounting his horse, Francis looked all around; but although the open plain stretched clear in all directions, he could not see the leper anywhere. . . . From that time on he clothed himself with a spirit of poverty, a sense of humility and a feeling of intimate devotion. Formerly he used to be horrified not only by close dealing with lepers but by their very sight, even from a distance; but now he rendered humble service to the lepers with human concern and devoted kindness in order that he might completely despise himself, because of Christ crucified, who according to the text of the

prophet was despised *as a leper* (Isa. 53:3). He visited their houses frequently, generously distributed alms to them and with great compassion kissed their hands and their mouths. (Bonaventure, *The Life of St.
Francis,* CWS, pp. 188-190)

VII ❧ SLAVERY

It has sometimes been argued that early Christian pastoral care witnessed
slavery without making any significant moral response. The following passages
indicate that care of souls included the care of those oppressed by slavery, and
in some cases that active resistance to the system of slavery was found in early
Christian pastoral care.

We begin with a powerful statement by John Chrysostom on the absurdity
of slavery, and an attempt to analyze the reasons why slavery has occurred.
Against those who would justify slavery as a natural expression of the human
condition, John Chrysostom argued that slavery was not part of the original
human condition as created by God:

> Should anyone ask, whence is slavery, and why it has found entrance
> into human life, (and many I know are both glad to ask such questions,
> and desirous to be informed of them), I will tell you. Slavery is the fruit
> of covetousness, of degradation, of savagery; since Noah, we know, had
> no servant, nor had Abel, nor Seth, no, nor they who came after them.
> The thing was the fruit of sin, of rebellion against parents. (Chrysostom,
> *Homilies on Ephesians,* Hom. XXII, NPNF 1, XIII, p. 159)

Similarly Augustine argued that servitude is not God's original intention for
any human being:

> He did not intend that His rational creature, who was made in His
> image, should have dominion over anything but irrational creation—not
> man over man, but man over the beasts. And hence the righteous men
> in primitive times were made shepherd of cattle rather than kings of
> men. . . . The condition of slavery is the result of sin. And this is why
> we do not find the word "slave" in any part of Scripture until righteous
> Noah branded the sin of his son with this name. It is a name, therefore,
> introduced by sin and not by nature. The origin of the Latin word for
> slave is supposed to be found in the circumstance that those who by the
> law of war were liable to be killed were sometimes preserved by their
> victors, and were hence called servants. And these circumstances could
> never have arisen save through sin. . . . But our Master in heaven says,
> "Everyone who sins is a slave to sin" (John 8:34). And thus there are
> many wicked masters who have religious men as their slaves, and who
> are yet themselves in bondage; for "they themselves are slaves of

depravity—for a man is a slave to whatever has mastered him" (2 Pet. 2:19). (Augustine, *The City of God,* Bk. XIX.15, NPNF 1, II, p. 411, NIV)*

One of the canons of the Apostolic Constitutions makes it clear that during the third and fourth century collections for the poor were being used to free slaves:

And such sums of money as are collected from them in the manner aforesaid, appoint to be laid out in the redemption of the saints, the deliverance of slaves, and of captives, and of prisoners, and of those that have been abused and of those that have been condemned by tyrants to single combat and death on account of the name of Christ. (*Constitutions of the Holy Apostles,* Bk. IV, Sec. I, ch. ix, ANF VII, p. 435)

It is noteworthy that a single exception was made to allow believers to attend pagan spectacles—on behalf of freeing slaves:

You are also to avoid their public meetings, and those sports which are celebrated in them. For a believer ought not to go to any of those public gatherings, unless to purchase a slave and redeem a soul. (*Constitutions of the Holy Apostles,* Bk. II, Sec. VII, ch. lxii, ANF VII, p. 424)*

Many former slaves became leading pastors of the early Christian community (among them the author of the *Shepherd of Hermas,* Pius, and Callistus, cf. Jerome, Letter lxxxii, NPNF 2, VI, p. 172), and canon law specifically provided a procedure for transition from bondage to ordination:

If any servant should appear to be worthy of receiving ordination, as our Onesimus appeared, and his masters agree and liberate him, and send him out of their house, he may be ordained (*Apostolic Canons,* Canon LXXXII, The Seven Ecumenical Councils, NPNF 2, XIV, p. 599)*

Although the New Testament injunction to "obey the powers that be" (Rom. 13:1) prevented early Christian pastors from engaging in any act of political insurrection, or in promoting rebellion on scriptural grounds (Council of Gangra, A.D. 325-381, Canon III, The Seven Ecumenical Councils, NPNF 2nd, Vol. XIV, p. 93), there were many slaves redeemed from bondage through the activities of Christian pastors. Palladius mentions eight thousand slaves freed (early fifth century, Lausaic History, Ch. 119). The deeper intention of the New Testament witness—that Jesus brings good news of release for captives and liberty for the oppressed (Luke 4:18), that in Christ there is no distinction between bond and free (Gal. 3:28), and that slave and master become brothers in Christ (Philemon)—did not receive wider political implementation and embodiment until the eighteenth century and following.

6 Care of the Dying

No act of soul care is more personal, more profound, more meaningful than care for the dying. The pastor is present in the midst of the approach of death, because Christ is present. Since God's own Word accompanies the faithful into the valley of the shadow of death, the representative ministry of that Word seeks to make Christ's presence knowable and experienced.

I ❧ Preparation for Death

The pastor's care for the dying begins not merely when serious illness occurs, but long before then, in assisting persons to reflect and meditate on their own vulnerability and mortality.

As it is impossible for a starving man not to think of bread, so it is impossible for a man eager to be saved not to think of death and judgment. (Climacus, *The Ladder of Divine Ascent,* Step 26, sec. 43, p. 195)

Contrary to modern cultural patterns that avoid any thought of death, John Climacus (c. 570-649) commended this daily act of remembrance that we are mortal as an aid to wisdom: Consider each day as if it were the last.

As of all foods, bread is the most essential, so the thought of death is the most necessary of all works. The remembrance of death amongst those in the midst of society gives birth to distress and meditation, and even more, to despondency. But amongst those who are free from noise, it produces the putting aside of cares and constant prayer and guarding of the mind. . . . He who with undoubting trust daily expects death is virtuous; but he who hourly yields himself to it is a saint. . . . The day is not sufficient to repay in full its own debt to the Lord.
It is impossible, someone says, impossible to spend the present day devoutly unless we regard it as the last of our whole life. And it is truly astonishing how even the Greeks have said something of the sort, since they define philosophy as meditation on death. (Climacus, *The Ladder of Divine Ascent,* Step 6, sec. 4, and Step 7, secs. 23-24, pp. 66-67, 69)

164

One way to prepare for death is to reflect upon the nature of sleep, learn to sleep, give up conscious control in sleep, and meditate on the trust assumed in sleep. In his treatise *On the Soul,* Tertullian speculated broadly on the analogy between sleep and death:

God has foreshadowed everything in the dispensation of His providence. . . . Thus He presents to your view the human body touched by the friendly gift of repose, stretched out by the kindly need of rest, immovably still in sleep as it was before life began and will be after life has closed, in proof of man's condition when he first was formed and after he has been buried—as if sleep awaited the soul before it was first bestowed on man and after it has been taken away.

In sleep, the soul acts as if it were present elsewhere for its future departure in death. . . . Thus, when the body awakens, it portrays before your eyes the resurrection of the dead by returning to its natural functions. There you have the natural explanation and the rational nature of sleep. Thus, by the image of death, you are introduced to faith, you nourish hope, you learn both how to live and die, you learn watchfulness even when you are asleep. (Tertullian, *On the Soul,* Ch. 43, secs. 11-12, FC 10, p. 278)

Preparation for death requires the focusing of consciousness upon the reality of death. That wisdom does not lie in death-avoidance is an ancient theme of pastoral care. Death is so much a part of human existence that it is one of the few experiences absolutely shared by all human beings. There could be no ongoing natural order without death, no birth without death, no life without death making space for new life. Yet, as Peter Chrysologus observed, before death, death does not exist, and after death there can be no grief.

To die is a matter of nature; it is necessary to perish. Our ancestors lived for us; we live for future men; no one lives for himself. It is the part of virtue to will what cannot be avoided. Willingly accept that to which you are being pressed with reluctance. Before death arrives it does not exist, but, when it has come, one no longer knows that it has arrived. Therefore, do not grieve about the loss of something about which, once you have lost it, you will have no more grief. (Peter Chrysologus, *Sermons,* 101, FC 17, p. 162)

The so-called "vulture syndrome," in which the family of a wealthy individual await his lingering death, is not a new phenomenon. It was encountered in the fifth-century ministry of Salvian the Presbyter, who spoke plainly about the phoniness of interpersonal relationships amid death which have been long distorted by inordinate wealth. He offered this pattern of pastoral care for those who are drawing toward death with twisted affections for their possessions. Those who have accumulated wealth are to be pastorally counseled to look candidly toward the loss of all that they have accumulated as an act of the realistic affirmation of life's limits. These words are spoken as if in preparation for death to one with much property:

Behold, behold, you are on the point of death. You are about to depart from the home of your body, not knowing where you will go, where you are to be taken. . . . This means: what will it profit you, O most unhappy man, if you possess the whole world or leave it to your near relatives, if you suffer the loss of your salvation and soul? (cf. Matt. 16:26). Damnation of the soul takes everything completely with it. Neither can a man possess anything whatsoever, who loses himself with the loss of his soul. . . . Though your Lord proclaims these facts to you who are already dying, O man, whosoever you are, you close your mind and ears and assert your faith with words alone. You think words suffice for you, instead of deeds. You think you have a sufficient strong basis in faith, if you seem to honor with lying words the God whom you despise in deeds and works. . . . Indeed, the reason for which you cannot listen to God is great. Your relatives and family stand around you when you are sick. The rich matrons of the family stand by. The distinguished men of the family stand close to you. A crowded multitude clothed in silken and ornamented garments lay siege to the bed of your sickness. . . . Indeed, you see men most rich and splendidly dressed weeping for you. You see people wearing a made-up sad appearance, but festive in dress, making a display of sorrow for you. . . . You see the faces of all fastened on you, as if they were blaming the slowness of your death.

O you, most unhappy and most wretched man, whose last breath is longed for by such a great crowd of relatives! I know and am very certain that the prayers of such people are of no avail whatsoever with God. . . . Scorn them who are lusting after your heritage and already dividing your substance among themselves. They love your patrimony, but not you. They curse you in greed for your possessions. While they impatiently thirst after your wealth, they hate you and regard your presence as a rival and adversary to themselves. They think the fact that you are alive is a barrier and obstacle to their greed. . . . Do not fear them, therefore; do not be terrified of them. Raise up your mind and take on the strength of holy power. For, if they strive so hard in order that you may perish, why do you not strive harder so that you may live? Be comforted and consult your own interests with an unchangeable mind. (Salvian, *The Four Books of Peter to the Church*, Bk. 3, secs. 18-19, FC 3, pp. 348-353)

Meditation on death is a central theme of the pastoral literature. This is dissonant with modern death avoidance habits. What follows is an example, admittedly somewhat extreme. Dame Julian of Norwich commended for Christian spiritual exercise the meditation on Christ's act of dying love. Although the realism of the medieval forms of these meditations are too stark for death-aversive moderns, there is something to be learned even from their exaggerations:

After this, Christ showed a part of his passion near his death. I saw his sweet face as if it were dry and bloodless, pale with dying. Next it became more pale and dead-looking with increasing weakness, and then it turned more dead-looking, to blue and then to brown blue as the flesh continued more and more to die. For his passion was visible to me most completely in his blessed face, particularly in his lips. There I saw these four colors, though they were previously fresh, ruddy, lifelike and pleasing to my sight.

This deep dying caused a change pitiful to watch. The nose clogged and dried as I watched, and the sweet body was brown and black, changed entirely from his own fair, lifelike color to dry dying. . . . This showing of Christ's sufferings filled me full of pain. I knew well that he had suffered only once, but that he willed to show his suffering to me, and to fill me with the experience of it. (Juliana of Norwich, *Revelations of Divine Love*, Chs. 16-17, pp. 108-111)

The contemplative here is beholding, picturing, imagining, and empathizing with the gradual dying of the Lord, as a spiritual exercise in preparation for one's own dying and trusting in the resurrection.

Reflection upon one's spiritual legacy is as important as writing a will for one's property, when death draws near:

I thought it would be well, my dearest companion in the service of the Lord, to give some consideration, even at this early date, to the manner of life that ought to be yours after my departure from this world, should I be called before you. I trust your own loyalty to follow the suggestions I shall offer. For if we pursue our purposes with such diligence when worldly issues are at stake, even drawing up legal instruments in our anxiety to secure each other's interests, ought we not to be all the more solicitous in providing for the welfare of those we leave behind us when there is question of securing their best advantage in matters concerning God and Heaven? Ought we not, acting as it were before the event, bequeath them legacies of loving-counsel and make clear our will respecting goods which constitute the eternal portion of their heavenly inheritance? (Tertullian, *To His Wife*, ACW 13, p. 10)

No temporal good is safe from accident. Nothing can be possessed or guaranteed in perpetuity. The pastor does well to remind the flock in advance of death of the vulnerability of all finite things:

For what flood of eloquence can suffice to detail the miseries of this life? Cicero, in the Consolation on the death of his daughter, has spent all his ability in lamentation; but how inadequate was even his ability here? For when, where, how, in this life can these primary objects of nature be possessed so that they may not be assailed by unforeseen accident? Is the body of the wise man exempt from any pain which may dispel pleasure, from any disquietude which may banish repose? The amputation or decay of the members of the body puts an end to its integrity, deformity blights its beauty, weakness its health, lassitude its vigour, sleepiness or sluggishness its activity—and which of these is it that may not assail the flesh of the wise man? (Augustine, *The City of God*, Bk. XIX.4, NPNF 1, II, p. 401)

As a rule, no one will die without love unless he has lived without loving. In Raymon Lull's *Book of the Lover and the Beloved* (i.e., of Christ and himself), the medieval poet dealt metaphorically with the relation of love and death, love and the acts of love, love and suffering, and love and God:

The Lover went to seek his Beloved and he found a man who was dying without love. And he said, "What a great sadness it is that any man should die without love!" So the lover said to the dying man, "Tell me, why are you dying without love?" And he answered, "Because I have lived without love."

The Lover asked his Beloved, "Which is greater—loving, or love itself?" The Beloved answered, "In creatures, love is the tree, and its fruit is loving. The flowers and leaves are trials and griefs. And in God, love and loving are one and the same thing, without either griefs or trials." (Raymon Lull, *The Book of the Lover and the Beloved*, secs. 85-86, p. 34)

That communion should be made available to the dying is a very old tradition pre-dating this canon of the Council of Nicaea:

Concerning the departing, the ancient canonical law is still to be maintained, to wit, that, if any man be at the point of death, he must not be deprived of the last and most dispensable Viaticum. (Council of Nicaea, A.D. 325, Canon XIII, The Seven Ecumenical Councils, NPNF 2, XIV, p. 29)

Viaticum refers to eucharist "on the way" toward imminent death. In proclaiming the grace that enables the faithful to face death non-defensively, the pastor does well to remain aware of the limits of his own faith. Among the soundest of medieval preachers on readiness for death is Guerric of Igny:

Brethren, how beautiful and blessed it is not only to be without fear of death but with the assurance of a good conscience to triumph over it; in the spirit and words of Martin [of Tours], to rebuke the foul beast if he dares to present himself, to open joyfully to the Judge when he comes and knocks. At that hour you may see unfortunates like me tremble, begging for a truce and having it denied them; wanting to buy the oil of penance for a sorrowing conscience and not having enough time. (Guerric of Igny, *Liturgical Sermons,* Vol. I, 3.1, CF 8, p. 15)

Unction (from *ungere,* to anoint) refers to the act of anointing with blessed oil to confer spiritual strength. By the medieval period, exteme unction (i.e., the ministry of readiness for death) was considered a sacrament in the western church, and was defined concisely as follows by Bonaventure:

As to the sacrament of extreme unction, this must be held: that it is the sacrament of those departing from this life, preparing and disposing them for perfect health; it is also effective in expunging venial sins and for the recovery of health if this is for the good of the infirm person. For the integrity of this sacrament, simple but consecrated oil is required, as are the recitation of prayers and the anointing of seven designated parts of the one who is sick, namely, the eyes, ears, nostrils, lips, hands, feet, and loins. This sacrament should be given only to adults who desire it, who are imminently in danger of death, and then only by the administration of a priest. From this it is evident that there is a sevenfold difference between this sacrament and confirmation, namely, in effect, matter, form, recipient, minister, place, and time. (Bonaventure, *Breviloquium,* p. 204)

Confirmation and unction are distinguishably similar in that confirmation readies one for life in Christ while unction readies one for death in Christ, in hope of resurrection. The aged Simeon was regarded as the biblical prototype of faithful preparation for death. We return to the wonderful homiletic imagination of Guerric of Igny, speaking to his monastic flock:

"When the days of purification were completed they took Jesus to Jerusalem" [Luke 2:22]. O how fortunate is he of whom it can be said: "the days of his purification have been completed," so that nothing remains for him but that they should carry him to the heavenly Jerusalem and offer him to the Lord. Such was Simeon, that old man of ours, as desirable as he was full of desires. Long before, I think, the days of his purification had been completed. Today the days of his expectation are also completed, so that now, according to the Lord's word, nothing remains for him after seeing Christ of the Lord, Christ the peace of God and man, but to be allowed to depart in peace and sleep in that same peace. This means to be taken to Jerusalem, the vision of eternal peace, and to be set before the Lord to contemplate the peace which surpasses all our understanding. O Simeon, man of desires, your desire of good things is fulfilled. O blessed old man, your youth is renewed like the eagle's. . . . The desire of the blessed old man is, then, fulfilled in good things, for the whole of his expectation and desire was the Expectation of the Nations and he who is desired by them. . . . Brethren, purge out the old leaven while you have time for purging; so that when the time comes for your purgation to be completed you too may be able to receive that joy which now fills Simeon's soul. (Guerric of Igny, *Liturgical Sermons,* Vol. I, 19.1, CF 8, pp. 127-128)

II ❧ SEARCHING FOR MEANING IN DEATH

That death is not absurd, and therefore that death, despite its pain and loss, has meaning, is a recurrent theme of pastoral care. If Christian faith had not been established so decisively on the resurrection of Jesus, the issue of the potential absurdity or meaning of death might have been more avoidable. But no Christian pastor will serve long without being asked: Why did this one die? And what relation does this death have to faith in the life, death, and resurrection of Jesus Christ? As the question is unavoidable today, so it was for classical pastoral thinkers. How did the early pastors think about meaning in death?

Lactantius (c. 240–c. 320) explored the fantasy question as to whether the human situation might have been improved if God had not created us subject to disease or death. The Epicurean (hedonic) position offered the more simple answer (definitely yes), to which Lactantius replied (no):

The Epicureans also complain that humanity is liable to diseases and to untimely death. They are indignant, it appears, that they are not born gods. . . . Since, therefore, humanity had to be formed by God as mortal and abiding in time, the matter itself required that human persons be made with a vulnerable and earthly body. . . . But let us suppose the opposite, as they wish, that it were possible that humans not be born under those conditions by which they are subject to disease or death, unless, having completed the course of their lives, they shall have arrived at the extremity of old age. They do not, therefore, see what would be the consequence if it were so arranged that it would be plainly impossible to die . . . They who complain of the frailty of humanity, make this complaint especially, that they were not born immortal and everlasting. (Lactantius, *On the Workmanship of God,* Ch. IV, ANF VII, pp. 284-285)*

The problem of Epicureanism (which moderns recognize as naturalistic hedonism) is that human beings tend to not affirm being creatures, even hating their status as creatures, wishing to be gods. Lactantius argued that creatureliness requires mortality, and a falsely based disgust with creatureliness requires a disgust at mortality. The answer lies in a new beginning point: seeing humanity from the viewpoint of divine providence:

> The Epicureans do not see the order of consequences because they have already committed an error in the main point itself. For the divine providence having been excluded from the affairs of human beings, it necessarily followed that all things were produced of their own accord. Hence they invented the theory of the fortuitious meeting and colliding together of minute seeds. For they did not see the origin of things. And when they had thrown themselves into this difficulty, necessity now compelled them to think that souls were born together with bodies, and thus were necessarily extinguished together with bodies. For they had already made the assumption that nothing was made by the divine mind. And they were unable to prove their theory in any other way than by showing that there were some things in which the system of providence appeared to be at fault. Therefore they blamed those things in which providence wonderfully expressed its divinity, such as those things which I have related concerning diseases and premature death. They ought rather to have considered (disease and death being assumed) what would be the necessary consequences if human beings were not liable to diseases, and did not require a dwelling, nor clothing. (Lactantius, *On the Workmanship of God,* Ch. IV, ANF VII, p. 285)*

The necessary consequence of being given finite life by God is being given that life within the limits of time, which implies birth and death. It is not an occasion of shame, in the Christian tradition, either to be born or to die.

The questions to Christian faith that are being raised today by modern skepticism were anticipated to a large degree by Epicurus, who sought to reassure his followers that death is hardly worth the wise person's thinking about because it is out of one's control. As modern skepticism relentlessly probes the vulnerable edges of modern Christian views of death, so did Epicurean views of death vex classical Christian views of death. Tertullian's response was that it is impossible to wish death away:

> It remains for us to speak of death, so that our discussion of the soul may end where the soul completes itself. Epicurus, according to his well-known doctrine, believed that death did not pertain to us. He says: "Whatever is dissolved is without sensation, and what is without sensation is nothing to us." But it is not death (but man) who experiences dissolution and the loss of sensation. And even Epicurus admits that the

man who dies suffers something. Besides, it is ridiculous to say that so great a force as death means nothing to the man for whom it means the separation of the soul and body and the end of sense knowledge. . . . If death means nothing to us, then neither does life. (Tertullian, *On the Soul,* Ch. 42, secs. 1-2, FC 10, pp. 274-275)*

Later in the same treatise, Tertullian reflected on why we die:

It is the acknowledged opinion of the whole human race that death is "the debt we owe to nature." This has been established by the voice of God, and everything that is born must sign this contract. This should be enough to refute the foolish opinion of Epicurus, who refused to acknowledge such a debt. It demolishes the mad doctrine of Menander, the Samaritan heretic, who thinks not only that death is no concern of his disciples but that it will never touch them. He pretends to have received from the Supreme Power on high the privilege that all whom he baptizes become immortal, incorruptible, and immediately ready for the resurrection. . . . What is this wonderful bath of Menander? Why, he seems to be a comedian, too. How does it happen that so few people know about it or use it? (Tertullian, *On the Soul,* Ch. 50, secs. 2-4, FC 10, p. 289)

Luther pointed out that death has the ironic meaning that it ends our proneness to evil:

With this one thing the Scriptures, which hold all others in contempt, associate fear, saying, "Remember thy end, and thou shalt never do amiss" (Ecclus. 7:40). Behold, how many meditations, how many books, how many rules and remedies have been brought together, in order, by calling to men's minds this one evil. . . . It is God's gift that we are moved thereby. For what true Christian will not even desire to die, and much more to bear sickness, seeing that, so long as he lives and is in health, he is in sin, and is constantly prone to fall, yea, is falling every day, into more sins. . . . God has appointed death, that this evil might come to an end, and that death might be the minister of life and righteousness. (Luther, *The Fourteen of Consolation,* WML I, pp. 120-122)

John Donne vigorously resisted the notion that a particular time of death comes directly and unambiguously from God:

How little soever I be, as "God calls things that are not, as though they were," I, who am as though I were not, may call upon God . . . Why dost thou melt me, scatter me, pour me like water upon the ground so instantly? . . . My God, my God, thou wast not wont to come in whirlwinds, but in soft and gentle air. Thy first breath breathed a soul into me, and shall thy breath blow it out? Thy breath in the congregation, thy word in the church, breathes communion and consolation here, and consummation hereafter; shall thy breath in this chamber breathe dissolution and destruction, divorce and separation? Surely it is not thou, it is not thy hand. The devouring sword, the consuming fire, the winds from the wilderness, the diseases of the body, all that afflicted Job, were from the hands of Satan; it is not thou. It is thou, thou my God, who hast led me so continually with thy hand, from the hand of my nurse, as that I know thou wilt not correct me, but with thine own hand. (John Donne, *Devotions,* pp. 14-15)

III ❧ Pastoral Care of the Terminally Ill

Lactantius offered a primitive description of what is occurring in death. Even while the body is failing the sensibility of the soul may remain, so the pastor does well not to assume that in the presence of a dying person that such a person has no levels of awareness, even though the limbs are growing cold:

They who are slain by disease are longer able to breathe forth their spirit. As the limbs grow cold, the soul is breathed out. For, since the living dimension of human existence is contained in the basic constitution of the blood (analogous to light being contained in oil), that living dimension is in death being consumed by the heat of fevers, so the extremities of the limbs are growing cold. The more slender veins are extended into the extremities of the body, and the extremely small streams are dried up when the fountain-spring fails.

It must not, however, be supposed that, because the perception of the body fails, the sensibility of the soul is extinguished and perishes. For it is not the soul that becomes senseless when the body fails, but it is the body which becomes senseless when the soul takes its departure, because it draws all sensibility with it. (Lactantius, *The Divine Institutes,* Bk. VII, Ch. XII, ANF VII, p. 209)*

The modern notion that anger and acceptance are stages of awareness prior to death was in a preliminary way anticipated by Richard Baxter:

Even the stoutest sinners will hear us on their death-bed, though they scorned us before. They will then let fall their fury, and be as gentle as lambs, who were before as untractable as lions. . . . It is a remark of Augustine, "He cannot die badly who lives well; and scarcely shall he die well who lives badly." (Baxter, *RP,* p. 103)

When an arduous dying process is anticipated, it may become a spiritual ordeal for all concerned. Calvin wrote of his own approaching death:

It may be thought that I am too precipitate in concluding my end to be drawing near, and that I am not so ill as I persuade myself; but I assure you, that though I have often felt myself very ill, yet I have never found myself in such a state, nor so weak as I am. When they take me to put me in bed, my head fails me and I swoon away forthwith. There is also this shortness of breathing, which oppresses me more and more. I am altogether different from other sick persons, for when their end is approaching their senses fail them and they become delirious. With respect to myself, true it is that I feel stupefied, but it seems to me that God wills to concentrate all my senses within me, and I believe indeed that I shall have much difficulty and that it will cost me a great effort to die. I may perhaps lose the faculty of speech, and yet preserve my sound sense. (Calvin, Testament, *SW*, pp. 40-41)

Lactantius reported inspiring deathbed communications and out of body experiences that in his view argued for the hypothesis of the immortality of the soul:

Why should I mention that we see many of the dying, not complaining that they are undergoing dissolution, but testifying that they are passing out and setting forth on their journey and walking? And they signify this by gesture, or if they still are able, they express it also by their voice. From which it is evident that it is not a dissolution which takes place, but a separation; and this shows that the soul continues to exist. (Lactantius, *The Divine Institutes,* Bk. VII, Ch. XII, ANF VII, p. 210)

The stage later described by Elisabeth Kübler Ross as the mature stage of acceptance of death was observed and described earlier by classic pastoral writers. Here is such a report from Luther, teaching the affirmability of death in the light of Christian hope:

The Christian's view of death is different from that of the great unbelieving mass of people in the world. Christians look at it as a journey and departure out of this misery and vale of tears (where the devil is prince and god) into yonder life, where there will be inexpressible and glorious joy and eternal blessedness. Diligently they study the art of looking at death in this way. Daily they practice it, and earnestly they ask our dear Lord Christ to grant them a blessed hour of departure and to comfort them in it with His Spirit, that they may commit their soul to Him with true faith, understanding, and confession. To such people death is not terrible but sincerely welcome. (Luther, *Ascription*, WA 48, pp. 63f.; in WLS 1, p. 382)

Those who are dying still often have remarkable powers to minister to others:

When the hour of his passing was approaching, he had all the friars who were there called to him and, consoling them for his death with words of comfort, he exhorted them with fatherly affection to love God. He long continued speaking about practicing poverty and patience and about keeping the faith. (Bonaventure, *The Life of St. Francis,* CWS, pp. 318-319)

Even in the case of a prolonged death, such as in the extended terminal illness of St. Catherine of Siena, this witness may be sustained to the end.

Meanwhile, every morning, after communion, she arose from the earth in such a state that anyone who had seen her would have thought her dead, and was thus carried back to bed. Thence, after an hour or two, she would arise afresh, and we would go to St. Peter's, although a good mile distant, where she would place herself in prayer, so remaining until vespers, finally returning to the house so worn out that she seemed a corpse. These were her exercises up till the third Sunday in Lent, when she finally succumbed, conquered by the innumerable sufferings, which daily increased, and consumed her body. (Catherine of Siena, *Transit of the Saint,* p. 337)

When persons experience an extremely hard death, it is not fitting that their whole life shall be judged by their last actions or words:

People often—especially at the time of death—turn so weak that their minds become and remain unsettled until the end. Speaking to them at length about the Word of God is futile. Such a death also seems to be dangerous and to offer little hope or comfort. . . . We are to look at the life these people led while they were still well and their reason was sound. If you find that they loved the Word, often heard it preached, did not despise the Sacrament, confessed and loved the Lord Jesus and comforted themselves with Him, then be satisfied, although they suddenly pass away. For though slips of weakness and sin were found in their lives, trust in the Lord Christ was there too. (Luther, "Sermon on Luke 7," WLS 1, p. 370; cf. Erlangen ed., vol. 3, pp. 552ff.)

Baxter offered these practical instructions on the pastoral on caring for the dying:

I will not stop to tell you particularly what must be done for men in their last extremity; but shall notice only three or four things, as specially worthy of your attention. (1) Do not wait till their strength and understanding are gone, and the time so short that you scarcely know what to do; but go to them as soon as you hear they are sick, whether they send for you or not. (2) When the time is so short, that there is no opportunity to instruct them in the principles of religion in order, be sure to ply the main points . . . . (3) If they recover . . . . put them in mind of what they said when they were stretched on a sick-bed. . . . (Baxter, *RP*, pp. 103-104)*

IV ❦ DEATH

The pastor is sometimes present when death occurs. The duty may evolve upon the pastor to care simultaneously for the dying and the grieving. Historically, the care of souls has viewed death not in a despairing way, but in the mode of hope.

What does it mean "to die"?

To die is to lose vital power, and to become henceforth breathless, in-animate, and devoid of motion, and to melt away into those [component parts] of [its] substance. But this event happens neither to the soul, for it is the breath of life, nor to the spirit, for the spirit is simple and not composite, so that it cannot be decomposed, and is itself the life of those who receive it. (Irenaeus, *Against Heresies,* Bk. V, Ch. VIII, sec. i, ANF I, p. 533)

Augustine spoke of the particular ambiguity of the notion of the "death" of the immortal soul:

Although the human soul is truly affirmed to be immortal, yet it also has a certain death of its own. For it is therefore called immortal, because, in a sense, it does not cease to live and to feel; while the body is called mortal, because it can be forsaken of all life, and cannot by itself live at all. The death, then, of the soul takes place when God forsakes it, as the death of the body when the soul forsakes it. (Augustine, *The City of God,* Bk. XIII.2, NPNF 1, II, p. 245)

While the body is destined for destruction, the soul is by definition that of the self that lives, and hence lives beyond the destruction of the body:

The function of death is obvious to all—the separation of the body and soul. There are some people, however, who . . . think that souls sometimes remain united to bodies after death. . . . But, not a particle of the soul can remain after death in the body, which itself is destined for destruction when time has finally dismantled the stage on which the body has played its part. (Tertullian, *On the Soul,* Ch. 51, secs. 1-4, FC 10, pp. 290-291)

There is much confusion amid modern medical technology as to when death occurs. According to classical pastoral teaching, if any life remains, death has not occurred:

Death also would have to be divided into stages if the soul could be divided into parts, with a part of the soul dying later; thus, a portion of death would have to wait behind for the part of the soul that remained. . . . If death is not complete, it is not death; if any of the soul is still there, there you have life. (Tertullian, *On the Soul,* Ch. 51, secs. 5-8, FC 10, p. 292)

Does the soul have senses after death?

It's true that souls hear, feel, and see after death, but how this occurs we don't understand. . . . If we try to figure this out according to [our conception of time in] this life, we're fools. (Luther, *Table Talk,* LW 54, #5534, pp. 446-447)

The reason why the sacrament is not to be offered to a dead body is set forth in the African Code of 419:

It also seemed good that the Eucharist should not be given to the bodies of the dead. For it is written: "Take, Eat," but the bodies of the dead can neither "take" nor "eat." Nor let the ignorance of the presbyters baptize those who are dead. (African Code, A.D. 419, Greek Canon XX, The Seven Ecumenical Councils, NPNF 2, Vol. XIV, p. 451)

V ✠ CHRISTIAN BURIAL

Grief may occur over any loss. Learning to deal with loss openly and realistically may serve the soul well when facing the loss of a loved one.

Maximus the Confessor grasped the powerful insight that grief is a feeling applicable to any loss, and not only to the loss of a person:

Some owners own with detachment; therefore, stripped of their goods they do not grieve, like the men who accepted with joy the seizure of their goods. Some own with attachment; wherefore, about to be stripped, they become grief-stricken, like the rich man in the Gospel, who "went away sad" (Matt. 19:22). And if in fact they are stripped they grieve till death. (Maximus the Confessor, *The Four Centuries of Charity,* Ch. 2, sec. 89, ACW 21, p. 171)

The *Recognitions of Clement* is an early Christian epic, a third century fictional treatment of the ministry of Peter. On one occasion it described the grief of Peter's congregation over the thought that he might leave them and not be seen by them again, and how the spirit of grief passes, as if contagious, from one to another. Pastors who serve the grieving must learn to deal with their own grief:

Therefore, on the day appointed, when they had ranged themselves before Peter, they said: "Do not think, O Peter, that it is a small grief to us that we are to be deprived of the privilege of hearing you." . . . When those twelve who had been sent forward had gone, Peter entered, according to custom, and stood in the place of disputation. And a multitude of people had come together, even a larger number than usual; and all with tears gazed upon him, by reason of what they had heard from him the day before, that he was about to go forth on account of Simon. Then, seeing them weeping, he himself also was similarly affected, although he endeavoured to conceal and to restrain his tears. But the trembling of his voice, and the interruption of his discourse, betrayed that he was distressed by similar emotion. (Clementina, *Recognitions of Clement,* Bk. III, ch. lxx, ANF VIII, pp. 132-133)

Among many early Christian prayers for the departed, here is one that reveals the liturgical heart of pastoral care for the grieving:

Let us pray for our brethren that are at rest in Christ, that God, the lover of mankind, who has received his soul, may forgive him every sin, voluntary and involuntary, and may be merciful and gracious to him, and give him his lot in the land of the pious that are sent into the bosom of Abraham, and Isaac, and Jacob, with all those that have pleased Him and done His will from the beginning of the world, whence all sorrow, grief, and lamentation are banished. Let us arise, let us dedicate ourselves and one another to the eternal God, through that Word which was in the beginning. (*Constitutions of the Holy Apostles,* Bk. VIII, Sec. IV, ch. xli, ANF VII, p. 497)

Early Christian burial was usually underground and without pomp:

Having summoned those who were there—they were two in number who had remained in the mountain fifteen years, practising the discipline and attending on Antony on account of his age—he said to them, "I, as it is written, go the way of the fathers, for I perceive that I am called by the Lord" (cf. Josh. 23:14). Be watchful and destroy not your long discipline, but as though now making a beginning, zealously preserve your determination. For you know the treachery of the demons, how fierce they are, but how little power they have. So do not fear them, but rather ever breathe Christ, and trust Him. Live as though dying daily. . . . Do not permit anyone to take my body to Egypt, lest perhaps they might place me in a pretentious tomb. For to avoid this I entered into the mountain and came here. Moreover you know how I always admonish those who had this custom, and exhorted them to cease from it. Bury my body, therefore, and hide it underground yourselves, and let my words be observed by you that no one may know the place but you alone." . . . And no one knows to this day where it was buried, save those two only. (Athanasius, *Life of Antony,* secs. 90-93, NPNF 2, IV, pp. 220-221)

Burial expenses were to be kept to a minimum. As shown in this early third-century account, Christians sought to protect the grieving from abuses and to prevent their grief from being exploited:

Let there be no heavy charge (*barein*) for burying people in the cemetery (*koimeterion*) for (*gar*) it is for all the poor; except (*plen*) they shall pay the hire of a workman (*ergates*) to him who digs and the price of the tiles (*keramos,* pl.). And (*de*) the bishop shall provide for the watchman there who takes care of it from what they offer at the assemblies, so that there be no charge to those who come to the place (*topos*). (Hippolytus, *The Apostolic Tradition,* Sec. XXXIV.1-2, pp. 60-61)

The duty to bury the poor was viewed as a signal office of piety. Since there were many displaced persons in the ancient world who were separated from their families, the burial of strangers was viewed as a solemn Christian duty, acting as surrogate family to the deceased, transcending all divisions of nation, class, or race:

The last and greatest office of piety is the burying of strangers and the poor, which subject those teachers of virtue and justice have not touched upon at all. For they were unable to see this, who measured all their duties by utility. . . . Therefore we will not suffer the image and workmanship of God to lie exposed as a prey to beasts and birds, but we will restore it to the earth, from which it had its origin; and although it be in the case of an unknown man, we will fulfil the office of relatives, into whose place, since they are wanting, let kindness succeed. (Lactantius, *The Divine Institutes,* Bk. VI, Ch. XII, ANF VII, p. 177).

The central pastoral task at the funeral—to comfort—is essentially an act of *presence*:

When one nears death . . . the priests shall chant and read unto them, until the hour when the death is borne forth, while they each hour pray, that comfort may be given to the sorrow of their hearts. (*Athanasian Canons,* sec. 100, p. 65).

In these passages we see that pastoral care of the dying and bereaved had many of the same challenges and tasks in its earlier as in its later stages of development. Its aim is to prepare the faithful for death, to interpret its meaning, to teach what death alone can teach, to comfort those experiencing loss, and to be present both personally and liturgically amid bereavement.

VI ❧ PASTORAL CARE IN ESCHATOLOGICAL PERSPECTIVE

The care of persons takes place within a vision of history that looks toward history's end. The perfection in love of which early pastors spoke is less a static *perfectus* than a dynamic *teleiosis*. "This is for us the perfection of love, to have confidence on the day of judgment, and this we can have, because even in this world we are as he is" (1 John 4:17). Perfect love, the final end of the Christian life, is seen under the aspect of hope. Early Christian pastors thought often and deeply about this end-time vision of fulfillment, and viewed this perspective as an integral part of their care for the living and the dying.

We call it "perfection" as needing nothing further, for what more does he need who possesses the knowledge of God? It would indeed be out of place to call something that was not fully perfect a gift of God. He is perfect; therefore, the gifts He bestows are also perfect. . . . The very fact that we believe in Him and are reborn is perfection of life. For God is by no means powerless. As His will is creation, which is called the universe, so His desire is the salvation of men, which is called the Church. He knows whom He has called. Whom He has called He has willed to save. Whom he has called he is able to save. The Apostle said: "It is written in the prophets: 'And they shall all be taught by God'" (John 6:45). Wouldn't it be wrong, therefore, for us to consider imperfect the teaching that is given by God? (Clement of Alexandria, *Christ the Educator,* Bk. I, Ch. 6.26-27, FC 23, pp. 26-27)*

For what do we pray when we say "Thy Kingdom come"?

The one who prays that the kingdom of God may come prays that the kingdom of God may spring up in him, bear fruit, and be rightly perfected. This is because every saint is ruled by God, obeys the spiritual laws of God, and dwells in himself as in a well-ordered city. The Father is present with him, and Christ rules with the Father in his perfected soul in accord with the verse we called to mind a little earlier, "We will come to him and make our home with him" (Jn. 14:23; cf. Mt. 13:23; Mk. 4:20; Lk. 8:15). And I think that the kingdom of God may be understood to be the blessed condition of the governing mind and the right ordering of wise thoughts. (Origen, *On Prayer,* XXV.1, CWS, p. 132)

The question of whether it is possible to imitate God in this life is raised by the Epistle of Diognetus. The metaphor becomes one of service as God has served humanity:

Do not be surprised that a man should be an imitator of God; he can, since God has willed it so. But happiness is not to be found in dominating one's fellows, or in wanting to have more than his weaker brethren, or in possessing riches and riding rough-shod over his inferiors. No one can become an imitator of God like that, for such things are wholly alien to His greatness. But if a man will shoulder his neighbour's burden; if he be ready to supply another's need from his own abundance; if, by sharing the blessings he has received from God with those who are in want, he himself becomes a god to those who receive his bounty—such a man is indeed an imitator of God. (*Epistle to Diognetus,* sec. 10, ECW, p. 181)

What God requires is not impossible:

God has, to be sure, commanded only what is possible. I concede that: but not every one of us can achieve all these possibilities. (Jerome, LCF, p. 188)

Theophilus painted a second century portrait of men and women living a mature and fulfilled Christian life. It does not seem outside of the range of possibility:

With them temperance dwells, self-restraint is practised, monogamy is observed, chastity is guarded, iniquity exterminated, sin extirpated, righteousness exercised, law administered, worship performed, God acknowledged: truth governs, grace guards, peace screens them; the holy word guides, wisdom teaches, life directs, God reigns. (Theophilus, *To Autolycus,* Bk. III, ch. xv, ANF II, p. 115)

Assuming the metaphor of a mirror that has the capacity to reflect God in this life, Theophilus argued that a darkened mirror reduces the capacity to make such a reflection:

When there is rust on the mirror, it is not possible that a man's face be seen in the mirror; so also when there is sin in a man, such a man cannot behold God. Do you, therefore, show me yourself, whether you are not an adulterer, or a fornicator, or a thief, or a robber, or a purloiner; whether you do not corrupt boys; whether you are not insolent, or a slanderer, or passionate, or envious, or proud, or supercilious; whether you are not a brawler, or covetous, or disobedient to parents; and whether you do not sell your children; for to those who do these things God is not manifest. (Theophilus, *To Autolycus,* Bk. I, ch. ii, ANF II, p. 89)

Gregory of Nyssa showed why the virtuous life is easier to describe than attain, and why it is less a state than a process of growth:

You requested, dear friend, that we trace in outline for you what the perfect life is. Your intention clearly was to translate the grace disclosed by my word into your own life, if you should find in my treatise what you are seeking. I am at an equal loss about my treatise or to show in my life the insights of the treatise. And perhaps I am not alone in this. Many great men, even those who excel in virtue, will admit that for them such an accomplishment as this is unattainable. . . .

Certainly whoever pursues true virtue participates in nothing other than God, because he is himself absolute virtue. Since, then, those who know what is good by nature desire participation in it, and since this good has no limit, the participant's desire itself necessarily has no stopping place but stretches out with the limitless. . . .

One should not disregard the commandment of the Lord which says, *Therefore be perfect, just as your heavenly father is perfect.* For in the case of those things which are good by nature, even if men of understanding were not able to attain to everything, by attaining even a part they could yet gain a great deal. We should show great diligence not to fall away from the perfection which is attainable but to acquire as much as is possible. To that extent let us make progress within the realm of what we seek. For the perfection of human nature consists perhaps in its very growth in goodness. (Gregory of Nyssa, *The Life of Moses,* CWS, p. 31)

There is a radical difference, yet potential correspondence, between human ideas of beauty and goodness, and God's own beauty and goodness. God's way of measuring is not to be judged by the measure of our passing, changing, alterable feelings.

Some think that God also, whom they measure with the measure of their own feelings, judges the same thing that wicked and foolish men judge to be subjects of praise and blame, and that He uses the opinions of men as His rule and measure, not taking into account the fact that, by reason of the ignorance that is in them, every creature falls short of the beauty of God. For He draws all things to life by His Word, from their universal substance and nature. For whether He would have good, He Himself is the Very Good, and remains in Himself; or, whether the beautiful is pleasing to Him, since He Himself is the Only Beautiful, He beholds Himself, holding in no estimation the things which move the admiration of men. That, verily, is to be accounted as in reality the most beautiful and praiseworthy, which God Himself esteems to be beautiful, even though it be contemned and despised by all else—not that which men fancy to be beautiful. (Methodius, "Three Fragments on the Passion of Christ," II, ANF VI, p. 400).

Origen proposed a simple test for asking oneself whether one is on the right road, the way to maturity and fulfillment in the Christian life:

We are on the road to perfection if straining forward to what lies ahead we forget what lies behind (cf. Phil. 3:14). (Origen, *On Prayer,* XXV.2, CWS, p. 133)

Clement of Alexandria argued that the good can be done habitually, and that there is no arbitrary limit to the power of grace to elicit good through the will:

This, then, is the perfect man's first form of doing good, when it is done not for any advantage in what pertains to him, but because he judges it right to do good; and the energy being vigorously exerted in all things, in the very act becomes good; not, good in some things, and not good in others; but consisting in the habit of doing good, neither for glory, or, as the philosophers say, for reputation, nor from reward either from men or God; but so as to pass life after the image and likeness of the Lord. . . . And when he shall do good by habit, he will imitate the nature of good, and his disposition will be his nature and his practice. (Clement of Alexandria, *The Stromata, or Miscellanies,* Bk. IV, Ch. XXII, ANF II, pp. 434-435)

Clement thought that it was not too much to expect that God's intention for humanity could be fulfilled:

Who then is perfect? First one who abstains from doing harm . . . . Those who strive after perfection, according to the apostle, must "put no stumbling block in anyone's path" (2 Cor. 6:3) . . . . "Since we have these promises, dear friends, let us purify ourselves from everything that contaminates body and spirit, perfecting holiness out of reverence for God" (2 Cor. 7:1). . . . The incomparably powerful God himself is providing the gifts to make this possible: "It was he who gave some to be apostles, some to be prophets, some to be evangelists, and some to be pastors and teachers, to prepare God's people for works of service, so that the body of Christ may be built up until we all reach unity in the faith and in the knowledge of the Son of God and become mature, attaining to the whole measure of the fullness of Christ" (Eph. 4:11-13). We are therefore to strive to reach this maturity as befits one who knows, and to be as completely responsive as we can while still abiding in the flesh. Our study in this life is to seek to concur as completely as possible with the will of God, so that the full nobility and maturity of the fullness of Christ may be restored in us. . . . Such being the case, the prophets are perfect in prophecy, the righteous in righteousness, and the martyrs in confession, and others in preaching. This is not to say that they do not share in other common virtues, but rather that they are proficient in those in which they are gifted. (Clement of Alexandria, *The Stromata, or Miscellanies,* Bk. IV, Ch. XXI, ANF II, pp. 433-434, NIV)*

Christianity does not assert that all believers are precisely equal in their responsiveness to God, or that all are at exactly the same point on the road from new birth to mature faith:

His disciples, accommodating their teaching to the minds of the people, according to the Master's will, delivered on the one hand to those who were able to receive it, the teaching given by the perfect master to those who rose above human nature. While on the other the side of the teaching which they considered was suitable to men still in the world of passion and needing treatment, they accommodated to the weakness of the majority, and handed over to them to keep sometimes in writing, and sometimes by unwritten ordinances to be observed by them. Two ways of life were thus given by the law of Christ to His Church. The one is above nature, and beyond common human living; it admits not marriage, child-bearing, property nor the possession of wealth, but wholly and permanently separate from the common customary life of mankind, it devotes itself to the service of God alone in its wealth of heavenly love! And they who enter on this course, appear to die to the life of mortals, to bear with them nothing earthly but their body, and in mind and spirit to have passed to heaven. Like some celestial beings they gaze upon human life, performing the duty of a priesthood to Almighty God for the whole race, not with sacrifices of bulls and blood, nor with libations and unguents, nor with smoke and consuming fire and destruction of bodily things, but with right principles of true holiness, and of a soul purified in disposition, and above all with virtuous deeds and words; with such they propitiate the Divinity, and celebrate their priestly rites for themselves and their race. Such then is the perfect form of the Christian life. And the other more humble, more human, permits men to join in pure nuptials and to produce children, to undertake government, to give orders to soldiers fighting for right; it allows them to have minds for farming, for trade, and other more secular interests. (Eusebius, *The Proof of the Gospel,* Bk. I, Ch. 8, pp. 48-49)

This study of care for the dying, and of classical pastoral care, concludes with a moving passage from Aelred of Rievaulx (1109-1167), who thought that the care of souls ends eschatologically only at an ironic point at which soul care has gone full circle, wherein those who have passed on from this life continue to care for those of us who remain in life and time. Aelred wrote a dialogue with an inquirer in which he discussed what happens in the departure of those perfected in faith:

John: That is true. Proceed with what you have begun about the departure of perfect souls. Aelred: We have said that as soon as some souls depart from the body they see themselves in the likeness of their bodies and experience punishment or consolation in places akin to corporeal places. But once the perfect soul, which lacks no perfection— such as that of a martyr—unloads the burden of its body, it finds itself outside corporeal limits, perhaps beyond the limits of all bodily forms and likeness, and in the Creator himself. It has no need of any creature either to travel from west to east or from earth to heaven, for wherever it is, it is, without a shadow of doubt, in him who fills heaven and earth with his luminous vision, his blissful love, his blessed eternity. John: Are some souls not more perfect than others, or are they all equal in one perfection? Aelred: Why did you think of asking this question? Did Our Lord not say: "In the house of my Father there are many mansions"? (Jn. 14:2)—thus distinguishing even between the perfect by a difference of degrees. John: How can anyone be perfect if another is considered more perfect? It is accepted that anyone who lacks something is not perfect. Whatever one is deficient in is possessed more fully by another. . . . To restore this ruin God in his compassion put forward a plan as marvellous as it was powerful. For how could he make a greater show of power than by bringing flesh to that place from which the spirits had fallen, and by finding a place for man in the heavens while the angels went plunging down to hell? . . . However, they will enjoy equal bliss, because as one love operates in all, each will have what all have, and all will have what each has. But that state of perfection will come about only when this corruptible body has put on incorruption and this mortal body has put on immortality. In the meantime, either the living are tested in this life, or the dead are released from their attachment to sin, or the less perfect, awaiting the redemption of their bodies, are consoled in their particular mansions. The living stand in need of our wise counsel, while the others by our prayers and the holy sacrifice of the altar or by almsgiving and the chanting of psalms have their glory increased or their sufferings diminished. Those, however, who are in all things perfect according to the state of souls after death, have no need of our care: it is they who plead for us. (Aelred of Rievaulx, *Dialogue on the Soul*, CFS 22, pp. 144-146)

Conclusion

THIS VOLUME OF THE Classical Pastoral Care Series reviews the tasks of soul care amid key moments of human crisis. These situations are characterized both by hazard and opportunity. We have sought to listen to classical pastoral wisdom amid six phases or series of human crises: interpersonal conflict, physical illness, despair over suffering, the crises of marriage and family living, poverty, and death. The pastor is called to be present in all these critical moments, mediating the presence of God amid human difficulties, and the love of God amid human distortions.

The crises faced by neolithic men and women do not differ fundamentally from the crises faced by modern men and women. When the stone age man stood beside the grave of his wife, the situation is fundamentally the same as when that occurs in modern life. Persons in ancient times also had interpersonal conflicts, had to deal with compulsive and addictive behaviors, and vocational decisions. They were not exempt from thoughts of suicide. They fell ill, and had to deal with the limits and vexations of suffering. They too faced problems with sexual bonding and parenting, abortion, adultery, and divorce. They faced poverty and economic vulnerability. They grieved over the loss of loved ones no less than we.

In all these ways the human condition has not changed. Christian pastoral care has now had two millennia of experience in dealing with these crises. Modern pastoral care stands to gain much by listening carefully to, even if in tension with, these remarkable sources.

Abbreviations

AAS   Acta Apostolicae Sedis, Acts of the Apostolic See. Rome, 1909ff.; follows Acta Sanctae Sedis. 41 vols. Rome, 1865–1908.

AC   Acta Conciliorum. Edited by J. Hardouin. 11 vols. Paris, 1714–1715.

ACO   Acta Conciliorum Oecumenicorum. Edited by E. Schwartz. 4 vols. Strassburg, 1914; Berlin, Leipzig, 1924–1971.

ACW   Ancient Christian Writers. Edited by J. Quasten, J. C. Plumpe, and W. Burghardt. 44 vols. New York: Paulist Press, 1946–1985.

AF   *The Apostolic Fathers.* Edited by J.N. Sparks. New York: Thomas Nelson, 1978.

AF-Ltft   The Apostolic Fathers. Edited by J. B. Lightfoot, revised by J. R. Harmer. London, New York: Macmillan, 1907.

ANF   Ante-Nicene Fathers. Edited by A. Roberts and J. Donaldson. 10 vols. 1866–1896. Reprint ed., Grand Rapids: Eerdmans, 1979.

Angl.   *Anglicanism, The Thought and Practice of the Church of England, Illustrated from the Religious Literature of the Seventeenth Century.* Edited by P. E. More and F. L. Cross. London: S.P.C.K., 1935.

AS   Acta Sanctorum. Edited by Camadet. 61 vols. Paris and Rome, 1863–83; first two volumes, Antwerp, 1643ff.

ASS   Acta Sanctae Sedis. 41 vols. Rome, 1865–1908; continued with Acta Apostolicae Sedis, 1909ff.

ASSB   Acta Sanctorum Ordinis S. Benedicti. Edited by J. Mabillon. 9 vols. Paris, 1668–1701.

BC   *The Book of Concord* (1580). Edited by T. G. Tappert. Philadelphia: Muhlenberg Press, 1959.

BCP   *Book of Common Prayer* (1662 unless otherwise noted). Royal Breviar's edition. London: S.P.C.K., n.d.

BKV   Bibliothek der Kirchenväter. Edited by F. Reithmayer and V. Thalhofer. Auswahl der vorzüglichsten patristischen Werke in deutscher Übersetzung. 90 vols. Kempten, 1869–1888.

BMKS   *Die Bedeutung der Medizin für die kirchliche Seelsorge im Selbstverständnis de sogenannten Pastoralmedizin: Ein bibliographisch-historische Untersuchung,* by Heinrich Pompey, Freiburg: Herder, 1968.

BOC   Bibliotheca Orientalis Clementino-Vaticana. Edited by J. S. Assemani. 4 vols. Rome, 1719–1728.

BPEC   Bibliotheca Patrum Ecclesiae Catholicae. Oxford: James Parker, 1853ff.

BPR   *Book of Pastoral Rule.* Gregory the Great, NPNF 2, XII, pp. 1–72.

BSP   Bibliotheca sanctorum Patrum. Edited by M. de la Bigne, later J. Vizzini. Rome, 1902ff.; continued in MBVP.

BVP   Bibliotheca veterum patrum antiquorumque scriptorum ecclesiasticorum. Edited by A. Galland. 14 vols. Venice, 1765–81.

CC   *Creeds of the Churches.* Edited by John Leith. Richmond: John Knox Press, 1979.

CCC   *Creeds, Councils, and Controversies.* Edited by J. Stevenson. London: S.P.C.K., 1966.

CCCM   Corpus Christianorum, Continuatio Mediaevalis. Turnhout, Belgium: Editions Brepols, 1966ff.

CCG   Corpus Christianorum. Series Graeca. Turnhout, Belgium: Editions Brepols, 1953ff.

CCL   *Code of Canon Law.* Edited by J. Coriden, T. Green, and D. Heintschel. New York: Paulist Press, 1985.

CE   Catholic Encyclopedia. 17 vols. New York: Encyclopedia Press, 1907–22.

CFHB   Corpus Fontium Historiae Byzantinae. 20 vols. Center for Byzantine Studies, Dumbarton Oaks, Washington, DC.

CFS   Cistercian Fathers Series. 44 vols. Kalamazoo, MI: Cistercian Publications, 1968ff.

CIC   Corpus Iuris Canonici. Edited by A. Friedberg. Leipzig, 1897; 2nd ed., Graz, 1955.

CLRC   Courtenay Library of Reformation Classics. 5 vols. Appleford, Abingdon, Berkshire, England: Sutton Courtenay Press.

COC   Creeds of Christendom. Edited by P. Schaff. 3 vols. New York: Harper & Bros., 1919.

COCL   Classics of the Contemplative Life. Edited by J. M. Hussey. 8 vols. London: Faber and Faber, 1960ff.

CPT   Cambridge Patristic Texts. Edited by A. Mason. Cambridge, 1899ff.

CR   Corpus Reformatorum. Melanchthon, vols. 1–28, ed. K. G. Bretschneider and E. Bindseil, Brunswick, 1834–60; Calvin, vols. 29–87, ed. G. Baum, E. Cunitz, and E. Reuss, Brunswick, 1863–1900; Zwingli, vols. 88ff., ed. E. Egli and G. Finsler, Berlin, 1905ff.

CS   *The Curate of Souls.* Edited by John R. H. Moorman. London, SPCK, 1958

CSCO   Corpus Scriptorum Christianorum Orientalium. Edited by J. Chabot, I. Guidi, H. Hyvernat, and B. Carra de Vaux. Louvain, Paris, 1903ff. There are four series: Syriac, Coptic, Arabic, and Ethiopic.

CSEL Corpus Scriptorum Ecclesiasticorum Latinorum. Edited by Academy of Vienna. 78 vols., 1866ff.; the "Vienna Corpus," reprinted by Johnson Reprint Corporation, New York.

CSHB Corpus Scriptorum Historiae Byzantinae. 50 vols. Edited by B. G. Niebuhr. Bonn, 1828–97.

CSS Cistercian Studies Series. 68 vols. Kalamazoo, MI: Cistercian Publications, 1968ff.

CST *Christian Social Teachings*. Edited by G. Forrell. New York: Doubleday, 1966.

CT The Church Teaches: Documents of the Church in English Translation. Edited by J. F. Clarkson et al. St Louis: Herder, 1955.

CW Carl G. Jung, Collected Works. 19 vols. Princeton, NJ: Princeton University Press, 1959ff.

CWMS *Complete Writings of Menno Simons* (c. 1496–1561). Edited by John C. Wenger. Scottdale, PA: Herald Press, 1956.

CWS Classics of Western Spirituality. 30 vols. to date. Edited by Richard J. Payne et al. New York: Paulist Press, 1978ff.

DDGC *Disciplinary Decrees of the General Councils*. Edited by H. J. Schroeder. St. Louis: Herder, 1937.

DIECH *Documents Illustrative of English Church History*. Edited by H. Gee and W. J. Hardy, 1896.

DNB *Dictionary of National Biography* (Great Britain).

ECF *Early Christian Fathers*. Edited by H. Bettenson. London: Oxford University Press.

ECW Early Christian Writers: The Apostolic Fathers. Translated by Maxwell Staniforth. London: Penguin Books, 1968.

EETS Early English Text Society. London, 1894ff.

ERS English Recusant Literature, 1558–1640. Edited by D. M. Rogers. 320 vols. London: The Scolar Press, 1970ff.

ES Enchiridion Symbolorum, Definitionum et Declarationum de Rebus Fidei et Morum. Edited by H. Denzinger, and later by C. Bannwart, I. B. Umberg, and K. Rahner, 1952ff. 31st ed., Freiburg, 1960.

ET English translation.

ETM Enchiridion Theologicum, or A Manual for the Use of Students of Divinity. 4 vols. Oxford: J. Fletcher, 1797.

FC Fathers of the Church. Edited by R. J. Deferrari. 69 vols. Washington, DC: Catholic University Press, 1947ff.

FIP Franciscan Institute Publications. Edited by E. M. Buytaert. 8 vols. St. Bonaventure, NY: The Franciscan Institute, 1950–55.

FER The Fathers for English Readers. 15 vols. London: SPCK, 1878–1890.

GCS Die Griechischen Christlichen Schriftsteller der ersten drei Jahrhunderte. Berlin: Akademie Verlag, 1897ff.

HC *A History of the Councils of the Church,* by Charles J. Hefele. Greek texts, transl., and commentary by W. R. Clark. Edinburgh: T. & T. Clark, 1895.

Heppe *Reformed Dogmatics,* by Heinrich Heppe. London: Allen & Unwin, 1959.

Inst. Institutes of the Christian Religion, by John Calvin. LCC XX-XXI. Philadelphia: Westminster Press, 1960.

KJV King James Version, 1611 (also called the Authorized Version).

LACT Library of Anglo-Catholic Theology. 99 vols. Oxford University Press, 1841–63.

LCC Library of Christian Classics. 26 vols. Edited by J. Baillie, J. T. McNeill, and H. P. Van Dusen. Philadelphia: Westminster Press, 1953–61.

LCF *Later Christian Fathers.* Edited by H. Bettenson. London: Oxford University Press, 1970.

LF A Library of Fathers of the Holy Catholic Church. Edited by E. B. Pusey, J. Kebel, J. H. Newman, and C. Marriott. 50 vols. Oxford: J. H. Parker, 1838–88.

Loeb Loeb Classical Library. Edited by Page, Capps, Rouse. Cambridge, MA: Harvard University Press, 1912ff.

LPT Library of Protestant Thought. Edited by John Dillenberger. 13 vols. New York: Oxford University Press, 1964–72.

LW Luther's Works. Edited by J. Pelikan and H. T. Lehmann. 54 vols. St. Louis: Concordia, 1953ff.

LXX Septuagint Version (Greek Old Testament).

MBVP Magna Bibliotheca Veterum Patrum. 14 vols. Cologne, 1616; continued by BSP. Later re-edited and supplemented in Maxima bibliotheca veterum patrum et antiquorum scriptorum ecclesiasticorum. 27 vols. Lyons, 1677; 2 vols., Paris, 1703; Index, Geneva, 1707.

MGH Monumenta Germaniae Historica. Edited by Georg Heinrich Pertz. 29 vols. Hanover and Berlin, 1872–98.

MPG J. B. Migne, ed. Patrologia Graeca. 162 vols. Paris: Migne, 1857–76.

MPL J. B. Migne, ed. Patrologia Latina. 221 vols. Paris: Migne, 1841–1865. General Index, Paris, 1912.

MPLS J. B. Migne, ed. Patrologia Latina: Supplementum. 4 vols. Edited by A. Hamman. Turnhout, Belgium: Editions Brepols.

MWS *Ministry, Word, and Sacrament: An Enchiridion,* by Martin Chemnitz (1595). St. Louis: Concordia, 1981.

NE *A New Eusebius: Documents Illustrative of the History of the Church to A.D. 337.* Edited by J. Stevenson (based on B. J. Kidd). London: S.P.C.K., 1957.

NEB New English Bible.

NIV New International Version.

NPB   Nova Patrum Bibliotheca. Edited by A. Mai. 8 vols. Rome, 1844-71.

NPNF   A Select Library of the Nicene and Post-Nicene Fathers of the Christian Church. 1st Series, 14 vols; 2nd series, 14 vols. Edited by H. Wace and P. Schaff. New York: Christian, 1887-1900. Reprint ed., Grand Rapids: Eerdmans, 1982ff.

OCC   Our Christian Classics. Edited by James Hamilton. London: Nisbet, 1858.

PA   Patres Apostolici. Edited by F. X. Funk. 2nd ed., 2 vols. Tübingen: Laupp, 1901.

PMS   Patristic Monograph Series. Philadelphia Patristic Foundation. 9 vols., 1968ff.

PO   Patrologia Orientalis. Edited by R. Graffin and F. Nau. 28 vols. Paris, 1903ff.

POS   S.S. Patrum opuscula selecta. Edited by H. Hurter. Innsbruck, Series I, 1865-1885, 48 vols; Series 2, 1884-1892, 6 vols.

PS   Patrologia Syriaca. Edited by R. Graffin. 3 vols. Paris, 1894ff.

PTS   Patristische Texte und Studien. Edited by K. Aland and W. Schneemelcher. 12 vols. Berlin: Walter de Gruyter.

PW   Practical Works, by Richard Baxter. 23 vols. London: James Duncan, 1830.

RAC   *Rules and Advices to the Clergy of the Diocese of Nown and Connor,* by Jeremy Taylor (1661), Works, ed. R. Heber, 1839, vol. xiv.

RD   *Reformed Dogmatics.* Edited by J.W. Beardslee. Grand Rapids: Baker, 1965.

RSV   Revised Standard Version.

SAOE   *Saint Augustine on Education.* Edited by G. Howie. Chicago: Henry Regnery, 1969.

SC   *Spiritual Conferences,* by St. Francis de Sales (1628). Westminster, MD: Newman, 1943.

SCG   Summa contra Gentiles, On the Truth of the Catholic Faith, by Thomas Aquinas. 4 vols. New York: Doubleday, 1955-57.

SCAC   Sacrorum Conciliorum Amplissima Collectio. Edited by J. D. Mansi. 31 vols. Florence, 1759-98; revised and continued by L. Petit and J. B. Martin. 53 vols. Lyons, Paris, 1899-1927.

Schmid   *The Doctrinal Theology of the Evangelical Lutheran Church,* by Heinrich Schmid. 3rd ed., Minneapolis: Augsburg, 1899.

SC   Sources chrétiennes. Edited by H. de Lubac and J. Danielou. Paris: Editions du Cerf, 1941ff.

SED   Standard English Divines. 19 vols. Oxford: Parker, 1855ff.

SLH   Scriptores Latini Hiberniae. Institute for Advanced Studies. Dublin, 1955ff.

SSW   *Selected Sacred Writings,* by Hugh of St. Victor. London: Faber and Faber, 1962.

SW   *John Calvin, Selections from His Writings.* Edited by John Dillenberger. Missoula, MT: Scholars Press, 1975.

TCL   Translations of Christian Literature. Edited by Sparrow Simpson and Lowther Clarke. London: SPCK, 1917ff.

TD   Textes et Documents pour l'Etude Historique du Christianisme. Edited by H. Hemmer and P. Lejay. Paris, 1904ff.

TG   *Theology of God — Sources.* Edited by K. Kehoe. New York: Bruce, 1971.

TPW   Taylor's Practical Works, by Jeremy Taylor. 2 vols. London: H. G. Bohn, 1854.

Trent   *Canons and Decrees of the Council of Trent* (1545–1563). Edited by H. J. Schroeder. St. Louis: Herder, 1941 (cf. J. Waterworth transl., in P. Schaff, *Creeds of Christendom*).

TRS   *A Treasury of Russian Spirituality.* Edited by G. P. Fedotov. Belmont, MA: Nordland, 1975.

TS   Texts and Studies. Edited by A. Robinson. Cambridge, 1891ff.

TU   Texte und Untersuchungen zur Geschichte der altchristlichen Literatur. Edited by O. von Gebhardt and A. Harnack. 15 vols. Leipzig, 1882–1897; New Series, 1897–1906, 15 vols.; Third Series, ed. A. Harnack and C. Schmidt, 1907ff.

VSH   Vitae Sanctorum Hiberniae. Edited by C. Plummer. 2 vols. Oxford, 1910.

WA   Weimarer Ausgabe, D. Martin Luthers Werke. Kritische Gesamtausgabe. Weimar, 1883ff.

WBD   *Webster's Biographical Dictionary.* Springfield, MA: Merriam, 1976.

W-Br.   Weimarer Ausgabe, D. Martin Luther. Briefwechsel, Kritische Gesamtausgabe. Weimar, 1930ff. (Letters)

WLS   What Luther Says. Edited by E. Plass. 3 vols. St. Louis: Concordia, 1959.

WML   Works of Martin Luther. Philadelphia Edition. 6 vols. Philadelphia: Muhlenberg Press, 1943.

WA-T   Weimarer Ausgabe, D. Martin Luther. Tischreden, Kritische Gesamtausgabe. Weimar, 1912ff. (*Table Talk*)

WSD   *Writings on Spiritual Direction.* Edited by J. M. Neufelder and Mary C. Coelho. New York: Seabury Press, 1982.

Appendix: The Pastoral Writers

Selected Biographical Summaries and Bibliography

These biographical sketches focus selectively on pastoral contributions and writings, varying in length according to their importance and frequency of reference in this collection. The biographical information may be further pursued in the following sources: *Catholic Encyclopaedia,* 17 vols., NY: Encyclopedia Press, 1907-22; *Dictionary of the Apostolic Church,* 2 vols., New York: Scribner's, 1915-1918; *Dictionary of Christian Biography,* 4 vols., London: 1887; *Dictionnaire de Théologie Catholique,* 15 vols., Paris: Letouzey et Ané, 1903-50; *Encyclopedia of the Lutheran Church,* 3 vols., Minneapolis: Augsburg, 1965; *Encyclopedia of Religion and Ethics,* 13 vols., New York: Scribner's Sons, 1908-28; *Evangelisches Kirchenlexikon,* 3 vols., Göttingen: Vandenhoeck & Ruprecht, 1955-61; *Lexikon für Theologie und Kirche,* 10 vols., Freiburg: Herder, 1957-65; *New Catholic Encyclopedia,* New York: McGraw-Hill, 1967; *New International Dictionary of the Christian Church,* 2nd ed., Grand Rapids: Zondervan, 1974; *The Oxford Dictionary of the Christian Church,* Oxford: University Press, 1974; *Die Religion in Geschichte und Gegenwart,* 3rd ed., 7 vols., Tübingen: J. C. B. Mohr, 1957-65; *Sacramentum Mundi: An Encyclopedia of Theology,* New York: Herder, 1968-70; *Webster's Biographical Dictionary,* Springfield, MA: Merriam, 1976; *Westminster Dictionary of Church History,* Philadelphia: Westminster Press, 1971; *Wycliffe Biographical Dictionary of the Church,* Chicago: Moody Press, 1982.

Abelard, Peter (1079–1142). Highly independent scholastic theologian of Brittany, debater and dialectician, who refuted the extreme realism of his former teacher William of Champeaux. Lectured to large audiences in Paris until his career was cut short in 1118 by the tragic issue of his celebrated love affair with Heloise, recounted in his *Story of My Misfortunes* (see *Letters to Heloise,* edited by C. K. S. Moncrieff, London, 1925). Trinitarian views condemned without hearing at the Council of Soissons (1124). Resumed teaching at Paris in 1136. Bernard of Clairvaux led the fight to condemn several of his views at the Council of Sens (1141). His *Sic et Non* arranged seemingly contradictory statements from scriptures and church fathers to elicit dialectical thinking among students, and influenced the process of teaching theology. His emphasis on sin as intent alone in his *Ethics* (edited by D. E. Luscombe, New York: Oxford University Press, 1971), tended to ignore the distinction between good and evil acts. His exemplarist (moral) theory of the atonement was later much admired by nineteenth century Protestant writers. Selections from

Exposition on Romans, Ethics, and Hymn for Saturday Vespers, in LCC IX. Latin texts in MPL clxxviii.

ADAM OF PERSEIGNE, (d. 1205). French Cistercian Abbot of Perseigne. *Letters,* CFS 21. MPL ccxi.

AELRED (AILRED, ETHELRED) OF RIEVAULX (c. 1109–1167). Missionary to Galloway Picts, abbot of Cistercian abbey of Rievaulx, in Yorkshire. Major pastoral work: *On Spiritual Friendship,* CFS 5, MPL xxxii. Wrote spiritual biographies of Edward the Confessor, Cuthbert of Lindisfarne, St. Ninian and St. Margaret. *Treatises,* Vol. I, *On Jesus at the Age of Twelve, Rule for a Recluse, The Pastoral Prayer,* CFS 2; *The Mirror of Charity,* CFS 17, MPL xxxii. His major work on psychology was *Dialogue on the Soul,* CFS 22, MPL cxxxv.

ALAN (ALAIN) OF LILLE, (1125–c.1203). Taught at Paris (c. 1157-70) and Montpellier (c. 1171-85). *The Art of Preaching,* CFS 23. MPL ccx.

ALBERTUS MAGNUS, (c. 1200–1280). German Dominican scholastic philosopher, scientist, and theologian, who sought to unite Aristotelian and Christian teaching, utilizing Arabic commentators. Taught at Paris (1245ff.) and Cologne (1248-54) where Thomas Aquinas was his pupil. Bishop of Regensberg (1260-62). Works include *Summa Theologiae, Summa de Creaturis* and commentary on Peter Lombard's Sentences. Opera omnia, ed. A. Borgnet, 38 vols., Paris, 1890-1899. MPL clxvi.

ALEXANDER OF HALES (c. 1186–1245). English Franciscan theologian, "Doctor Irrefragabilis." Wrote *Summa Theologica,* 4 vols, ed. by V. Douchet, and the Franciscans of Quarrachi: 1924-48.

AMBROSE, ST. (340–397). Bishop of Milan, born in Gaul. His father was prefect of one of the four major prefectures of the Roman empire, which included Gaul, Britain, Spain, and a portion of Africa. After a legal education in Rome, and practice in the Roman courts, he was appointed governor of a large territory that had its seat in Milan. On the occasion of the death of Auxentius, the Arian bishop of Milan who had persecuted Catholic subjects for two decades, the people of Milan demanded that Ambrose, an unbaptized catechumen, be made bishop. Ambrose received baptism, and by an extraordinary procedure, passed directly through intermediary offices, to be consecrated at age thirty-five in 374 the bishop of Milan, where for twenty-three years he labored as chief pastor. Began the serious study of theology only after he became bishop, yet in due course became one of the four great Latin Christian theologians. Orthodox in doctrine, deeply caring and empathetic in human relations, eminently practical in mind, he became one of the great preachers and pastoral writers of his age, being in part responsible for the conversion of Augustine, who revered him deeply. Ambrose acquired a mastery of Greek language and literature, and was familiar with the Eastern tradition, especially Origen and Basil. Remembered as a model bishop, of whom the Emperor Theodosius said, "I know of no bishop worthy of the name, except Ambrose."

His most important work on pastoral care is *De officiis Ministrorum* (On the Duties of Clergy, NPNF 2, XX, pp. 1-91), the form of which was based on Cicero's moral instructions, but with many biblical allusions interspersed. His major work on psychology was entitled *Isaac, or the Soul* (FC 65). Ambrose contributed significantly to hymnody, introducing congregational singing and the style of music known as the Ambrosian chant, as well as to church architecture, as the one who guided the original building of the Ambrosian basilica of Milan. His funeral discourses on Valentinian II (392) and Theodosius (395) are considered models of this genre (FC 22). His style of Christian counsel is seen in his *Letters*, FC 26. Among other pastoral works he wrote treatises On Penance, On Baptism, *De Mysteriis* on the sacraments, and an essay on Death as a Blessing. See Theological and Dogmatic Works, FC 44. He wrote exegetical and homiletical commentaries on the patriarchs, Psalms, and Luke. See Seven Exegetical Works, FC 65; and Hexameron, Paradise, and Cain and Abel, FC 42. MPL xiv-xvii.

AMES, WILLIAM (1576-1633). Puritan theologian and casuist. Served as chaplain to the English governor of Brill in Holland, and contributed to the formulations of the Synod of Dort. In 1622 he become professor of theology at the University of Franeker. His last days were spent serving as pastor of the English church at Rotterdam. Attacked Arminianism and defended predestinarian Dort in *The Marrow of Sacred Divinity* (*Medulla Theologiae*, 1623, ET 1642), and developed the first systematic Reformed attempt at moral casuistry in *Conscience with the Power and Cases Thereof* (*De Conscientia*, 1632, ET 1639, English Experience Series, New York: Johnson Reprints, 1975).

ANDREWES, LANCELOT (1555-1626). Bishop of Chichester (1605), Ely (1609), and Winchester (1619), patristic scholar, privy councilor for England and Scotland, one of ten Westminister translators of Pentateuch. Author of *Ninety-Six Sermons* (1629), *Pattern of Catechetical Doctrine* (1630), and *Preces Privatae*, private devotions published posthumously (ed. Richard Drake, 1648). Closely associated with Richard Hooker and George Herbert, both of whom influenced Anglican pastoral practice deeply. Resisted Puritan rigorism, held a high doctrine of ministry and sacraments, stressed reasonable balance and Catholic rootage of Anglican pastoral care. See *Andrewes Complete Works*, 11 vols., LACT, 1854; *Sermons*, 5 vols, SED; and selections in *Angl*.

ANSELM, ST. (1033-1109). Abbot of Bec (1063), Archbishop of Canterbury (1093). Leading scholastic thinker, author of *Monologion* and *Proslogion*, who argued that properly conceived the idea of perfect necessary being requires the existence of that being than which nothing greater can be conceived. Wrote monumental essay on atonement, *Cur Deus Homo?* (*Why God Man?*, 1097) while in exile resulting from conflict with William II (Rufus) in defense of the independence of the pastoral office (*St. Anselm: Basic Writings*, transl. S. N. Deane, LaSalle, IL: Open Court, 1962). Anselm's writings on free choice, sin and sacraments are in *Trinity, Incarnation, and Redemption*, ed. J. Hopkins and H. Richardson, Edwin Mellen Press, 1970. *Concerning Truth* and *On Freedom of Choice* (1080-1085), and *The Fall of Satan* (1085-1090) are in *Truth, Freedom and Evil*, ed. J. Hopkins and H. Richardson,

Edwin Mellen Press, 1967. Selections in LCC, vol. X. MPL clviii, clix. Opera Omnia, F. S. Schmitt, 4 vols., Edinburgh: Thomas Nelson, 1946-1961.

※

ANTHONY THE GREAT, ST. (c. 251–356). Hermit and founder of Egyptian anchorite monasticism. In 285, after having given away all his possessions, he lived alone for twenty years as a hermit in the Egyptian desert. In c. 305 he founded a monastic community at Scetis for his disciples. In the Arian controversy he sided with Athanasius and Nicaea. He died in 356 at the age of 105. His life was recorded by Athanasius (NPNF 2, IV). His major contributions to the tradition of Christian counsel were penetrating self-examination with accurate self-description, consistent self-monitoring, and rigorous application of ascetic disciplines of prayer and self-denial. Anthony was chief spiritual guide of the Desert Fathers. *Seven Letters of St. Anthony,* transl. by D. Chitty, London: S.L.G. Press, 1975. MPG xi, 977-1000. See also the *Sayings of the Desert Fathers,* Kalamazoo, MI: Cistercian Publications, 1975.

※

APHRAHAT (APHRAATES), (c. 280–345). First Syriac Church Father, the "Persian Sage," a Persian monk and perhaps a bishop. His twenty-three treatises, *Select Demonstrations* (ca. 337-345), provide an early picture of pastoral practices in the Syriac Church. See esp. "Of Pastors," NPNF 2, XIII, pp. 383-387. Patrologia Syriaca, vols. 1-2, edited by J. Parisot, Paris, 1895, 1907.

※

AQUINAS, *See:* THOMAS AQUINAS, ST.

※

APOSTOLIC CONSTITUTIONS, Constitutions of the Holy Apostles. A collection of church canons compiled between 350-400, probably of second and third century, and chiefly Syrian, origin. Of eight Books, the first six are based on the now lost *Didaskalia Apostolorum,* from the early third century, of Greek origin. The first Book constitutes moral instructions for laity. The second Book serves as a manual of guidance for clergy, includes duties of bishops, priests and deacons, and stands as an important precursor of penitential discipline. Subsequent Books deal with care of widows, diaconal duties, baptism, the care of the poor, problems of heresy, schism, persecution and martyrdom. The seventh Book of moral and liturgical instruction was partially adapted from the second century *Didache.* Parts of Books seven and eight are ordination and liturgical materials taken in part from the *Apostolic Tradition* of Hippolytus (c. 200-220) and from the Antiochene liturgy and further developed. The work purports to be the writing of the apostles compiled by Clement of Rome, although it has seldom been regarded as of apostolic origin. The compiler may have been the fourth century interpolator of St. Ignatius' Letters, working probably between 341 and 390. The Trullan Council of 692 rejected its apostolic origin. There are occasional evidences of semi-Arian influence in the redaction. The collection reveals valuable insights into pastoral and liturgical practice of the Ante-Nicene period. *Apostolic Constitutions,* transl. D. O'Leary, TCL. See MPG i, 509-1156. The 1870 translation of James Donaldson appears in *The Constitutions of the Holy Apostles,* ANF VII.

※

ARNDT, JOHANN (1555–1621). Lutheran Pastor of Badeborn (1583), forerunner of pietism, primary influence upon Philipp Jakob Spener, author of *Four Books of True Christianity* (1606; *True Christianity,* transl. A. W. Boehmna and C. F. Schaeffer, Philadelphia: Smith, English, 1868; also in CWS), which stressed the work of Christ in the heart in contrast to forensic views of the atonement.

※

ARNOBIUS OF SICCA, THE ELDER, (d. c. 327). African Christian apologist of the time of the Diocletian persecution (305f.); teacher of rhetoric, one of his pupils was Lactantius; defended Latin Christianity, distinguishing it from pagan wisdoms and follies in his *Disputationes Adversus Nationes, The Case Against the Pagans,* ACW 7,8. Sought to defend the plausibility of Christian teaching in a hostile cultural environment, arguing that Christianity is consonant with the best wisdom of ancient philosophers and psychologists. Provided one of the earliest attempts at a platonizing Christian psychology in his treatise on the nature of the soul (ANF IV, 405ff.). CSEL, IV; MPL v, 349ff.

※

ATHANASIUS, ST. (c. 295–373). Bishop of Alexandria, defender of orthodox trinitarian doctrine against Arius. As a catechist in his native city of Alexandria, living out of the catechetical tradition of Pantaenus, Clement and Origen, he became arch-deacon and secretary to Bishop Alexander. Treatise Against the Pagans and Treatise on the Incarnation of the Word were written about 318 (MPG xxv). As a young presbyter, he attended the first ecumenical council at Nicea (325), and was soon to become a chief defender of trinitarian orthodoxy. At youthful age became bishop of Alexandria and metropolitan of all Egypt and Libya in 328, and soon was embattled in the Arian controversy. Banished four times from his church by powerful Arian influences on the Emperor Constantine and others, he spent a total of twenty-three years in exile. His importance in the history of pastoral care hinges significantly on his friendship with early leaders of the monastic movement, Pachomius and Serapion, and as biographer of the greatest among the Desert Fathers, St. Antony, whose pattern of spiritual direction was widely influential (*Life of St. Anthony,* ACW 10 and CWS with A Letter to Marcellinus). Although Athanasius is largely remembered for his defense of the Nicene trinitarian formulation, his life was spent as a bishop, in episcopal visitations, pastoral correspondence and preaching, and pastoral care, or in various extended periods of exile defending the faith. In addition to his treatise *On the Incarnation of the Word of God* and *Orations Against Arius* (LF 8; NPNF 2, IV), his *Festal Epistles,* LF 39 (see also *Resurrection Letters,* ed. Jack N. Sparks, Nashville: Thomas Nelson, 1979) are of special pastoral importance. Historical Tracts, LF 13. Writings, NPNF 2, IV; LF 8, 13, 19; MPG xxv–xxviii. The Athanasian Canons (*The Canons of Athanasius of Alexandria,* ed. W. Riedel, London: Williams and Norgate, 1904) are of uncertain authorship.

※

ATHENAGORAS (second century). Christian philosopher and apologist of Athens, went to Alexandria and began the prototype for its famed Christian academy. Wrote *A Plea for the Christians* (about 177, ANF II, 123ff., ACW 23), refuting calumnies urged against Christians of that day, claiming for Christians the benefit of toleration in the Roman Empire; and *The Resurrection of the Dead* (ANF II, 149ff; ACW 23). MPG vi, 889ff.

AUGUSTINE, AURELIUS (354–430). Bishop of Hippo, theologian, doctor of the church, unequalled contributor to the western theological tradition, shepherd of souls. Considered by most Catholics and Protestants alike to be the greatest theologian of the western Church, was born in Tagaste, North Africa, to a pagan father and a Christian mother, Monica. Had a Christian education, but turned to profligate living and pagan philosophy in his late teens and twenties. During this time he took a concubine, to whom he remained faithful for many years, and by whom he had a son, Adeodatus, in 372. In 373 became and for nine years remained a Manichaean, attracted by their rejection of the Old Testament, their attempt rationally to demonstrate the orderly workings of nature, and their explanation of the origin of evil in two conflicting principles. He returned to Tagaste to teach rhetoric, and subsequently at Carthage (374), Rome (383), and finally Milan (384). In 383 he left Manichaenism and became strongly influenced toward Neo-Platonism through Plotinus and Porphyry. Began attending the preaching of Ambrose, and in September, 386, converted to Christianity. Baptized the next year, he then returned to Tagaste and lived in a close-knit community with Christian friends. Was ordained priest in Hippo in 391 by popular acclaim. Moved his community there, which became the core of what is considered one of Africa's first monasteries, out of which were to come many of Africa's future bishops. Was bishop of Hippo from 396 until his death in 430.

Augustine's pastoral-theological contribution is deeply tied with his struggle against three heresies: Manichaeans (A.D. 396ff., FC 56; NPNF 1, IV) Donatists (400ff.; NPNF 1, IV), and Pelagians (415ff.; NPNF 1, V). A prolific writer, his two best known works were *Confessions* (shortly before 400; LCC 7, NPNF 1, I, FC 21, LF 14, MPL xxxii, CSEL 33), and *The City of God* (413-426; FC 8, NPNF 1, II, LF 12, MPL xli, CSEL 40). He wrote many sermons, epistles, and theological and philosophical writings which significantly informed and shaped the western theological tradition and pastoral practice. From the early 390s until his death he was a leader in the church and involved in all of its administrative, preaching, teaching, liturgical, and pastoral activities. He is one of the first great pastoral theologians of the church and his writings reveal his profound grasp of the pastoral task. His pastoral views may especially be seen in works that emerged out of the Donatist controversy, in his *De Catechizandis Rudibus* (399-400; NPNF 1, III, ACW 2, FC 8, MPL xl), and in Book four of *On Christian Doctrine* (396; NPNF 1, II, FC 2, LC 9, MPL xxxiv), in which his views on preaching and religious instruction were developed, as well as in numerous sermons, epistles and letters.

Other major pastoral works: Admonition and Grace (A.D. 426-427; NPNF 1, II, FC 2, LF 15, MPL xliv), The Christian Combat (396; FC 2, MPL xl, CSEL 41), Commentary on the Lord's Sermon on the Mount (394; NPNF 1, VI, FC 11, ACW 5, LF 8, MPL xxxiv), On the Freedom of the Will, (388-96; FC 59), The Problem of Free Choice (ACW 22, MPL xxxii, CSEL 74). Enchiridion (423; LCC 7, ACW 3, FC 2, NPNF 1, III, LF 9, MPL xl).

Early works on the soul include: On the Greatness of the Soul (387-388; ACW 9, Magnitude of the Soul, FC 4, MPL xxxii), On the Immortality of the Soul (387; FC 4, MPL xxxii), On the Two Souls (392; NPNF 1, IV, MPL xlii, CSEL 25, 1), and a later work, On the Soul and Its Origin (419-421; NPNF 1, V, LF 12, MPL xliv, CSEL 60).

The Teacher, The Free Choice of the Will, Grace and Free Will (FC 59). Against the Academics (386; FC 5, ACW 12, MPL xxxii, CSEL 63). The Happy Life, Answer to Skeptics, Divine Providence and the Problem of Evil, Soliloquies (FC 5). Letters (FC 12, 18, 20, 30, 32; also NPNF 1, I, LF 6, MPL xxxiii, and CSEL 35, 44, 57, 58). On Lying (395; FC 14). Against Lying (429; NPNF 1, III, FC 16, MPL xl, CSEL 60). On the Spirit and the Letter (412; LCC 8, NPNF 1, V, LC 4, MPL xliv, CSEL 60). On the Trinity (399-419; LCC 8, NPNF 1, III, PF 45, LF 7, MPL xlii). Patience (417; FC 16, NPNF 1, III, MPL xl, CSEL 41). Homiletic and expository writings include: Sermons for Christmas and Epiphany (ACW 15), On the Psalms (ACW 29, 30, LF 24, 25), On St. John (LF 26, 29, 30, 32, 37), On the Literal Meaning of Genesis (ACW 41, 42), Sermons (LF 16, 20), Sermons on the Liturgical Seasons (FC 38), Retractions (426-427; FC 60, MPL xxxii, CSEL 36), Short Treatises (LF 22, MPL xxxii-xlvi).

❧

BAKER, AUGUSTINE (1575-1641). Benedictine priest, mystic, spiritual writer; remembered for his study of the development of the Benedictine order in England, and for his posthumous ascetical writing, *Holy Wisdom* (2 vols., 1657).

❧

BARCLAY, ROBERT (1648-1690). Scottish theologian and major apologist of early Quaker tradition. Nominal governor of East New Jersey (1682-88). Author of *A Catechism* and *Confession of Faith,* and of the standard exposition of Quaker tenets, *An Apology for True Christian Divinity* (1678), Philadelphia: Friends' Bookshop, 1908 (note especially: "Concerning the Ministry," pp. 260-328).

❧

BARROW, ISAAC (1630-1677). Professor of Greek, Cambridge, 1660; Chaplain to Charles II, 1670; vice-chancellor of Cambridge, 1675. Wrote numerous sermons, and treatise on "The Divinity of the Holy Spirit." *Works of Isaac Barrow,* 3 vols., New York: Riker, 1845.

❧

BASIL, ST., THE GREAT (330-379). Bishop of Caesarea (370) following Eusebius, and archbishop of Cappadocia overseeing fifty bishoprics. One of three Cappadocian Fathers, the brother of Gregory of Nyssa, and life-long confidant of Gregory of Nazianzus. Lived as a hermit near Neo-Caesarea (358), and later introduced monastic system into Pontus. Set forth the Rule of St. Basil (358-364) which viewed asceticism as a way to perfect the service of God in community life under obedience organized around hours of liturgical prayer and work, yet without the more extreme austerities of the desert hermits. Trusted widely as conciliatory mediator between east and west. Attentive to the needs of the poor, Basil built and provided oversight for a hostelry for indigents, another for lepers, a hospital, and an elaborate system for poor relief. Ascetical Works, FC 9; Letters, FC 13 and 28; Exegetic Homilies, FC 46; Letters and Select Works, NPNF 2, VIII. Ascetic Works of St. Basil, transl. by W. Clarke, London: 1918. *On the Holy Spirit,* Crestwood, NY: St. Vladimir's Press, 1980.

❧

BAXTER, RICHARD (1615-1691). Puritan divine, pastor at Kidderminster, author of almost 200 works on pastoral theology, ethics, liturgics and preaching. Born in Rowton, Shropshire, became well versed in the Bible in his parents' home, was baptised and confirmed in the Church of England. He did not attend university,

but excelled in private studies. In his early twenties, was influenced by Nonconformists Walter Craddock and Joseph Symonde. Despite his Latitudinarian views
and moderate Calvinism, was ordained an Anglican priest in 1638. In 1641 began
his career at Kidderminster as curate, teacher, pastor, catechist, and ecumenist.
He served admirably the poor population of hand-loom workers, and put his proto-
ecumenism to work by persuading the ministers of various churches to work together toward a common cause. When the Civil War broke out in 1642 Baxter,
who sided with Parliament, left Kidderminster, and served for a time as an army
chaplain. Attained instant recognition through his *The Saints' Everlasting Rest*
(1650). He returned to Kidderminster until 1660 when he went to London as
Chaplain to Charles II, who had been moved by his preaching. He was offered the
bishopric of Hereford, but his scruples against the episcopacy caused him to refuse,
a refusal which debarred him from ecclesiastical office. He was one of 2000 pastors
to leave the Church of England in 1662 in opposition to the Act of Uniformity.
Spent the next twenty-six years without a charge, suffering persecution and imprisonment for espousing toleration of moderate dissent within the Church of
England. Led Nonconformists at the Savoy Conference in considering modifica-
tions of the Book of Common Prayer. He married Margaret Charlton in September of 1662, who was so supportive that she went with him not only into exile, but
into prison. Baxter was imprisoned in 1685 for preaching without permission, and
again in 1686 for writing his *Paraphrase of the New Testament.* Was one of those
directly responsible for the Society for the Propagation of the Gospel. After years
of suffering, imprisonment, persecution and bereft of a regular charge, the Act of
Toleration (1688), which allowed Non-Conformists the right to worship, enabled
Baxter to enjoy three peaceful years before he died in 1691 (cf. *Autobiography,* New
York: E. P. Dutton, 1931).

Baxter, one of Protestantism's greatest pastoral theologians, wrote prolifically.
Among his most widely read works were *The Reformed Pastor* (1656, abbr. RP,
Carlyle, Pa: Banner of Truth, 1979), *Christian Directory* (1673), *Catholic Theology*
(1675), *Methodus Theologiae Christianae* (1681), *Family Catechism* (1683), and his *Reli-
quiae Baxterianae* (1696). See *The Practical Works of the Rev. Richard Baxter* (PW), 23
vols., ed. W. Orme, London: James Duncan, 1830.

❧

BEDE, ST. (C. 673–735). "The Venerable." Monk of Jarrow, "Father of English
History." Entered monastery at Wearmouth at age 7 under the Benedictine Rule,
and transferred to Jarrow shortly thereafter. Spent his life in Northumbria in scientific pursuits (*De Natura Rerum*), biblical exegesis, hymns, and especially history
(*Ecclesiastica Gentis Anglorum,* Ecclesiastical History of the English People, 731, and
his *Six Ages of the World*). His pastoral thought stressed episcopal visitation, confirmation and frequent communion. MPL xc-xcv. Collected works, edited by J.
Giles, 12 vols., London: 1843-44.

❧

BELLARMINE, (BELLARMINI, BELLARMINO), ROBERT (1542–1621). Counter-Reformation apologist, archbishop of Capua (1602), Jesuit theologian, professor of theology
at Louvain and Rome. His *Disputationes de Controversiis Christianae Fidei* (3 vols.,
Ingolstadt, 1586-93) defined the sacramental and pastoral implications of the
Council of Trent. See also *De Laicis: Or, the Treatise on Civil Government,* transl. by K. E.

Murphy, Westport, Conn: Hyperion Press, 1979. Opera Omnia, Paris, 1870.

※

BENEDICT, ST., OF NURSIA (c. 480–c.543). Founder of monasticism in western Europe. Established Monte Cassino (c. 529) which became the leading monastery of the Benedictine Order. Formulated the *Rule of St. Benedict* (in Latin and English, London: Burns & Oates, 1932) under the influence of earlier rules by John Cassian and Basil, to regulate the life of monks, giving spiritual authority to the abbot to be elected by vote. The vow called for works of mercy, possessions to be held in common, and residence in one place. MPL lxvi, 215-358.

※

BERNARD OF CLAIRVAUX (1091–1153). Monastic reformer, mystic, founder and first abbot of Cistercian monastery of Clairvaux. Hostile to rationalism (such as that of Peter Abelard), he stressed contemplation, ascetic discipline, self-denial, and orthodoxy shaped by mystical experience. Influential in the spread of Cistercian Order which had established 530 secluded abbeys by the end of the twelfth century. Treatises, Vol. I: *Apologia to Abbot William, On Precept and Dispensation,* CFS 1; Treatises, Vol. II: *The Steps of Humility, On Loving God,* CFS 13; LCC 13. Treatises, Vol. III: *On Grace and Free Choice, In Praise of the New Knighthood,* CFS 19; *Sermons on Conversion: A Sermon to Clerics, Lenten Sermons on Psalm 91,* CFS 25; *Five Books on Consideration; Advice to a Pope,* CFS 37. *The Letters of St. Bernard of Clairvaux,* transl. B. S. James, London: Burns & Oates, 1953. The Life and Works of St. Bernard, ed. Dom John Mabillon, 4 vols., London: J. Hodges, 1889-96. MPL clxxxii, clxxxiii.

※

BEVERIDGE, WILLIAM (1637–1708). Bishop of St. Asaph. Wrote commentary on the Thirty-Nine Articles of Religion. Complete Works, 12 vols., SED.

※

BEZA (BEZE, DE BESZE), THEODORE (1519–1605). French Protestant theologian, successor to Calvin at Geneva (1564). Defended right of magistrates to revolt against tyrannical government, urged rigorous church discipline, and contributed to textual criticism of scripture. *Confession de la foi chretienne* (1560). *Tractationes Theologicae* (1570-1582). *Histoire ecclesiastique,* (1580), edited by E. Cunitz, 3 vols., Paris, 1883-89). *Opera,* 3 vols, Geneva: 1582.

※

BOETHIUS, ANICIUS MANLIUS TORQUATUS SEVERINUS (c.480–524). Roman philosopher and statesman. Born in Rome and educated in Athens and Alexandria. In 510 he became a Consul under Emperor Theodoric. Accused of treason, Boethius was imprisoned in Italy where he wrote *The Consolation of Philosophy* (ed. H. F. Stewart, Cambridge: Harvard University Press, 1936; another edition edited by E. Edman, New York: Random, 1943), which became a model of the genre of consolation literature. Wrote treatises on logic, music, arithmetic and theology. Beheaded in 524. His commentaries on Aristotle became a major source of knowledge of Platonic and Aristotelian ideas in the Middle Ages. *The Theological Tractates,* trans. H. Steward and E. Rand, Loeb. MPL lxxxi.

※

BONAVENTURE, ST. (1217–1274). Leading medieval theologian, called "the angelic doctor," leader of Franciscan Order, and Cardinal. *The Mind's Road to God,* transl.

George Boas, New York: Bobbs, 1958, provided clear statement of the steps of contemplative prayer (cf. *The Soul's Journey to God, The Tree of Life,* and *The Life of St. Francis,* all in CWS, ed. Ewert Cousins). *The Works of St. Bonaventure,* transl. J. De Vinck, 5 vols., Paterson, NJ: St. Anthony Guild Press, 1960-70. *Breviloquium,* London: Herder, 1946. *Rooted in Faith: Homilies to a Contemporary World,* transl. M. Schumacher, Chicago: Franciscan Herald Press, 1974. *The Character of the Christian Leader,* Ann Arbor: Servant, 1978. *Disputed Questions Concerning Christ's Knowledge* (Excerpts in LCC X, pp. 379-402). MPL clxxxv.

❧

BORROMEO, FEDERIGO (1564-1631). Cardinal of Milan. *Pastorum instructiones, monitiones ad clerum atque epistolae,* ed. E. Westhoff, Muenster: n.p., 1860.

❧

BOUDEWYNS, MICHAEL (1601-1681). An early Dutch exemplar of the tradition of "pastoral medicine." *Ventilabrum medico-theologicum, quo omnes casus tum medicos, tum aegros, aliosque concernentes eventilantur* (Antwerp, 1666). Cf. BMKS.

❧

BROWNE, THOMAS (1605-1682). English writer and physician; trained in medicine at Oxford; after extensive travelling, settled in Norwich in 1637 where he became a leading physician, philosopher of science, and Anglican religious writer. Wrote *Religio Medici* (1632; Cambridge: University Press, 1963), which reveals a highly independent mind conjoining a pragmatic, skeptical outlook with piety and faith in revelation; and *Pseudodoxia Epidemica or Inquiry into Vulgar and Common Errors* (1646), seeking to demythologize science in a period of transition from an age of authority to an age of scientific inquiry. Combining originality with wide learning, Browne was fascinated with paranormal phenomena, alchemy, primitive anthropology, esoteric burial customs, and witchcraft. Collected writings edited by C. Keynes, 6 vols., London: Faber and Gwyer, 1928-1931.

❧

BRUNFELS, OTTO (C. 1488-1534). German Carthusian priest, pastor in Steinau, physician in Bern; forerunner of modern botany. *Catalogus illustrium medicorum sive de primis medicinae scriptoribus* (1530); *Herbarium vivae icones* (Strassburg, 1532); *Jatrion Medicamentorum Simplicium* (Strassburg, 1553).

❧

BUCER, (BUTZER), MARTIN (1491-1551). Reformer of Strasbourg. Entered Dominican order in 1506, in 1517 began studies in Heidelberg where he became an ardent follower of Erasmus. Met Luther in 1518 and began correspondence. In 1521 he received papal dispensation from his vows, and in 1522 was one of the first priests to marry among those who became Reformers. His Reformed ministry began in 1523, the year of his excommunication, with his move to Strasbourg, where Reformed views had already been introduced. He remained there for over twenty years, taught Protestant theology and church practice, initiated congregational singing, wrote catechisms, contributed to liturgical development, began the Protestant practice of confirmation, helped to open the first Protestant Gymnasium (1538) and Seminary (1544). Major works pertaining to pastoral care: *Instruction in Christian Love* (1523) and *Pastorale, das ist von der wahren Seelsorge und dem rechten Hirtendienst* (1538). Mediated between Luther and Zwingli in their eucharistic dispute. Calvin was significantly influenced by Bucer's ecclesiology and pastoral care. When Zwingli died in 1531 Bucer became the Reformed leader not only of Strasbourg but also of southern Germany and Switzerland. His work in Strasbourg inspired reforms in Geneva and Hesse, while his understanding of liturgy had wide influence in Geneva and Scotland. Remembered as a key Protestant mediator with Catholics in conferences in Leipzig (1539), Worms and Hagenau (1540) and Ratisbon (1541), his most successful encounter with Catholic theology came at the 1541 conference at Regensburg. Exiled when he refused to recognize the 1548 Interim of Augsburg, Bucer proceeded to England on the invitation of Thomas Cranmer to aid in the English Reformation, influencing especially the Anglican Ordinal of 1550. He lectured as a professor of Theology at Cambridge from 1549 until his death on February 28, 1551. *Deutsche Schriften,* edited by Robert Stupperich, 4 vols., Gütersloh: 1960ff. *De Regno Christi,* ET by Wilhelm Pauck, LCC XIX, pp. 155-395. *Common Places of Martin Bucer,* CLRC 4. *The Psalter of David,* 1530, Courtenay Facsimilies, Appleford: Sutton Courtenay Press.

※

BULLINGER, JOHANN HEINRICH (1504-1575). Swiss Reformer, successor to Zwingli, one of the authors of the First and Second Helvetic Confessions and the Consensus of Zurich, which sought common ground among Reformed groups in Switzerland. Wrote *Of the Holy Catholic Church,* LCC XXIV, pp. 283-327; *Bericht der krancken: Wie man by den Krancken un sterbenden Menschen handeln,* Zürich: C. Froschoeur, 1538; *Compendium Christianae Religionis decem libris comprehensum,* Tiguri: 1559.

※

BUNYAN, JOHN (1628-1688). Puritan writer and pastor, author of *Pilgrim's Progress.* Born in 1628 at Elstow, joined the army while still a teenager; later a tinker. Converted to Christianity by his wife, was baptised in 1655 and began to preach in the Bedford Baptist Church. Imprisoned in 1660 for preaching without permission. During his twelve year stay in prison he wrote *Pilgrim's Progress* (1678). After his release he was pastor in Bedford for the rest of his life. Other works include *Grace Abounding to Chief of Sinners* (1666) and *The Greatness of the Soul and the Unspeakableness of the Loss Thereof;* see *Works of John Bunyan,* Philadelphia: Bradley, 1870.

※

BURNET, GILBERT (1643-1715). Scottish-born Anglican bishop of Salisbury, historian, Nonconformist. Following his education at Aberdeen where he studied theology, law and the arts, he traveled extensively through England, France and Holland. Upon his return home he was ordained in the Church of Scotland and given a charge at Saltaun (1664-1669). Wrote an *Exposition of the Thirty-Nine Articles* (1669) and *A Memorial of Diverse Grievances.* This latter book almost led to his excommunication because of his sharp critique of immorality among ecclesiastical office-holders. Professor of theology at Glasgow (1669-1674). In 1674 lectured at St. Clements and became chaplain of the Rolls Chapel. While at first in good standing with the court, he was ousted by Charles II after criticizing his life-style. When James II came into power in 1687, Burnet was outlawed. He then moved to the Hague in Holland where he supported William of Orange with whom he returned to England in 1688. He became William and Mary's chaplain and in 1689 assumed the bishopric of Salisbury. Wrote a three volume historical work *History of the Reformation in England* (1679-1714) and *History of His Own Time* (1723-34). His major contribution to pastoral care is his 1692 work *A Discourse on the Pastoral Care* (London: W. Baynes, 1818; cf. selections in CS, pp. 81ff.).

✻

CAESARIUS OF ARLES, ST. (470–543). Archbishop of Arles, primate of Gaul and Spain, who urged his clergy to preach in the town and country simply, often and briefly. Espoused lay administration of church finances, congregational singing, and memorization of scripture. Convened the Second Council of Orange in 529, ending the Semi-Pelagian controversy by developing a position nearer to Augustine than John Cassian, advocating prevenient grace and baptismal regeneration, and rejecting double predestination. Sermons, 2 vols., FC 31, 47.

✻

CALIXTUS, GEORG (1586–1656). Protestant ecumenist, Lutheran Professor of theology, Helmstedt (1614-1656). Sought reconciliation between Catholics and Protestants on the basis of the faith of the Ecumenical Councils of the first five centuries, interpreted in the light of the Vincentian canon. Sought to diminish differences and emphasize fundamental articles of faith in *Epitome Theologiae, Theologia Moralis,* and *De Arte Nova Nihusii.* Orthodox Lutherans thought him too Catholic; Catholics thought him too Lutheran.

✻

CALOVIUS, ABRAHAM (1612–1686). German Lutheran theologian, taught at Koenigsberg and Wittenberg. Opponent of Calixtus, Socinianism, Pietism and Grotius. Chief dogmatic work, *Systema locorum theologicorum,* 12 vols. 1655-1677, became the major statement of seventeenth century Lutheran scholasticism, covering many points in pastoral theology, church, ministry and sacraments. Selections in M. Schmid, *Doctrinal Theology,* Minneapolis: Augsburg, 1961.

✻

CALVIN, JOHN (1509–1564). French Reformer and theologian, born in Noyen, the second child of Gerard Cauvin, an advocate of the city of Noyen, where he practiced civil and canon law. Received an excellent ecclesiastical education. Was tonsured in 1521, the only order he was ever given. Studied for the priesthood in Paris until 1528, when he began law studies at Orleans. Showed early humanist interests in his first book, a commentary on Seneca's *De Clementia* (Paris, 1532). After experiencing a "sudden conversion" in 1533, Calvin considered himself to be aligned with the Reformers. When in November 1533 his friend Nicholas Cop, rector of the University of Paris, gave a speech which expounded Reformation views, Calvin was forced to flee because it was assumed that he helped Cop write the speech. After a period of imprisonment (in Noyon) and wandering to Nerac (where he encountered Le Fevre), to Paris, and with Canon du Tillet to Metz, Calvin arrived at Strasbourg where Bucer was exercising strong influence. Published first edition of his famed *Institutes of the Christian Religion* in 1536. In that year joined William Farel in Geneva to help establish the reformation there. In 1537 Farel and Calvin published their "Articles Concerning the Organization of the Church and of Worship" which dealt with discipline and the Lord's Supper, requiring a profession of faith of all Genevans. Banished from Geneva in 1538, returned to Strasbourg to pastor a church of French refugees. During his three years there he developed a new edition of the Institutes (1539; LCC XX, XXI), wrote the first of his many commentaries on scripture, and published his *Reply to Sadolet* (1539), and the *Short Treatise on the Lord's Supper* (1540). Returned to Geneva in 1541 when a new government pleaded for him to come back. His *Ecclesiastical Ordinances* began to be enforced in Geneva in 1552.

Calvin is remembered along with Luther as one of the two leading Protestant reformers and the founder of Reformed theology and pastoral practice. The *Institutes* clearly stand out as the most significant systematic work on theology, church, and ministry to come out of the early Reformation. Calvin authored some 2300 sermons, and numerous commentaries on the Old and New Testaments (Commentaries, 22 vols., Grand Rapids, MI: Baker, 1979). CR, xxix-lxxxvi. LCC XX-XXIII. Calvin Translation Society: *Calvin's Tracts,* ed. H. Beveridge, 3 vols, Edinburgh: 1844-51. *Letters of John Calvin,* ed. J. Bonnet, 2 vols., Edinburgh: T. Constable, 1855-1857. *Calvin: Selections from His Writings,* ed. J. Dillenberger, Missoula: Scholars' Press, 1975, abbr. SW.

❧

CASSIAN, JOHN (C.360–C.435). Monk, ascetic writer of Southern Gaul, the first to introduce the rules of Eastern monasticism into the West. The place of birth is unclear, but some speculate that he was born in Scythia, Romania, or Provence. After being educated in a monastery in Bethlehem, he and his friend Germanus left for Egypt to study spiritual guidance and ascetic practices. While travelling through Constantinople in 403 he was ordained deacon, and became a leading disciple of John Chrysostom. In 405 went to plead Chrysostom's case to Pope Leo in Rome. Leo later asked him to write a work refuting Nestorius. Around 430 Cassian wrote *De Incarnatione Domini,* a work comprised of seven books against Nestorius, in which these views were first made available to the Western world. In around 415 Cassian founded the monastery of St. Victor and a nunnery near Marseilles. His *Conferences* describe what he had learned of the ascetic life from hermits while travelling through Egypt. His *Institutes* (425-430) describe the art of spiritual guidance developing in early monasticism. He was an exponent of Semi-Pelagianism, a view that moderates between Augustine's view of radical human fallenness and Pelagius' view of the natural goodness of humanity (Semi-Pelagianism was rejected in 529 by the Council of Orange). The *Institutes and Conferences* LCC XII, NPNF 2, XI, influenced the Benedictine rule. MPL xlix.

❧

CATHERINE, ST., OF GENOA (1447–1510). Italian mystic and renowned hospital care-giver. *Purgation and Purgatory, The Spiritual Dialogue,* CWS.

❧

CATHERINE, ST., OF SIENA (1347–1380). Italian mystic. After a vision at the age of seventeen Catherine entered into a life of complete dedication, becoming in 1365 a Dominican Tertiary. She devoted herself to asceticism and care for the poor and sick. In 1376 she travelled to France where she helped to persuade Gregory XI to return to Rome, and after the 1378 Great Schism, supported Urban VI. Remembered for her spirituality, prophecies and visions, she left behind a number of prayers and letters which clearly express the depth of her piety and energies as a spiritual guide. *St. Catherine of Siena as Seen in Her Letters,* ed. Vida Scudder, London: J. M. Dent, 1905. *Prayers,* CWS; ET of *Legenda Major,* London: W. Caxton, 1493. *The Dialogue,* CWS.

CHEMNITZ, MARTIN (1522–1586). Lutheran theologian, born in Brandenburg, educated at Magdeburg (1539-42), Frankfurt, and Wittenberg (1545) where he came under the influence of Luther and began a life-long friendship with Melanchthon. Became rector of the Kneiphof school and in 1550 was made librarian to Duke Albert at the ducal library. Returned to Wittenberg in 1553 on the philosophical faculty. After his ordination in 1554 he went to Brunswick where he became superintendent of the church. Although offered other posts, he remained in the pastorate until ill health forced his retirement in 1584. He defended Luther's view of the Lord's Supper, writing in 1561 his *Repetito Sanae Doctrinae de Vera Praesentia*. Chemnitz assisted in the reorganization of the Prussian Churches after controversies surrounding Osiander, and became a central figure in the drafting and final approval of the 1577 Formula of Concord. In *Examen Concilii Tridentini* (1565-1573) he set forth Lutheran teaching in response to Trent. His *Loci Theologici* were published after his death (1591). An erudite, centrist, Melanchthonian, Lutheran pastoral theologian, his major pastoral work is *Ministry, Word and Sacrament: An Enchiridion,* 1595 (St. Louis: Concordia, 1981), abbr. MWS.

❧

CHRYSOLOGUS, ST., PETER (C. 400–450). Bishop of Ravenna. Selected Sermons, FC 17.

❧

CHRYSOSTOM, JOHN (C. 347-407). Bishop of Constantinople, Doctor of the Church, Patron of Preachers. Born in Antioch into a wealthy family. His father, an army officer of high rank, died shortly after his birth. Studied law and rhetoric under the eminent Antiochene orator, Libanius. Met Meletius, Bishop of Antioch, at age eighteen and was baptized three years later and shortly thereafter ordained as lector. During four years in the mountains engaged in study and ascetic exercises under the Pachomian rule. Ordained deacon in 381 by Meletius, with responsibilities of pastoral care for the sick, poor, widowed, and catechumens. During the twelve year period after his ordination to the priesthood by Flavian (386-398), he preached in the Antioch cathedral and published numerous biblical expositions, a series of Homilies on the Statues, (LF 9) and Homilies on Galatians and Ephesians (LF 6), Romans (LF 7), Matthew (LF 11, 15), Philippians (LF 14), Corinthians (LF 27), John (LF 28,29), and Acts (LF 33,35). These homilies (also in NPNF 1, IX-XIV) established John Chrysostom as one of Christianity's leading biblical expositors. By his eloquence and character he soon was widely recognized as a preacher of unexcelled quality. During these years he also wrote numerous pastoral letters, among them a letter of consolation to Stagirius, and a moving admonition to a young widow. As a young priest (before 392), he wrote one of Christianity's most important treatises on ministry *De Sacerdotio* (*On the Priesthood,* London: S.P.C.K., 1964, republished by St. Vladimir's Seminary Press, 1977), which sets forth a high view of the priestly calling and responsibility.

Against his wishes Chrysostom was consecrated Patriarch of Constantinople in 398. Worked for the relief of the sick and poor, and for church reform. In 401 he presided over a council at Ephesus. Incurred the disfavor of Empress Eudoxia through his preaching against extravagance. Amid politics and intrigue, was exiled in 403 and again in 404 to Cucusus in Asia Minor. Maintained correspondence with supporters as he endured great physical hardships. Died in 407 en route to a place of further exile.

John Chrysostom is considered one of the greatest Doctors of the Greek Church. He is remembered, above all, for the eloquence of his preaching which earned him the name Chrysostom ("Golden-Mouthed"). His 102 works of homilies, treatises and letters exhibit constant pastoral concerns. Hence he ranks among the greatest of pastoral theologians. *Baptismal Instructions*, ACW 31; *Homilies*, 2 vols., FC 33, 41. NPNF 1, IX-XIV. MPG xlvii-lxiv. NPB iv. *On Wealth and Poverty*, Crestwood, NY: St. Vladimir's Seminary Press, 1984.

❧

CLARE, ST., OF ASSISI (1194–1253). Founder of the Franciscan nuns, often called Order of the Poor Clares. *The Complete Works*, CWS.

❧

CLEMENT OF ALEXANDRIA (CLEMENS TITUS FLAVIUS) (C. 150–C.215). Among the greatest of the Alexandrian theologians; probably born in Athens, became pupil of Pantaenus of Alexandria, whom he succeeded in 190 as head of the Alexandrian school. When forced to flee from persecution, was succeeded by his pupil Origen. Major works are *Protrepticus* (*Exhortation to the Heathen*), ANF II, pp. 163-207; *Paedagogus* (*Christ the Educator*), FC 23, on Christian life and manners, or *The Instructor*, ANF II, pp. 207-299; *Stromata, or Miscellanies*, ANF II, pp. 299-569. LCC II; and *Who Is the Rich Man That Is Being Saved?*, TCL. MPG viii and ix.

❧

CLEMENT OF ROME, ST. (fl. c. 96). Bishop of Rome. His Epistle to the Corinthians is among the oldest of post-apostolic writings, written in the last decade of the first century. ANF I, ACW 1, FC 1, ECW, AF.

❧

CLEMENTINA, Clementine Literature, Clementine Homilies and Recognitions, Clementine Pseudo-writings (early third century source, fourth century redaction). The names given to didactic novels falsely ascribed to Clement of Rome, which come down to us in two forms. The *Recognitions* may date as early as 211-231 on the assumption that they were referred to by Origen in his Commentary on Genesis. The twenty Greek *Homilies* are very similar in content to the Latin abridgment by Rufinus, called *The Recognitions of Clement*. Both were redacted before 380, and probably depend upon a Jewish-Christian document from the early third century. Scholars debate whether they depend upon an earlier work, *The Sermons of Peter* (cf. Walter Bauer, *Orthodoxy and Heresy in Earliest Christianity*, 1972, pp. 257-271), and/or whether the Homilies may display Ebionitic or Jewish Gnostic tendencies. In any case they provide invaluable information on pastoral practice among exponents of Jewish Christianity in the third and fourth centuries. ANF, VIII, 75-361; in MPG, ii, 19-468.

The Homilies were written in the form of a religious romance which Clement is presumed to have sent to James of Jerusalem from Rome. The premise: Clement, an educated Roman with links of kinship to the Emperor Domitian, despairing over pagan idolatries, in his search for truth travels to Judea and meets the Apostle Peter, is converted by him, and accompanies him on his missionary journeys, recording his sermons. The action of the story centers around Peter's contests with Simon Magus, the great deceiver and arch-heretic. Some interpreters view the romance as a thinly veiled advocacy of Judaising Christianity against Pauline hellenizations. Jerusalem remains the center of Christianity, Peter is accountable to James, the Lord's brother, and Christianity is presented as the restoration of the primitive religion of Adam, Enoch, Noah, Abraham, and Moses, purged by Christ of demonic corruption. The work refers to letters from Peter and Clement, and suggests considerable legendary material about Clement's family. The Recognitions add additional details concerning Clement's family and their eventual reunion after their recognition by Peter. Among curious aspects of the Clementina are Peter's vegetarianism, use of water instead of wine in the Eucharist, and repudiation of celibacy.

❈

COLET, JOHN (1467–1519). Dean of St. Paul's and instructor at Oxford. *Works,* ed. J. Lupton, London: Bell, 1867. *Daily Directions,* OCL III.

❈

COMENIUS (KOMENSKY), JOHN AMOS (1592–1670). Moravian educational reformer, ecumenical pioneer. Studied theology in Herborn and Heidelberg. After ordination as a Moravian (Bohemian Brethren) pastor, served churches in Prerau and Fulneck. When Brethren were banished from Moravia he moved to Lissa in Poland, where as principal of a high school, began the educational reform for which he became famous. The reform began with his Latin textbook *Janua Linguarum Reserata* (1631), an elementary encyclopedia, and then his *Didactica magna* (1657, Great Issues in Education, Vol. I, Chicago: Great Books, n.d.). Author of over 150 books, three others must be singled out as crucial to his contributions to pedagogy: *Via Lucis* (1641-42) in which he advocated the founding of "pansophic colleges" in which students would learn an integrated wisdom; *De rerum humanarum emendatione Consultatio* (1645); and *Unum Necessarium* which stressed the important role education could play in the eventual unification of religious diversity. Comenius deeply influenced nineteenth-century pedagogical theories, and the educational systems of England, Holland, Sweden, Hungary and Poland. Sense experience was emphasized, coercion avoided, understanding was stressed more than rote learning, and education was viewed as a cradle-to-grave effort.

❈

CONNOR, BERNARD (1666?–1698). Oxford physiologist, exponent of pastoral ("mystical") medicine. *Evangelium Medici: seu Medicina mystica* (London: Wellinton, 1697).

❈

CONSTANTINE AFRICANUS (C. 1015–1087). African medical writer. Born in Carthage, travelled widely, studied Arabian medicine. Became Benedictine at Monte Cassino. Wrote *Pantegni* (a translation of an Arabic medical text), *Liber de oculis, Megatechne et Microtechne* (c. 1080), and in effect began the second epoch of Salernitan School of Medicine. Works (Basel: 1536).

❈

COSIN, JOHN (1594–1672). Bishop of Durham, a leading figure in the development of Anglican theology and pastoral practice. *Collection of Private Devotions* (1627). Leader of Savoy Conference, 1661-2. Collected edition, 5 vols., LACT; Correspondence edited by Surtees Society, 2 vols., 1868-1870.

CYPRIAN, ST. (THASCIUS CAECILIANUS CYPRIANUS) (C. 200–258). Bishop of Carthage, Martyr, Saint. Born in Carthage to wealthy pagan parents, apparently his father was a high ranking Roman army officer who saw to it that his son received the best Greek education possible. Cyprian went on to become a wealthy and well-known rhetorician in Carthage. In 246 when already middle aged he converted to Christianity. He studied Tertullian and the Scriptures diligently. Two years later he was made the Bishop of Carthage. Shortly after becoming bishop the Decian persecutions began in the autumn of 249 in which Christians were forced to offer sacrifices to the Emperor Decian. Cyprian fled the city but maintained contact with his congregations, comforting and encouraging them through letters. When he returned to Carthage in 251 he found that many Christians had lapsed and that they were being readmitted into the Church by presbyters in Carthage. In 251 presided over a Council which determined that the lapsed could be readmitted into the Church, but only after rigorous penitence. In 252 a severe plague broke out which led to an alarming resurgence of anti-Christian sentiment. Fearing further persecution Cyprian readmitted all the lapsed back into the Church. Out of the Decian persecutions there arose the Novatian schism and the rebaptism controversy. Cyprian engaged in controversial correspondence with Bishop Stephen of Rome over this issue. Stephen's death in 257 and Valerian's persecution prevented Cyprian's excommunication. During the Valerian persecution Cyprian was summoned to appear for trial at Utica. He failed to appear, was banished to Curubis, and beheaded a year later outside Carthage on September 4, 258.

Cyprian is remembered not so much as a philosopher and theologian but rather as a popular and practical writer. His most famous works are *De Lapsis* (c. 251, ACW 25) written just after the Decian persecution, and *De Catholicae Ecclesiae Unitate* (251, Unity of the Catholic Church, ACW 25) written during the rebaptism controversy. He authored a number of short treatises and letters (ACW 43). Of importance for an understanding of his views on pastoral care are his treatises on prayer, alms, patience, jealousy, and envy. Treatises, FC 36, LF 3; Letters, FC 51, LF 17. Writings, ANF V. *The Lord's Prayer,* TCL. *Select Epistles,* TCL.

✳

CYRIL OF JERUSALEM, ST. (C. 310–386). Bishop of Jerusalem, Doctor of the Church. Born in or near Jerusalem to Christian parents. Macarius made him a deacon in 330. He later renounced the priestly orders which were given to him by Maximus in 343. During this period Cyril was charged with the instruction of catechumens and exhibited warmth and skill in this pastoral role. It was for his catechumens that he wrote his famous *Catechetical Lectures* (c. 347-348; FC 64; NPNF 2, VII; LCC IV) which dealt with the essentials of Christian teaching and practice. Of importance to pastoral care are his expositions on baptism, chrismation, and the Eucharist. The Arian controversy began while Cyril was still young. When he was made the Bishop of Jerusalem in 349 he came into conflict with the Arian Bishop of Caesarea, Acacius. Due to his opposition to Arianism, Cyril was exiled in 358, when charges were levelled against him for selling church furniture to feed the poor and needy during a famine. Restored in 359 by the Synod of Selucia, he was again exiled in 360. When Julian came into power in 361 he returned to Jerusalem, but was banished in 367. During his eleven years of exile, he cooperated with pro-Nicene bishops led by Melitius of Antioch. In 378 he returned to the see of

Jerusalem, "the mother of all the churches," as one who had long struggled against Arianism. Procatechesis, Catechesis 1-12, FC 61. St. Cyril's Lectures, LF 2.

❊

DESCARTES, RENÉ (1596–1650). French philosopher and scientist, founder of Continental Rationalism. Born and studied in France, spent his most productive years in Holland, and died in 1650 in Sweden. Author of *Discourse on Method* (1637) and *Meditations on the First Philosophy* (1641), his principal contribution to psychology and to the soul care tradition is his work on *The Passions of the Soul* (1649).

❊

DESERT FATHERS. Third and fourth century literature that emerged among the monks in the deserts of Egypt, Syria and Palestine, first through oral transmission, then in Coptic, Syriac, Greek and later Latin manuscripts. *Apophthegmata Patrum,* MPG lxv, 71-440 (cf. also MPL lxxiii, 851-1052); see *The Sayings of the Desert Fathers: The Alphabetical Collection,* transl. by Benedicta Ward, SLG, Kalamazoo: Cistercian Publications, 1975; *The Wit and Wisdom of the Christian Fathers of Egypt,* transl. W. Budge, Oxford, 1934. Selections translated by Owen Chadwick, LCC XII; *The Wisdom of the Desert: Sayings from the Desert Fathers of the Fourth Century,* transl. T. Merton, Norfolk, Conn: New Directions, 1960; and Helen Waddell, *The Desert Fathers,* London: Constable & Co., 1936. See also bibliographical references to Anthony, Athanasius, Basil, John Cassian, Dorotheus of Gaza, Evagrius Ponticus, Jerome, John Climacus, Maximus, Pachomius, Palladius, and Rufinus. MPL xxi, 387-462.

❊

DIDACHE, THE. Early Christian manual on morals and Church practice. ACW 6; ANF I; AF, pp. 305ff; ECS, pp. 233ff.

❊

DIONYSIUS (THE AREOPAGITE, PSEUDO-DIONYSIUS, DENIS; c. 500). Syrian mystical theologian who sought to christianize Neo-Platonic influence. *The Divine Names and the Mystical Theology,* TCL, 1920; SPCK, 1940. Works, transl. J. Parker, 2 vols., London: 1897, 1899. MPG iii, iv; MPL cxxii, 1023-1194 (Erigena's translation).

❊

DODDRIDGE, PHILIP (1702–51). Nonconformist, Congregationalist pastoral theologian. Entered dissenting Academy at Kibworth near Leicestershire, about 1719, where he became pastor and teacher; called to Harbarough in 1725 and to Northampton in 1730, where he became a leading figure in the training of Independent ministers. Founded a hospital and charity school at Nottingham. *Lectures on Preaching* (London: Baynes & Son, n.d.) is important for pastoral care. Other works are *Lectures on Pneumatology, Ethics, and Divinity, Sermons on Regeneration, Sermons to Young People, Rise and Progress of Religion in the Soul, Family Expositor.* Collected edition of Works, Leeds, 1802, 10 vols.

❊

DODWELL, HENRY (1641–1711). Born in Ireland, Dodwell was professor of ancient history at Oxford (1688-1691). Siding with nonjuring bishops, he lost his professorship when he refused to pledge allegiance to William and Mary. Among pastoral writings are his *Two Letters of Advice, for the Susception of Holy Orders* (1672; CS, pp. 27ff.).

Donne, John (1573-1631). Metaphysical poet, clergyman, dean of St. Paul's Cathedral in London. Born and raised in a staunch Catholic family, he studied at Oxford and Cambridge, and became an Anglican in 1592, while preparing for a career in law. Unable to settle down, he went to Cadiz with Essex and Raleigh in 1596 and the following year to the Azores. During these travels he wrote a number of celebrated poems. In 1598 became private secretary to the lord chancellor, Sir Thomas Egerton, until he eloped in 1601 with Anne More, Egerton's niece, lost his post and was imprisoned. His break with Roman Catholic piety became clear in *Pseudo Martyr* (1610), and with Jesuit theology in *Conclave Ignati* (1611), and he was ordained in the Church of England in 1615. Not only did King James secure him a post as royal chaplain, but also persuaded an unwilling University of Cambridge to grant Donne a doctorate. He became rector of Sevenoaks and then lector in theology at Lincoln's Inn. As dean of St. Paul's in London beginning in 1621, his sermons were considered to be among the finest of the seventeenth century. In 1623 an illness was the occasion for the reflections recorded in his profound work of *Devotions Upon Emergent Occasions* (1624; Ann Arbor: Univ. of Mich, 1959). His last years were spent in preaching and writing his *Divine Poems* which earned him the name of the finest of the "metaphysical poets." *Biathanos* (a tolerant argument on suicide) was published posthumously in 1644.

Dorotheus of Gaza, St. (sixth century). Monk of Palestine. Wrote *Didaskaliai Psychopheleis,* spiritual instructions for monks of a monastery near Gaza about 540. *Discourses and Sayings,* CSS 33.

Durandus, William (1230-1296). Bishop of Mende, canonist, whose *Rationale divinorum officiorum* was a medieval compendium of liturgical and pastoral instruction. ET with notes on first book of the *Rationale* by J. M. Neale and B. Webb in *The Symbolism of Churches and Church Ornaments,* 1843; and of the third book by T. H. Passmore, *The Vestments,* 1899.

Ecumenical Councils, Seven. NPNF 2, XIV. Seven councils are commonly held both by eastern and western Christianity to be ecumenical, i.e., representative assemblies of bishops and ecclesiastics from the whole world whose decisions on apostolic faith and practice have been universally received by the church and are considered binding on all Christians. These and the heresies they renounced are: Nicaea, 325 (Arianism); Constantinople I, 381 (Apollinarianism); Ephesus, 431 (Nestorianism); Chalcedon, 451 (Eutychianism); Constantinople II, 553 (Monophysitism); Constantinople III, 680-681 (Monothelitism); Nicaea II, 787 (Iconoclasm). MPL lxvii. Cf. COC, ES and HC. Cf. DDGC, and William Beveridge, Works, VIII, LACT, 1848.

Ephraim (Ephraem) Syrus, St. (c. 306-c.373). Syrian theologian, author, hermit, and hymnist, Doctor of the Church. The most important writer of the ancient church in Syria, ordained deacon in 338 in Nisibis, moved to Edessa during the Persian occupation. Lived as an ascetic in a cave, preached to monks, helped the poor. Attended the Council of Nicaea as a young man. Spent several years in Egypt among ascetics. Became leading teacher of the catechetical school at Nisibis. Wrote works against Marcion, Mani and Julian the Apostate. His numerous (more than 1000) writings include Biblical commentaries (some in verse), homilies, treatises and hymns. His pastoral concern can be seen in his treatise "On Admonition and Repentance" (NPNF 2, XIII, 330-336), and in his homilies in seven-syllable lines—the Ephraemic meter. *Rhythms on the Nativity,* and *On Faith, LF* 41. *Select Metrical Hymns and Homilies of Ephraem Syrus,* transl. H. Burgess, London: Blackader, 1835.

※

ERASMUS, DESIDERIUS (c. 1466–1536). Dutch humanist, leading patristic and classical scholar of North European renaissance. Born in Rotterdam, educated by the Brethren of the Common Life in Deventer from 1475 to 1484. Augustinian monk from 1486 to 1491, was ordained a priest in 1492 and studied in Paris and Orleans from 1495 to 1499. On a journey to England shortly thereafter was persuaded by John Colet to apply his humanist views and excellent knowledge of Greek to scripture and the early church. After a trip to Italy (1506-09) during which he studied the classics, he returned to England and became a professor of Greek and theology at the University of Cambridge. There he finished his edition of his Greek New Testament (1516). In 1521 moved to Basel, living in the home of the printer Froben, where he wrote a number of books advocating reform including *In Praise of Folly* and *The Enchiridion (Handbook of the Christian Soldier)* which contains wide implications for pastoral care. In 1524 he parted with Luther in *On Free Will.* Although articulating reformist views through his scholarly writings, Erasmus did not join with the Reformers in their break with Catholicism. Lived from 1529 to 1535 in Freiburg-im-Bresgau; died in Basel in 1536. Collected Works of Erasmus, Toronto: University of Toronto Press, esp. vol. 31, Adages, 1982.

※

EUSEBIUS OF CAESAREA (EUSEBIUS PAMPHILI) (c. 265–339). Bishop of Caesarea, Father of Church History. Pupil of scholar-martyr Pamphilus, after whose death he fled to Tyre, and was imprisoned in Egypt. Unanimously elected bishop of Caesarea about 314. Led moderate party during Arian controversy. Offered but refused bishopric of Antioch. His *Ecclesiastical History (Church History,* London: S.P.C.K., 1927f.; NPNF 2, I; Books 1-5, FC 19; Books 6-10, FC 29), is the principal source of church history from the Apostolic Age to his own time. Contains long tracts from earlier writers. Written in Greek, it survives in Armenian, Latin and Syriac versions. Other writings include *The Martyrs of Palestine* (the Diocletian persecution, 303-310 A.D.); a Chronicle of universal history; commentaries on Psalms and Jeremiah; *Omnasticon,* a biblical topography; a life of Constantine; *Preparation for the Gospel,* which explains why Christians accept the Hebrew tradition; and *Proof of the Gospel,* which attempts to validate Christianity through the Old Testament promises (TCL). MPG xix-xxiv.

※

EVAGRIUS PONTICUS (346-399). Monk and writer of ascetic wisdom. Ordained lector by Basil and deacon by Gregory of Nazianzus, he became widely known as a preacher in Constantinople. Attended the Ecumenical Council of 381, assisting Bishop Nectarius. Due to a developing relationship with a married woman, Evagrius left Constantinople for Jerusalem, and in 382 went into the Nitrian desert where he spent the remainder of his life, first as a disciple of Macarius and later as a teacher of Palladius, Rufinus, probably John Cassian, and others. He is among the first of monks who also was a scholar and writer. Very influential mystical theologian, but whose Origenist tendencies caused his teaching to be rejected in part by the Fifth Ecumenical Council (Constantinople, 553). *Praktikos and Chapters on Prayer,* CSS 4. MPG, xl, 1213ff, lxxix, 1165-1200.

※

FENELON, FRANCOIS DE SALIGNAC DE LA MOTHE (1651-1715). Archbishop of Cambrai, French spiritual advisor. Jesuit educated, ordained in 1675, conducted a mission to Huguenots for several years. Wrote *Traité de l'education des filles* (1687). Tutor to the Duke of Burgundy, for whom he wrote the novel *Telemaque* (written 1693, publ. 1699). Made archbishop of Cambrai in 1695. Had become associated with the Quietist mystic Madame Guyon in 1688. Defended her, but in 1696 signed Articles of Issy condemning Quietism. In 1697 published *Explication des maximes des saints,* on true and false mysticism, which Fenelon was later forced to burn, and which was later condemned by the Holy See, 1699. His influence on pastoral care rests largely on his ten volumes of Letters of Spiritual Counsel published after his death (see *Spiritual Letters,* transl. M. W. Stillman, Cornwall-on-Hudson: Idlewild, 1945), his "Traité du ministère des pasteurs," twenty-four pastoral charges, *Dialogue on Eloquence* (transl. W. S. Howell, Princeton: Univ. Press, 1950), and *Christian Perfection,* New York: Harper, 1947.

※

FOX, GEORGE (1624-1691). Founder of the Society of Friends. Rejected church attendance and religious rites, preaching truth as found in "the inner light," the voice of God speaking to the soul. Frequently imprisoned, he developed the discipline of religious silence. He fought for religious toleration, and undertook missionary journeys to Ireland and America. *Journal,* Cambridge: Univ. Press, 1941, published postumously in 1694 (see also N. Penney ed., 1911); *George Fox's Book of Miracles,* ed. H. Cadbury, 1948).

※

FRANCIS OF ASSISI, ST. (1182-1226). Founder of the Franciscans. Born in Assisi into a wealthy family, was disowned by his father when in 1203 he put on beggar's clothing and devoted his life to a ministry to the poor and sick. In 1208 he set out with a group of followers to put into practice Jesus' radical teaching in Matthew 10:7-19. During his lifetime he journeyed three times to the Holy Land to win souls for Christ and helped found several orders. The Franciscan Rule was composed in 1209, and by 1212 the order had gained the approval of Pope Innocent III. Known as Friars Minor, they went about preaching, caring for the poor, lepers, sick and outcast. The brotherhood spread rapidly. In 1212 he helped St. Clare found a community for women. St. Francis went to Morocco, Syria and Egypt in 1213, 1214, 1219. Among the writings usually attributed to St. Francis are "Canticle to the Sun," *Twenty-eight Admonitions, Testament,* seven letters, and a paraphrase of the Lord's Prayer. Among the most beloved of all saints, St. Francis is remembered for his love of nature, commitment to poverty, and deep spirituality. *Francis and Clare: The Complete Works,* CWS; *The Little Flowers, Life of St. Francis,* and *Mirror of Perfection,* London: J. M. Dent, 1910.

※

FRANCIS DE SALES, ST. (1567-1622). Leader of the Counter-Reformation, Bishop of Geneva, Doctor of the Church, co-founder of Visitandines, the Order of the Visitation of Mary. Against his family's desire that he enter a secular career, he was ordained a priest in 1593. That same year he embarked upon the hazardous task of trying to convince the people from his native Chablais to return from Calvinism to Catholicism, a task in which he was successful. Precursor of quietism, his writings influenced Molinos and Fenelon. Many of his literary works grew directly out of his pastoral concerns, esp. *Introduction to the Devout Life* (1608, New York: E. P. Dutton, 1961) which influenced King James I and John Wesley, among many others; *Treatise on the Love of God* (1616); *The Spiritual Conferences* (1628, abbr. SC); and *Spiritual Letters to Persons in Religion* (transl. H. B. Mackey, Westminster, MD: Newman, 1943). He became St. Jane Frances de Chantal's spiritual advisor after meeting her in 1603. Together they founded the Order of the Visitation in Annecy in 1610. ET of Works ed. by J. C. Hedley, 6 vols., 1883-1908. *Selected Letters,* COCL.

※

FRUCTUOSUS, ST. (600–665). Bishop of Braga. Rule for the Monastery of Compludo, General Rule for Monasteries, (ca. 660) FC 63, Iberian Fathers, Vol. II.

※

FULLER, THOMAS (1608–1661). Anglican divine, rector of Cranford. *The Cause and Cure of a Wounded Conscience* (1647), London: W. Tegg, 1867; *Collected Sermons,* 2 vols., ed. J. E. Bailey and W.E.A. Axon, London: Gresham Press, 1981.

※

GERHARD, JOHANN (1582–1637). German orthodox Lutheran dogmatician. General Superintendent of churches of Coburg, responsible for development of revised Lutheran church polity. In 1616 became Professor at Jena, where he spent the remainder of his life as one of Lutheranism's leading theologians. Author of *Loci Theologici* (9 vols., 1610-1621, 1863 ed. by E. Preuss, Berlin, 1863ff.), a standard scholastic work on Lutheran theology, ethics, and issues of church, ministry and sacraments; *Doctrina Catholica et Evangelica*; *Meditationes Sacrae (Sacred Meditations,* transl. C. W. Heisler, Philadelphia: 1896); and numerous commentaries.

※

GERSON, JEAN LE CHARLIER DE (1363–1429). French theologian, conciliarist and mystic. After receiving his doctorate in theology at the University of Paris in 1394 he became a canon of Notre Dame and chancellor of the University. During his teaching career his stress was not upon the theoretical but rather upon the practical and pastoral. He was the author not only of mystical writings but also of pastoral works which include his *On Bringing the Little Ones to Christ* and *On the Art of Dying.* He devoted himself to trying to remedy the Great Schism by taking part in both the Council of Pisa (1409) and the Council of Constance (1415-17). Opera omnia, ed. E. Dupin, 5 vols, Antwerp, 1706. Oeuvres completes, ed. Msgr. Glorieux, 4 vols., Paris: Desclée, 1960ff.

※

GRATIAN (twelfth century). Italian canonist. Virtually the father of canon law. His *Concordia discordantium canonum* (probably c. 1150), popularly known as the *Decretum,* arranged conciliar decrees and papal pronouncements and became the standard text for canon law in the west. Selections in LCC X, pp. 243-247.

GREGORY I, ST. (c. 540-604), GREGORY THE GREAT. Pope from 590, leading pastoral theologian of the western church. Son of a senator, became prefect of the city of Rome, sold all possessions and gave them to the poor about 575. Built six monasteries in Sicily. Appointed ambassador to the imperial court at Constantinople, 578-585. Returned to become abbot of monastery of St. Andrew. Upon accession to papacy wrote the most influential treatise on pastoral care in the Christian tradition, *Liber regula pastoralis,* or *Book of Pastoral Guidance* (c. 591, ACW 11, *Pastoral Care*; NPNF 2, XII, *Book of Pastoral Rule,* abbr. BPR), which became the textbook of pastoral care for the middle ages, also revered by Protestant pastoral writers. First monk to become pope. Initiated mission of St. Augustine (later of Canterbury) to England. Wrote *Dialogues* (c. 593; *Dialogues of St. Gregory the Great,* an Old English Version, ed. by H. Coleridge, London: Burns & Oates, 1874), on the lives and miracles of St. Benedict and other early Latin saints; *Moralia on Job* (595 A.D., LF 18, 21, 23, 31) which expounds Job in allegorical and moral senses, providing a wealth of observations on moral theology; Twenty-two Homilies on Ezekiel (601), Forty on the Gospels, and Two on the Song of Songs; 848 extant letters reveal him as counselor, administrator, and moral thinker. ET in NPNF 2, XII, XIII.

❧

GREGORY NAZIANZUS, ST. (c.329-390). Gregory the Theologian, Bishop of Constantinople, Cappadocian Father, Orator and Poet. Son of the Gregory, bishop of Nazianzus. He received a good education, studying first in Caesarea in Cappadocia where he became acquainted with Basil. He then studied in Caesarea in Palestine and at Alexandria. At the University of Athens he again studied with Basil who became a life-long friend. In 358 he finished his studies and returned to Nazianzus where he at first worked as a rhetorician, helped his father and then spent time with Basil in monastic retreat. When Gregory was baptised by his father in 358 his desire was to engage in a monastic way of life but circumstances prevented him from doing so. Much against his own will he was ordained a priest in 362 and shortly thereafter preached his *On the Flight (Oration 2).* This oration speaks of the duties and responsibilities of the pastor. It greatly influenced John Chrysostom's *On the Priesthood* and Gregory the Great's *Pastoral Care.* For the next ten years he helped his aging father carry out his ministerial activities until his death in 374. After his father's death and until 379 he went into seclusion at Seleucia in Isauria. In 379 he was asked to go to Constantinople to take over a small church. He built up this church and became famous as a biblical expositor. At the Council of Constantinople in 381 he was made Archbishop of Constantinople. Still wishing nothing other than the monastic life he retired from this appointment after about a year, returning to Nazianzus where he lived until his death in 390. Gregory is remembered above all as being one of the greatest preachers and theologians of the Eastern Church. He also wrote prolifically. His writings include a large number of poems; 45 Orations which include his *Five Theological Orations* (ed. A. Mason, in CPT, Cambridge: 1899) and *Funeral Orations,* FC 22; and 243 letters which include numerous letters of pastoral counsel and consolation.

❧

GREGORY OF NYSSA, ST. (c.330-395). Bishop of Nyssa, Cappadocian Father. One of the leading theologians of the fourth century, was born into a wealthy Christian family in Caesarea. He was younger brother of St. Basil, who supervised Gregory's education. It seems that Gregory was intended for an ecclesiastical career, but after a short period as a lector in the church, became a teacher of rhetoric (c.360-65). During this period of time he also married. When his wife, Theosebia, died, Gregory of Nazianzus persuaded him to enter Basil's monastery. In 371 he reluctantly accepted Basil's bestowal upon him of the title of Bishop of Nyssa. In 376 he was exiled by the Arian bishops because of his support of the Nicenes and did not return to Nyssa until the death of Valens in 378. When his brother died the following year Gregory carried on his work, soon becoming known as a staunch supporter of Nicene theology in the face of Arianism. In 379 he attended the Council of Antioch and later that year exhibited skill as a pastoral guide when he visited the Church of Syria and helped them to overcome their schisms. In 381 he was one of the leading spokesmen for Nicene views at the Council of Constantinople, delivering the inaugural address. Gregory was the first clearly to distinguish between *ousia* (essence) and *hypostasis* (persons) in trinitarian debates. Although overshadowed by his brother Basil who is one of the four "ecumenical" doctors of the Greek Church, Gregory surpassed him in knowledge, originality and the capacity for speculative thought. His corpus is large; besides 26 letters, sermons and homilies it contains a number of exegetical, theological and ascetical works. *Lord's Prayer and Beatitudes,* ACW 18; *Life of Moses,* CWS; *From Glory to Glory: Texts from Gregory of Nyssa's Mystical Writings,* ed. H. Musurillo, St. Vladimir's Seminary Press, 1979; *Easter Sermons of Gregory of Nyssa,* ed. A. Spir and C. Klock, PMS 9. Exegetical works on Psalms, Song of Songs, Beatitudes, etc., MPG xliv. Dogmatic works, MPG xlv, include *Oratio catechetica magna,* 9-116, *De anima,* 187-222, *Epistola canonica,* 221ff., *De perfecta christiani forma,* 251-286, *De mortuis,* 497-538. Ascetical Works, FC 58; Dogmatic Treatises, NPNF 2, V; The Catechetical Oration, TCL (see also NPNF 2, V and An Address on Religions Instruction, LCC III, pp. 268-327).

※

GREGORY PALAMAS, ST. (c. 1296–1359). Greek theologian, Doctor of the Eastern Church, and principal exponent of Hesychasm, the view that one is able through ascetic discipline, especially involving perfect quiet of body and mind, to behold the vision of the Uncreated Light of the Godhead. Born at Constantinople, was taught Hesychasm by the monks at Mt. Athos, ordained priest in 1326, retired as hermit to mountain near Beroea, and to Mt. Athos in 1331. Wrote a defense of Hesychasm in 1338 (*De Hesychastis,* MPG cl, 1101-1118). Called as bishop of Thessalonica. In response to critics who thought that the doctrine of Uncreated Light approached pantheism, Palamas argued that God's essence could not be known, but God's energies and evidences could be, and that human consciousness, even the physical eye, can behold the light of God. The council of Constantinople in 1341 debated, and the Blacherna Synod of 1351 affirmed the teaching of the Uncreated Light. Later The Synod of 1368 canonized Palamas as "Father and Doctor of the Church." *The Triads,* CWS; forty-three homilies, MPG cli.

※

GREGORY THAUMATURGUS, ST. (c. 213–c.270). Bishop of Neo-Caesarea in Pontus, "Wonder-worker." Heard Origen's lectures in Caesarea (Palestine). Attended Synod of Antioch in 265. Wrote "On the Subject of the Soul," "Four Homilies," and "On the Trinity," in ANF VI; also Panegyric on Origen, see TCL: *Gregory Thaumaturgus (Origen the Teacher): the Address of Gregory to Origen, with Origen's Letter to Gregory.*

※

GROSS, (GROSSE), JOHANN GEORG (1581-1630). *Compendium medicinae, et scriptura sacra demonstrata* (Basel: 1620).

※

GUERRIC OF IGNY (1075?-1157). Abbot of Igny (1138-1157). Lived at Clairvaux with Bernard as his abbot; influenced by Odo of Cambrai. Wrote *Liturgical Sermons,* 2 vols., CF 8, 32, outstanding for their balance and spiritual value, organized around the feast days of the Christian year. Sermons for monks constitute a powerful example of pastoral care through preaching. MPL clxxxiv.

※

HALL, JOSEPH (1574-1656). Bishop of Norwich, moral philosopher, casuist, Dean of Worcester. Sent in 1618 as moderate, irenic, Anglican representative to the Synod of Dort. Wrote *Heaven Upon Earth* (1606), later reprinted by John Wesley in his *Christian Library; Sacred Polemics* (1611); *The Old Religion* (1628); *Christian Moderation* (1639); *Episcopacy by Divine Right Asserted* (1641); *Resolutions and Decisions of Cases of Conscience* (1649); *Holy Decency and in the Worship of God* (posthumous); *Via Media, The Way of Peace;* and his courageous statement, *Humble Remonstrance to the High Court of Parliament* (1641), for which he was sent to the Tower, after which he lived in poverty until his death. Collected Works edited by Philip Wynter, 10 vols., 1863.

※

HENRY, MATTHEW (1662-1714). Biblical Commentator, Nonconformist minister, devotional writer. After studying law, ordained Presbyterian minister in 1687; showed exceptional pastoral skill in his churches in Chester (1687-1712) and in Hackney (1712-1714). Remembered for his six volume *Exposition of the Old and New Testaments* in which he explicated the practical implications of scripture for sermon preparation, still widely used. His views on pastoral care have been gathered by Colin McIver in *Rev. Matthew Henry's Aphorisms on the Ministry* (Princeton: Thompson, 1847).

※

HERBERT, GEORGE (1593-1633). Anglican clergyman and leading metaphysical poet, author of one of the major works on pastoral care in the Christian tradition, *The Country Parson.* Born in the Castle of Montgomery in Wales, younger brother of the famous deist philospher, Lord (Edward) Herbert of Cherbury. Educated at Westminister school and Trinity College, Cambridge; a gifted musician and classicist; held the position of public orator of the University from 1619 to 1627. Sustained close friendships with John Donne, Nicholas Ferrar and Francis Bacon, and served as a courtier for King James I. Herbert may have at one time wished for a career in the King's court, but with the death of James I in 1625, the option of a career in service of the state was closed to him. It was the influence of his friend Nicholas Ferrar, as well as the death of his mother, which led him to turn to the study of theology and a quiet but regrettably brief life as country parson. In 1626 he was made a prebendary in Huntingdonshire where he helped rebuild the church. In 1630 he was ordained a priest and made the rector of Bermerton near Salisbury where he died just three years later. Devoted himself zealously and selflessly to the pastoral care of his rural congregation. Besides writing a number of hymns Herbert wrote a collection of poems published in 1633 under the title *The Temple*. The poems, influenced by John Donne, are among the most important devotional poems of the Church of England, and were destined to influence both Coleridge and Vaughan. Of significance to pastoral care is his prose work, *A Priest to the Temple: or, the Country Parson*. This work remains a classic manual of pastoral care in which the activities and duties of the priest are described in a beautiful language and style which conveys the deep piety of the author. *The English Works of George Herbert*, ed. G. H. Palmer, Boston: 1905.

❦

HICKES, GEORGE (1642–1715). Non-juring bishop. Wrote *The Case of Infant Baptism* (1683), *Of the Dignity of the Episcopal Order* (1707). His principal contribution to pastoral care was his treatise *Of the Christian Priesthood* (in *Works*, ed. I. Barrow, LACT, 3 vols., 1847-1848).

❦

HILARY OF POITIERS, ST. (c. 315–367). Bishop of Poitiers, Doctor of the Church, known as the "Athanasius of the West" for his ardent defense of triune teaching against Arianism. In this cause he suffered exile (356-360) in Phrygia, where he wrote *On the Trinity* (FC 25, NPNF 2, IX). Also wrote a commentary on Psalms, and a book of lyrics that mark him as one of the church's first hymnists. MPL ix, x.

❦

HILDEGARD, ST., OF BINGEN (1098–1179). Abbess of convent of Rupertsberg, near Bingen on the Rhine. *Causae et curae* (ca. 1160), edited by P. Kaiser, Leipzig: B. G. Teubneri, 1903. *Physica* (c. 1080; see P. Riethe, *Naturekunde*, Salzburg, 1959); *Liber divinorum operum simplicis hominis* and Letters in MPL cxcvii.

❦

HILTON, WALTER (d. 1396). English mystic, Canon of Augustinian Priory at Thurgarton, Notts, author of *Epistle to a Devout Man in Temporal Estate* (printed 1506); *Scale of Perfection*, edited by I. Trethowan, London: Geoffrey Chapman, 1975; *The Goad of Love* (transl. of *Stimulus Amoris* by Clare Kirchberger), COCL, London: Faber. *Minor Works of Walter Hilton*, ed. Dorothy Jones, London: Orchard Books, 1927.

❦

HIPPOLYTUS OF ROME, ST. (c. 170–c. 236). Doctor of the Church, apologist, the most important early third century Roman theologian. A noted preacher whom Origen reports having heard, he reproved Pope Zephyrinus (198-217), and his successors, Popes Callixtus, Urban and Pontianus (217-235), for their leniency in disciplinary matters. A rigorous disciplinarian like the Montanists and later the Novatians, he opposed the relaxation of penitence to accommodate the influx of pagan converts in large numbers. Exiled to the mines of Sardinia for establishing himself as anti-pope, he was probably reconciled before his death, since the Liberian Catalogue (c. 255) considers him a Catholic martyr. His principal work is the *Refutation of All Heresies* (or *Philosophumena*, TCL), ANF V, 9-163. See also Fragments from Commentaries, ANF V, 163-203; *Treatise on Christ and Antichrist*,

ANF V, 204ff.; and *The Apostolic Tradition* (ed. G. Dix, London: SPCK, 1937; see AF-Ltft, I, 2, 1980, pp. 317-477). MPG x, 583ff.

HIPPOLYTUS, CANONS OF ST. A collection of canons redacted in the early sixth century consisting of liturgical and disciplinary instructions, probably of fifth century Greek origin. The original Greek text is lost, but survives in Ethiopic and Arabic manuscripts made from Coptic translations. Dependent upon the *Apostolic Tradition* of Hippolytus, to whom they were mistakenly attributed.

HOOKER, RICHARD (c. 1554–1600). Church of England theologian and apologist. Born near Exeter, attended Exeter and Corpus Christi College in Oxford, where he taught Hebrew and logic from 1579 until 1584. In 1581 he was ordained but did not take his first charge until 1584 when he became the rector of Drayton Beauchamp; Master of the Temple in London (1585), rector of Boscombe, Wilts (1591), and of Bishopsbourne (1595-1600). Influenced the pastoral tradition largely through his *Treatise on the Laws of Ecclesiastical Polity,* written as a pastor during the 1590s (Cambridge, MA: Harvard Univ. Press, 1977, 1980), one of the classics of its period, written as an Anglican response to Puritan claims. Hooker reappropriated the natural law tradition in relation to church/state issues, affirmed Anglican continuity with patristic and medieval traditions, and defended the polity and doctrine of the Church of England. Relying heavily upon Thomist categories incorporating reason and revelation in theological discourse, Hooker showed that questions of church polity could be decided without claiming superficial scriptural justification for every detail, and also without needing to justify medieval practices. He held that the church is a developing, organic reality, not a static expression of legalism, and that its government will change according to circumstances, in the light of natural reason, in the light of which all scriptures must be interpreted. Although Hooker is remembered as one of the Church of England's greatest theologians, his theological and apologetic abilities have overshadowed the equally important fact that he was a pastor. His views on ministry, ordination, pastoral care and counseling are exhibited especially in the fifth book of his *Treatise on the Laws of Ecclesiastical Polity,* first published in 1597. Collected works edited by J. Keble, 3 vols., 1888.

HUGH OF ST. VICTOR (c. 1096–1141). Medieval theologian, exegete, philosopher and mystic. Of noble birth, against his parents' wishes Hugh took the habit of the Canons Regular of St. Augustine at Hamersleven. He did not finish his novitiate there but travelled in 1115 to the newly founded monastery of St. Victor in Paris, where he studied, wrote and taught, soon becoming leading master of the school, and was made prior in 1133. Hugh rarely left the confines of the monastery and died there in 1141. Hugh's most famous work, *On the Sacraments of the Christian Faith* (1134; Cambridge, MA: Medieval Academy of America, 1951), is a rich contribution to liturgical and moral theology in the service of ministry. He influenced rules for exegesis, and the discussion of natural reason and faith in revelation (see MPL clxxv, clxxvi). *The Didascalicon of Hugh of St. Victor,* ed. J. Taylor, NY: Columbia University Press, 1961, discusses the interpenetration of arts and sciences with scripture and tradition, with insightful understanding of the psycho-somatic relationship, and of the unity of knowledge.

❊

HUS, JOHN (C. 1373-1415). Bohemian Reformer, professor and preacher at Prague, elected Rector of University of Prague in 1409, martyr. Convicted of heresy at the Council of Florence in 1415 and burned at the stake. *On the Unity of the Church.* Collected works edited by E. H. Gillett, 3rd ed., 2 vols., Boston, 1871.

❊

IGNATIUS OF ANTIOCH (C. 35-C. 115). Bishop of Antioch. Known through seven highly regarded letters written while traveling from Antioch to Rome. Traveling under armed guard to be executed in Rome at the Colosseum, he was welcomed by Polycarp and others at Smyrna, whence the letters to Ephesus, Magnesia, Tralles and Rome were written. Later from Troas he wrote to the Philadelphians and Smyrnaeans and to Polycarp (see ANF I; LCC I; ECW; MPG v). Strongly urged cohesive teaching of the three-fold order of bishops, presbyters and deacons amid hazards of persecution. Probably a native of Syria, direct heir to the apostlic tradition, had important influence in the development of monarchial episcopal authority in the early church, and was among the first to use the term "Catholic Church." According to Origen, he was the second bishop of Antioch, and direct successor to Peter.

❊

IGNATIUS OF LOYOLA, ST. (1491-1556). Founder and First General of the Society of Jesus, leading figure in the Counter-Reformation, Ignatius was born in 1491 in the family castle of Loyola in Spain. He spent his youth at the Court of King Ferdinand serving in the army. His military career came to an end in 1521 when he was severely wounded. While recuperating he read biographies of the saints and Lundolph of Saxony's *Life of Christ.* These led to his conversion and desire to devote his life to God. He went to Montserrat, confessed, threw away his swords, and put on the clothing of a beggar. He spent the following year (1522-23) in a monastery in Manresa where he engaged in prayer and ascetic exercises. Here he wrote the bulk of his influential *Spiritual Exercises* (transl. A. Mottola, New York: Doubleday, 1964). In 1523 he journeyed to Jerusalem, but, because of the Turkish occupation, was forced to turn back. Studied at the Universities of Barcelona, Alcala, Salamanca, and finally in Paris where in 1535 he received a degree in philosophy. While in Paris he continued to fast, engage in spiritual exercises, live a life of poverty, and minister to the sick and poor. His dedication and his *Spiritual Exercises* prompted a group of young men to follow him. In 1534 he and six others joined together unofficially to found the Society of Jesus, taking upon themselves the four vows of chastity, obedience, poverty and service to God in the Holy Land or elsewhere under the direction of the Pope. Founded the Roman College (1551) and the German College (1552), and numerous orphanages and homes for unwed mothers.

❊

IRENAEUS OF LYONS, ST. (C. 130-200). Early Church Father, Bishop of Lyons, possibly a martyr. Irenaeus may have been born in Smyrna, in Asia Minor, the town in which Polycarp was bishop. A disciple of Polycarp, he studied in Rome and may even have taught there. Marcus Aurelius was reigning over Lyons when

Irenaeus moved there and became presbyter of the Church. Served as envoy to Eleutherus in Rome in 177/78 where he pleaded that toleration be shown to the Montanists. The Church of Lyons suffered great persecution and its bishop, Pothinus, was martyred while Irenaeus was away. Upon his return from Rome he was made bishop of Lyons. Showed remarkable ability as an administrator and pastor over a large diocese. Gregory of Tours wrote that he converted almost the entire population of Lyons as well as many areas of eastern Gaul to Christianity. Not only was he involved in pastoral care, correspondence and missionary outreach in his capacity as bishop, but he is also remembered for his plea in 190 to Pope Victor I against the excommunication of the Asian Quartodecimans (who observed Easter according to the Jewish calendar), as well as his staunch and extremely effective opposition to Gnosticism. Only two of his works are still extant: Against All Heresies, *Adversus Omnes Haereses* (c. 185, ANF I, 309ff; J. Keble transl., LF, 1872) contains an examination and refutation of Gnosticism and other challenges to early Christianity. *Proof of the Apostolic Preaching* (ACW 16; translated in TCL as *The Apostolic Preaching of Irenaeus*), which came to light in Armenian translation, examines the New Testament in the light of Old Testament prophecy. He forms an important link between eastern and western Christianity. He strongly emphasized the episcopacy and was instrumental in defining the received canon of scripture. He argued that the true teaching of the church is handed down through an unbroken succession of apostolic witnesses whose bishops can be traced back to the beginning. He stressed the authority of the church of Rome, whose Petrine and Pauline teaching lay claim to apostolicity. His teaching of recapitulation (*anakephalaiosis*) taught that humankind, originally free yet fallen in Adam, is recapitulated in Christ the New Adam and reconciled with the Father, so as to summarize the human story, thereby giving positive significance to the full humanity of Jesus. He stressed the co-ordinate authority of all four evangelists. He died about A.D. 200 and was reported by Jerome to have been martyred. See also "Fragments from the Lost Writings of Irenaeus," ANF I, 568-578. MPG vii.

❧

Ivo, St. (c. 1040–1116). Bishop of Chartres. *Panormia* and *Prologue to the Decretum* (LCC X, pp. 238-243), influenced early medieval canon law. MPL clxi.

❧

Jerome (Eusebius Hieronymus), St. (c. 342–420). Biblical scholar and translator, Doctor of the Church, monastic advocate. Born at Strido near Aquileia, studied in Rome where he became proficient in Latin, Greek, ancient literature and rhetoric. Spent several years as an ascetic at Treves in Gaul, in Aquileia, and near Rome, where he knew Rufinus. Longing for deeper engagement in the Christian tradition, he made a journey through the east, to Pontus, Galatia, Cappadocia and Cilicia, and finally to Antioch, where he met Evagrius. He became very ill, and through a vision, dedicated himself unconditionally to the study of scripture, as distinguished from philosophy. He retired to a cave near Antioch and a converted Rabbi taught him Hebrew. Ordained a priest in Antioch, he studied in Constantinople under Gregory Nazianzus and Gregory of Nyssa, translated the works of Eusebius, Origen and others, and in 382 became secretary to Pope Damasus in Rome, under whose direction he began translating the Bible into Latin. Work began in Rome (382-384), but after the death of the Pope he moved to a monastery in Bethlehem, where he spent the last thirty five years of his life as spiritual director of the monastery for men, assisting in the direction of a monastic order for women, and continuing his incessant scholarly work. He was frequently engaged in controversy concerning Pelagius, Origen, Rufinus, and Augustine. His pastoral work included the development of an inn for travellers and a school for the local children. Unsurpassed by anyone in the early church in proficiency in languages and biblical scholarship, he is remembered not only for his Latin Vulgate, many Biblical commentaries, and translations of Eusebius, Origen and Didymus, but also for his work as a counselor and spiritual director, of which we have much evidence in his correspondence. NPNF 2, VI; Homilies, FC 48, 57; Dogmatic and Polemical Works, FC 53; Select Letters, transl. F. A. Wright, Loeb; MPL xxii-xxx.

❀

JOHN CLIMACUS (JOHN OF THE LADDER), ST. (C. 570–649). Monk of Sinai, later abbot of St. Catherine's monastery, mystic, ascetic writer. Received a good education, travelled to Mt. Sinai, then a famous center of Christian monasticism, and at first studied and practiced the spiritual life under the guidance of Martyrius. Upon his teacher's death he went into solitude for 20 years during which he engaged in spiritual exercises and studied the lives of saints. When he was approximately seventy-five years of age he was persuaded to become the abbot of the monastery of Mt. Sinai. So skilled was he in this role that he came to the attention of Pope Gregory the Great, who assisted him in the building of a hospital. While abbot he wrote *Ladder of Divine Ascent* (ed. L. Moore, Boston: Holy Transfiguration Monastery, 1978; also in COCL and CWS) in response to the request of John, Abbott of Raithu, for anchorites and cenobites. Each of the thirty steps of the ladder correspond to one of the "hidden" years of Jesus' life before his baptism and each speaks of a Christian virtue. Climacus was abbot for only four years after which he returned again to the hermitage to spend the rest of his life in isolation. He died in the hermitage of Mt. Sinai in 649. *To the Pastor,* COCL. MPG lxxxviii, 1165-1210.

❀

JOHN OF THE CROSS, ST. (1542–1591). Spanish mystic, co-founder with St. Teresa of Avila of the Discalced Carmelites, Doctor of the Church. Born in Hontiveros Avila, Spain, of a poor family of noble origin, John grew up in poverty and attended an elementary school for the poor in Medina del Campo. To support himself for his education at a Jesuit school, he worked at a hospital where he served the poorest of patients. In 1563 he joined the Carmelites, studied theology at Salamanca, and in 1567 was ordained priest. The following year he met Teresa of Avila, and concurred with her desire to reform the Carmelites through adoption of the "Primitive Rule." In 1568 he began the "Teresian Reform" among the brothers, and joined the first of the Discalced Houses in Duruelo. From 1570 to 1572 John was rector of the newly established Carmelite College at Alcalca de Henares. From 1572 to 1577 he served as Director and Confessor of Teresa's Convent of the Incarnation at Avila. In 1577 he was imprisoned at Toledo by recalcitrant Carmelites. It was during his nine-month imprisonment that he wrote most of his *Spiritual Canticle.* In 1578 he made a remarkable escape to the monastery of Calvario, and subsequently helped put Discalced reform into practice in monasteries at Baeza, Granada, Cordova, and Segovia. Among key influences upon his mysticism were Thomas Aquinas, and the Arabian mystics whom he studied in Granada in 1581. His *The Ascent of Mount Carmel, The Dark Night of the Soul* (1577ff.; New York: Doubleday, 1959), *The Spiritual Canticle, In an Obscure Night,* and *The Living Flame of Love* (1585; New York: Doubleday, 1962) were written for those seeking ascetic instruction and those charged with the spiritual welfare of others. He dealt with the purgation of the human spirit through the dark night of the soul, through which the soul through grace is sustained in pure faith. After a second purification, often accompanied by intense suffering, the soul becomes energized by the fully illuminating divine presence. He taught that the soul must be emptied of itself in order to be filled with God. The end of John's life was fraught with difficulties. His superiors, who disliked and distrusted him, sent him to Ubeda where he died in 1591. Collected Works, transl. by E. A. Peers, 3 vols., 2nd ed., London: 1953.

JOHN OF DAMASCUS, ST. (C. 675–C. 749). Greek theologian, among the greatest of the Eastern Church Fathers. Served as Christian representative in the Islamic court of the caliph of Damascus. Entered monastery near Jerusalem. Defended in three treatises the rich tradition of Christian iconography (*Against Those Who Reject Images,* 726-730; *On the Divine Images,* Crestwood, NY: St. Vladimir's Seminary Press, 1980). His *Fount of Wisdom* (or Sources of Knowledge) was a summary of philosophy, heretical views, and orthodoxy, the last third of which has been often the pattern of Christian theological reasoning subsequently. This last part, the *Exposition of the Catholic Faith (De Fide Orthodoxa),* or *The Orthodox Faith* (NPNF 2, IX; MPG xciv, 789-1228), consists of 100 chapters, and became a pattern for Peter Lombard, Thomas Aquinas, and other medieval theologians. It is a succinct summary of major teachings of the Greek Fathers on God, Trinity, Creation, Man, Providence, Incarnation, Sacraments and Ministry, Images, and Eschatology. It included a fully developed Mariology. It has been called the first systematic theology. Wrote *De virtutibus et vitiis, De institutione elementari,* and *De duabus voluntatibus,* MPG xcv, 85-186. Also wrote *A Commentary on the Epistles of St. Paul,* 13 homilies, various ascetic treatises, poems, and hymns (MPG xcvi). *Barlaam and Ioasaph,* ed. by G. R. Woodward and H. Mattingly, Loeb. MPG xciv-xcvi; BVP, xiii, 272ff.

JOHNSON, JOHN (1662–1725). Nonjuring English theologian and canonist. *Johnson's English Canons,* 2 vols., SED.

JULIAN OF NORWICH (C. 1342–after 1413). English mystic, Benedictine nun, anchoress who lived in a cell built into the wall of the Norman Church of St. Julian's Church, Norwich, England. In 1373, when seriously ill, received fifteen revelations, or showings, in a single day, and another the following day, and was healed. Twenty years later wrote *Revelations of the Divine Love* (entitled *Showings* in CWS), primarily focusing upon visions of the Lord's Passion and the Holy Trinity.

JUSTIN MARTYR, ST. (C. 100–C. 165). Philosopher, martyr, the most important second century Christian apologist. Born in Nablus (ancient Shechem in Samaria) to pagan parents. After studying Greek philosophy, became a Christian in 132 and spent the rest of his life as a travelling teacher and apologist of Christian thought, serving for a time at Ephesus where he engaged in his *Dialogue with Trypho*, the Jew (c. 135), and later at Rome where he taught Tatian and others. He is remembered for three principal works: *First Apology* (c. 152), addressed to the Emperor Antoninus Pius in which he sought to reconcile Greek philosophy and Christian revelation by showing that Christianity is not a new revelation, but rather the oldest and fullest revelation. Considered Christianity to be the true philosophy. Of special importance to pastoral thought in this essay is his account of contemporary baptismal and eucharistic practice. His *Second Apology,* addressed to the Roman Senate shortly after the ascension of Marcus Aurelius (161), speaks out against the persecution of Christians, and rebuts charges against them. *Dialogue with Trypho* argues the vocation of the gentiles to continue and transmute the covenant of God with Israel. Sought to reconcile the claims of faith and reason, arguing that traces of the truth are found in all humanity, since all share in the *logos spermatikos,* the germinative Word, of which Christian confession is the incarnate fulfillment. Upon refusing idolatrous sacrifice, Justin was, according to Tatian, scourged and beheaded in Rome in 165. Works, ANF I, LF 40, LCC I, pp. 225ff. MPG vi.

※

KNOX, JOHN (c. 1505–1572). Scottish Reformer. Educated Glasgow and St. Andrews, ordained 1536. By 1543 he had been converted to Protestantism by his tutor, Thomas Gilyem. His zeal and sense of prophetic vocation came from his association with John Rough and George Wishart (martyred in 1546). Was among rebels who held and preached in St. Andrews in 1547; imprisoned as a galley slave for nineteen months. After release in 1549, preached Reformed teaching at Berwick, and at the royal court in 1552, opposed kneeling during communion. Following the ascension of Catholic Queen Mary in 1553, Knox fled to the continent, met Bullinger in Zurich, learned extensively from Calvin's experiment in Geneva, and preached to refugee Protestant congregations in Frankfurt in 1554, and Geneva beginning in 1556. His work *First Blast of the Trumpet Against the Monstrous Regiment of Women* (1558), arguing that female sovereignty contravened natural law, alienated not only Queen Mary but also Elizabeth. In the same year he argued for lawful rebellion against idolatrous magistrates. His *Treatise on Predestination* appeared in Geneva in 1560. When he returned to Scotland in 1559 he became a leader of the Reformed movement, resisting the Roman rite, and proposing that monasteries and Catholic churches be closed. The *Book of Common Order* (1556-64) and the *First Book of Discipline* were largely his work. When in 1560 the Catholic queen regent, Mary of Lorraine, died, Protestantism became the established religion. He had numerous conflicts with the new queen, Mary Stuart from 1560-1567. Knox was arrested for treason but acquitted. Wrote *Scottish Confession* and *History of the Reformation of Religion Within the Realm of Scotland* (first published 1587, suppressed, first complete edition, 1644). His pastoral concerns can be seen in his treatises "On Prayer" and "A Fort for the Afflicted" as well as in his numerous pastoral letters. *Works,* ed. D. Laing, 6 vols., 1846-64. Collected *Writings,* London: Religious Tract Society, n.d.

※

KORTHOLT, CHRISTIAN (1632–1694). Professor of theology at Rostock (1662) and Kiel (1666), Lutheran pastoral writer. Wrote in opposition to Bellarmine, Spinoza, Hobbes, and Herbert of Cherbury. Wrote one of the first Protestant books in the genre of pastoral theology: *Pastor fidelis sive de officiis ministrorum ecclesiae opusculum,* Hamburg: S. Seylii & JI. Leibezeiti, 1696.

※

LACTANTIUS (LUCIUS CAECILIUS FIRMIANUS) (C. 240–C. 320). Christian Apologist. Born to pagan parents in North Africa, studied under Arnobius the Elder, and became a skilled rhetorician. Arrested the attention of the Emperor Diocletian and was asked to be a teacher of rhetoric in Nicomedia. He was converted to Christianity in 300 at nearly sixty years of age. When Diocletian issued his first edict against the Christians, Lactantius was forced to give up his teaching position. When in 303 the persecution of Christians began in earnest he was forced to leave the city. His first theological work, *De Opifico Dei* (303/304, see ANF VII, *On the Workmanship of God, or the Formation of Man*) was an attempt to prove the existence of God from the remarkable nature of the human body and from natural phenomena, an early attempt at natural theology. It sets forth a rudimentary early Christian psychology. His most famous work was his Seven Books of *Divinae Institutiones* (304-311, FC 49, Divine Institutes, ANF VII), one of the earliest systematic accounts of the Christian life, addressed to intellectuals of his day, sought to show the inability of pagan philosophy and reason to come to an adequate knowledge of God. In 314 his *De Ira Dei* (On the Anger of God) argued for the divine punishment of human misdeeds. *De Mortibus Persecutorum* (Death of the Persecutors, c. 318), which vividly described the deaths of persecuted Christians, is an important source of information on the last great persecution. The Emperor Constantine in 317 asked him to become tutor of his son Crispus. When Crispus was made Caesar, Lactantius followed him to Trier where he died in 320. Jerome called Lactantius one of the most learned men of his time, in his *De Viris Illustribus.* Minor Works, FC 54. MPL vi, vii.

※

LANGTON, STEPHEN (d. 1228). Archbishop of Canterbury. Wrote commentary on Peter Lombard's Sentences. Helped obtain the Magna Carta. Selections in LCC X, pp. 352-375.

※

LATIMER, HUGH (C. 1485-1555). Anglican Bishop of Worcester, Reformation theologian, martyr. Born in Thurcaston, Leicestershire. An ordained priest, wrote eloquent sermons against social and ecclesiastical corruption that showed the early influence of Reformation views in England. In 1534 when Henry VIII broke with Rome, Latimer became one of his chief advisors. In 1535 he became the Bishop of Worcester, but was forced to resign in 1539 when he refused to accept the pro-Roman Six Articles. Mary arrested him and had him confined to the Tower in 1553. He was burned at the stake with Ridley on the Oxford square in October, 1555 when he refused to accept the doctrine of transubstantiation. *Sermons,* edited by H. C. Beeching, 1906. *The Works of Hugh Latimer,* ed. by C. E. Corrie, 2 vols., New York: Johnson Reprints, 1844-1846 ed.

※

LAUD, WILLIAM (1573-1645). Archbishop of Canterbury. Born in Reading, England, son of a tailor, educated at St. John's College. When he was made Archbishop of Canterbury in 1633, he took vigorous measures against Presbyterians, suppressed Puritans with heavy penalties, and maintained the divine right of kings. When in 1637 he attempted to impose medieval liturgical practices upon the Church of Scotland, the entire country rebelled with the Civil War following in 1642. 400,000 Puritans fled England and went to New England and the Caribbean during his reign as Archbishop. His formulation of the "etcetera oath" led to his impeachment by the Long Parliament in 1640 and imprisonment to the Tower in 1641 under the charge of treason. He was executed at the Tower, January 10, 1645. His contributions to pastoral care are found in *A Summary of Devotions* (1667, posthumous); *Visitation Articles* (selections in CS); Speeches and Sermons. See *Works of Archbishop Laud,* edited by W. Scott-J. Bliss, LACT, 7 vols., 1847-60.

⁂

LEO I (THE GREAT), ST. (d. 461). Pope (440-461). Born in Rome, became deacon in 431. Leo's papacy ranks as the most important in the early Church next to that of Gregory the Great. During his twenty-one year reign he reshaped the papacy by placing primary stress on Petrine authority, sought unity in the church, opposed Pelagian theology, and engaged in many important diplomatic missions, successfully persuading the Vandals and Huns not to sack Rome in 452 and 455. Stressed the importance of the task of preaching and of private confession. The *Tome of Leo,* accepted as orthodox teaching at Chalcedon, 451, emphasized that Jesus Christ is fully human, fully God. Works extant are 143 Letters (FC 34), 96 sermons, and various selections in NPNF 2, XII. Critical ed. of Letters in E. Schwartz, ACO II, 4, 1932. MPL liv-lvi.

⁂

L'ESTRANGE, HAMON (1605-1660). Anglican religious writer. *God's Sabbath* (1641); *The Alliance of Divine Offices* (1659; LACT). Selections in *Angl.*

⁂

LULL, RAYMON (C. 1232-C. 1315). Apologist, philosopher, poet, mystic, Franciscan missionary to the Muslims, martyr. Born in Majorca, educated as a knight, at the age of 30 he devoted himself to the conversion of Muslims and Jews. Wrote apologetic arguments for Christianity in *Ars Magna* and lectured in Spain, France (Paris and Montpellier), and Italy. His method contrasted with scholastic methods of Thomism at that time. Sought to demonstrate the unity of all truth, sought the reunification of eastern and western Christianity, and the reunification of all mankind through Christianity. In 1267 began the study of Arabic and then went to North Africa as a missionary. Probably the first western medieval theologian to write in a language other than Latin (Catalan and Arabic) for his major works. Twice banished from Tunis for attempts to convert Muslims. He was mainly responsible for the addition of a faculty of oriental language study in five universities. A major influence on the thought of St. Teresa and St. John of the Cross. A prolific writer of some 290 books (of which 240 have survived), they include *The Book of the Lover and the Beloved* (translated by Kenneth Leech), *The Art of Contemplation, Tree of Life, The Book of the Beasts, True Art of Invention,* and *The Great Art.* He is thought to have been martyred in 1315.

⁂

LUTHER, MARTIN (1483-1546). German Reformer, primary influence in the shaping of Protestant pastoral care. Born in Eisleben, in 1501 he enrolled in the University of Erfurt where he studied under the nominalists, receiving his masters degree in 1505. Luther was preparing for a career in law, but in a storm swore to St. Anne to become a monk, and entered the Augustinian monastery at Erfurt. Ordained a priest in 1507, he began teaching at the University of Wittenberg in 1508. His teaching and doctoral studies at the University were interrupted for a period of time in 1510 when he travelled to Rome, where he was disturbed by abuses he saw in sacramental and penitential practice. In 1512 he received his doctoral degree in theology and was made a professor of Scriptural Theology at the University of Wittenberg, a post he held for the rest of his life. During this period he lectured on Psalms, Romans (LCC XV), Galatians and Hebrews. A new understanding of Christianity began to emerge in which the Bible became sole authority, each individual had direct access to divine revelation through scriptures, and each person was justified not by works but by faith through God's grace. Luther did not at first understand these teachings to conflict with papal teachings. He fully intended to remain within the Catholic Church and would have were it not for a series of events which eventually led to his excommunication. In response to the indulgence-selling of the popular Dominican preacher Tetzel, Luther wrote his "Ninety-five Theses upon Indulgences" and fastened them to the door of the Castle church at Wittenberg on October 31, 1517. The issue soon shifted away from indulgences and toward papal authority. The three pamphlets which he wrote in 1520—*An Appeal to the Nobility of the German Nation, On the Babylonian Captivity of the Church,* and *Christian Liberty*—were widely read, rallying much of Germany behind his reforms (cf. Early Theological Works, LCC XVI). After Luther's excommunication in 1521, he was asked to appear at the Diet in Worms, where he refused to recant. On May 25, 1521 he was declared an outlaw. Frederick the Wise, however, kidnapped him on his way from Worms and took him to Wartburg where he remained in hiding (1521-25), and where his career as a Reformer began in earnest. His most significant achievement during this period was his translation of the Bible into German. In 1524 he discarded his religious habit and in 1525 married Katherina von Bora, a former Cistercian nun. Together they raised six children. He sided with the princes in suppressing the Peasant Revolt of 1524-25. His strict adherence to the doctrines of original sin and predestination also caused him to lose many of his humanist followers when in 1524 he wrote *The Bondage of the Will* in response to Erasmus' *On Free Will* (LCC XVII). His debate with Zwingli in 1529 over the Eucharist and Calvin's differences with him resulted in a split within Protestantism between Reformed and Lutheran wings.

Luther's Reformation was not only doctrinal but also pastoral and practical (see especially *Letters of Spiritual Counsel,* LCC XVIII). Luther's pastoral concerns are evident in his *Greater Catechism* and *Smaller Catechism, Table Talk,* and numerous sermons. We quote from various editions: *Luther's Works,* ed. Jaroslav Pelikan, 54 vols. (St. Louis: Concordia, 1953ff.; abbr. LW); *Works of Martin Luther,* 6 vols. (Philadelphia: Muhlenberg Press, 1943; abbr. WML); *What Luther Says,* ed. Ewald Plaas, 3 vols. (St. Louis: Concordia, 1959; abbr. WLS); the Weimar Edition of Luther's Works, ed. J. K. F. Knaake (abbr. WA, or the *Tischreden,* abbr. WA-T; or Letters, abbr. WA-Br.); and *Martin Luther: Selections from His Writings,* ed. J. Dillenberger, 4 vols. (New York: Doubleday, 1961); *Theologia Germanica,* CWS.

MACARIUS, ST. OF EGYPT (c. 300–c. 390). Ascetic spiritual guide, also called Macarius the Elder, Macarius the Great, or Macarius the Egyptian. Lived sixty years in the wilderness of Scete, heart of Egyptian monasticism during the most crucial time of its formation. The *Lausaic History* of Palladius and Rufinus' history of monasticism provide our primary sources for Macarius' life, yet neither mention his writings; nonetheless numerous sayings are attributed to him that were destined to become staple sayings of the monastic tradition of spiritual guidance (cf. MPG xxxiv, 449-822; *Fifty Spiritual Homilies of St. Macarius the Egyptian,* edited by A. J. Mason, TCL, including themes on patience, discretion and perfection of spirit; *Sayings of the Desert Fathers,* trans. B. Ward, London: A. R. Mowbray, 1975; LCC XII).

❦

MARTIN OF BRAGA (BRACARA) (c. 520-579). Abbot of Dumio, Archbishop of Braga, Spain. Wrote on canon law, liturgy, cardinal virtues, anger, and the church calendar. Chief pastoral work is *Collectio orientalium canonum* (c. 561), which treats of ordination and the duties of the clergy. See FC 62 (The Iberian Fathers, Vol. I). MPL lxxii-lxxiv. Critical edition of works edited by C. W. Barlow, New Haven: Yale Univ. Press, 1950. In his *De correctione rusticorum,* he resisted superstitions of popular culture of his time.

❦

MARTIN OF TOURS, ST. (c. 335-397). Bishop of Tours, patron saint of France, among the earliest leaders of western monasticism. Founded monastery of Liguge, the first in Gaul. Sought to evangelize the neglected poor of the countryside; introduced rudimentary parochial system. MPL xviii, 9ff; BVP vii, 599ff. Life of St. Martin written by Sulpicius Severus (see MPG xx, 159-222).

❦

MATHER, INCREASE (1639-1723). Colonial minister, educated at Harvard and Dublin, pastor of North Church, Boston, 1664-1723, President of Harvard, 1685-1701. Advocated half-way covenant which provided a modified form of church membership for children of believers unable to meet full tests prescribed by Congregational polity. Wrote *An Essay for Recording of Illustrious Providence* and *Cases of Conscience concerning Witchcraft.*

❦

MAXIMUS THE CONFESSOR, ST. (c. 580-662). Greek theologian, monk, hymnist, and writer. Born of a distinguished family in Constantinople, left a promising political career (as secretary to the Emperor Heraclius) in 615 to become a monk in the monastery of Chrysopolis where he eventually became abbot. Fled to North Africa during the Persian invasion in 626, where he became the chief opponent of Monothelitism (rejected by sixth Ecumenical Council of Constantinople, 680). In 653 he was tortured and exiled to Thrace and in 661 exiled to Caucasus on charges of treason against Emperor Constantius II. Among the most prolific authors of eastern orthodoxy, he wrote some ninety works, some of which deal with soul care, ascetic discipline, ethics, liturgy and doctrine as well as commentaries on scripture. MPG xc, xci, iv, xix, 1217-80. *The Ascetic Life* and *The Four Centuries of Charity,* ACW 21. *Selected Writings,* CWS.

❦

MELANCHTHON, PHILIP (1497-1560). Protestant Reformer, collaborator with Luther. While a professor of Greek at the University of Wittenberg where he was known for his humanistic scholarship, Melanchthon became a follower of Luther, attended the Leipzig Disputation (1519), the Diet of Speyer (1529), the Colloquy of Marburg (1529), and was principal Lutheran spokesman at the Diet of Augsburg (1530). When Luther was in hiding in Wartburg (1521) and after Luther's death in 1546, Melanchthon assumed leadership of the Reformation movement. Was the first to organize and systematize Luther's teachings in his 1521 commentary on Romans, *Loci Communes* (LCC XIX, 1959, and in an earlier edition by C. L. Hill, Boston: 1944); and was principally responsible for writing the 1530 Augsburg Confession. Collected Works edited by K. G Bretschneider and E. Bindseil, CR, i-xxviii, Brunswick, 1834-60.

❦

MENNO SIMONS (1496–1561). Dutch Anabaptist, biblical expositor, leader of the Mennonites. Born in Witmarsum, Holland, son of dairy farmers who wished him to enter the priesthood. In 1524 he was ordained a priest in the Roman Catholic Church, serving in the town of Pingjum. During his first year he became disturbed while administering communion, especially concerning the doctrine of transubstantiation. He began searching the Scriptures and writings of Luther. A second religious crisis occurred when Sicke Freerks Snijder was martyred in 1531 because he had been "re-baptized." This led Simons to question the biblical basis for infant baptism. He concluded that the Scriptures supported believers' baptism. Still he did not leave the Roman Catholic Church, and from 1532 to 1536 served in his home church in Witmarsum. A third crisis arose in the year 1535 when hundreds of Anabaptists, his brother Peter Simons among them, who had attempted to found a "New Jerusalem" in Muenster were slaughtered. In agreement with Anabaptist views and in outrage over their persecution Menno Simons decided to join them. In 1536 he left the Roman Catholic Church, and in 1537 was rebaptized by the leading Anabaptist Obbe Philip and became the leading figure among the Anabaptists. He wandered from place to place in Holland, preaching secretly at night. He was soon asked to become an elder, and devoted the rest of his life to the administrative task of organizing the northern Anabaptists, to pastoral care, preaching, and expounding Anabaptist teaching in pamphlets which he printed on his own clandestine printing press. He authored many books, now collected in the *Complete Writings of Menno Simons* (abbr. CWMS, Scottdale, PA: Herald Press, 1956). Among leading works that pertain to pastoral care are *Foundation of Christian Doctrine* (1539); *A Kind Admonition on Church Discipline* (1541); *Confession to Distressed Christians* (1552); *The Nurture of Children* (c. 1557); and numerous letters of consolation and pastoral care. His views bore close kinship with the Swiss Brethren. They included believer's baptism, a primitive congregational polity, rejection of the Christian magistracy, and the ethics of non-resistance to violence. The English separatist baptists exiled in Holland were in close touch with scattered Mennonite communities.

❦

METHODIUS OF OLYMPUS (d. c. 311). Probably bishop of Olympus, martyred in Chalcis. Only complete extant work in Greek is the *Symposium, or Banquet of the Ten Virgins* (*The Symposium: A Treatise on Chastity*, ACW 27), modeled on Plato's Symposium, extolling chastity as Plato extolled eros. MPG xviii, 9-408; ANF VI, 309ff.

❦

MINUCIUS FELIX (lived before 250). Latin apologist, Roman lawyer, author of the

Latin dialogue *Octavius* (ANF IV, 173-198; ACW 39, FC 10, Loeb, MPL iii) in which the Christian Octavius refutes the arguments of the pagan Caecilus, converting him to Christianity.

※

MOLINA, LUIS DE (1535-1600). Spanish Jesuit theologian. Principal work: *Concordia liberi arbitrii cum gratiae donis* (Lisbon: 1588), the central argument of which is that free human cooperation with the gift of grace is divinely foreknown without the diminishing of freedom. Divine foreknowledge embraces all hypothetical future contingents that could be elicited by free decisions (sometimes called *scientia media* or Molinism). This extremely precise argument was written as a commentary on Thomas Aquinas, ST, I-1ae, QQ xiv, xix, xxii, xxiii, was resisted by Dominicans, but exonerated by Paul V in 1607. His *De justitia et jure* (Cuenca, 1593) constituted a significant attempt to discuss economic justice and church-state relationships. Critical edition of works edited by F. Stegmueller, BGPMK xxxii, Muenster: Aschendorff, 1935.

※

MOLINOS, MIGUEL DE (1640-1697). Spanish quietist. Became one of the leading spiritual directors of his era, and counselor to many prelates, among them the future Pope Innocent XI. Wrote *Spiritual Guide* (1675, Glasgow: Thompson, 1885), read by Protestants (esp. A. H. Francke and Gottfried Arnold) as well as Catholics. Sought to reconcile the contemplative and active life. Perceived by Catholic leadership as too mystical, and as having too close an affinity with Protestants and pietists. Condemned by the pope in 1685 and forced to recant, he was placed in confinement in a Dominican monastery until his death in 1697. Taught that perfect spiritual peace was possible through abnegation of the will by means of rigorous meditative discipline, making the soul indifferent to sense and desire.

※

MORE, THOMAS, ST. (1458-1535). English lord chancellor, author of *Utopia,* on the ideal political state. Came into conflict with Henry VIII (whom he probably helped to write a defense of the seven sacraments) over his marriage annulment to Catherine of Aragon, refused to take an oath renouncing the authority of the pope, and was sent to the tower and executed. During his confinement in the Tower, wrote one of the greatest works in the genre of consolation literature: *A Dialogue of Comfort against Tribulation,* ed. L. Miles, Bloomington: Indiana University Press, 1965. *Works* ed. by Wm. Rastell, London: John Cawod, 1557.

※

NEMESIUS OF EMESA (4th century). Christian philosopher and psychologist, probably Bishop of Emesa (Homs), Syria. Wrote *On the Nature of Man* (LCC IV), the most detailed psychology of the eastern church fathers. Although few facts of his life can be learned from this work, it is evident that Nemesius was a man of considerable education who was well versed not only in philosophy, but also in medicine. It would also seem that the book was written at the end of the fourth century since Nemesius had clearly read Origen but did not know that Origen's orthodoxy had been questioned. This work, which influenced John of Damascus, Albert the Great, and Thomas Aquinas, consists of a thorough explication of the *psyche* from a Christian point of view. In it Nemesius argues against Plato's view of the soul as quite separate and distinct from the body, and Aristotle's view which tends to reduce soul to material substance. He rather views the soul as an incorporeal substance which is self-moving and acts upon the body. In the same way in which he views the world as a graded order, he sees the soul also as composed of a series of levels with unconscious impulses at the natural or libidinal level, seeking organization and intentionality through reasoning. In the second part of the work Nemesius explores the possibility of free will rejecting the determinisms of his day. MPG xl.

❧

NICETA, ST. (c. 335–414). Hymnwriter, missionary, Bishop of Remesiana in the Balkans, c. 370. Wrote on Liturgical Singing, on the Vigils of the Saints, and several essays on theology: "An Instruction on Faith," "The Power of the Holy Spirit," "An Explanation of the Creed," in FC 7; MPL xvii, 579ff.

❧

NICHOLAS I, MYSTIKOS, ST. (852–925). Patriarch of Constantinople. *Miscellaneous Writings,* Greek text and ET, L. G. Westerink, Washington, DC: Center for Byzantine Studies, 1981.

❧

NICOLAS OF CUSA (1401–1464). Cardinal, philosopher, scientist, ecumenist. Supported independence of princes in secular matters; anticipated Copernicus by teaching the revolution of the earth around the sun; argued for a plurality of worlds; worked for reconciliation of the Hussites. *De Concordantia Catholica* (1431-36) sought broad reforms in the church; and *De Docta Ignorantia* (1440, ET, G. Herron, 1954) argued that since divine truth is one, absolutely simple, and fully present to God, it is unknowable by man. Human knowledge is relative, complex, divided, partial. The way to knowing the truth must lead through and beyond reason by means of the principle of contradiction to God in whom all contradictions are understandable in a *coincidentia oppositorum.* God is neither three nor one, but triune, being both center and circumference of the world, both everywhere and nowhere. Collected works edited by Henric-Peters, 3 vols., Basel, 1565. *The Vision of God,* Chicago: Ungar, 1960. *Unity and Reform: Selected Writings of Nicholas de Cusa,* ed. J. Dolan, Notre Dame: University Press, 1962.

❧

ODO OF CLUNY, ST. (879–942). Cistercian reformer, second abbot of Cluny. Born near LeMans, France, brought up in the family of William of Aquitaine who founded the influential abbey of Cluny in 910. Educated at Aquitaine, St. Martin of Tours, and Paris, joined the Cluniac community at Baume, was later charged with the monastery school. Became abbot of Cluny in 927. Reform included complete liberation of the church from secular direction and abolition of clerical marriages and simony. Several Cluny-trained monks became popes who continued these reforms. Peacemaking diplomat between King Hugo of Italy and Alberic of Rome. Works include *Occupatio* (ed. A. Swoboda, Leipzig, 1900), an epic poem on redemption; *Collationes,* three books of moral and political essays; *Moralia in Job;* sermons; hymns; and biographies of St. Gerald of Aurillac and Gregory of Tours. MPL cxxxiii, 105-845.

Odon (Oda the Good), St. (d. 959). Bishop of Ramsbury, Wiltshire (927), appointed Archbishop of Canterbury during the reign of King Edmund, 942. A Dane, he converted and became a Benedictine. His *Constitutiones* (MPL cxxxiii, 931ff.; SCAC, xviii) published as Archbishop provide instructions for bishops, priests, deacons, monks, fasting, tithing, support of the poor, and secular political authority. Life by Eadmer in Wharton, Anglia Sacra, II, pp. 78-87 and in Mabillon, ASSB, 1685.

❧

Origen (c. 185–c. 254). Alexandrian theologian, Biblical scholar. Held to three senses of scripture: historical (somatic), moral (psychic), and speculative (pneumatic). Born in Egypt of a Christian family. Origen's father, Leonides, gave Origen an excellent education in both sacred and secular literature. Probably studied under Clement at his catechetical school in Alexandria. When the persecution of Septimius Severus broke out in 202, his father was martyred. He received permission in 203 to re-open the catechetical school of Clement who had been forced to flee during the persecution. Within a short time the school flourished. Crowds flocked to hear Origen teach, and the school soon became a famous center of learning. Besides teaching, he diligently studied scripture, began his prolific literary career, and engaged in an extreme form of asceticism. Devoted himself to visiting and ministering to the imprisoned in spite of danger to his own life. Undertook journeys to Rome, and to Arabia; fled in 215 to Caesarea during a political uprising. Was recalled by Bishop Demetrius to Alexandria where from 218 to 230 he continued to teach, and produced numerous books. He was exiled by Demetrius in 230 after being ordained in Caesarea. Origen spent the remainder of his life teaching in exile in Caesarea where he opened another influential school. During the Decian persecution in 250 Origen was imprisoned, tortured, and killed.

One of the most prolific writers of Christian history, his writings may have numbered as many as 6,000 volumes, many now unfortunately lost, partly because some of his teachings were later considered heretical and the originals destroyed. Origen is remembered for his famous six column version of the Old Testament, the *Hexapla* (ed. F. Field, 2 vols., Oxford, 1872; MPG xv, xvi); the first systematic exposition of Christian doctrine in *De Principiis* (On First Principles, ANF IV; Harper Torchbook Edition, 1966, ed. by G. W. Butterworth); Commentaries on most books of the Bible (MPG xvii), see *Song of Songs, Commentary and Homilies,* ACW 26; an important apologetical work entitled *Against Celsus* (MPG xi, 641-1632); *Exhortation to Martyrdom* (ACW 19; CWS; MPG xi, 563ff), written in 235 during persecution; and *On Prayer* (ACW 19; CWS; LCC), an early exegetical approach to the Lord's Prayer. MPG xi-xviii. TU i. ANF IV and X.

❧

Orosius, Paulus, (c. 385–d. after 418). Apologist, historian. Upon Augustine's request, wrote a history of the world designed to provide a theological clarification of the meaning of Alaric's sack of Rome, as a history of providence; see *Adversus Paganos,* Seven Books Against the Pagans, FC 50. MPL xxxi. Also wrote polemical essays against Pelagius, Origen, and Priscillian.

❧

Owen, John (1616–1683). Dissenting theologian, devotional writer, Congregationalist pastor. Left Queen's College in 1637 because of Laud's statutes, became pastor of a church in Fordham, Essex (1643). When in 1647 he became pastor at Coggeshall, he sought to institute a Congregational method of government. He was chaplain to Cromwell (1649-51) during the Civil War period, and then dean of Christ Church (1651) and vice chancellor of Oxford University (1652-1657). After the Restoration in 1660 he was permitted to continue preaching, and in 1673 became minister of Leadenhall in London. From this time until his death in 1683 he was the leading figure in the Protestant Nonconformist movement. A prolific author of devotional writings, biblical commentaries and polemical works against the Arminians and Socinians, he also wrote on pastoral care and church polity—see *The True Nature of a Gospel Church and Its Government* (1689), *The Doctrine of Justification by Faith, On the Holy Spirit, The Divine Origin of Holy Scripture, Saint's Perseverance, Union Among Protestants,* and *Christologia.* Collected Works edited by T. Russell, 21 vols., 1826.

※

PACHOMIUS, ST. (C. 290–346). Founder of the cenobitic system of monasticism. Built monastery on the Nile (c. 320), which served as model for the Rule of St. Basil. Founded eleven monasteries housing more than 7,000 monks and nuns. Noted in Palladius, his Rule has survived through Jerome (MPL xxiii, 61-99; see A. Boon and L. Lefort, ed. Pachomiana Latina, 1932). *Pachomian Koinona,* I-III: *The Lives,* CCS 45; *The Chronicles and Rules,* CSS 46; *The Instructions, Letters and Other Writings of St. Pachomius and His Disciples,* CSS 33. MPG xxiii, xl.

※

PALLADIUS (C. 365–425). Bishop of Helenopolis, Christian writer on early monasticism. Probably born in Galatia, entered a monastery in Jerusalem, then to Egypt to devote himself to ascetic discipline. After an illness in 399 returned to Palestine, and in 400 was made Bishop of Helenopolis. Exiled in 406 after he defended his friend John Chrysostom at the Synod of the Oak (403). Authored a dialogue on the life of Chrysostom. In 412 returned to Helenopolis and in 417 moved to the diocese of Aspuna where he authored the single most significant treatise on early monasticism, *Historia Lausaica* (419-420, MPG xxxiv; BVP viii, 259), *The Lausaic History,* ed. C. Butler, TS VI, Cambridge, 1898; ACW 34. *Life of Chrysostom,* TCL.

※

PAPIAS, ST. (C. 60–130). Bishop of Hierapolis, companion of St. Polycarp of Smyrna. Fragments, MPG v, 1255-62. AF (Lightfoot), pp. 514-535. ANF I, 151-159.

※

PARACELSUS (PSEUDONYM OF PHILIPPUS AUREOLUS THEOPHRATUS BOMBASTUS VON HOHENHEIM, 1493-1541). Swiss medical doctor, scientist, alchemist, theosophic writer. Born and raised in Switzerland, studied medicine in Germany, and practiced medicine thoughout Europe until 1526 when he took a teaching position at the University of Basel. Lost this job in 1528 and spent the remainder of his life living in numerous places, engaged in scientific research in which he made unparalleled contributions to the fields of chemistry, medicine, and psycho-somatic theory. Influenced by kabbalistic and hermetic writers, Paracelsus argued that man was a microcosm that brought together all of the macrocosm of nature into a single organism. *Selected Writings,* ed. J. Jacobi, Princeton: Princeton University Press, 1958.

※

PASCHASIUS RADBERTUS (C. 785–860). French Benedictine theologian, abbot of Adalhard, 844. Wrote commentaries on Matthew, Psalms, and Lamentations. Treatise on *De Corpore et Sanguine Domini,* 831, an early monograph on the Eucharist, which in maintaining the Real Presence of Christ, specified it further as the flesh born of Mary, miraculously multiplied at each consecration. Although insisting on the spiritual mode of Christ's Presence, his teaching later became further formulated as the doctrine of transubstantiation. The physical realism of these views was later opposed by Ratramnus and Rabanus Maurus, yet later approved by the Fourth Lateran Council. Collected works edited by J. Sirmond, Paris, 1618; MPL, cxx.

※

PATRICK, ST. (C. 389–C. 461). Celtic missionary to Ireland, "Apostle to the Irish." Probably born near Scottish town of Dumbarton, captured at sixteen by marauders from Ireland, became a slave in East Antrim, where his eyes were opened to his calling to convert Ireland. After six years in captivity, returned to Scotland; a vision called him back to Ireland, and he returned about 432, preaching, and converting enormous numbers, according to legend. Founded monastery at Armagh. Works of St. Patrick; St. Secundius, Hymn on St. Patrick, ACW 17; *St Patrick: His Writings and Life,* TCL; MPL liii, 789ff; BVP, x, 159ff.

※

PATRICK, SIMON. (1626–1707). Bishop of Ely, latitudinarian. Wrote *A Full View of the Doctrines and Practices of the Ancient Church* (1688). "A Letter of the Bishop of Chichester to His Clergy, 1690," and "The Work of the Ministry" (1692), in *CS,* 49ff. Collected works edited by A. Taylor, 9 vols., Oxford, 1858.

※

PAULINUS OF NOLA, ST. (353–431). Bishop of Nola, foremost Christian Latin poet of the period. Lived self-sacrificially, built hospital for poor, and water works for city of Nola in Campania. Carried on extensive correspondence with Ambrose, Augustine, and others that revealed his pastoral discernment, Letters, 2 vols., ACW 35, 36; *Life of Ambrose,* FC 15; *Poems,* ACW 40. MPL lxi.

※

PEARSON, JOHN (1612–1686). Lady Margaret Prof. of Divinity and Master of Trinity College, Cambridge, 1662, Bishop of Chester, 1673. *Exposition of the Creed* (1659); *Vindiciae Espistolarum S. Ignati* (1672, LACT, 2 vols.); *Annales Cyprinici* (1682).

※

PELAGIUS (d. c. 424). British monk. In Rome (383–410) opposed Augustine's doctrine of will. Father of Pelagianism, rejected by the council of Ephesus in 431. Held the freedom of will to be the power of alternate choice. Rejected original sin, affirming each person has perfect freedom to do good or evil. Hence a sinless life was thought possible, and the church was considered an adult community committed to perfectionist ideals, with Christ as example. Sought to discredit asceticism and moral pessimism. Sharply attacked by Augustine and Jerome. Wrote *On*

Free Will, Faith in the Trinity, Exposition on Thirteen Epistles of Paul, TS 9.1–9.3. MPL xxi. 1155ff. CSEL 42, 60.

PERKINS, WILLIAM (1558–1602). Puritan theologian, Cambridge casuist. Influenced practical divinity in continental pietism and English puritanism. *The Whole Treatise of the Cases of Conscience,* London: Pickering, 1611.

PERPETUA, ST. (d. 7 Mar. 203). African martyr of the Carthaginian church. Imprisoned after baptism and condemned to execution in the arena of Carthage. The *Passion* of St. Perpetua records her visions and martyrdom. Authorship uncertain, perhaps edited by Tertullian (see Latin edition by J. A. Robinson, Texts and Studies, I, No. 2, Cambridge, 1891). ANF III, 697ff., MPL iii, 13ff.

PETER DAMIAN, ST. (1007–1072). Benedictine reformer, Doctor of the Church, Cardinal, Bishop of Ostia. Born in Ravenna, in 1035 he entered the Benedictine hermitage, and in 1043 was made prior of the monastery. He applied his reforms to the church at large when he was made cardinal in 1057. Ally of Cardinal Hildebrand and his reforms. He has left behind a number of treatises, sermons, letters, vitae, prayers and hymns. Wrote one of the few medieval treatises on homosexuality, *Liber Gomorrhianus* (The Book of Gomorrah). MPL cxliv, cxlv. *Selected Writings on the Spiritual Life,* ed. P. McNulty, COCL.

PETER LOMBARD (c. 1095–1159). Medieval scholastic theologian, "Master of the Sentences." Born in Lombardy, educated at Bologna, Rheims and Paris, became Bishop of Paris. Known chiefly for his Four Books of Sentences (*Libri Quatuor Sententiarum,* 1157, (LCC X, Selections, pp. 334-352), a compendium of citations of church fathers organized in a sequential argument that moves from the triune God to creation and sin, to incarnation and the virtues, to the sacraments (essentially the same sequence used by John of Damascus). Peter Lombard was the first to designate the number of sacraments as seven, later accepted by the Fourth Lateran Council (1215). His work strongly influenced the remainder of medieval theology, where *The Sentences* became a standard text. Numerous commentaries were written on the sentences. MPL cxci, cxcii. Text of sentences and commentary on them is found in Bonaventure's work. Also wrote *Commentary on the Psalms,* MPL cxci.

POLYCARP, ST. (c. 69–c. 155). Bishop of Smyrna. Disciple of the Apostle John, friend of Ignatius, teacher of Irenaeus. "Letter to Philippi," AF 123ff.; "The Martyrdom of Polycarp," ECW 151-169; AF 138ff.

PROSPER OF AQUITAINE, ST. (c. 390–c. 463). Augustinian theologian and poet. Secretary to Pope Leo I. *On Grace and Free Will,* FC 7; *Defense of St. Augustine,* ACW 32. MPL, li, 1-868.

PRUDENTIUS, AURELIUS CLEMENS (348–c. 410). Latin Poet and Hymnist. Applied classical Latin poetic style to Christian spiritual instruction. Wrote *Psychomachia* (The Struggle of the Soul), an allegory of the battle between virtue and vice for the soul of humanity. Poems, 2 vols., FC 43, 52. MPL lix, 775ff., lx. CSEL 61.

※

QUENSTEDT, JOHANN ANDREAS (1617–1688). Professor of Theology at Wittenberg. Wrote major compendium of Lutheran orthodoxy: *Theologia didactico-polemica sive Systema theologicum* (1685). Pastoral theology contained in *Ethica Pastorum et Instructio Cathedralis* (1678; 3rd. ed. Wittenberg: Michael Wendt, 1708).

※

QUINISEXT SYNOD (692). So-called because it occurred between the Fifth and Sixth General Ecumenical Council, hence Quinisext (fifth-sixth), also called Trullan Synod, or Council of Trullo. Among its 102 canons are many on spiritual, penitential and marital counsel, the rejection of fees for pastoral counseling, and liturgical decisions. See Ecumenical Councils.

※

RABANUS MAURUS (776–856). Abbot of Fulda, Archbishop of Mainz, author and poet, one of the greatest theologians of his age. Born in Mainz, became a Benedictine, ordained a priest in 814 and Abbot of Fulda from 822-842, he instigated many reforms. When made Archbishop of Mainz in 847 he engaged in missionary work in Germany, presided over three synods and wrote an important work for pastoral care entitled *De Institutione clericorum* (840, ed. A. Knoepfler, Munich: Lentner, 1900, MPL cvii), a priest's manual dealing with sacraments, prayer, fasts and discipline, influenced strongly by Gregory the Great and Augustine. Wrote *Tractatus de anima,* and *Paenitentiale,* MPL cx; *De ecclesiastic disciplina, Liber de sacris ordinibus,* MPL cxii; and *De Rerum Naturis* (MPL, cvii-cxii), and numerous commentaries on scripture.

※

RAYMOND OF PENAFORT, ST. (c. 1185–1275). Dominican Spanish canonist, Professor of law at Barcelona and Bologna. Helped found the Mercedarian Order dedicated to the redeeming of captives. As confessor and chaplain to Gregory IX, was commissioned to organize papal decretals, a standard work completed in 1234. Wrote *Summa de poenitentia* (1223-1238, cf. also *Summa casuum*), a pastoral handbook on penance. Commissioned Thomas Aquinas to write SCG. Founded schools of Hebrew and Arabic in missionary efforts. Collected works edited by J. R. Serra, Barcelona, 1945ff.

※

RICHARD OF ST. VICTOR (d. 1173). Scottish born scholar and leading mystical theologian. Pupil of Hugh of St. Victor, prior of St. Victor. Discussed contemplation in stages, influenced Bonaventure and Gerson. *Benjamin Major* and *Benjamin Minor* became standard manuals of medieval spiritual guidance. Chief theological work, *De Trinitate,* prepared the way for Thomas Aquinas. CWS edition has *The Twelve Patriarchs, The Mystical Ark, Book Three of the Trinity.* Selections in LCC, Vol. X, pp. 319-332, and *Selected Writings on Contemplation,* COCL, transl. by Clare Kirchberge, London: Faber & Faber, 1962. MPL clxxv-clxxvii, cxcvi.

※

RIDLEY, NICHOLAS (c. 1500–1555). Bishop of London, Oxford martyr. Chaplain to Thomas Cranmer. Assisted in establishing Protestant views at Cambridge, and in compiling BCP of 1549. After Oxford disputations of 1554, was excommunicated, and burned with Latimer at Oxford, Oct. 16, 1555. Selections in Fathers of the English Church, iv, (1809), pp. 31-267; and in ETM I.

❧

ROLLE OF HAMPOLE, RICHARD (C. 1295–1349). Yorkshire mystic, hermit, spiritual advisor to Cistercian nuns. Studied at Oxford and Paris; rebelled against scholasticism; led a wandering life of contemplation and solitude. One of the earliest religious authors to write in the vernacular for the common people concerning spiritual formation. Wrote *Incendium Amoris,* (ed. by Margaret Deanesly, Manchester, 1915), *Melos Amoris* (ed. by E. Arnould, Oxford: Blackwell, 1957) and *Emendatio Vitae* (London: Watkins, 1922). Also wrote commentary on psalms, devotional poetry, and meditation on the Lord's Passion. *Selected Works,* edited by E. C. Heseltine, London: Longmans, Green, 1930.

❧

RUFINUS, TYRANNIUS (C. 345–410). Presbyter of Aquileia, Latin church historian, translator of Greek works into Latin, notably Origen's *De principii,* Origen's commentaries, the Clementina, and works by Basil, Gregory of Nazianzus and Eusebius. Engaged in controversy with former friend Jerome on the value of Origen's works. Founded monastery in Jerusalem. Wrote commentary on the Apostles' Creed (ACW 20). NPNF 2, III, pp. 405ff. MPL, xxi, 1123ff.

❧

RUPERT OF DEUTZ (C. 1070–1129). Benedictine theologian, medieval exegete, abbot of Deutz about 1120. Wrote *De Divinis Officiis* (ed. R. Haacke, CCCM 7, 1967; MPL clxix), a treatise on the Christian year, and numerous commentaries, especially on the prophets. MPL, clxvii-clxx. Opera Omnia, edited by M. Pleunich, 4 vols., Venice, 1748-51.

❧

RUYSBROECK, JAN VAN (1293–1381). Flemish Augustinian theologian, mystic. Founded Augustinian monastery of Groenendaal, 1350; influenced Johannes Tauler, Geert de Groote (founder of the Brethren of the Common Life), and others. In *The Spiritual Espousals,* ed. by E. Colledge, COCL, he sought to combine the active life, the inner life, and the beatific vision. Collected works ed. by J. Van Mierlo, 4 vols., 1944-48.

❧

SALVIAN THE PRESBYTER (C. 400–C. 480). Born to Christian parents in Cologne, Salvian later separated from his wife, Palladia, in order that both of them might become devoted to the religious life, first at Lerins (from c. 424), then Marseilles (from c. 439) where he was a presbyter. Wrote *De Gubernatione Dei* (after 439, FC 3, see *The Governance of God,* trans. J. O'Sullivan, New York: Cima Publ., 1947), a work in eight books in which he contrasts the corruption of Roman society with that of the barbarians. Also still extant are nine letters (FC 3) and a treatise, *Ad Ecclesiam,* on the giving of alms; *Four Books of Timothy to the Church,* FC 3; MPL, liii, 25-238.

❧

SARCERIUS, ERASMUS (1501–1559). Lutheran Theologian, pastor of Leipzig, Magdeburg. *De consensu verae ecclesiae et ss. Patrum* (1540). Wrote on ordination, systematic pastoral visitation, and catechetical instruction. *Pastorale oder Hirtenbuch,* Frankfurt: n.p., 1565.

SAYINGS OF THE DESERT FATHERS. *See* DESERT FATHERS.

❧

SERAPION, ST. (d. after 360). Bishop of Thmuis, Egypt (c. 339); friend of Athanasius, lived in desert with Anthony. Wrote *Against the Manichees* (Harvard Theol. Studies 15, 1931), and a sacramentary, *Bishop Seraphion's Prayer Book*, TCL, transl. J. Wordsworth, London: SPCK, 1899.

❧

SEVEN ECUMENICAL COUNCILS. NPNF 2, XIV. *See* ECUMENICAL COUNCILS.

❧

SHEPHERD OF HERMAS, THE, OR PASTOR OF HERMAS. (Second century). A slave emancipated in Rome prospered, lost property, and in a vision is shown the way of repentance and faith. Written in the second century, so named because an angel in the form of a shepherd visited Hermas and revealed to him the necessity of repentance. The Muratorian Canon indicates that his brother was Pius, bishop of Rome (140-154). Possibly composed in stages, perhaps by several authors, the work consists of five Visions, twelve Mandates, and ten Similitudes. It was included in early canonical lists of the third century in the eastern tradition, and was at times used in the instruction of catechumens. Among its chief themes is the difficulty and necessity of radical repentance. ANF I; AF, pp. 155-263; FC 1.

❧

SPARROW, ANTHONY (1612–1685). Anglican bishop of Exeter. Fellow of Queens' College, Cambridge 1633-1644, until fellowship was rejected on the grounds of his Royalism, reinstated 1662. Wrote *A Rationale Upon the Book of Common Prayer* (1655); *A Collection of Articles, Injunctions, Canons of the Church of England* (1661). Selections in *Angl.*

❧

SPENER, PHILLIP JAKOB (1635–1705). Lutheran pastor, founder of Pietism. Born in Alsace, studied theology in Strassburg, served Lutheran churches in Strassburg (1663), Frankfurt (1666), Dresden (1686) and Berlin (1691). While a minister in Frankfurt his concern for the inner religious life led him to form small study groups called "Collegia Pietatis" from which Pietism as a movement took its name. He set down his views on church renewal in *Pia Desideria* (1675, ed. T. Tappert, Philadelphia: Fortress Press, 1954). He stressed the necessity of conversion and holy living, small group biblical study and accountability, sometimes known as conventicles or *ecclesiolae in ecclesia* (the churches within the church), lay mission, the priesthood of all believers, avoidance of divisive disputation, devotional literature, evangelical preaching, practical works of love, emphasis on spiritual formation in pastoral education, restoration of confirmation, and setting aside of days of prayer and fasting. As a friend of King Frederick I of Prussia he helped found the University of Halle in 1694, and was an important promoter of missionary activity, prayer meetings, catechetical instruction and Sunday school. Wrote *Das geistliche Priesterthum* (The Spiritual Priesthood, 1677, ET in Henry E. Jacobs, ed., *A Summary of the Christian Faith*, Philadelphia: General Council Board of Publication, 1905, pp. 581-595). *Letzte Theologisches Bedencken*, Halle: Waeysenhauses, 1721. Collected works, *Theologische Bedencken*, 4 vols., Halle, 1700-1702; *Letzte Theologische Bedencken*, ed. Baron von Canstein, 3 vols., Halle, 1711. *Hauptschriften*, edited by Paul Gruenberg, Gotha: F. A. Perthes, 1889. Wrote on the impediments to theological study

(*Hauptschriften,* pp. 184-231). *Speners Kleine Geistliche Schriften,* ed. J. Steinmetz, 2 vols., Magdeburg, 1741.

❧

SUAREZ, FRANCISCO DE (1548-1617). Spanish canonist, leading Jesuit theologian. Born at Granada, studied canon law at Salamanca, Professor at Coimbra, Portugal. Wrote *De legibus* (1612). Helped formulate an early theory of international law, positing a "law of nations" (*jus gentium*); repudiated James I's theory of divine right of kings, influenced Protestant canonists. Commented extensively on Thomas Aquinas, proposing a "congraduism" of grace, that God gradually draws persons by grace toward salvation though stages which by foreknowledge God knows will be useful (*De vera intelligentia auxilii efficacis,* 1605, published 1655). As in Luis de Molina, God does not cause human free acts, but foresees them, and by his special foreknowing (*scientia media*) provides means of grace gradually necessary for spiritual growth. His theory of grace and freedom was fully developed in *De necessitate gratiae* (1619), *De gratia habituali* (1619), and *De gratia actuali* (1651). Opera, 23 vols., 1740-51. *Selections,* Oxford: Clarendon, 1944.

❧

SULPICIUS SEVERUS (C. 360–C. 420). Lawyer until c. 392, became monk, priest, and a leading Latin ecclesiastical historian. Disciple of St. Martin of Tours, and his biographer. Among the earliest Christian writers to try to provide an interpretation of universal history, from the creation of the world to 400 A.D. *Chronicle* written about 403. Writings, FC 7, NPNF 2, XI, pp. 3-122. MPL xx, 95ff.

❧

SYLVESTER II (GERBERT, C. 940-1003). Pope from 999, anticipated numerous themes of Renaissance humanism. Among earliest medieval writers to acquire knowledge of medicine, as well as other scientific subjects. Considered an antecedent of the tradition of "pastoral medicine" (BMKS). MPL cxxxix, 57-338.

❧

SYMEON THE NEW THEOLOGIAN (C. 949-1022). Abbot, Byzantine mystical theologian in the tradition of Evagrius, Maximus the Confessor and John Climacus. *Theological and Practical Treatises and Three Theological Discourses,* CSS 41; *Discourses,* CWS. Wrote on themes of sobriety and attention, modes of prayer, and the relation of body and soul. MPG cxx. *Hymns of Divine Love,* transl. Geo. Maloney, Denville, NJ: Dimension Books, 1976.

❧

SYNESIUS OF CYRENE (C. 370–C. 414). Bishop of Ptolemais (c. 410-414). Native of Cyrene, ambassador to Imperial Court of Constantinople. Wrote on political activity at Constantinople, a satirical eulogy on baldness, and a defence of the life of learning. Wrote a treatise, *De Insomniis* (MPG lxvi, 1281-1320), on the causes and meaning of sleep and dreams, and a treatise on providence (ibid., 1209ff.). Collected works in Latin, edited by Petavius, Paris, 1612, include 155 letters and 10 hymns. MPG lxvi, 1021-1756. ET of Letters, edited by A. FitzGerald, London, 1920.

❧

TARNOW, JOHANN (1586-1629). *De sancrosancto Ministerio,* 3 vols., Rostock: n.p., 1623.

TATIAN (c. 110–172). Syrian Christian apologist, pupil of Justin Martyr at Rome, engaged in defense of faith against pagan misrepresentation in *Oratio ad Graecos, Address to the Greeks* (c. 160, ANF II), refuting Greek prejudices in a polemical style. Wrote *Diatessaron,* a harmony of the four gospels, used liturgically in Syrian Church until the fifth century. ANF II. MPG vi, 801ff.

TAYLOR, JEREMY (1613–1677). Devotional writer, Anglican Bishop. Cambridge born and educated, Taylor was ordained in 1633, became chaplain of All Soul's College, Oxford (1636), and rector of Uppingham, Rutland (1638). When the Civil War broke out in 1642 Taylor, closely associated with Archbishop Laud, became a chaplain to the royalist army. He was imprisoned three times during the Commonwealth, for some time in the Tower. In 1644 he moved to Wales where he spent 10 years of forced exile until Charles II returned in 1660. These years in Wales, in which he was the Earl of Carbery's chaplain and principal of a school in Newton Hall, Carmarthenshire, were his most productive years. There he wrote *Liberty of Prophesying* (1647), *An Apology for Authorized and Set Forms of Liturgy* (1647), *The Great Exemplar* (1649), *The Life of Christ* (1649), *Holy Living* (1650), *Holy Dying* (1651), as well as many letters and sermons. Taylor went to Ireland in 1658 where he served English churches in Lisburn and at Portmore, near Dublin. In 1660 he received the bishoprics of Down and Connor. He also served as the vice-chancellor of the University of Dublin. In 1660 he published his massive, casuistic *Ductor Dubitantium,* covering numerous cases of conscience faced by the pastor, often considered his best work. His days as a bishop were fraught with difficulty with both Presbyterian and the Roman Catholic opposition. Remembered chiefly for eloquent sermons, he has been called the "Chrysostom of England." Noting his superb rhetorical abilities, Coleridge spoke of him as the "Spenser of prose," and Emerson called him the "Shakespeare of the divines." *The Whole Works of the Rev. Jeremy Taylor,* edited by R. Heber, revised C. P. Eden, 10 vols., London: Longman, 1851. *Practical Works,* 2 vols., London: H.G. Bohn, 1854. Of importance for his views on pastoral care and counselling are his *Rules and Advices to the Clergy* (1661; Whole Works XIV; see CS, 5ff.; ETM II); Sermon on "The Minister's Duty in Life and Doctrine" (PW I, pp. 442ff.); and *The Golden Grove: A Manual of Daily Prayers and Litanies,* (1655, PW II, pp. 224ff.); and *Christian Consolations, Discourse on Friendship,* and *Letters* (PW II, pp. 505ff.).

TERESA OF AVILA, ST. (1515–1582). Spanish mystical writer; founder of Discalced Carmelites; the first woman Doctor of the Roman Catholic Church. Born in Spain, Teresa joined the Carmelites in 1533. After an illness accompanied by mystical experiences, she received permission in 1562 to found a monastery in Avila based on the "Primitive Rule." She spent the rest of her life, amid much opposition, establishing Reformed Discalced houses and writing her famous books on spirituality and prayer: *The Way of Perfection* (Doubleday, 1964), *The Interior Castle* (CWS), and her autobiography *The Life of St. Teresa of Jesus* (London: 1916). Complete Works, transl. E. A. Peers, 3 vols., London: Sheed and Ward, 1946.

TERTULLIAN, QUINTUS SEPTIMIUS FLORENS (c. 160–c. 220). African theologian, Apologist, Montanist. Born as son of a Roman officer stationed in Carthage in 160;

received an excellent education in literature, philosophy, law and rhetoric. Spent the years prior to his conversion as a lawyer in Rome. His conversion to Christianity in 195 was sudden and dramatic, whereupon he and his wife returned to Carthage where he was ordained a presbyter and became a teacher of catechumens. Here he became a prolific Christian writer. His writings from the period around 206 show the influence of Montanism on his thought. It was not, however, until the year 212 that he finally broke with the official church and joined the Montanists. He later became the leader of his own sect, the Tertullianists, which lasted until c. 400 when St. Augustine finally brought them back into the church. As a Montanist his asceticism and disipline were severe, forbidding second marriages, denying that certain sins such as blasphemy, homicide and adultery could ever be forgiven, and instituting compulsory fasts. He was the first major Christian thinker to write in Latin and is acknowledged as the father of Latin Christian theology. He is a major contributor to the formation of early Christian theological language, having been among the first to explain the Godhead in terms of one substance and three persons. Besides his contributions to the doctrine of Trinity and Christology he is the founder of the doctrine of traducianism, the idea that the human soul is transmitted by parents to children (*On the Soul,* ANF III, pp. 23-41). His *Apologia* (c. 197) is considered a classic defense of Christianity against paganism. His polemical works include his treatise *De Praescriptione Haereticorum* (c. 200), *Against Marcion* (207), *Against Praxeas* (ANF III, TCL), and *Treatise Against Hermogenes* (ANF III, ACW 24). Many of his practical and ascetical works were written during the period in which he was teaching catechumens. These include *De paenitentia* (200, ACW 28) and *De pudicitia* (c. 217-22), *Ad uxorem* (200) and *De exhortatione castitatis* (204-212) in which widows are advised not to remarry. ET of *Treatises on Marriage and Remarriage, To His Wife, Exhortation to Chastity,* and *On Monogamy* are in ACW 13. Also among his practical writings are one of the earliest analyses of the Lord's Prayer; the first extant treatise on baptism, *De Baptismo* (c. 198-211); *De spectaculis* (c. 197-202) in which Christians are forbidden to attend secular activities; and *De Idololatria* (c. 211-212) in which Christians are instructed on which professions they may not engage in, including military service of any kind. *De Anima* (c. 210) is among the earliest books on psychology ever written by a Christian. LF 10; CSEL xx; ANF III; Moral Treatises, ACW 12; ACW 13; Disciplinary, Moral and Ascetical Works, FC 40. Apologetic Works, FC 10. *Tertullian's Treatises Concerning Prayer, Concerning Baptism,* TCL. MPL i, ii.

※

THEODULF OF ORLEANS (c. 750–821). Bishop of Orleans, succeeded Alcuin in 804 as chief theological advisor to Charlemagne. Wrote *Directions to the Priests of the Diocese, De Spiritu Sancto* in defense of the Filioque, and *De Ordine Baptismi.* MPL cv, 191-380.

※

THEONAS OF ALEXANDRIA (fl. 300). Bishop of Alexandria, c. 283-301. Only writing remaining (and its authenticity is debated) is his *Epistle to Lucianus,* a letter of vocational advice on the duties of an office, addressed to the chief chamberlain of the Emperor (probably Diocletian). ANF VII, 158-161. Cf. TU IX, iii (Harnack, 1903).

THEOPHILUS, ST. (second century). Bishop of Antioch, 169-c. 181. *Apology, addressed to Autolycus,* presents the case of the Christian life to pagan society, emphasizing *logos* doctrine. MPG vi, 1023-1168; ANF II, 87ff; BKV; BVP ii, 77ff.

THOMAS À KEMPIS (C. 1380-1471). Devotional writer and spiritual advisor. Born in Germany, at the age of twenty he joined the Augustinian Convent of Mt. Saint Agnes near Zwolle in Holland. He spent his entire life in this house, becoming a priest in 1413 and subprior in 1429. As a copyist he copied the Bible at least four times, wrote a number of works and was known for his spiritual and pastoral counsel. He is remembered above all for the writing of one of Christianity's most celebrated devotional works, *The Imitation of Christ* (New York: Doubleday, 1955). Collected works edited by M. J. Pohl, 7 vols., 1902-1922.

THOMAS AQUINAS, ST. (C. 1225-1274). The "Angelic Doctor," leading theologian and philosopher of the Middle Ages; Doctor of the Church; Italian Dominican theologian; patron of Catholic schools. Born in Naples, the youngest son of Landulph, Count of Aquino, at five or six years of age was sent by his parents as an oblate to the Benedictine Monastery at Monte Cassino. In 1244, at the age of nineteen, and after having studied for five years at the University of Naples, Thomas conceived of an intellectual apostolate, and joined the Dominicans in Naples. While travelling from Rome to Bologna, Thomas was abducted by his older brother and returned to his home. During the next fifteen month "imprisonment" his mother, Theodora, tried to dissuade him from becoming a Dominican friar. He returned to the Dominicans in 1245. The time was not entirely lost, for he had managed to study the Bible, Aristotle's *Metaphysics,* and Peter Lombard's *Sentences.* After prounouncing his vows he was sent first to Paris and then to Cologne to study. Between the years 1245 and 1252 he received the best theological education possible in that time under Albert the Great. When in 1252 two chairs opened at the University of Paris, Albert recommended that Thomas prepare for a doctorate and the chair. Thomas began lecturing at the University of Paris in the fall of 1252. Between the years 1256 and 1259 Thomas taught at the University of Paris where teachers and students alike were amazed by the breadth of his knowledge and his skill in dealing with intricate issues. In 1259 he returned to Italy where he held teaching posts in Ostia, Viterbo, Anagni, Perugia, Bologna and the "studium generale" in Rome. Here he wrote prolifically, finished his *Summa Contra Gentiles* and conceived his plan for his *Summa Theologica.* In 1269, he was asked to return to Paris to confront the problems created by Latin Averroism and the continuing Mendicant controversy. Here he also began working diligently on his *Summa Theologica.* Thomas returned to Naples shortly after Easter in 1272 where he helped set up a Dominican school and continued to work on *Summa Theologica.* On December 6, 1273 while still at work on the third part of the *Summa* and after a Mass during the feast of St. Nicholas, he had a religious experience which made him believe that all his efforts at writing were but "straw" in comparison with what had been revealed to him by God. He put away his pens and never wrote again. In early 1274 he was asked to attend the Second Council of Lyons whose goal it was to seek unity between the Greek and Latin Churches. He died while journeying there in the Cistercian Monastery of Fossanuova on March 7, 1274.

Built upon an extensive knowledge of scripture, the Thomistic synthesis was a remarkable integration of many influences. His pastoral theology was affected by virtually all the then known works of the Greek and Latin Church Fathers, especially Augustine, Peter Lombard, and Boethius, and above all Aristotle. He wrote over sixty works which fall into the categories of scriptural, apologetic, philosophical and theological works. Wrote Commentaries on Aristotle, *Quaestiones Disputationes, Quodlibeta, Summa Contra Gentiles* (abbr. SCG), *Truth of the Catholic Faith* (4 vols., ed. C. J. O'Neil, A. Pegis, V. J. Bourke, New York: Doubleday, 1957ff.), and *Summa Theologica* (abbr. ST; quotations in this selection largely taken from the English Dominican edition, 3 vols., New York: Benziger, 1947-48. See also *Summa Theologiae,* edited by T. Gilby and T. C. O'Brien, 40 vols., New York: McGraw Hill, 1963ff., for Latin and English texts in correlation). Thomas was a man of prayer, a counselor to spiritual counselors, and a writer of hymns. His *Summa Theologica* is not merely a manual of Christian theology, but also a handbook filled with practical wisdom for pastors.

※

TRAVERS, WALTER (c. 1548-1635). Puritan Presbyterian Theologian. Provost of Trinity College, Dublin. Refused Anglican orders. Wrote *Declaration of Ecclesiastical Discipline* (1574), defending presbyterian polity.

※

USSHER, JAMES (1581-1656). Anglican Archbishop of Armagh, primate of Ireland, Professor of Divinity, Trinity College, 1607, vice-chancellor of University of Ireland, 1615. Wrote *Discourse of the Religion anciently professed by the Irish (1623); Brittanicarum Ecclesiarum Antiquitates* (1639); *A Body of Divinity* (1645); and the work for which he is famous, *Chronologia Sacra* (1660). Collected works ed. by C. R. Elrington and J.H. Todd, 17 vols., Dublin and London: 1847-1864.

※

VALDES, JUAN DE (1500-1541). Spanish theologian and reformer; one of the first Spaniards to adopt in part the ideas of the Reformation, in his *Dialogue on Christian Theology* (1529). *The Christian Alphabet,* LCC XXV, pp. 353ff.

※

VALERIAN, ST. (d. c. 460). Bishop of Comenelum during barbarian resettlement of Gaul. *Homilies,* FC 17.

※

VINCENT OF LERINS, ST. (d. before 450). Presbyter of monastery on isle of Lerins, near Cannes. *Commonitorium* (434, FC 7, MPL 1, 625ff), set forth the Vincentian Canon, a three-fold test of catholicity: *quod ubique, quod semper, quod ab omnibus creditum est* (what has been believed everywhere, always and by all). By this three-fold test of ecumenicity, antiquity, and consent, the church may discern between true and false traditions. NPNF 2, XI, pp. 123ff.; see translations in LCC IX, TCL; cf. BKV.

※

VOETIUS, GISBERT (OR VOET) (1588-1676). Dutch Reformed dogmatic theologian, Utrecht and Leiden. Anti-Arminian defender of Dort. *Concerning Practical Theology,* RD 265ff.; Collected works: *Selectae Disputationes Theologicae,* 5 vols., ed. A. Kuyper, 1887.

※

WALTON, IZAAK (1593–1683). Biographer of eminent Anglican clergymen, esp. of John Donne (1640), Richard Hooker (1662), George Herbert (1670), and Robert Sanderson (1678). *Waltonia,* edited by R. H. Shepherd, London, 1878. Most famous work, *The Complete Angler* (1653).

WATTS, ISAAC (1674–1748). Nonconformist hymn writer. Born in Southhampton, Watts served as a pastor of the Independent congregation in London. His *Rules for the Preacher's Conduct,* is found in *Young Minister's Companion,* Boston: S. T. Armstrong, 1813, 642ff.; and in John Brown, ed., *Christian Pastor's Manual,* 198ff. Collected works edited by D. Jennings and P. Doddridge, 6 vols., London, 1753.

WERMULLERUS, OTTO (1488–1568). Treatise on Death, pp. 37-135 of *The Remains of Miles Coverdale,* Cambridge: University Press, 1846.

WILLIAM OF ST. THIERRY (1085–1148). Benedictine abbot of St. Thierry, mystical theologian who attempted to synthesize eastern and western forms of spiritual direction, especially those of Gregory of Nyssa and Augustine. *On Contemplating God, Prayer, and Meditations,* CFS 3; *The Enigma of Faith,* CFS 9; *The Golden Epistle,* CFS 12; *The Mirror of Faith,* CFS 15; *Exposition on the Epistle to the Romans,* CFS 27; *The Nature and Dignity of Love,* CFS 30.

WOLLEBIUS, JOHANNES (1586–1629). Reformed pastoral theologian. *The Abridgement of Christian Divinitie,* transl. A. Ross. London: T. Longman, 1650; cf. RD.

WYCLIF (WICLIFFE), JOHN (c. 1329–1384). English Reformer, philosopher, writer, martyr. Called "The Morning Star of the Reformation," Wyclif was born in Yorkshire, educated at Oxford, master of Balliol College, rector of Lutterworth. Advocated Scripture as sole authority, denied the infallibility of the Pope; teachings akin to those of the later Reformation. After his writings were condemned by the Pope in 1377, he retired and spent the rest of his life translating the Vulgate Bible into English and writing a number of books. Of interest to pastoral care is his *Tractatus de Officio Pastorali* (*On the Pastoral Office,* c.1378; edited by G.V. Lechner, Leipzig: A. Edelmannum, 1863; cf. LCC XIV) which expounds the view that the clergy are not to lord over, but rather to serve their congregations. Collected works edited by J. Loserth, 4 vols., London: 1887- 1890. ET Selections, edited by H. E. Winn, Oxford, 1929.

ZONARAS, JOHN (12th century). Monk of Mt. Athos, Byzantine chronicler and canonist. His importance for the history of pastoral care hinges on his voluminous commentary on the apostolic canons, and canons of various oriental synods, including moral and penitential writings of the Fathers of the third and fourth centuries. Complete edition in MPG cxxiv-cxxxviii. *Commentaria in SS. Canones,* MPG cxxxvii-cxxxviii. *Expositio canonum Damasceni,* MPG cxxxv, 421ff.

ZWINGLI, HULDREICH (1484–1531). Swiss Reformer. Born in Wildhaus, Switzerland, educated for the priesthood at Berne, Vienna, and Basel. Ordained a Roman Catholic priest in 1506. From 1506 to 1516 pastor of a church at Glarus where he came under the influence of Erasmus. While a military chaplain (1513-1515) he was exposed to abuses of medieval sacramental practices. Became minister of the Great Church in Zurich from 1518 until his death. He began the Reformation in Switzerland in 1523 with the publication of his "Sixty-Seven Articles." In 1525 his break with Catholicism became complete when he administered a Protestant communion service in the Great Church. He engaged in disputes with both Anabaptists and the Lutherans. Disagreed with Luther's teaching on the Eucharist at the Synod of Marburg in 1529. Authored a number of works, the most famous of which are his *Commentary on True and False Religions* (1525); and *An Exposition of the Faith* (1531), LCC XXIV, ed. G. Bromiley. Selections in H. Hillerbrand, *The Reformation: A Narrative History Related by Contemporary Observers and Participants,* NY: Harper & Row, 1964; and C. Manschreck, *A History of Christianity: Readings,* Englewood Cliffs, NJ: Prentice-Hall, 1965. Samuel Jackson, ed., *Selected Works of Huldreich Zwingli,* Philadelphia: Univ. of Penn. Press, 1901. Of particular importance to his views on pastoral care is *Der Hirt* (Basel: C. Detloff, 1884). *Huldreich Zwinglis saemtliche Werke,* 14 vols., CR, vols. 88ff., edited by E. Egli et al., Berlin: C. A. Schwetschke, 1905ff.

Acknowledgments

THE AUTHOR IS GRATEFUL to the following for the use of the selections listed below in the four volumes of this series.

Benziger Bros., Inc.: Thomas Aquinas, *Summa Theologica*.

Catholic University of America: R. J. Deferrari, ed., Fathers of the Church Series.

Cistercian Publications, Inc., Kalamazoo, MI: Cistercian Studies Series, Cistercian Fathers Series.

Concordia Press: J. Pelikan, ed., Martin Luther, *Luther's Works;* E. Plass, ed., *What Luther Says*.

Faber and Faber, Inc.: Classics of the Contemplative Life Series.

Herald Press: Menno Simons, *Complete Writings of Menno Simons*.

Holy Transfiguration Monastery Press: John Climacus, *Ladder of Divine Ascent*.

Muhlenberg Press: Works of Martin Luther.

Oxford University Press: John Dillenberger, ed., Library of Protestant Thought; and E. B. Pusey et al., eds., A Library of Fathers of the Holy Catholic Church; Library of Anglo-Catholic Thought.

Paulist Press: Richard J. Payne, ed., Classics of Western Spirituality; and J. Quasten et al., eds. Ancient Christian Writers Series.

Scholars Press and the American Academy of Religion: John Dillenberger, ed., *John Calvin: Selections from His Writings*.

SPCK: S. Simpson and L. Clarke, eds., Translations of Christian Literature, The Fathers for English Readers; and P. W. Moore and F. L. Cross, eds., *Anglicanism*.

Thomas Nelson: Jack Sparks, ed., *The Apostolic Fathers: New Translations of Early Christian Writings*.

University of Michigan Press: John Donne, *Devotions Upon Emergent Occasions*.

Viking-Penguin Inc.: *Early Christian Writings: The Apostolic Fathers,* trans. Maxwell Staniforth.

Westminster Press: J. Baille, J. T. McNeill, and H. P. Van Dusen, eds., The Library of Christian Classics.

Index

Abelard, Peter
on nonverbal
confession, 2:136
on recognizing the need
for counseling,
3:84–85
on repentance without
restitution, 2:153
Abortion counsel, 4:141–43
Accusations, dealing with
false, 2:216–22
Active versus contemplative
life, 1:52–53
Admonition
dynamics of internal
resistance to,
3:178–80
gentleness in, 3:167–70
pastoral duty of,
3:160–62
the practice of, 3:172–76
as a preservative of
community,
3:182–85
private and public,
3:176–78
responsibility of,
3:165–67
Adultery, 4:116–18
Aelred of Rievaulx
on abortion counsel,
4:142
on accurate empathic
listening, 3:11
on animal psychology
versus human
psychology, 3:276
on friendship, 3:33
on pastoral formation
and moral
development, 1:178
on prayer for the
pastor's own needs,
2:9

on soul care in
eschatological
perspective, 4:185
African Code of 419
on death and the
sacraments, 4:177
African Council
on the clergy entering
taverns, 1:182
Age restrictions for clergy,
1:107, 126, 140
Alan of Lille
on decoding deceptions,
3:157
on hospitality to
strangers, 4:160
on marriage, the
meaning of, 4:104
on the metaphor of
Jacob's ladder,
2:35–36
on the pastor's use of
homilies, 2:40
on pastoral care through
preaching, 2:29, 47
on the political ethics of
the pastor, 2:196
on priestly care, 1:93
on the process of self-
examination, 3:44
Alcoholism and addictive
behaviors, counsel
on, 4:16–19
Alexander of Alexandria
on God's order and
design, 3:91
Ambrose, Saint
on accurate empathic
listening, 3:8, 10
on the act of baptism,
2:125
on the active versus
contemplative life,
1:53

on admonition
the pastoral duty of,
3:160–61
the practice of,
3:175–76
on anger, 3:27
on authority in ministry,
1:57
on Christ as the "couch"
of the saints, 3:251
on comparing a musical
instrument with a
well-attuned soul,
3:102–3
on the conscience,
rewards for
following, 3:191
on the consecration of
the bread and wine,
2:162
on counsel, 1:13, 73–74
choosing good, 3:66
the exquisite timing
of seasonable
counsel, 3:127
flexibility of
response in,
3:121–22
language used in,
3:138
using individual
treatment consistent
with doctrinal unity,
3:111
on the curative power of
self-disclosure,
3:23–24
on deception
decoding, 3:159
probing the layers
of, 3:151
on the duties of a priest,
1:98
on friendship, 3:32–33

betrayal of, 3:34
on the "gentle warrior"
metaphor, 3:77
on God's own empathic
understanding,
3:13–14
on guilt as moral
indebtedness, 3:196
on hospitality to
strangers, 4:159
on the journey of the
pilgrim (soul), 4:7
on learning to trust
oneself, 3:19, 20
on the limits of human
freedom, 3:268
on ministry being "set
apart," 1:87, 88–89
on nurturing
characteristics of the
pastor, 3:78–79
on parents, pastoral care
of, 4:120
on the path to
ordination, 1:114
on the poor, care of,
4:145–46
averting the
dependency
syndrome in,
4:149–50
on priestly sacrifice,
1:96, 97
on public demeanor and
double standards in
the ministry, 1:181
on rejection of fees for
pastoral service,
2:205
on the sacred ministry,
1:90–91
on sibling rivalry,
parental response
to, 4:124–25
on the soul most ready
for confession,
2:137–38
on strength found amid
weakness, 4:36–37
on the struggle between
passion and virtue,
3:243

on sublimation, 3:252
on suffering
the meaning of,
4:72–73
the pedagogy of,
4:69
on unconditional
accepting love, 3:28,
29
on visitation of the sick,
4:32
on young people,
pastoral care for,
4:135–36, 137
Ammonius
resistance to the
pastoral calling,
1:28–29
Andrewes, Lancelot
pastoral study habits of,
1:156
Angelic and demonic
influences, 4:92–94
Anonymous
on communion counsel,
2:138–39
on the hard remedy
of confession,
2:135
on interpersonal crisis
counseling and
conflict
management, 4:14
on the recipients of
baptism, 2:116
Anselm of Canterbury, Saint
on the parable of the
mill, 3:208
Anthony, Saint
as congruent with his
own feelings, 3:16
on excessive judgment,
2:151
and his gift of healing,
4:54
on grace and effort,
3:212
on health of the soul,
4:50–51
on habit modification,
3:230–32

on the limits of
openness, 3:25–26
need for quiet
meditation with
God, 1:157
and paranormal visions,
3:283
preparation for the
ministry, 1:152–54
on self-knowledge, 3:36
on temptation
being less severe
than former
generations, 4:88
potentially
constructive uses of,
4:89
Apollonius
on marriage, breaking
the covenant of,
4:115
on public demeanor and
double standards in
the ministry, 1:180
on rejection of fees for
pastoral service,
2:204–5
Apostolic Canons
on slaves becoming
pastors, 4:163
Apostolic tradition of soul
care, 1:62–65
Apostolicity and succession,
1:59–62
Aquinas, Thomas, Saint
on almsgiving, 3:81–82;
4:144, 148
on behavioral change
strategies, 3:245–46
on children, loving our
own more than
others, 4:126
on choice, 3:273–74
on counsel
the gift of, 3:82
given with regard to
circumstance, 3:120
good, 3:48–50, 51
prudent, 3:80–81,
134–36
suicide, 4:22, 23–24

wise, 3:136, 137
on delight perfecting
    action, 3:248
on fraternal correction,
    3:162–63, 164,
    165–66
on habit formation,
    3:238–39
on interpersonal crisis
    counseling and
    conflict
    management,
    4:13–14
on love, 3:29, 30, 31
on obeying a spiritual
    guide, 3:65
on pastoral intercession,
    2:81
on pastoral supplication,
    2:79–80
on the poor, care of,
    4:145
on priestly care, 1:93
on prayer
    the elements of, 2:76
    the language and
    forms of pastoral
    prayer, 2:86–87
    public, 2:93–94
on questioning God's
    providence, 3:98
on rejection of fees for
    pastoral service,
    2:201
on restitution, 2:152–53
on the sacraments, 2:61
    the necessity of,
    2:163–64
    ordination as,
    1:117–18
on suspicion, 3:152
on tithes and offerings,
    2:208–9
on understanding, 3:9
Arnobious of Sicca
on moral progress and
    regress in humanity,
    3:209
Ascesis and spiritual
    athleticism, 3:213–17
Astrology and magic as

anathema, 3:280–83
Athanasian Canons
on ancillary orders of
    ministry, 1:112
on astrology and magic
    as anathema, 3:282
on the authority to
    approach the altar,
    2:64
on burial, Christian,
    4:179
on the clergy drinking
    wine, 1:182
on communion for the
    sick, 4:46–47
on the contact between
    bishop and
    presbyters, 1:131
on divorce counsel,
    4:138
on inquiry into pastoral
    abuses, 2:223
on leaving the ministry,
    2:17
on pastoral care through
    institutions, 2:185
on pastoral
    disengagement from
    worldly
    preoccupations,
    2:205–6
on the pastoral ordering
    of worship, 2:67
on the presbyter's
    responsibilities,
    1:127, 129
on tithes and offerings,
    2:211, 212
on visitation of the sick,
    timing of, 4:33
Athanasius, Saint
on angelic and demonic
    influences, 4:93
on astrology and magic
    as anathema, 3:283
on baptismal heresy,
    2:121
on the benefits of
    pastoral study and
    meditation, 1:157
on burial, Christian,

4:178–79
on cohesion and
    catholicity amid
    diverse ministries,
    1:66
on congruence of inner
    spirit with outer
    behavior, 3:16–17
on Christ as "living
    Counselor," 1:78
on comprehending God
    by becoming
    attuned to one's own
    soul, 3:101–2
on decoding deceptions,
    3:156
on the empathy of God,
    3:12
falsely accused, 2:220
on fault-finding,
    avoiding, 3:171–72
on the gift of healing,
    4:54
on God's way of teaching
    through
    incarnation, 2:171
on habit modification,
    3:230–32
on hospitality to
    strangers, 4:161
on Jesus as a model for
    teaching, 2:178
on the language and
    forms of pastoral
    prayer, 2:88
on the management of
    pain, 4:45
on pastoral formation
    and moral
    development, 1:174
on the path to
    ordination, 1:114
on the political ethics of
    the pastor, 2:194–95
on the poor, cruelty to,
    4:154
on role models for
    ministry, 1:52–54
on Scripture as source of
    good counsel, 3:105
on soul care

of the emotionally
ill, 3:262–63
and music, 2:102–4,
105
on why God permitted
the will to fall, 4:63
Athenagoras
on abortion counsel,
4:142
on idolatry, 3:260
Augustine, Saint
on accurate empathic
listening, 3:10
on admonition
gentleness in, 3:168
as a preservative of
community, 3:183
on adultery, 4:117–18
on avoiding unfit or
premature
ordinations, 1:104–5
on baptism
conferred by an
unworthy minister,
2:129, 130
and conversion,
2:112
the recipients of,
2:114
on behavioral change
strategies, 3:244
on the body of Christ
metaphor, 1:72
on the care of the world,
2:197
on counsel
moral, 3:197
suicide, 4:22–23, 25
on death
of the immortal
soul, 4:176
preparation for,
4:168
on false accusations,
dealing with, 2:219
on fraternal correction,
3:164
on freedom
and grace, 3:286–87
and the layers of
necessity, 3:268

the self-alienation
of, 3:277
on the Holy Spirit as
Counselor, 3:102, 103
on humility, 3:224
on inquiry into pastoral
abuses, 2:223–24,
225
on the interpretation of
Scripture, 3:108
on involuntary acts and
degrees of consent,
3:291–92
on the omnipotence of
God, 4:62–63
on the pastor
accountability of,
1:45–46
as moral role model,
1:187
on pastoral intercession,
2:81–82, 83
on prayer
effectual, 2:85–86
the Lord's Prayer as
pattern for, 2:90–91
public, 2:93–94
on probing the layers of
deception, 3:151
on public demeanor and
double standards in
the ministry, 1:180
on the purpose of
language, 3:145
on questioning God's
providence, 3:99
on self-examination,
3:38
on self-knowledge, 3:40
on slavery, 4:162–63
on the soul
guidance of, 3:60
the progress as a
developmental
process of, 3:57
on the unworthy
partaking of a
sacrament, 2:130
on vindicating the
justice of God amid
pain, 4:67–68

on why God permitted
the will to fall,
4:61–62
on widows, the care of,
4:157–58
Authority
in ministry, 1:55–59
for soul care, 1:54–80

Baker, Augustine
on choosing a soul
guide, 3:66
on learning to trust
oneself, 3:20
Baptism
the act of, 2:122–26
by a care-giver, 2:107–12
confirmation of,
2:131–33
the deacon's role in,
1:123
the effects of, 2:126–29
pastoral care through,
2:107–33
preparation for,
2:119–22
recipients of, 2:112–16
water as the sign of,
2:117–19
Barrow, Isaac
on communion
frequency of,
2:161–62
worthiness to
receive, 2:159
on the conscience,
3:187–88
on health of the soul,
4:52–53
Basil, Saint
on the curative power of
self-disclosure,
3:21–22
on the qualities of a
spiritual guide, 3:62
Baxter, Richard
on accurate empathic
listening, 3:10–11
admonition
dynamics of internal
resistance to, 3:178

gentleness in,
3:169–70
as a preservative of
community, 3:184
private and public,
3:176, 177–78
responsibility of,
3:167
on the characteristics of
a good care-giver,
1:150–51; 3:79–80
on confirmation of
baptism, 2:133
on the correlation
between quality of
self-disclosure and
truthfulness of
preaching, 3:23
on counseling
circumstances in,
3:120
recognizing the
need for, 3:85–86
on the dispossessed, 1:20
on families, pastoral care
of, 4:122–23, 125–26
on good counsel, 3:50
on habit formation,
3:239
on habit modification,
3:233
on healing the
corruptions of
sacred ministry, 2:24
on knowing each
parishioner
personally, 3:75–76
on living well in addition
to preaching well,
2:43
on ministry being "set
apart," 1:89
on the pastor as moral
role model, 1:188
on the pastor's books,
1:163
on the pastor's relation
to other pastors,
2:192–93
on the pastor's use of
homilies, 2:44

on the pastor's use of
scientific studies,
1:172–73
on the pastoral calling,
1:35, 36
on pastoral counsel,
3:74–75
a variability
principle used in,
3:116–17
on the pastoral duty of
admonition, 3:162
on pastoral preaching,
2:37, 38–39, 46
on pastoral study and
meditation, the
benefits of, 1:157
on pastoral visitation,
4:28–29
on the poor, care of,
4:148
on positive thinking in
ministry, 2:17
on public demeanor
and double
standards in the
ministry, 1:181
on reinforcement
techniques, 3:237
on representative
ministry, 1:84
on role models for
ministry, 1:154–55
on self-awareness,
3:41–42
on serving the poor,
2:212
on soul care
the sphere of,
1:24–25
of the terminally ill,
4:173, 175–76
on teaching
by example, 1:178
from experience,
1:176
through families
under pastoral
guidance, 2:169
plain speaking in,
2:169–70

by questioning the
learner, 2:170
on the temptation of
ministers, 2:12
on the therapeutic
function of
confession, 2:137
on time distribution for
pastoral priorities,
2:186, 187–88
Behavior modification. *See*
Habit modification
Benedict of Nursia, Saint
on admonition,
gentleness in, 3:170
on the difficulties in
ministry, 2:11
on the hard remedy of
confession, 2:137
on the mandates for the
spiritual pilgrim,
3:139–40
on probing the layers of
deception, 3:153
Benefits of pastoral study
and meditation,
11:155–59
Beveridge, William
on the language and
forms of pastoral
prayer, 2:88
Bishop
office of, 1:129–32
tasks of, 1:132–36
Black Moses
on "dying to one's
neighbor," 3:223–24
on pastoral formation
and moral
development, 1:175
Body of Christ, metaphor of,
1:71–73
Boethius
on developmental stages
as variables of
seasonable counsel,
3:130
on fate versus
providence, 3:286
Bona, John Cardinal
on the curative power of

self-disclosure, 3:22
on trying to be one's
own spiritual guide,
3:63
Bonaventure, Saint
on the deliberation of
good, 3:275
on extreme unction,
4:169
on hospitality to
strangers, 4:161–62
on marriage, questions
concerning, 4:105–6
on the ministry of those
who are dying, 4:175
on the pastoral calling,
1:38
resistance to, 1:28
on penance, the three
steps of, 2:144
on reparenting and
transference,
3:253–54
on self-examination, the
process of, 3:42–44
on the three "orders" of
ministry, 1:111
Book of Common Prayer
on the visibility of
church and ministry,
1:70–71
Books used in pastoral study,
1:159–64
Bramhall, John
on the pastoral ordering
of worship, 2:67
Breaking of bread, 2:160–65
Browne, Thomas
on virtue, 1:14
Bucer, Martin
on the deacon's care for
the poor and sick,
1:124; 4:152
on divorce counsel,
4:141
on premarital pastoral
counsel, 4:98
Burial, Christian, 4:177–80
Burnet, Gilbert
on admonition
connected to

receiving the Lord's
Supper, 3:174
on Christian education,
2:168
on Jewish pedagogy,
2:168
on the language of
curacy, 1:29–32
on the pastor's books,
1:160–61
on pastors caring for
one another, 2:9
on public prayer, 2:92
on the sphere of soul
care, 1:23–24
on visitation
pastoral, 4:27, 28
of the sick, 4:29–30
Burnout, pastoral, 2:13–17

Calvin, John
on ancillary orders of
ministry, 1:113
on communion
children partaking
of without
instruction, 2:132
the ministry of,
2:155
on the deacon's care for
the poor and sick,
1:124–25
defining ministry as
priesthood, 1:91–92
on false accusations,
dealing with, 2:218
on his calling to the
pastoral ministry,
1:17–18
on his own approaching
death, 4:174
on the office of pastor,
1:21
inquiry into the
abuses of, 2:224
on the ordinal
examination,
1:105–6
on ordination
avoiding unfit or
premature, 1:103

the path to, 1:116
on representative
ministry, 1:84
on sacraments conferred
by an unworthy
minister, 2:131
on sickness causing
spiritual self-
examination,
4:37–38
on visitation of the sick,
4:32
timing of, 4:33–34
Candor as a pastoral virtue,
3:180–82
Care-giving
difficulties in, 2:10–13
for the pastor, 2:7–9
Cassian, John
on the care of souls
facing temptation,
4:91
on the curative power of
self-disclosure, 3:22
on grace and freedom,
3:288
on reinforcement
techniques, 3:238
on unsolicited
counseling, 3:87
Catherine of Siena, Saint
on admonition, as a
preservative of
community,
3:184–85
on angelic and demonic
influences, 4:94
on communion
the ministry of,
2:155–56
the recipients of,
2:158
on empathy, 3:8–9
on fairness in language,
1:142
on God's own empathic
understanding, 3:14
on the management of
pain, 4:45–46
on the ministry of those
who are dying, 4:175

on pastoral burnout,
2:13
on reverence for an
unworthy minister,
2:18
on self-knowledge,
3:40–41
on servant ministry, 1:55
on temptation
the limit of demonic
power in, 4:90–91
and responsible
freedom, 4:87
Chalcedon
on the age limitations
and ordinal
examination of a
deaconess, 1:140
on the care-giver as
baptizer, 2:111
on clergy suing other
clergy, 1:182
on leaving the ministry,
2:20
on the pastoral study of
Scripture, 1:167
Characteristics of a good
care-giver, 1:148–51
Charismatic gifts, 1:99–101
Charles I, King
on the tasks of episcopal
care, 1:134–35
Chemnitz, Martin
on candor as a pastoral
virtue, 3:182
on cohesion and
catholicity amid
diverse ministries,
1:69
on the ministry of the
Word, 2:29
on ordination
the act of, 1:118
the laying on of
hands in, 1:117
the path to, 1:114–15
on the pastor
the church
removing a, 2:17–18
the office of, 1:20,
21

on the pastoral calling,
1:33–34, 35
on pastoral disengage-
ment from worldly
preoccupations,
2:207
on representative
ministry, 1:83–84
Chrysologus, Peter, Saint
on death, 4:165
on the pastor as the
physician of souls,
3:56
on the priesthood of all
baptized Christians,
1:82–83
Chrysostom, John
on the active versus
contemplative life,
1:52
on admonition, the
practice of, 3:173
on the affirmation of
divine mystery, 4:65
on the authority of the
Word, 2:31–32
on avoiding unfit or
premature
ordinations, 1:102,
103, 105
on behavior
modification, 3:235
on the care of the world,
2:197
on communion
the ministry of,
2:154
the recipients of,
2:157
on the consecration of
the bread and wine,
2:162–63
on counseling
pastoral
discernment in,
3:123
premarital pastoral,
4:99, 100
recognizing the
need for, 3:84
on criticism, dealing

with, 2:212–14
on deception and self-
deception, 3:149
on the difficulties in
ministry, 2:10
on divorce counsel,
4:139
on the equality of souls
beyond sexual
differences, 1:143
on false accusations,
dealing with,
2:219–20
on freedom, the social
consequences of
taking seriously,
3:284
on healing the
corruptions of
sacred ministry, 2:26
on health of the soul,
5:51
on interpersonal crisis
counseling and
conflict
management, 4:9–10
on lying, 3:153–54
on marriage
the meaning of,
4:102–3
second, 4:106
trust in, 4:115
on the ordinal
examination, 1:106
on the pastor
accountability of,
1:44–45, 46–47
attentiveness of,
1:50, 51
care for, 2:8
and the metaphor
of the military
logistics
coordinator, 3:118
negligence of,
1:47–48
the office of, 1:22
political ethics of,
2:193
on the pastor's use of
homilies, 2:39

on pastoral care of parents, 4:122

on pastoral preaching, 2:36, 37–38

on pastoral uses of the law, 3:204

on physical attraction in selecting a spouse, 4:97

on preparation for soul care compared to athletic fitness, 1:149

on preparation for the ministry, 1:13

on priestly care, 1:92, 93, 94

on public demeanor and double standards in the ministry, 1:180, 181

on the reception of sermons, 2:42–43

on repressed anger, 3:249

on responsible parenting, 4:127

on self-examination, 3:34

on the shepherding metaphor, 1:43

on slavery, 4:162

on teaching by instruction and example, 1:175

on testing the strength of a ministry, 2:16

on the urgent need for soul care, 1:15–16

on widows, the care of, 4:158

on women, the gifts of, 1:144–45

on young people, pastoral care for, 4:133

Church, defined as Catholic, 1:65–66

Church reformability, pastor's expectations of, 1:73–75

Clement of Alexandria

on alcoholism and addictive behaviors, 4:16–17, 18

on the analogy between energetic youth and new birth in Christianity, 4:134–35

on angelic and demonic influences, 4:93

on astrology and magic as anathema, 3:282–83

on baptism, the effects of, 2:127, 128

on the bishop's pastoral care of the church, 1:130

on communication through the tone of one's voice, 3:144

on communion, the recipients of, 2:157–58

on continence, 4:97

on counseling
the function of silence in, 3:142
humor in, 3:45
language used in, 3:144–45
moral, 3:198
the unity and coherence of situational, 3:114
using individual treatment consistent with doctrinal unity, 3:112
and the various means used in offering aid, 3:128

on divorce counsel, 4:140–41

on the duties of an effective counselor, 3:72

on the equality of souls beyond sexual differences, 1:142–43

on the face reflecting holiness, 3:143

on fairness in language, 1:141–42

on fasting, 3:218

on freedom, 3:246
growth of, through discipline, 3:207
the social consequences of taking seriously, 3:284

on good counsel, 3:50
Scripture as source of, 3:104

on grace and effort, 3:212

on the Holy Spirit as Counselor, 3:101

on Jesus as Educator, 3:72, 73

on the love of God, 3:277–78

on marriage
breaking the covenant of, 4:114
happiness and fulfillment in, 4:111
the meaning of, 4:102, 104
sex and, 107, 108–9
single, 4:140

on the ordinal examination, 1:106

on pain as a corrective function, 3:235

on the pastor
as educator of the soul, 2:167, 171; 3:71
and the metaphor of the navigator, 3:117
as the physician of souls, 3:54–55, 56

on the pedagogy of suffering, 4:69

on the possibility of doing that which God intended for us, 4:183–84

on rational analysis of
the passions,
3:255–58
on reason and will, 3:273
on the soul
guidance of, 3:58–60
sickness testing the
strength of, 4:36
on soul care
in eschatological
perspective, 4:180
and the use of
secular psychologies
and therapies,
3:227–28
by word and
counsel, 2:45
on the spoken versus
written word, 3:146
on the teaching methods
of his own teachers,
2:172–73
on visitation of the sick,
4:30
on women, the gifts of,
1:145
on young people,
pastoral care for,
4:133–34
Clement of Rome, Saint
on admonition,
dynamics of internal
resistance to,
3:178–79
on apostolicity and
succession, 1:59, 60
on confession, 2:140
on inequalities in
created beings,
4:77–78
on integrity in pastoral
leadership,
2:185–86
on the pastoral ordering
of worship, 2:66
on pastoral supplication,
2:77–78
on role models for
ministry, 1:152
on the three "orders" of
ministry, 1:110–11

on unconditional
accepting love, 3:29
Clement, Second, Book of
on admonition, the
pastoral duty of,
3:161
on deception and self-
deception, 3:149–50
on developmental stages
as variables of
seasonable counsel,
3:131
on self-control, eliciting
disciplined, 3:206
on teaching by example,
1:178
Clementina
on adultery, 4:117
on apostolicity and
succession, 1:61–62
on astrology and magic
as anathema,
3:280–81
on authority in ministry,
1:55–56
on behavioral change
strategies, 3:243
on behavioral
excellences of
ordinands, 1:108
on care of the
emotionally ill, 3:261
on the conscience, as a
universal human
capacity, 3:189
on demon-possession,
3:214–15
on the equality of souls
beyond sexual
differences, 1:143
on the exquisite timing
of seasonable
counsel, 3:128–29
on framing the question
of theodicy, 4:58–59
on free association,
3:251
on freedom
and the layers of
necessity, 3:268, 272
the self-alienation

of, 3:278, 279
the social
consequences of
taking seriously,
3:284
on the gift of healing,
4:54–55
on grace and effort,
3:212
on grief, 4:178
on idolatry, 3:260–61
on language
in ministry,
constraints on the
use of, 3:142
the use and abuse
of, 3:147
on the limits of rational
argument amid
suffering, 4:57
on marriage, covenant
faithfulness in,
4:113–14
on ministry to inquirers,
2:166–67
on the need for ordered
ministry, 1:85, 86
on the office of deacon,
1:120
on ordinal prayer, 1:119
on pastoral care
of parents, 4:121
of the poor, 4:145
on pastoral
disengagement from
worldly
preoccupations,
2:206
on pastoral formation
and moral
development, 1:179
on present relationships
recapitulating past
relationships, 3:254
on rejection of fees for
pastoral service,
2:203
on self-knowledge,
3:36–37, 39
on the three "orders" of
ministry, 1:109

on visitation of the sick,
4:30–31
on women in ministry,
1:138, 140
on the workman
metaphor, 1:128
Climacus, John, Saint
on admonition,
dynamics of internal
resistance to, 3:178,
180
on anger, 1:12
on choosing a soul
guide, 3:63, 64
on communicating
concern and care
without words, 3:143
on congruence of inner
spirit with outer
behavior, 3:17
on counseling
moral, 3:198
pastoral discern-
ment in, 3:122, 123
recognizing the
need for, 3:84
timing in, 3:126
vocational, 4:20
wisdom versus com-
plexity in, 3:137
on death, preparation
for, 4:164
on deception and self-
deception, 3:149
on discernment of
oneself, 3:125
on distinguishing
between guile and
honesty, 3:17–18
on fault-finding,
avoiding, 3:171
on good works, 2:55–56
on governing hunger,
3:217
on habit modification,
3:230, 232
on humility, 3:222–23,
325
on interpersonal crisis
counseling and
conflict manage-
ment, 4:15

on the limits of
openness, 3:26–27
on maturation, stages of,
3:204–5
on the ministry of
pardon, 2:147–48
on one good action
overcoming many
evils, 3:208
on the pastor
attentiveness of, 1:51
care for, 2:8
and the metaphor of
the surgeon, 3:118
on the pastor's use of
homilies, 2:39
on prayer
effectual, 2:86
the elements of, 2:75
the temporal
ordering of, 2:98
on the responsibility of
the care-giver, 3:62
on the soul
guidance of, 3:62
health of, 4:51
on suffering, the
meaning of, 4:70
on temptation
prayer as a defense
against, 4:91
and responsible
freedom, 4:86–87
to try to do the
impossible, 4:90
Coherence in educating the
soul, 2:173–76
Cohesion and catholicity
amid diverse
ministries, 1:65–69
Colet, John
on covenant faithfulness
in marriage, 4:113
Comfort, divine, 2:49–52
Commodianus
on giving food to the
needy, 4:146
Communion
counsel, 2:138–41
the deacon's role in,
1:123

the ministry of, 2:154–57
for the sick, 4:46–48
Community, care of the,
2:184–99
Confession
and communion
counsel, 2:134–65
the hard remedy of,
2:134–38
Conscience, 3:186–89
care of the distraught
and anguished,
3:191–94
as a universal human
capacity, 3:189–91
*Constitutions of the Holy
Apostles*
on abortion counsel,
4:142
on adultery, fornication,
and homosexuality,
4:117
on admonition
gentleness in,
3:168–69
as a preservative of
community, 3:183
on ancillary orders of
ministry, 1:113
on apostolicity and
succession, 1:60–61
on astrology and magic
as anathema, 3:280,
282
on authority in ministry,
1:56–57, 59
on baptism
the act of, 2:124–25,
126
by the care-giver,
2:111
the prayer of, 2:122
preparation for,
2:120–21
recipients of, 2:113
sin after, 2:128
on burial, Christian,
4:178
on care of the
emotionally ill, 3:264
on the catholic church,
definition of, 1:70

on charismatic gifts,
1:101
on counselors
deficient personal
qualities to be
pruned away,
3:77–78
viewed as "spiritual
parents," 3:63–64
on the "golden rule,"
3:201
on healing the
corruptions of
sacred ministry,
2:25–26
on the Holy Spirit as
Counselor,
3:100–101
on interpersonal crisis
counseling and
conflict
management, 4:12
on Jesus as the pattern
for ministry, 1:79
on language, the use
and abuse of, 3:147
on law and gospel,
3:201
on marriage
the covenant of,
4:103
sex and, 4:108
on the ministry of
pardon, 2:146
on moral progress and
regress in humanity,
3:209
on the office of deacon,
1:121
on the ordinal
examination, 1:106
on the ordinal prayer
of a deacon,
1:122–23
of a deaconess,
1:137–38
of a presbyter, 1:126
on ordinands
behavioral
excellences of, 1:107
the marital status of,
1:109

on ordination
of the bishop,
1:131–32
the path to, 1:114,
116
on overly permissive
parents, 4:121
on the pastor
accountability of,
1:45
as moral role model,
1:186
negligence of,
1:48–49
as the physician of
souls, 3:52, 53
and his relation to
other pastors, 2:190,
191–92
and the Sunday
service, 2:72
on pastoral
disengagement from
worldly
preoccupations,
2:206
on pastoral visitation,
4:27
on the poor, care of,
4:145
on the positioning of
clergy and laity in
the church, 2:96
on prayer
the Lord's Prayer as
pattern for, 2:90
the temporal
ordering of, 2:97, 98,
99, 100–101
on the presbyter and
deacon, the differ-
ence between, 1:125
on the presbyter's
responsibilities,
1:129
on the priesthood of all
baptized Christians,
1:81, 82
on priestly sacrifice, 1:95
on reinforcement
techniques,
3:234–35

on the sacraments,
substitution of, 2:162
on the sacred ministry,
1:90
on self-harm, 3:216
on the shepherding
metaphor, 1:41–42
on slavery, 4:163
on tithes and offerings,
2:209–11
on vocational counsel,
4:19–20
on widows, the care of,
4:156
on women in ministry,
1:138, 39
on worship
the order of, 2:71–72
preparing for, 2:62
Cosin, John
on confirmation of
baptism, 2:132
on pastoral intercession,
2:82–83
on the temporal
ordering of prayer,
2:97
on venial sins versus
mortal sins, 2:138
Council of Ancyra
on abortion counsel,
4:143
on leaving the ministry,
2:20
on the pastor's relation
to other pastors,
2:192
Council of Antioch in
Encaeniis
on the presbyter's
responsibilities,
1:129
Council of Carthage, Fourth
on the gifts of women,
1:147
Council of Chalcedon
on cohesion and cath-
olicity amid diverse
ministries, 1:68
on the pastor's relation
to other pastors,
2:192

on pastoral
disengagement from
worldly
preoccupations,
2:206–7
Council of Constantinople,
First
on soul care to
penitents, 2:145–46
Council of Constantinople,
Second
on apostolic tradition of
soul care, 1:65
on the pastor's relation
to other pastors,
2:190
on pastoral formation
and moral
development, 1:178
Council of Neocaesarea
on minimal age for
presbyterial
ordination, 1:126
Council of Nicea
on communion for the
dying, 4:168
on the pastor's relation
to other pastors,
2:191
Council of Sardica
on inquiry into pastoral
abuses, 2:225
Crisis, the pastor's presence
amid, 4:3–6
Crisis counseling
on alcoholism and
addictive behaviors,
4:16–19
conflict management
and interpersonal,
4:9–15
special situations of,
4:3–25
for the suicidal, 4:21–25
Criticism, dealing with,
2:212–16
Crow, as metaphor of
abandonment, 2:19
Cudworth, Ralph
on the ministry of the
Word, 2:29–30

Curacy, language of, 1:29–32
Cyprian, Saint
on friendship, 4:10
on the shepherding
metaphor, 1:42
Cyril of Alexandria
on the ministry of
communion, 2:154
Cyril of Jerusalem, Saint
on baptism
as a happy occasion,
2:111
preparation for,
2:121
water as the sign of,
2:118
on coherence in
educating the soul,
2:173–74, 176
on cohesion and
catholicity amid
diverse ministries,
1:65–66
on ministry to inquirers,
2:167–68, 169
on Scripture as source of
good counsel, 3:105,
106
on self-knowledge, 3:39

Damiani, Pietro
on homosexuality and
sexual norms in the
ministry, 1:183,
184–85
Deacon
and care for the poor
and sick, 1:124–25
office of, 1:120–23
and role in liturgy,
1:123–24
Death, 4:176–77
preparation for,
4:164–70
searching for meaning
in, 4:170–73
Deception
decoding, 3:156–59
probing the layers of,
3:150–53
and self-deception,
3:148–50

Didache
on astrology and magic
as anathema, 3:281
on baptism, the act of,
2:122
on the breaking of
bread, 2:160–61
on charismatic gifts, 1:99
on confession
and communion,
2:60
and a right spirit in
prayer, 2:137
on individual counseling
consistent with
doctrinal unity,
3:112
on pastoral visitation,
4:26
on plain speech as the
remedy for
deception, 3:158
on requisite personal
qualities of the
pastor, 1:13
on tithes and offerings,
2:209
Discipline, growth of
freedom through,
3:206–9
Divine mystery, the
affirmation of,
4:63–65
Divorce counsel, 4:137–41
Doddridge, Philip
on care of the gravely ill,
4:49
on public prayer,
2:92–93
on visitation of the sick,
4:31
as a pastoral service,
4:34–35
Donne, John
on the conscience, 3:189
on death, searching for
the meaning in,
4:172–73
on freedom, the social
consequences of
taking seriously,
3:285

on healing the
corruptions of
sacred ministry, 2:27
on the management of
pain, 4:45
on physical illness, 4:48
prayer during, 4:50
spiritual effects of,
4:39–41
on the process of self-
examination, 3:42
on the relationship
between physician
and pastor, 4:42–43
on sudden illness
revealing human
vulnerability, 3:129

Earle, John
on the characteristics of
a good care-giver,
1:151
Early Liturgies
on pastoral supplication,
2:78–79, 80; 4:3
Eckhart, Meister
on good counsel, 3:50
Ephesus
on perseverance in the
ministry, 2:12–13
Epistle of Barnabas, The
on accepting all
experiences as
blessings, 3:15
on admonition, the
practice of,
3:173–74
on apostolic tradition of
soul care, 1:63
on decoding deceptions,
3:156–57
on the temple of
worship, 2:64–65
Epistle to Diognetus, The
on apostolic tradition of
soul care, 1:63
on the care of the world,
2:197–98
on the characteristics of
a good care-giver,
1:149–50

on imitating God in this
life, 4:181
on self-harm, 3:215
Erasmus, Desiderius
on counseling
averting mistakes in,
3:83
circumstances in,
3:121
unsolicited, 3:87
on deception and self-
deception, 3:150
on friendship, 3:33–34
on growth of freedom
through discipline,
3:208–9
on reinforcement
techniques, 3:239
on self-controlled
speech, 3:26
Eucharist, ministry of. *See*
Communion
Eugippius
on pastors in the
presence of
governmental
power, 2:196
Eusebius of Caesarea
on astrology and magic
as anathema,
3:281–82
on Christians being at
different maturity
levels of faith, 4:184
on communion
the authority to
administer, 2:160
as a symbol of
sacrifice, 2:164
on deception and self-
deception, 3:148
on Jesus
the biblical images
of, 1:79–80
the ministry of, 1:77
on vindicating the
justice of God amid
pain, 4:66–67

Faith and possessions,
4:153–56

False teaching. *See* Teaching,
false
Families, shepherding of,
4:122–26
Fault-finding, avoiding,
3:170–72
Fees for pastoral service,
rejection of,
2:200–205
Felix, Minucius
on abortion counsel,
4:143
on the conscience, as a
universal human
capacity, 3:189–90
on the Holy Spirit as
Counselor, 3:101
on human caring
grounded in God's
care, 3:90–91, 92
on the pastor's presence
amid crisis, 4:4
First Council of
Constantinople. *See*
Council of Constan-
tinople, First
First Council of Nicea. *See*
Council of Nicea,
First
Forbes, William
on communion for the
sick, 4:47
on the mystery of
Christ's presence in
the sacrament,
2:156–57
Forgiveness without
responsiveness,
2:149–51
Fourth Council of Carthage.
See Council of
Carthage, Fourth
Francis, Saint
God's calling of, 1:38
problems with his father,
3:253–54
struggle with pastoral
calling, 1:28
Francis de Sales, Saint
on admonishing pastors
and spiritual guides,
3:166–67

on antipathy, 4:14–15
on choosing a soul
    guide, 3:64
on humor in counseling,
    3:46
on learning to trust
    oneself, 3:18–19
on role models for
    ministry, 1:152
on the various types of
    care-givers, 3:17
Fraternal correction,
    3:162–65
Freedom
    Christian, 2:52–55
    and grace, 3:286–88
    and the layers of
        necessity, 3:266–69
    the self-alienation of,
        3:276–80
    the social consequences
        of taking seriously,
        3:283–86
    and temptation, 4:83–87
    of will as a premise of
        soul care, 3:269–72

General ministry versus
    sacred ministry of
    the church, roles of,
    1:81–101
Gerson, Jean
    on curiosity and
        singularity in
        pastoral care,
        1:173–74
Gilbert of Hoyland
    on the congruence
        between word and
        facial gesture,
        3:147–48
God's own caring, 3:89–108
    human caring grounded
        in, 3:89–96
Good works, 2:51–52, 55–57
Grace
    and effort, 3:211–14
    and freedom, 3:286–88
Gregory of Nyssa, Saint
    on baptism
        defining, 2:109

the effects of, 2:128
on gaining experience
    and knowledge in
    counseling, 3:133
on ministry being "set
    apart," 1:87–88
on the virtuous life as a
    process of growth,
    4:182
Gregory of Sinai
    on pastoral discernment,
        3:125–26
Gregory the Great
    on the active versus
        contemplative life,
        1:52
    on admonition, the
        practice of, 3:174,
        175
    on candor as a pastoral
        virtue, 3:180–81
    on the conscience, care
        of the distraught
        and anguished,
        3:192–93
    on counseling
        using individual
        treatment consistent
        with doctrinal unity,
        3:111, 113
        specific varieties of
        situational
        differences in,
        3:115–16
    on decoding deceptions,
        3:159
    on the episcopal office,
        1:130
    on forgiveness without
        responsiveness,
        2:149
    on governing hunger,
        3:219–20
    on habit modification,
        3:232–33
        strategies of,
        3:241–42
    on health of the soul,
        4:51–52
    on humility, 3:221
        self-deception and
        false, 3:221–22

on interpersonal crisis
    counseling and
    conflict manage-
    ment, 4:9, 13
on the journey of the
    pilgrim (soul), 4:7
on the limits of
    openness, 3:24–25
on marital happiness
    and fulfillment,
    4:109
masochism, avoiding the
    trap of, 4:73–74
on the pastor
    care for, 2:8
    and the metaphor of
        the wrestler, 3:119
    negligence of, 3:27
    requisite personal
        qualities of, 1:12
on the pastoral duty of
    admonition, 3:161
on pastoral formation
    and moral
    development, 1:179
on physical affliction
    having spiritual
    meaning, 4:35, 36
on probing the layers of
    deception, 3:150–51
on recognizing the need
    for counseling, 3:83
on reinforcement
    techniques, 3:235,
    236
on repressed speech,
    3:249–50
on restitution, 2:152
on servant ministry, 1:55
on vindicating the
    justice of God amid
    pain, 4:66
Guerric of Igny
    on the authority of the
        Word, 2:35
    on death, preparation
        for, 4:169–70
    on pastoral formation
        and moral
        development, 1:177
    on soul care to
        penitents, 2:144

Guido
on the pastoral study of
Scripture, 1:167
Guilt as moral indebtedness,
3:195–97

Habit modification,
3:230–34
strategies of, 3:240–48
Hall, Joseph
on the benefits of
pastoral study and
meditation,
1:157–59
on the characteristics of
a good care-giver,
1:151
on confirmation of
baptism, 2:132–33
on the conscience, 3:187
on divorce counsel,
4:137
on Jesus and the
ministry of the
church, 1:79
on the language and
forms of pastoral
prayer, 2:87
on moderation,
3:220–21
on music and soul care,
2:104–5
on worship, 2:58–59
the pastoral
ordering of, 2:66–67
Healing, the gift of, 4:53–56
Helvetic Confession, Second
on celibacy, 4:119
Herbert, George
on admonition, private
and public, 3:177
on the age for receiving
confirmation and
first eucharist, 2:133
clarifying events and
celebrations of the
Christian year, 2:100
on crisis, the pastor's
presence amid, 4:5
on false accusations,
dealing with, 2:222

on fasting, 3:219
on humor in counseling,
3:47
love of music, 2:104
on ministry to inquirers,
2:170
on the pastor
and his ministry
while travelling,
3:127–28
as the physician of
souls, 3:55
and the Sunday
service, 2:72–73
on the pastor's books,
1:163–64
on the pastor's use of
homilies, 2:41–42,
44
on the pastoral blessing,
2:60–61
on pastoral care through
institutions, 2:187,
189
on pastoral counsel, 3:75
on the pastoral study of
Scripture, 1:166
on pastoral visitation,
4:29
on the poor, care of,
4:147–48
averting the
dependency
syndrome in,
4:150–51
on preaching too long,
2:44
on reinforcement
techniques, 3:237
Hermeneutics. *See*
Interpretation of
Scripture
Hippolytus of Rome, Saint
on baptism
the act of, 2:122–24
confirmation of,
2:131–32
on the breaking of
bread, 2:163
on burial expenses,
4:179

on false teaching, 2:181
on the office of deacon,
1:122
and baptism, 1:123
and communion,
1:123
on ordination
by confession, 1:120
of a presbyter,
1:125–26
on the tasks of episcopal
care, 1:135–36
Holy Spirit
in admonition,
discipline, and
comfort, 3:160–85
as Counselor, 3:99–103
Homilies, the pastor's use
of, 2:39–44
Homosexuality and sexual
norms in the
ministry, 1:182–85
Hooker, Richard
on charismatic gifts,
1:99–100
on the deacon's role in
liturgy, 1:123–24
on priestly sacrifice, 1:97
on the tasks of episcopal
care, 1:132, 133–34
on the three "orders" of
ministry, 1:109–10
Hospitality to strangers,
4:158–62
Hugh of St. Victor
on the analogy of the
emotive flood and
Noah's ark, 4:4–5
on charity, 3:213–14
on fault-finding,
avoiding, 3:172
on focussing on long-
range good rather
than immediate
setbacks, 3:127
on learning wisdom and
wise counsel, 3:138,
139
on love, 3:29–30
on marital happiness
and fulfillment,
4:111–12

on the metaphor of
  flowering, 3:132
on the pastor's use of
  scientific studies,
  1:173
on the pastoral study of
  Scripture, 1:164–65
on self-control, eliciting
  disciplined, 3:205–6
on temptation and
  responsible
  freedom, 4:85
on wealth, the
  disadvantages of,
  4:155
Humility, 3:221–25
Humor in counseling,
  3:45–47
Hunger and fasting,
  3:217–21

Ignatius of Antioch
  on apostolicity and
    succession, 1:62
  on the bishop's pastoral
    of the church, 1:131
  on Christian worship,
    2:59
  on communion
    the authority to
      administer, 2:159
    the ministry of,
      2:156
  on counseling
    developmental
      stages as variables of,
      3:130
    the function of
      silence in, 3:141
    using individual
      treatment consistent
      with doctrinal unity,
      3:112–13
  on God's spirit being
    undeceived,
    3:152–53
  on interpersonal crisis
    counseling and
    conflict
    management, 4:11
  on Jesus as the Physician,
    3:54

on ministry to inquirers,
  2:167
on the need for ordered
  ministry, 1:86–87
on the nurturing
  relationship, 3:76
on the pastor
  and his relation to
    other pastors, 2:191
  as teacher, 2:172
on the path to
  ordination, 1:113
on the poor, lack of
  caring for, 4:153
on rejecting bad
  counsel, 3:66
on representative
  ministry, 1:84
on the shepherding
  metaphor, 1:42
on the three "orders" of
  ministry, 1:110
on women
  in ministry, 1:139
  the treatment of,
    1:144
Ignatius of Loyola, Saint
  on admonition, private
    and public, 3:177
  on almsgiving, 4:149
  on cautious teaching of
    controversial
    Christian subjects,
    2:182
  on the conscience
    care of the
      distraught and
      anguished, 3:194
    vulnerability of the
      over-scrupulous,
      3:197
  on consolation versus
    desolation, 4:73
  on crisis, times of, 4:5–6
  on the curative power of
    self-disclosure, 3:21
  on the pastoral calling,
    1:38–40
  on pastoral formation
    and moral
    development,
    1:176–77

on prayer, 2:65–66
  the Lord's Prayer as
    pattern for, 2:91
on the priesthood as an
  immutable choice,
  2:19
on reinforcement
  techniques, 3:237
on restitution, 2:153
on temptation hitting
  one's greatest
  weaknesses and
  vulnerabilities, 4:89
on worldly goods,
  3:216–17
Inequalities in created
  beings, 4:76–83
Inquirers, ministry to,
  2:166–70
Isaacson, Henry
  on hospitality to
    strangers, 4:158–59
Institutions, pastoral care
  through, 2:184–89
Intercession, pastoral,
  2:80–83
Interpretation of Scripture,
  2:47–49
Involuntary acts and
  degrees of consent,
  3:288–93
Irenaeus of Lyons, Saint
  on the acquisition of
    moral good, 3:244
  on authority in ministry,
    1:58
  on the authority of the
    Word, 2:33–34
  on death, 4:176
  on distinguishing good
    from evil, 3:275
  on freedom
    and grace, 3:287
    the self-alienation
      of, 3:279
    the social
      consequences of
      taking seriously,
      3:284–85
  on freeing the soul from
    bondage, 3:69–70

on God's own empathic
understanding,
3:12–13
on the negligent pastor,
1:50
on the practice of
scriptural
counseling, 3:106–7
on preparing for
worship, 2:63
on the presbyter's
responsibilities,
1:127, 128
on reason and will,
3:274
on the timely fulfillment
of prophecy,
3:132–33
on vindicating the
justice of God amid
pain, 4:66
on women in the history
of salvation, 1:146
Irish Canons of 1634
on communion counsel,
2:139
Isaacson, Henry
on the benefits of
pastoral study and
meditation, 1:156
Isidore of Pelusium
on receptivity to
guidance, 3:66–67

Jean de Paris
on authority in ministry,
1:58
on the tasks of episcopal
care, 1:133
Jean of Paris. *See* Jean de
Paris
Jerome, Saint
on dealing with
criticism, 2:215
on the office of
presbyter, 1:126
on the possibility of
doing that which
God requires, 4:181
Jesus
ministry of, 1:75–77

and the ministry of
the church, 1:77–80
as Physician, 3:54
as Priest, 1:98–99
John of Avila
on recognizing the need
for counseling,
3:86–87
John of Damascus
on apostolic tradition of
soul care, 1:65
on the elements of
prayer, 2:75–76
on questioning God's
providence, 3:98
on worshipping God
through visible
images and
representations,
2:95–96
John of the Cross
on choosing a soul
guide, 3:67
on recognizing the
need for
counseling, 3:86
Julian of Norwich
on the affirmation of
divine mystery, 4:64
on care of the gravely ill,
4:49–50
on death, preparation
for, 4:167
on the gift of healing,
4:55–56
Justin
on the pastor and the
Sunday service, 2:71

Lactantius
on admonition,
dynamics of internal
resistance to, 3:179
on the burial of
strangers, 4:179
on the characteristics of
a good care-giver,
1:148–49
on civil disobedience,
3:191
on counsel

the limits of
situational wisdom
in, 3:131
the unity and
coherence of
situational,
3:113–14
on Epicureanism,
3:96–97; 4:170
versus divine
providence, 3:97–98;
4:171
on evil, why God
permitted, 4:62
on forgiveness without
responsiveness,
2:150
on God as Creator,
3:94–95
on hospitality to
strangers, 4:160–61
on how the eyes "tell all,"
3:143
on the immortality of
the soul, 4:174
on intuitive reasoning,
3:266
on the journey of the
pilgrim (soul), 4:7–8
on the meaning of
suffering, 4:71–72
on probing the layers of
deception, 3:152
on reinforcement
techniques, 3:235
on religion as
projection, 3:259
on soul care
of the emotionally
ill, 3:262
of the terminally ill,
4:173
on teaching
by untrustworthy
teachers, 2:178
true, 2:176, 177–78
on virtue, 3:247–48
and vices, 3:242–43
Language
of the body, learning to
read, 3:142–44

in counsel, use and
abuse of, 3:144–48
fairness in, 1:141–42
and silence and gesture
of counsel, 3:141–59
Latimer, Hugh
on dealing with
criticism, 2:215–16
on the pastor's
attentiveness,
1:50–51
on potentially
constructive uses of
temptation, 4:88
Laud, William
on care of the gravely ill,
4:48–49
on the pastor as moral
role model, 1:187
on the pastor's
expectations of
church
reformability, 1:75
on pastoral visitation,
4:28
on rejection of fees for
pastoral service,
2:203
Law
and gospel, 3:199–201
pastoral uses of, 3:202–4
Leaving the ministry,
2:17–20
L'Estrange, Hamon
on the ministry of
pardon, 2:147
Life of Pachomius, The
on befriending, 3:32
Liturgical tradition,
continuity in,
2:73–74
Lord's Prayer, as pattern for
Christian prayer,
2:89–91
Lord's Table, the. *See also*
Communion
invitation to, 2:157–60
Lull, Raymond
on the difficulties in
ministry, 2:10–11
on how the eyes speak
from the heart, 3:143

on love, 3:31
and death, 4:168
on self-knowledge, 3:44
on virtues offered to the
believer in true
contrition, 3:248
on worship, preparing
for, 2:63–64
Luther, Martin
on admonition, necessity
of, 3:169
on the affirmation of
divine mystery, 4:64
on alcoholism and
addictive behaviors,
4:19
on angelic and demonic
influences, 4:92
on authority in ministry,
1:57
on the authority of the
Word, 2:32
on baptism
the act of, 2:125–26
the effects of, 2:128
neglect of, 2:128–29
the recipients of,
2:112–13, 114, 116
the recollection of,
2:107–8
water as the sign of,
2:118–19
on behavioral
excellences of
ordinands, 1:107
on the body of Christ
metaphor, 1:71, 72,
73
on candor as a pastoral
virtue, 3:181
on the characteristics of
a good care-giver,
1:149
on children
hurting their
parents, 4:132
as the most pleasant
aspect of marriage,
4:127
on Christian education,
2:168

on Christian freedom,
2:53–55
on Christian worship,
2:60
on cohesion and
catholicity amid
diverse ministries,
1:68
on comfort, 2:138
on communion
as a free act, 2:161
the ministry of,
2:157
preparation for,
2:162
worthiness to
receive, 2:158
on confession
the confidentiality
of, 2:141
the hard remedy of,
2:135, 140–41
on the conscience,
3:186–87
care of the
distraught and
anguished, 3:192,
194
on continuity in
liturgical tradition,
2:73
on counseling
premarital pastoral,
4:96, 98–99, 100
the use of metaphor
in, 3:146
on criticism, dealing
with, 2:213, 214
on the crow metaphor,
2:19
on dancing, 4:136, 137
on the deacon's care for
the poor and sick,
1:125
on death, 4:177
acceptance of, in
light of Christian
hope, 4:174
judging people by
their last actions or
words before, 4:175

searching for the
meaning in, 4:172
on deceivers, various
types of, 3:157–58
on the difficulties in
ministry, 2:10, 11, 12
on divorce counsel,
4:138, 141
on faith, 2:50, 52–53
on false teaching,
2:182–83
on families, pastoral care
of, 4:125
on fasting, 3:218–19
on fault-finding,
avoiding, 3:170–71
in children,
4:131–32
on forgiveness without
responsiveness,
2:149–50
on fraternal correction,
3:163
on the gift of prophecy,
1:101
on good works, 2:56–57
on grace and effort,
3:211
on guilt as moral
indebtedness, 3:195
on healing the
corruptions of
sacred ministry, 2:21,
26, 27
on his ordination, 1:119
on human caring
grounded in God's
care, 3:91–92
on idolatry, 3:260
on the indelibility of the
priesthood, 2:19, 20
on interpersonal crisis
counseling and
conflict
management, 4:10
on Jesus
and the ministry of
the church, 1:78
as Priest, 1:98–99
on law
and gospel,
3:199–200

pastoral uses of,
3:202
on learning to trust
oneself, 3:21
on the limits of rational
argument amid
suffering, 4:58
on the management of
pain, 4:46
on marriage
breaking the
covenant of, 4:115
consent in, 4:106
covenant
faithfulness in,
4:112–13
legalism in, 4:110
the meaning of,
4:101, 104–5
questions
concerning, 4:107
sexual intercourse
before, 4:98
on masochism,
avoiding the trap
of, 4:74
on the meaning of the
word "Amen," 2:80
on the ministry of
pardon, 2:148–49
on the ministry of the
Word, 2:28, 30, 31,
42
on the need for ordered
ministry, 1:85–86
on the nurturing
relationship, 3:77, 78
on the office of the
priesthood, 1:94, 95
on ordinal prayer, 1:119
on overemphasizing
church numbers
rather than spiritual
strength, 2:188–89
on parents
honoring our, 4:124
pastoral care of,
4:120–21
responsible, 4:127
strictness and
leniency of, 4:130

on the pastor
accountability of,
1:47
care for, 2:7
formation and
moral development
of, 3:1:179
opposition to, 1:74
political ethics of,
2:193–94, 195
relationship between
physician and, 4:42
the service of, 3:76
and the Sunday
service, 2:72
as teacher, 2:171
on the pastor's books,
1:159–60, 161–62
on the pastor's
expectations of
church
reformability, 1:73,
74
on the pastor's use of
homilies, 2:39, 40
on the pastor's use of
scientific studies,
1:170–71
on pastoral burnout,
2:13–14, 15–16
on the pastoral calling,
1:32, 37
resistance to, 1:26,
27–28
on pastoral care through
institutions, 2:186
on pastoral
disengagement from
worldly
preoccupations,
2:207
on the pastoral ordering
of worship, 2:66
on pastoral preaching,
2:36, 37, 38, 45–46
on pastoral study and
meditation, the
benefits of, 1:156
on the path to
ordination, 1:116
on the priesthood of all

baptized Christians,
1:81–82
on reason, 3:258, 259
on rejection of fees for
pastoral service,
2:201
on representative
ministry, 1:83
on resting, 2:101
on Scripture
the interpretation
of, 3:107
the pastoral study of,
1:165, 166
on servant ministry, 1:54
on the soul
coherence in
educating, 2:174–75,
176
the equality of, 1:144
freed from bondage,
3:68
on soul care
music and, 2:104,
105–6
to penitents,
2:142–43
the sphere of,
1:22–23, 25
through
unconditional
accepting love, 3:28
on spoiling a child,
4:120
on strength found amid
weakness, 4:37
on suffering
the meaning of,
4:70–71
the pedagogy of,
4:69, 70
praising God amid,
4:72
on suicide, 4:21–22
on temptation
potentially
constructive uses of,
4:88
and responsible
freedom, 4:83
on the visibility of

church and ministry,
1:71
on visitation of the sick,
timing of, 4:34
on women
the faith of, 1:144
as preachers, 1:141
on worship
modes of, 2:69, 70
preparing for,
2:62–63
on young people,
pastoral care for,
4:132, 134, 135

Macarius the Great
on admonition,
gentleness in, 3:168
on the exquisite timing
of seasonable
counsel, 3:127
on humility, 3:222
Marie of the Incarnation
on the curative power of
self-disclosure, 3:22
Marital status requirements
of ordinands, 1:109
Marriage
adultery in, 4:116–18
covenant of
breaking, 4:114–16
keeping faithful,
4:112–14
and family counseling,
4:96–143
happiness and
fulfillment in,
4:109–12
the meaning of,
4:100–105
questions concerning,
105–7
sex and, 107–9
Martyr, Justin, Saint
on the effects of
baptism, 2:127
on the deacon's role in
the eucharist, 1:123
on inquiry into pastoral
abuses, 2:223
on philosophy, 1:171

on soul care
and the use of
secular psychologies
and therapies,
3:228–29
Masochism, avoiding the
trap of, 4:73–76
Maximus the Confessor,
Saint
on candor as a pastoral
virtue, 3:182
on friendship, 3:33
on grief, 4:177
on moral progress and
regress in humanity,
3:210
on moral self-
examination, 2:64
on pastoral discernment,
3:124
on the poor, equally
caring for all, 4:148
on reinforcement
techniques, 3:239
on vices, development
of, 3:245
on temptation
and responsible
freedom, 4:87
why God permits,
4:68
Mede, Joseph
on ancillary orders of
ministry, 1:112
on the history of the
word "priest," 1:92
Methodius of Olympus
on discovering spiritual
wisdom, 3:20
on judging by God's
standards, 4:182
on music and soul care,
2:105
on the pastor as moral
role model,
1:186–87
on single life, affirming
the, 4:119
Moral counseling and the
nurture of
responsible
freedom, 3:186–225

Moral development,
    pastoral formation
    and, 1:174–79
Moral progress and regress
    of humanity, 3:209
Moral role model, the pastor
    as, 1:185–88
Music and soul care, 2:102–6

Nazianzen, Gregory
    on the principle of
        variable
        responsiveness,
        3:109–10
Nemesius of Emesa
    on alcoholism and
        addictive behaviors,
        4:16
    on astrology and magic
        as anathema, 3:280
    on choice versus desire,
        3:270
    on fate versus
        providence, 3:285
    on free will, 3:267
        reason and,
        3:275–76
    on God's providence,
        3:93, 94
    on involuntary acts and
        degrees of consent,
        3:288–91
    on the pastor as the
        physician of souls,
        3:54
    on vindicating the
        justice of God amid
        pain, 4:66
Nicholas de Cusa
    on cohesion and
        catholicity amid
        diverse ministries,
        1:67–68
Nicholas of Cusa. *See*
    Nicholas de Cusa

Ordered ministry, need for,
    1:85–87
Ordination, 1:102–36
    the act of, 1:116–20
    and ancillary orders of
        ministry, 1:111–13

and the bishop's pastoral
    care of the church,
    1:129–32
caution toward, 1:102–5
examination for, 1:105–7
and the office of deacon,
    1:120–23
and the office of
    presbyter, 1:125–26
the path to, 1:113–16
and requirements
    concerning marital
    status, 1:109
and the three "orders" of
    ministry, 1:109–11
Origen
    on the acquisition of
        moral good, 3:245
    on admonition,
        dynamics of internal
        resistance to, 3:179
    on apostolicity and
        succession, 1:62
    on the benefits of
        pastoral study and
        meditation, 1:155
    on care of the
        emotionally ill,
        3:263–64
    on the choice between
        good and evil,
        3:273
    on crisis, the pastor's
        presence amid, 4:4
    on education as a
        developmental
        process, 2:172
    on fairness in language,
        1:142
    on free will, 3:267–68,
        270–71, 274
    on the "gentle rain"
        metaphor referring
        to speech, 3:146
    on God as Creator,
        3:98–99
    on God's love
        complementing
        humanistic
        psychology and
        philosophy, 3:229

on the Good Shepherd,
    1:41
on guidance of the soul,
    3:60–61, 70
on guilt as moral
    indebtedness, 3:195,
    196
on habit modification,
    3:233–34
on the healing
    physician metaphor,
    3:129–30
on the Holy Spirit as
    Counselor, 3:100
on human caring
    grounded in God's
    care, 3:89–90
on inequalities in
    created beings, 4:77,
    78–79, 80–82
interest in scientific
    studies, 1:168, 172
on interpersonal crisis
    counseling and
    conflict
    management,
    4:10–11, 12–13
on Jesus' ministry, 1:76
on the journey of the
    pilgrim (soul), 4:6, 8
on learning to trust
    oneself, 3:19
masochism, avoiding the
    trap of, 4:75–76
on parents
    communicating with
    children on their
    own level, 4:123
on the pastor
    as the physician of
        souls, 3:53
    and his use of
        scientific studies,
        1:169
on pastoral care in
    eschatological
    perspective, 4:180
on pastoral intercession,
    2:81
on the pedagogy of
    suffering, 4:70

on prayer
  effectual, 2:83–84
  the elements of,
    2:74–75
  the Lord's Prayer as
    pattern for, 2:90
  posture for, 2:95
  public, 2:93
  the temporal
    ordering of, 2:98–99
on Scripture
  the interpretation
    of, 2:47–49
  as source of good
    counsel, 3:105–6
on self-examination,
  3:35, 37
on the social metaphor
  of blackness, 1:19
on the soul's perception
  of truth, 3:154, 155
on striving for Christian
  maturity and
  fulfillment, 4:183
on the support of
  ministries, 2:210
on temptation
  potentially
    constructive uses of,
    4:87–88
  and responsible
    freedom, 4:84,
    85–86
virtues of, 1:175–76
on young people,
  pastoral care for,
  4:136
Orosius, Paulus
  on self-deception, 3:153
Overall, John
  on apostolicity and
    succession, 1:60

Pain
  the management of,
    4:45–46
  vindicating the justice of
    God amid, 4:65–68
Palladius
  on dealing with false
    accusations,
    2:220–22

on the gifts of women,
  1:145–46
on resistance to the
  pastoral calling,
  1:28–29
Pambo
  on humility, 3:224–25
Papias, Saint
  on Jesus' ministry,
    1:75–76
Pardon, the ministry of,
  2:146–49
Parenting
  responsible, 4:126–29
  strictness and leniency
    in, 129–32
Parents, pastoral care of,
  4:119–22
Passions, rational analysis of
  the, 3:255–59
Pastor
  as educator of the soul,
    2:166–83; 3:70–74
  as guide of the soul's
    journey, 3:58–63
  obligation to care for
    oneself, 2:7–27
  office of, 1:20–22
    inquiry into the
      abuses of, 2:222–25
  openness to his own
    experiencing
    process, 3:14–18
  opposition to, 1:74
  ordination of, 1:102–36
  as physician of souls,
    3:52–57
  political ethics of,
    2:193–96
  and his relation to other
    pastors, 2:189–93
  relationship between
    physician and,
    4:41–45
  as shepherd, 1:41–53
    accountability of,
      1:43–47
    attentiveness of,
      1:50–51
    negligence of,
      1:47–50

of souls, 1:41–43
and the Sunday service,
  2:71–73
Pastor of Hermas, The. See
  Shepherd of Hermas,
  The
Pastoral calling, the, 1:11–40
  and identification with
    the dispossessed,
    1:18–20
  inward and outward,
    1:32–34
  resistance to, 1:26–29
Pastoral counsel
  circumstances in,
    3:120–22
  developmental stages as
    variables of,
    3:129–31
  discernment in,
    3:122–26
  the function of silence
    in, 3:141–42
  good, 3:48–52
  the language, silence,
    and gesture of,
    3:141–59
  the limits of situational
    wisdom in, 3:131–33
  metaphors applying the
    principle of variable
    responsiveness in,
    3:117–21
  the nature of, 3:48–88
  premarital, 4:96–100
  prudent, 3:80–83,
    133–36
  timing in, 3:126–29
  the unity and coherence
    of situational,
    3:113–17
  use and abuse of
    language in,
    3:144–48
  using individual
    treatment consistent
    with doctrinal unity,
    3:111–13
  wisdom in, 3:13640
Pastoral visitation and care
  of the sick, 4:26–56

Patrick of Ireland, Saint
 on astrology and magic
  as anathema, 3:282
 on his calling to the
  pastoral ministry,
  1:36
Peter of Alexandria
 on decoding deceptions,
  3:158
 on the preservation of
  original apostolic
  writings, 1:77
Poemen
 on accurate empathic
  listening, 3:10
 on choosing a soul
  guide, 3:65
 on the limits of
  openness, 3:26
 on pastoral formation
  and moral
  development, 1:174
 on self-harm, 3:215
 on self-knowledge, 3:36
Political ethics of the pastor,
 2:193–96
Polycarp, Saint
 on compassion, 1:11–12
 on courtesy, 1:12–13
 on inquiry into pastoral
  abuses, 2:223
Poor, care of the, 4:144–63
 averting the dependency
  syndrome in,
  4:149–53
Praise of God, preparing the
 soul for, 2:62–66
Prayer
 effectual, 2:83–86
 elements of, 2:74–77
 the language and forms
  of pastoral, 2:86–89
 the Lord's Prayer as
  pattern for, 2:89–91
 and meditation,
  1:156–57
 ordinal, 1:119, 122–23,
  126, 137–38
 for the pastor's own
  needs, 2:9
 pastoral care through,
  2:58–106

public, 2:91–94
 the spatial ordering of
  the community at,
  2:94–96
 the temporal ordering
  of, 2:96–101
Presbyter
 office of, 1:125–26
 responsibilities of,
  1:127–29
Priesthood
 of all baptized
  Christians, 1:81–83
 as an immutable choice,
  2:19
 ministry of the, 1:91–95
 sacrifice under the old
  and new covenant,
  1:95–99
Prosper of Aquitaine, Saint
 on children dependent
  on parental wisdom,
  4:122
 on grace and effort,
  3:212–13
 on inequalities in
  created beings, 4:79
 on pastoral preaching,
  2:46–47
 on understanding the
  will of God, 3:95
Providence, questioning
 God's, 3:96–99
Psychoanalysis, anticipations
 of, 3:249–52
Psychotherapy, anticipations
 of, 3:226–65
Public demeanor and
 double standards in
 the ministry,
 1:180–82
Public prayer, 2:91–94

Quinisext Synod
 on the clergy
  age restrictions for,
  1:107, 140–41
  operating taverns,
  1:182
  clothing of, 1:182
  the sexual values of,
  1:183

on marriage, breaking
 the covenant of,
 4:116
on music and soul care,
 2:106
on the office of deacon,
 1:121
on the pastor as the
 physician of souls,
 3:56–57
on priestly descent, 1:98
on rejection of fees for
 pastoral service,
 2:202
on restrictions on laity in
 teaching Christian
 doctrine, 2:178–79
on the tasks of episcopal
 care, 1:134
on using church
 property for making
 money, 2:189

Reason and will, 3:273–76
Reformability of the church,
 pastoral realism
 concerning, 1:73–75
Reinforcement techniques,
 3:234–40
Relationship, conditions of a
 helping, 3:7–47
Religion as projection,
 3:259–61
Reparenting and
 transference,
 3:252–54
Representative ministry,
 1:83–84
Restitution, 2:151–53
Reynolds, Edward
 on the urgent need for
 soul care, 1:16–17
Richard of St. Victor
 on moral counsel, 3:198
 responsibility of
 admonition, 3:167
Ridley, Nicholas
 on healing the
 corruptions of
 sacred ministry,
 2:21–22

Role models for ministry,
1:152–55
pastors as moral,
1:185–88

Sacraments, conferred by an
unworthy minister,
2:129–31
Sacred ministry, 1:89–91
healing the corruptions
of, 2:21–27
Salvian the Presbyter
on behavioral change
strategies, 3:248
on death, preparation
for, 4:166
on faith and possessions,
4:154–56
on moral progress and
regress in humanity,
3:210
on overemphasizing
church numbers
rather than spiritual
strength, 2:188
on parental vices passed
on to children, 3:254
on the poor
averting the
dependency
syndrome among,
4:151
the effects of tax
policy on, 4:152–53
on responsible
parenting, 4:129
on strength found amid
weakness, 4:40
Sancroft, William
on the pastor's
expectations of
church
reformability, 1:73
Sanderson, Robert
on scruples, 3:193
Sandys, George
on governing hunger,
3:218
Scholasticus, Socrates
on the abuse of
preaching, 2:38

on avoiding unfit or
premature
ordinations, 1:103–4
on dealing with
criticism, 2:214
on healing the
corruptions of
sacred ministry,
2:25
on modes of worship,
2:68–69
Scientific studies, pastoral
use of, 1:167–74
Scriptural counseling, the
practice of, 3:106–8
Scripture
pastoral study of,
1:164–67
as source of good
counsel, 3:103–6
Second Council of
Constantinople. *See*
Council of
Constantinople,
Second
Second Helvetic Confession.
See Helvetic
Confession, Second
Self-awareness, deepening
of, 3:37–42
Self-control, eliciting
disciplined, 3:204–6
Self-disclosure
constraints upon
compulsive, 3:24–27
the curative power of,
3:21–24
Self-examination
the call to, 3:34–37
the process of, 3:42–45
Servant ministry, 1:54–55
Severin, Saint
in the presence of
governmental
power, 2:196
Sex and marriage, 107–9
Shepherd
metaphor of, 1:41–53
pastor as. *See* Pastor, as
shepherd
Shepherd of Hermas, The

on angelic and demonic
influences, 4:94
on the limits of
situational wisdom,
3:131–32
on pastoral uses of the
law, 3:203–4
on self-control, 3:203
on truth-telling, 3:155
Silence in counsel, the
function of, 3:141–42
Simons, Menno
admonition, gentleness
in, 3:167
on communion, the
recipients of, 2:159
on corruption in the
ministry, 2:23
on divorce counsel,
4:138–39
on false accusations,
dealing with,
2:217–18
on hypocrisy among
clergy, 2:15
on the need for ordered
ministry, 1:86
on parenting
responsible,
4:128–29
strictness and
leniency in, 4:131
on the pastor
accountability of,
1:43
negligence of, 1:49
on the pastoral calling,
1:34–35, 36, 37
resistance to,
1:26–27
on pastoral
disengagement from
worldly preoc-
cupations, 2:207–8
on pastoral formation
and moral
development, 1:179
on peace, 4:14
on rejection of fees for
pastoral service,
2:202–3, 204

the secret ministry of,
3:123–24
on spiritual effects of
physical illness, 4:39
on widows, the care of,
4:157
Single life, affirming the,
4:118–19
Sisoes
on grace and effort,
3:211
on the pastoral duty of
admonition, 3:160
Slavery, 4:162–63
Soul(s)
freed from bondage,
3:68–70
health of, 4:50–53
as neither male nor
female, 1:142
as pilgrims, 4:6–9
Soul care
through accurate
empathic listening,
3:8–12
as compared to
God's empathic
understanding,
3:12–14
apostolic tradition of,
1:62–65
authority for, 1:54–80
through befriending,
3:31–34
through Christian
worship, 2:58–62
distinguishing the
sphere of, 1:22–25
of the dying, 4:164–85
in eschatological
perspective,
4:180–85
of the emotionally ill,
3:261–65
freedom of will as a
premise of, 3:269–72
of the gravely ill,
4:48–50, 173–76
the internal witness of
conscience as a
premise of, 3:186–89

music and, 2:102–6
through nurturing
relationships,
3:76–80
to penitents, 2:142–46
personal qualities
requisite to, 1:11–13
through prayer,
2:58–106
through preaching,
2:28–57
preparation for,
1:148–88
benefits of pastoral
study and
meditation in,
1:155–59
books used in,
1:159–64
pastoral formation
and moral
development in,
1:174–79
the pastoral use of
scientific studies in,
1:167–74
studying Scripture
in, 1:164–67
recognizing the need
for, 3:83–88
study of, 1:13–14
through unconditional
accepting love,
3:28–31
urgent need for, 1:14–18
and the use of secular
psychologies and
therapies, 3:227–30
through word and
counsel, 2:44–47
Soul guide, instructions for
choosing a, 3:63–68
Sparrow, Anthony
on communion for the
sick, 4:47
on the relationship
between physician
and pastor, 4:41
Staupitz, Johann von, 1:26
Strength found amid
weakness, 4:36–41

Suffering
the enigma of, 4:57–95
the meaning of, 4:70–73
the pedagogy of, 4:68–70
Suicide counsel, 4:21–25
Sunday service, the pastor
and, 2:71–73
Supplication, pastoral,
2:77–80
Symeon the New
Theologian
on choosing a soul
guide, 3:67
Symeon of Thessalonica
on the meaning of
marriage, 4:101
Synod of Laodicea
on astrology and magic
as anathema, 3:280
Synod of Quinisext. *See*
Quinisext Synod

Tatian
on the relationship
between physician
and pastor, 4:41–42
Taylor, Jeremy
on admonition,
gentleness in, 3:168
on almsgiving, 4:146–47
on the conscience, care
of the distraught
and anguished,
3:194
on continuity in
liturgical tradition,
2:73–74
on episcopal visitation to
the congregation,
1:131
on false teaching, 2:181
on fraternal correction,
3:165
on love, 3:31
on the ministry of the
Word, 2:30–31, 42
on the pastor
the leadership of,
2:186
as moral role model,
1:185

and his relation to
other pastors, 2:190
on the pastor's books,
1:161
on prayer
public, 2:94
the temporal
ordering of, 2:99
on receiving one's own
counsel, 3:71
on rejection of fees for
pastoral service,
2:204
on soul care by word and
counsel, 2:44–45
on the use of technical
or ornate language
in sermons, 2:41
on visitation of the sick,
timing of, 4:33
Teaching
true, 2:176–79
false, 2:179–83
Teaching of the Apostles,
The
on apostolic tradition of
soul care, 1:64
"Teaching of the Twelve
Apostles, The"
on ambivalences in
counseling, 3:78
Temptation
the care of souls facing,
4:89–91
potentially constructive
uses of, 4:87–89
and responsible
freedom, 4:83–87
Teresa of Avila, Saint
on prayer and
meditation,
1:156–57
on recognizing the need
for counseling, 3:85
Tertullian
on abortion counsel,
4:142
on adultery, 4:116
on angelic and demonic
influences, 4:94
on baptism

the authority to
administer, 2:115
as a happy occasion,
2:111
misunderstandings
concerning,
2:111–12, 113
preparation for,
2:120
recipients of,
2:114–15, 116
the simplicity of,
2:108–9
time or season to
administer, 2:122
water as the sign of,
2:117, 118
on charismatic gifts,
1:100
on Christian worship,
2:59
on cohesion and
catholicity amid
diverse ministries,
1:66, 67
on the conscience, as a
universal human
capacity, 3:190–91
on continence, 4:97
on death, 4:176, 177
preparation for,
4:165, 167
searching for the
meaning in,
4:171–72
on divorce counsel,
4:140
on fairness in language,
1:141
on false teaching,
2:179–80
on forgiveness without
responsiveness,
2:150–51
on grace and freedom,
3:287
on the hard remedy of
confession, 2:136
on marital happiness
and fulfillment,
4:111

on moral counsel, 3:197
on the pastor
accountability of,
1:44
and his use of
scientific studies,
1:169, 170, 172
on patience, 1:174–75
on the practice of having
multiple spouses,
4:139–40
on prayer
effectual, 2:84, 85
the Lord's Prayer as
pattern for, 2:89
the temporal
ordering of, 2:97–98
on rejection of fees for
pastoral service,
2:202
on the sacred ministry,
1:91
healing the corrup-
tions of, 2:22–23, 27
on Scripture
interpretation of,
3:108
as source of good
counsel, 3:104
on single life, affirming
the, 4:118, 119
on soul care
apostolic tradition
of, 1:63–64
historical experience
and, 1:14
to penitents, 2:142
on trusting your soul,
3:15, 16
on why God permitted
the will to fall,
4:59–61
"Testaments of the Twelve
Patriarchs"
on the limits of
openness, 3:26
Thaumaturgus, Gregory,
Saint
on the pastor's use of
scientific studies,
1:168, 172; 3:255

on virtues, 1:175–76
Theodora, Amma
on potentially
constructive uses of
temptation, 4:89–90
Theodoret of Cyrus
on priestly sacrifice,
1:95–96
Theonas of Alexandria
on the care of books,
1:162–63
on counsel
Scripture as source
of good, 3:106
vocational, 4:20–21
on the pastor's fiscal
accountability, 2:185
Theophilus, Saint
hospitality to strangers,
4:158
on language in counsel,
the use and abuse
of,3:145
on reflecting God in our
lives, 4:181
Thirty-Nine Articles of
Religion (1563)
on cohesion and
catholicity amid
diverse ministries,
1:68
on the office of pastor,
1:21
on sacraments conferred
by an unworthy
minister, 2:130–31
on speaking in tongues,
1:100
on the visibility of
church and ministry,
1:70
Timing of good counsel,
3:109–40
Tithes and offerings,
2:208–12
Traherne, Thomas
on the benefits of
pastoral study and
meditation, 1:159
on pastoral supplication,
2:78

Trithemius, Johannes
on the pastor's books,
1:164
on the pastoral study of
Scripture, 1:167
Tronson, Louis
on the metaphor of
complete pouring
out of conscience,
3:22–23
on resistance to asking
for help, 3:86
True teaching. *See* Teaching,
true
Trusting oneself, 3:18–21
Truth-telling, 3:153–56

Valerian, Saint
on alcoholism and
addictive behaviors,
4:19
on the ordination vows,
1:105
on praying for the poor
but doing nothing,
4:153
Visibility of church and
ministry, 1:69–71
Visitation
pastoral, 4:26–29
of the sick, 4:29–33
timing of, 4:33–34
Vocational counsel, 4:19–21

Walton, Isaac
on clarifying events and
celebrations of the
Christian year,
2:100
on the elements of
prayer, 2:77
on music and soul care,
2:104
Wake, William
on ordination as a
sacrament, 1:118
Westminster Confession
on admonition, as a
preservative of
community,
3:183–84

on the assurance of
salvation, 2:50–51
on the authority of the
Word, 2:34–35
on baptism, the ministry
of, 2:110
on Christian freedom,
2:52
on communion, the
ministry of,
2:154–55
on divorce counsel,
4:138
on freedom
and grace, 3:286
and the layers of
necessity, 3:269
on good works, 2:51–52
on Jesus and the
ministry of the
church, 1:78–79
on law
and gospel,
3:200–201
pastoral uses of,
3:202–3
on marriage
homosexuality and
bigamy in, 4:106
the meaning of,
4:100
on the political ethics of
the pastor, 2:194
on repentance, 2:143–44
on the sacraments,
2:164–65
on Scripture
the interpretation
of, 3:107
as source of good
counsel, 3:103–4
on the visibility of
church and ministry,
1:69–70
on why God permitted
the will to fall, 4:61
on worship, modes of,
2:69–70
White, Francis
on the four purposes of
confession, 2:134–35

on the language and
    forms of pastoral
    prayer, 2:89
Widows, care of, 4:156–58
Will
    being permitted by God
        to fall, 4:59–63
    the psychological
        dynamics of the,
        3:266–93
William of St. Thierry
    on choosing a soul
        guide, 3:67–68
    on the counselor
        modeling his own
        counsel, 3:87–88
    on the curative power of
        self-disclosure, 3:24
    on self-awareness, 3:42
    on the vices of humanity,
        3:240

Wilson, Thomas
    on pastoral care for the
        poor, 4:146
Women in ministry,
    1:137–47
    and the equality of souls,
        1:142–44
    and fairness in language,
        1:141–42
    gifts of, 1:144–47
Word, the
    authority of, 2:31–36
    interpreting, 2:47–49
    ministry of, 2:28–31
Workman, metaphor of the,
    1:128
World, care of the, 2:196–99
Worldly preoccupations,
    pastoral
    disengagement
    from, 2:205–8

Worship
    and the care of souls,
        2:59–62
    modes of, 2:67–70
    the pastoral ordering of,
        2:66–67
Wyclif, John
    on the pastor's
        accountability, 1:47
    on withholding money
        from corrupted
        clergy, 2:187

Young people, pastoral care
    for, 4:132–37

DATE DUE
